THE DYNAMIC FRAME

FILM AND CULTURE

FILM AND CULTURE

A series of Columbia University Press

Edited by John Belton

For a complete list of titles, see page 351.

THE DYNAMIC FRAME

*Camera Movement in
Classical Hollywood*

PATRICK KEATING

Columbia University Press
New York

Columbia University Press
Publishers Since 1893
New York   Chichester, West Sussex
cup.columbia.edu

Library of Congress Cataloging-in-Publication Data
Names: Keating, Patrick, 1970– author.
Title: The dynamic frame : camera movement in classical Hollywood /
    Patrick Keating.
Description: New York : Columbia University Press, [2019] | Series: Film and
    culture | Includes bibliographical references and index.
Identifiers: LCCN 2018037319 (print) | LCCN 2018050507 (ebook) |
    ISBN 9780231548953 (e-book) | ISBN 9780231190503 (cloth : alk. paper) |
    ISBN 9780231190510 (pbk. : alk. paper)
Subjects: LCSH: Cinematography—United States—History. | Motion pictures—
    Aesthetics. | Motion pictures—United States—History—20th century.
Classification: LCC TR848 (ebook) | LCC TR848 .K43 2019 (print) |
    DDC 777—dc23
LC record available at https://lccn.loc.gov/2018037319

♾

Cover design: Milenda Nan Ok Lee
Cover photo: Courtesy Everett Collection

For Lisa ❧

CONTENTS

ACKNOWLEDGMENTS

When I was a teenager, my father, Dennis, drove me to the Los Angeles County Museum of Art to see a 35-millimeter screening of a silent movie: *Sunrise.* More than thirty years later I am still thinking about that movie; this book is the result. Dad, thanks for the ride, and thanks for all of your love and support over the years. Thanks also to my sisters, Coleen and Amy, and my late and much-loved mother, Maria, who helped this project in countless ways, never once making me feel odd for spending so much of my childhood watching old movies.

I began to research this project in earnest in 2011. Since then, I have received the support of several generous institutions. First, the Academy of Motion Picture Arts and Sciences provided me with an Academy Film Scholars grant. Thanks to Shawn Guthrie, who guided me through the grant process with care, and to John Bailey, who expressed warm interest in my work. Thanks also to the staff at the academy's Margaret Herrick Library, where Barbara Hall, Faye Emerson, and others helped me locate valuable and sometimes bizarre documents and photographs.

In 2011, I received a summer fellowship from the Harry Ransom Humanities Research Center at the University of Texas at Austin, where curator Steve Wilson pointed me in the direction of much interesting research.

In 2014, the American Council of Learned Societies (ACLS) awarded me a Frederick Burkhardt Fellowship for Recently Tenured Scholars, which supported a nine-month residency at the Radcliffe Institute for Advanced Study at Harvard University, where Judith Vishniac and Liz Cohen ran a magnificent program. I discussed my ideas with many gifted fellows, including V. V. Gane-shananthan, Heather Hendershot, Ben Miller, João Pedro Rodrigues, Felix Warnekan, and Jennifer Quick. Haden Guest, Jeremy Rossen, and Liz Coffey helped me conduct research at the Harvard Film Archive. Thanks to Derek Miller for letting me sit in on his class, to Eric Rentschler for inviting me to give a talk at Harvard's film studies colloquium, and to Matthew Goldfeder at the ACLS.

My employer, Trinity University, provided summer research stipends in 2011, 2013, and 2015. Thanks to Jennifer Henderson, Mike Fischer, and Mark Brodl for endorsing an extra sabbatical year after I completed my fellowship at Rad-cliffe, and thanks to Deneese Jones, David Ribble, and the Department of Communication at Trinity for providing a generous subvention to support the cost of the illustrations. The book would not be the same without their support. Elizabeth Poff helped me set up a website where readers can view clips from the films discussed in this book (www.thedynamicframe.net).

Most of the illustrations in this book are frame grabs, but the pictures of dollies and cranes draw on the extraordinarily rich collections of the Bison Archives Photographs Collected by Marc Wanamaker, the Everett Collection, and the Academy of Motion Picture Arts and Sciences. I thank them for the permission to reprint those images here.

Support from Trinity enabled me to take several research trips to archives around the country. At the Lilly Library at Indiana University–Bloomington, I reviewed the Orson Welles Papers; at the George Eastman House in Rochester, New York, I watched silent films; at the Warner Bros. Archive at the University of Southern California, I consulted scripts and other documents; at the Department of Special Collections at the University of California–Los Angeles, I examined RKO materials; and at the Department of Special Collections at the University of Tennessee–Knoxville, I worked with the Clarence Brown Collection. During my visits to Los Angeles, I greatly enjoyed the hospitality of Jordan Hoffman, Rachel Pinto, and my sister Amy and brother-in-law Aaron.

At Columbia University Press, Chuck Maland and an anonymous reader provided detailed responses to the entire manuscript. Their insights were unfailingly sharp, and I truly appreciate their generosity. Annie Barva was a superb copy editor, consistently improving the manuscript's clarity and consistency. Thanks also to Philip Leventhal and Jennifer Crewe, who showed great enthusiasm for the project from beginning to end. Thanks to Miriam Grossman for all her help and to the graphic designer for crafting a beautiful cover. The Everett Collection provided the image.

In addition to Columbia's excellent readers, several scholars read portions of this manuscript over the years. John Belton, David Bordwell, and Dana Polan read almost every word; Adam Hart, Daniel Morgan, and Xinyu Dong also read substantial sections. I am truly grateful that such brilliant minds were willing to share their ideas about camera movement with me.

I have presented portions of this book's argument to several audiences over the years. Lisa Dombrowski invited me to cochair a panel on camera movement at the Society of Cinema and Media Studies way back in 2006. Joel Burges encouraged me to present at a conference in Rochester, and Vince Bohlinger invited me to speak at Rhode Island University. Jordan Schonig and Daniel Morgan asked me to participate in their wonderful conference "Seeing Films, Seeing Movement" at the University of Chicago, where I learned from all of my esteemed fellow panelists; John Peponis invited me to give a talk at Georgia Tech; Kerry Hegarty hosted me at Miami University for a presentation on my research in progress; and Ben Singer invited me back to my alma mater, the University of Wisconsin–Madison, for a colloquium. Thanks to everyone who invited me and to everyone who listened to my talks.

In 2015, I attended Middlebury College's workshop on videographic criticism sponsored by the National Endowment for the Humanities. There, Christian Keathley, Jason Mittell, Catherine Grant, and my fellow participants taught me to put my ideas about camera movement in audiovisual form. Christian, Jason, John Gibbs, and Miklós Kiss subsequently helped me publish video essays based on some of the examples analyzed in this book.

Over the years, I have been lucky to discuss my ideas with many outstanding scholars, including Lea Jacobs, Ben Brewster, Jeff Smith, Kristin Thompson, Masha Belodubrovskaya, Kristi McKim, Leger Grindon, Malcolm Turvey, Corey Creekmur, Julie Turnock, Chris Cagle, Christopher Lucas, Rick Jewell, and Janet Bergstrom. I greatly admire each one as a scholar, and I am tremendously grateful for their ideas and insights.

At Trinity, I have had many inspiring students since I arrived in 2007. The students in my fall 2017 class on the video essay pushed me to refine my ideas about *The Magnificent Ambersons*. Anthia Liu helped me start a large database of clips, which proved to be an invaluable resource. At Academic Technology, Rob Chapman ensured that my database did not get lost. Throughout my years at Trinity, I have had the pleasure of discussing my work with several wonderful faculty colleagues, including Kathryn O'Rourke, Curtis Swope, Jarrod Atchison, Corinne Pache, Michael Schreyach, and Andrew Kania.

Finally, I offer my deepest thanks to Lisa Jasinski, who supported me throughout this process even as she was finishing her own ambitious project. Her expert wordsmithing improved my writing, and her astute thinking sharpened my ideas. Lisa, you are a brilliant scholar, a careful reader, a formidable chef, an energetic travel companion, and a wonderful friend at the movies. As we pass our tenth wedding anniversary, I cannot believe how lucky I am to spend the rest of my life with you.

THE DYNAMIC FRAME

INTRODUCTION

During the studio years, Hollywood filmmakers routinely complained about the moving camera. The director Rouben Mamoulian said, "Moving shots just for the sake of moving shots and with no reason are silly."[1] The cinematographer James Wong Howe charged, "The average moving-shot results in injecting a sort of false movement into a scene or sequence. It interrupts the progress of the story."[2] Darryl F. Zanuck, the head of production at Twentieth Century-Fox, advised director Joseph L. Mankiewicz, "It is my opinion that prolonged scenes where the camera moves back and forth are more harmful than helpful."[3] The director George Cukor said, "You should never move the camera unless you have to."[4] All four characterized the moving camera as an ever-looming mistake.

Don't believe it. The moving camera was an integral part of Hollywood's filmmaking technique, and Mamoulian, Howe, Zanuck, and Cukor knew it. Many of the same filmmakers who denounced the technique in print employed the moving camera quite daringly onscreen. Mamoulian was one of the industry's leading innovators of camera movement in the early sound period, as in his musical *Applause* (1929). Howe later gained fame for his willingness to experiment with the moving camera, as when he donned roller skates to film the fight scenes in *Body and Soul* (1947). Zanuck's attempts to restrain his employees proved to be only partly successful: the film he was advising on, *Somewhere in the Night* (1946), featured several extended subjective sequences, and the studio boss was obliged to send memos to recalcitrant directors more than once over the next few years. As for Cukor, even if he did believe that you should never move the camera unless you have to, his films suggest that he had to, many times—witness the extended dolly shots in *The Women* (1939), *Edward, My Son* (1949), and *A Star Is Born* (1954).

Here we have a puzzle. When we look to the rhetoric alone, we find Hollywood filmmakers cautioning against camera movement. When we look to the films, we find that the high-powered studio system enabled some of the most fluid camerawork in the world. Historians have explained Hollywood's adoption of many technologies by invoking a dialectic of display and restraint. After new tools are introduced (such as sound, color, and widescreen), filmmakers initially flaunt the technology, only to shift toward moderation, subordinating each device to the limitations of narrative.[5] But "restraint" is not the right metaphor in the case of camera movement. The moving camera became standard equipment—an easily available option when shooting just about anything. Although a few distinguished filmmakers insisted that dollies and booms were empty distractions, many more learned to use camera movement with energy and purpose. They applied the technique to a wide range of contexts, from musical numbers to dramatic turning points, from explosions of violence to moments of quiet recognition. The demands of dramatic storytelling made the dolly seem more useful, not less. Mamoulian, Howe, Zanuck, and Cukor were not Luddites, arguing against dollies and cranes as a matter of principle. They were arguing against camerawork that seemed careless, deployed for no good reason. The guiding ideal was not efficiency but efficacy.

This book tells the story of camera movement in classical Hollywood cinema, covering the years from 1924 to 1958. I offer a historical poetics of the technique: a "poetics" because I am concerned with the principles of film construction; "historical" because I explain those principles by situating the technique within the context of the Hollywood studio system. David Bordwell has outlined the basic premises of the historical poetics approach: "We can explain important aspects of how movies work by considering filmmakers as creative agents working with craft practices within a community."[6] The framework of historical poetics is broad enough to include interpretation, and this book explains how disputes about *meaning* shaped the history of the moving camera. Artisans and engineers solved the technological problems relatively quickly. The challenge for filmmakers lay not in the how but in the why. A history of camera movement must be a history of ideas about camera movement.

These ideas found expression both on- and offscreen. In the pages of the trade journals, directors such as F. W. Murnau and Alfred Hitchcock and cameramen such as James Wong Howe and A. Lindsley Lane at Metro-Goldwyn-Mayer (M-G-M) produced a brief but provocative body of writings, offering their peers working theories of camera movement. These theories engaged in substantive debates. Whereas some filmmakers insisted that the camera's movements should mimic the movements a person might perform, others believed that the camera should move about the stage with a freedom denied to human observers. Whereas some filmmakers argued that the best way to tell a story was to reveal the most relevant information at all times, others delighted in the mobile frame's ability to conceal events for dramatic effect. Whereas some filmmakers used the camera to offer an objective view of each scene, others pondered the ways a camera might mimic a character's subjective states. These conceptual tensions—imitation and liberation, revelation and concealment, subjectivity and objectivity—shaped the history of camera movement by changing the ways that filmmakers imagined their art.

But an examination of written statements can take us only so far. When it came time to put the camera in motion, filmmakers did not consult back issues of *American Cinematographer*. They asked: How might a judicious movement contribute to this particular story? Here, I turn to the interpretation of individual films, where my approach draws inspiration from V. F. Perkins's discussion of worldhood in the cinema. "Selection by the camera," Perkins writes, "asserts significance. The image is displayed not only to relay information but to claim that it matters and to guide us towards the ways in which it matters."[7] Because a film represents a world, we may always ask, "Why is the movie showing us this and not that?" This observation applies to any Hollywood film, whether it uses a dolly or not, but films that foreground camera movement make the act of selection uniquely salient, using the mobile frame to provide a visibly shifting viewpoint on the events of the storyworld. Analyzing this viewpoint (in the literal sense of the term *viewpoint*) allows us to characterize a film's viewpoint (in the philosophical sense): its attitudes, its values, its sense of irony, and its tone.[8]

To be sure, there is some tension between these two interpretive projects. My discussion of the theories of camera movement examines how working filmmakers expressed general ideas about the cinema, but my close analysis of the practice of camera movement examines how individual works expressed attitudes and themes that were particular to specific storyworlds. To bridge this gap between the general and the particular, I rely on the concept of the shared strategy. As a group, Hollywood filmmakers shared familiar methods of moving the camera to address recurring storytelling situations. These shared methods were strategies rather than rules; they encompassed a wide range of tactics. The best films featured complex variations on familiar techniques, each suited to the needs of the work at hand.

Consider one of the most familiar conventions of camera movement: the dolly-in toward a character's face. The convention seems so familiar that its function seems obvious, barely worth discussing. Why does the camera dolly in? To emphasize the character's facial expressions, of course. However, the convention could take many forms, evoking many different ideas, as in two examples from the 1940s: *Phantom Lady* (1944) and *Mrs. Miniver* (1942). Produced by Joan Harrison, Robert Siodmak's film *Phantom Lady* features an unusually vigorous variation on the prototype. The protagonist, Kansas (Ella Raines), must solve a crime to free her unjustly accused boss from prison. Stumped, she is standing on the street when she happens to notice a hotel porter carrying a hat box. The low-angle camera briskly dollies in from a medium shot to a close-up, and Kansas smiles: she has figured out what to do next (fig. I.1a–b). What the shot lacks in subtlety it gains in expressive force. Departing from the emerging norm of the femme fatale, Kansas is a sympathetic, courageous protagonist.[9] The low angle allows her to dominate the frame, and the brisk movement evokes her intelligence by suggesting that the idea has come to her in a flash. Kansas is enjoying her stint as a detective, and this exhilarating shot sweeps us up in her enjoyment.

A shot from William Wyler's film *Mrs. Miniver* deploys the same convention—the dolly-in to a woman's face—with beautiful restraint. The title character (Greer Garson) is pointing out that her new daughter-in-law, Carol (Teresa Wright), seems happy. Carol agrees, even though she knows that her husband, a pilot in the Royal Air Force, is in danger. The camera remains stationary for most of Carol's monologue, but then with the slightest push it begins to move toward her (fig. I.2a). "I will be very happy," Carol says, "every moment that I have him. If I must lose him, there'll be time enough for tears. There'll be a lifetime for tears." Then the camera rests (fig. I.2b). The scene depicts a moment of self-recognition. At first, Carol answers her mother-in-law's question about her feelings simply. But then Teresa Wright adds another layer to her performance, suggesting that Carol is learning about herself as she speaks. She starts out by saying that she is happy in spite of her belief that her husband might die, but she gradually realizes that she is willing herself to be happy in order to defend against that belief. The shift is subtle, and so is the

I.1 In *Phantom Lady*, the camera swoops in for a moment of recognition.

I.2 In *Mrs. Miniver*, the camera moves forward gently for a recognition that dawns more slowly, but more deeply.

camerawork—truly, the gentlest dolly-in imaginable. In *Phantom Lady*, Kansas comes up with a new plan in a flash; the dolly zips from medium shot to close-up in less than three seconds. In *Mrs. Miniver*, Carol struggles toward a difficult truth; it takes the dolly grip almost fifteen seconds to move the camera less than a foot.

Clearly, these shots follow a familiar pattern; each is a dolly-in during a moment of recognition. In that sense, they have deployed a shared resource. Every Hollywood filmmaker knew that it was a good idea to dolly in during a moment of recognition. Yet these shots look so different, producing such different effects! The shared strategy set the stage for a series of subsequent choices: dramatic choices (Who is experiencing the moment of recognition? When? How long does the moment last?) and technical choices (When should the camera start moving? When should it stop? How fast should it move? How close should it get?). The results may be exuberant, as in *Phantom Lady*, or suffused with sympathy and respect, as in *Mrs. Miniver*, but they take on their meanings in the context of their unfolding stories.

The same shot may draw on more than one shared strategy. Unlike *Mrs. Miniver*'s Carol, who experiences a private moment in a domestic space, *Phantom Lady*'s Kansas experiences her moment of recognition on a New York City sidewalk, sparked by an ephemeral connection with the possessions of a random stranger. The vigorous dolly-in expresses not just what it feels like to have an idea but also what it feels like to have such an idea in the middle of a bustling modern city. Just as filmmakers discovered that the dolly-in could serve as a powerful tool of emotional emphasis, they learned that the cinema's uniquely mobile frame could in the right context evoke the frenetic energy of contemporary life.

Here, I make no claims that camera movement inevitably says something about cities or that it inevitably conveys information about character psychology. The technique accomplishes these functions only in context. The narrative theorists Meir Sternberg and Tamar Yacobi have written eloquently about the Proteus principle. In Yacobi's words, "Given the endless variability of context, the same form or formal pattern can always serve as means to different effects, and vice versa."[10] Throughout this book, I insist on this variability. We cannot know what a camera movement means in advance; we must interpret each shot in the moment. But that does not mean that Hollywood filmmakers were free to move the camera in any way at any time. They worked within the limits of their industrial and cultural contexts, starting with shared conventions and then modifying them to express different shades of meaning. Far from leaving works open to any interpretation whatsoever, the Proteus principle provides the foundation for a culturally specific historical poetics approach. Once we assume that techniques and meanings are *not* fixed, then we may ask how, when, and why they change.

Chapter Outline

Through the lens of this historical, interpretive approach, I examine several factors that shaped the history of camera movement from 1924 to 1958: technologies that facilitated certain uses of the moving camera and discouraged others; a division of labor that allowed Hollywood crews to master those technologies; cultural shifts that provided filmmakers with suitably dynamic subjects and themes; and individual filmmakers such as F. W. Murnau, Orson Welles, and Alfred Hitchcock, who pushed their peers to think about the moving camera in new ways. I have chosen 1924 as a starting point because it was the year American producers first saw Murnau's film *The Last Laugh*.[11] The film's subsequent American release was not a financial success, but Murnau's example inspired many Hollywood filmmakers to experiment with the moving camera more boldly. Chapter 1, "American Cinema, German Angles," examines this shift in the cultural status of camera movement over the course of the 1920s. In the first half of the decade, the technique had a low cultural status, associated with the fast-paced stunts of slapstick comedy. After Murnau, the technique's cultural connotations suddenly ascended—perhaps too much, evoking the artistry and pretensions of the German imports. Chapter 2, "Purposes and Parallels," analyzes the working theories of camera movement in the 1930s as articulated in the pages of *American Cinematographer* and other trade journals. Though some skeptics railed against camera movement, many filmmakers made sense of the technique by appealing to two different kinds of logic: means–end thinking and analogical thinking. The first justified camera movement by listing the various effects the technique might serve; the second prescribed specific variants of the technique by modeling the camera's movements on those a person might perform. Chapter 3, "Dynamism, Seriality, and Convergence," argues that Hollywood filmmakers found in the moving camera a powerful tool for the representation of American modernity. Without sacrificing their commitment to storytelling, several key films of the 1930s and 1940s explored three distinct aspects of contemporary culture: the dynamism of urban spaces, the seriality of mass production, and the convergence of crowded spaces that brought diverse groups of strangers together.

These first three chapters focus on the industry's complex, contradictory response to the work of Murnau, whose films offered a multifaceted model for Hollywood filmmakers to follow—or reject. The remaining three chapters examine Hollywood's long-range response to a group of filmmakers who came to prominence in the 1940s, including Hitchcock and Welles. Chapter 4, "Constructing Scenes with the Camera," explains how filmmakers photographed their scenes in three different ways. Many of the decade's filmmakers continued the standard practice of shooting master-and-coverage scenes, but Hitchcock and Welles vividly demonstrated the advantages of two alternatives: cutting in the camera and the long take. In so doing, they encouraged observers to think of camera movement as a director's technique rather than as a collaborative creation. Chapter 5, "Between Subjective and Objective," looks at various trends that came to fruition in the postwar period, ranging from the point-of-view experiments of *Lady in the Lake* (1947) to the semi-documentary style of *The Naked City* (1948). Although Hollywood's theorists routinely posited a sharp distinction between subjective and objective technique, the period's films problematized this distinction, exploring techniques of camera movement that were more ambiguous than they appeared. Chapter 6, "An Art of Disclosures," examines how the long-take films of the late 1940s and the early widescreen films of the 1950s forced filmmakers to rethink the camera's contribution to four perennial purposes: revelation, concealment, emphasis, and understatement. A well-designed long take fulfilled these functions without difficulty, but widescreen technologies posed a deeper problem, offering an immersive experience at odds with the craft of cinematic storytelling, which remained grounded in the careful control of what was onscreen and what was off. The book concludes with an analysis of the celebrated opening shot of *Touch of Evil* (1958).

The chapters proceed in a rough chronological order, from 1924 to 1958. However, my primary goal is not to construct a perfectly linear timeline but to offer a multifaceted look at the history of camera movement. Each chapter approaches the history from a slightly different perspective, bringing a new aspect of camera movement to the fore: cultural status (chapter 1), the advantages and disadvantages of comparing a camera to a person (chapter 2), representations of modernity (chapter 3), scene construction (chapter 4), subjectivity and objectivity (chapter 5), and the relationship between onscreen and offscreen space (chapter 6). This structure mandates occasional shifts from short-term claims (about trends that lasted for a year or two) to long-term claims (about trends that have lasted as long as Hollywood has been in the business of making commercially driven narrative films). For instance, the theorists of the early 1930s often compared the camera to a person, hoping to provide a model for the camera's movements. But this analogy persisted long after the transition to sound was complete; my examination of the camera–person analogy in chapter 2 inevitably gestures toward issues that recur in subsequent decades. Similarly, Orson Welles's innovations in scene construction, discussed in chapter 4, must be understood against a longer history of filmmakers working within (and revolting against) master-and-coverage technique.

Most broadly, I use the history of camera movement to offer some general observations about the nature of cinematic storytelling in classical Hollywood. The early chapters register my skepticism about a particular way of theorizing camera movement—the idea that the Hollywood camera typically moves in the manner of an all-seeing observer. Working filmmakers often invoked this figure in their theories, but I think that the ideals of anthropomorphism (the camera is like a person) and omniscience (the camera sees or knows everything) failed to capture the complexity of their own practice. In the later chapters, I spell out an alternative account of what Hollywood filmmakers were doing when they moved the camera, grounded in the idea of sequential disclosures. A Hollywood film is a sequence of pictures; these pictures have frames; and these frames set in motion a play of revelation and concealment, thereby manipulating the ever-shifting gap between the known and unknown. Like the theory of the "all-seeing observer," this alternative finds historical support in the working theories of Hollywood practitioners, and I think it does a better job explaining how Hollywood filmmakers made concrete, context-specific decisions about moving the camera: they were taking full advantage of the cinema's dynamic frame, offering changing pictures of a changing storyworld. The camera cannot show everything at once; herein lies its power.

Types of Camera Movements

Before starting the story, let us meet the characters. The category "camera movement" includes several techniques—most notably, pans, tilts, dollies, and cranes. This list can be widened to include zooms, handheld work, shots taken on moving vehicles, and effects produced with postproduction tools. This book focuses on the first four—pans, tilts, dollies, and cranes—with occasional references to other techniques. This section describes all of the basic moves with

the help of illustrations. Interested readers may also consult my website (www
.thedynamicframe.net/clips), where I post short fair-use videos of the most
important examples.

Sunset Boulevard (1950) usefully illustrates all of the basic moves. Directed
by Billy Wilder and photographed by John F. Seitz, this classic film noir uses
pans, tilts, dollies, and cranes to control what we see and when. In so doing, it
demonstrates a core principle of this book: cinematic storytelling is an art of
disclosures. A film may reveal information in many ways, but the moving camera makes the act of revelation (or concealment) unusually salient.

Early in the film, the struggling screenwriter Joe Gillis (William Holden)
pulls his car into the derelict garage of what appears to be an abandoned house.
Adjacent to his vehicle, he notices an old car and walks over to take a closer
look; the camera *pans* to follow him, swiveling from left to right. Note that the
camera remains in its original position, close to Joe's car, even as it angles toward
the old car (fig. I.3a–b). We might compare a pan to the movement of a person
turning his or her head while standing in one spot, but the anthropomorphic
analogy is not quite right. A person does not look at the world through a rectangular frame, and the presence of a frame is essential to the shot's effect. Joe's
car is in the frame, and then it is out; the battered older vehicle is out of the
frame, and then it is in. In this way, the film foreshadows a later plot point: Joe
will lose ownership of his car and become a passive passenger in this soon-to-
be-refurbished relic.

The term *pan* is short for *panorama*, and it usually refers to lateral movements, as in this left-to-right example. When the camera changes the direction
of its angle up or down without shifting its position, the result is a *tilt*. There is
a brief tilt at the beginning of the car shot, but a clearer example appears later
in the film, after Joe has revealed his sordid secret to Betty (Nancy Olson). Joe
watches Betty leave the mansion; then he turns around (fig. I.4a). On Joe's turn,

I.3 In *Sunset Boulevard*, the camera pans to follow Joe as he notices an older car.

I.4 The camera tilts up to reveal that Norma is watching Joe.

the camera tilts up and through the ornate gate reveals Norma (Gloria Swanson) watching from the second floor (fig. I.4b). The tilt up emphasizes Norma's ominous power by making her presence a jolting surprise: she is offscreen, then shockingly on. At the same time, the precise framing evokes her weakness: the bars of the gate form a series of rectangles, one of which encloses Norma. The symbolism is affecting. The house is a prison for Norma just as much as it is for Joe. Earlier she declared, "I am big. It's the pictures that got small." Now she seems miniscule, a dwarfed figure locked in a tiny rectangle, enclosed within the screen's much larger frame.

In the simple pan or tilt shot, the camera points in a different direction without moving its position. In the simple dolly shot, the camera changes its position in space, though the direction it points may remain the same. An earlier scene shows Joe pacing by Norma's bed while he is waiting for Betty to arrive (fig. I.5a). When the doorbell rings, Joe exits, and the camera *dollies* forward to frame a closer view of Norma, sitting up and revealing a gun by the pillow (fig. I.5b). Here, the frame changes because the camera has advanced toward Norma, not because its direction of view has changed. The resulting camerawork offers another play of revelation and concealment by displaying the presence of a gun. In the previous two examples, the pattern of disclosures echoed Joe's experiences. The pan revealed the old car when Joe noticed it, just as the tilt revealed Norma's presence when Joe turned to look at her. Here, the camera's movement is detached from Joe's: he walks away from Norma, but the camera moves in. This detachment underscores a crucial difference in knowledge: we now know that Norma is lying next to a gun, but Joe does not. Hollywood parlance might describe this shot as an "unmotivated" movement, as the camera fails to follow a walking figure, but the term is misleading. The dolly serves a very clear purpose, drawing our attention to a detail that the protagonist has overlooked.

I.5 Joe paces by Norma's bed; after he exits, the camera dollies in toward Norma—and the gun.

I.6 When Joe explores the grounds of the mansion, the camera cranes up to reveal a decaying garden.

Dollies are also known as "tracking shots," referring to the rails laid on the ground to guide the camera's movement, in the manner of a model train set. With or without tracks, the dolly shot encompasses many types of movement: in or out, left or right, in a straight line or along an arc. In the crane shot, the camera changes its position in space by moving up or down. *Sunset Boulevard* features a striking *crane* after Joe leaves his car in the decrepit garage. Joe ascends the stairs (fig. I.6a), and the camera vaults upward, revealing a dried-out swimming pool and an overgrown garden (fig. I.6b). Again, the movement of the camera delicately manages the timing of the disclosures. As Joe discovers this vast space for the first time, the upward movement expresses a sense of grandeur while exposing the reality of its decay. The timing aligns our knowledge with Joe's—but not perfectly. Recall that *Sunset Boulevard* opens with Joe's corpse floating in the swimming pool, and Joe is now narrating this story from beyond the grave. When the camera cranes up to reveal the swimming pool, we know already that Joe is destined to die in that pool; the Joe depicted onscreen does not. This dramatic irony undercuts Joe's cynical, knowing persona as he looks at the space with disgust.

Pans, tilts, dollies, and cranes constitute the four prototypical movements that are the subject of this book. Of course, drawing these distinctions can be somewhat artificial: many shots combine several kinds of movement. Technologies encouraged these combinations. Some dollies came equipped with small boom arms, allowing for miniature crane motions. Cranes were capable of traveling laterally, producing a dollylike movement. And any camera placed on a crane or dolly could be mounted on a standard tripod head, enabling the full complement of pans and tilts. Flexibility supports complexity, as in the scene when Norma mistakes Joe for an undertaker. She leads him into her bedroom, where a recently deceased pet monkey lies, awaiting burial. The camera *pans* to follow Norma as she walks through the door and into the bedroom, *booms* up slightly as Norma ascends a couple steps, and *dollies* forward as Norma and Joe approach the corpse. This intricate movement—a pan, a boom, and a dolly—aligns the spectator's experience with Joe's complex reaction. Joe is amazed to find himself in a bedroom with a bizarre older woman and a dead monkey, yet he is strangely fascinated, cautiously stepping forward and leaning in to learn more. Fittingly, the camerawork offers the spectator a surprise followed by an incomplete disclosure, panning quickly to reveal the eerie new room and then moving forward gradually to explore that space while keeping the identity (and species) of the corpse a mystery.

One more example will complete this survey of basic camera movements before turning to the history proper. Unusually for a film of the period, *Sunset Boulevard* contains a handful of zooms, apparently executed in-camera (as opposed to "optical zooms," which are produced by enlarging the image in postproduction). Right after Joe discovers the garden in the previously discussed crane shot, Norma calls to him from her second-story bedroom window. He looks up, and the film cuts to a long shot of Norma, wearing sunglasses even as she stands behind window shades (fig. I.7a). The camera *zooms* in slightly, just enough to draw attention to Norma, but not enough to reveal any details (fig. I.7b). In a simple zoom such as this, the camera does not change its position or the direction of its angle. Instead, the operator changes the lens's focal length, producing visible differences in scale. A zoom shifts from a wide angle of view to a narrow (telephoto) angle of view or vice versa; the effect is either to enlarge or to demagnify the image. Not exactly a camera movement, a zoom is an adjustment of the lens, changing its focal length to alter its field of view. Norma's image grows bigger, but only slightly, thereby evoking Joe's shift of attention—and failure of recognition.

I.7 After Joe looks up, the camera zooms in.

At first glance, it is easy to mistake a zoom-in for a dolly-in, but they look quite different.[12] When in doubt, take a closer look at relative sizes and overlaps as they appear onscreen. Consider figure I.5a again. Notice the cherub sitting on the orb, just to the left of Norma. If you were to measure the occlusion size of the orb onscreen and compare it to the occlusion size of Norma's head, her head would be slightly larger.[13] Sounds trivial, I know, but look at figure I.5b. Notice that the occlusion sizes have changed: Norma's head is now much bigger than the orb. Meanwhile, the cherub overlaps a different part of the background curtain. These changes in overlap and relative size show that the camera has moved in space, altering the geography with respect to the viewpoint. By contrast, in a zoom shot, overlaps and relative sizes remain the same. Take a look at figure I.7a again. On the right, the fronds of the palm tree overlap an Ionic column. As the camera zooms in (fig. I.7b), the overlaps do not change at all, even though the palm tree is at least ten feet in front of the column. Similarly, the relative sizes remain identical: the image of Norma gets bigger, but so does the image of the palm tree, and they both get bigger at exactly the same rate. The zoom is a magnification rather than a movement proper.[14]

Looking at overlaps also provides a useful way to recognize when you are looking at pans and tilts, on the one hand, and lateral dollies and cranes, on the other. In the former pairing, the camera remains in position; overlaps remain largely the same. In the latter, the camera changes its position in space, resulting in shifting overlaps. In figure I.4a, on the right side of the frame, the bars form a decorative pattern, overlapping the top of a middle-ground lamp. After the camera tilts up (fig. I.4b), the ornamental bars and the lamp are now in the lower-right corner—but their overlaps remain unchanged. By contrast, during the crane-up in figure I.6 the overlaps shift constantly: in the first half of the shot, the wall occludes the trunks of the palm trees, which become visible in the second half. A lateral dolly works the same way: foreground objects occlude background objects, but the patterns of occlusion shift constantly.

These illustrations may help us recognize the differences among the various camera movements, but what purposes do those movements serve? Here, an ahistorical, narrowly formal analysis might propose specific correlations between style and function. Perhaps the dolly-in is inevitably immersive, giving the spectator the illusion of moving forward through space. Perhaps the zoom-out is inevitably distancing, giving the spectator the sense of looking at a constantly diminishing picture. However, I think it is more useful to approach techniques from a contextualist perspective. The pans, tilts, dollies, cranes, and zooms of *Sunset Boulevard* perform functions that are specific to this film, even as they draw on strategies shared throughout Hollywood. The strategy of gradual revelations echoes Joe's step-by-step discovery of Norma's disintegrating world. Wilder and his collaborators align the camera's movements with Joe's, revealing details as he encounters them, but the flashback structure guarantees that the result is not identification but irony. A film with a different temporal structure, without the ironic voiceover, might deploy the same combination of pans, tilts, dollies, and cranes to very different effect.

Indeed, this potential for variation is why we need a *history* of camera movement. If the dolly or the pan were to have a single consistent meaning, then the analyst could point to a single film and generalize from there. But the meanings of the moving camera were subject to constant reinvention from decade to decade and even from film to film. By looking at the discourse and the practice of camera movement, shifting and turning from 1924 to 1958, this book offers such a history.

CHAPTER 1

AMERICAN CINEMA, GERMAN ANGLES

I n 1926, the *Film Daily* reporter Maurice Kann wrote several editori-
als championing the dynamic camerawork of recent German films,
most notably F. W. Murnau's *The Last Laugh* (1924) and E. A. Dupont's
Variety (1925). Both directors had signed contracts with Hollywood studios, and
Kann hoped that they could teach Hollywood filmmakers how to use the
camera more creatively. Toward the end of the year, however, a note of ambivalence began to appear in Kann's prose. His admiration for the German works
remained undiminished ("It will be rather generally agreed that it was the
German influence in camera work that served to jog Hollywood out of a complacent rut"), but he charged that some filmmakers had taken the idea of the
roaming camera too far: "The appeal that goes with innovations has taken
hold too strongly. This has resulted in the insertion of camera pranks where
they don't belong."[1] The title of Kann's editorial was significant: "Tricks." He
feared that the celebrated German "angles" were being reduced to trick shots.

Journalists would later credit Murnau as the inventor of the moving camera.[2] This claim is demonstrably untrue: the innovation had many precursors,
in Germany (e.g., Lupu Pick's film *Sylvester* [1924]), in France (e.g., Abel Gance's
film *La Roue* [1923]), and even in Hollywood.[3] But if Murnau did not invent the
moving camera, he did give the device new cultural significance for Hollywood
filmmakers. In the early 1920s, moving-camera shots were the specialty of slapstick cinematographers, who described their work as the making of "trick
shots"; a bit ashamed, they longed for the day when they might produce the
painterly, static compositions that were the mark of the serious drama. Dupont's

and Murnau's films seemed fresh because they inverted the cultural connotations of the mobile frame, replacing the low status of slapstick with the high status of European drama.

Such a shift did not guarantee the widespread acceptance of the moving camera; if anything, the German intervention made the device more contentious. Debates about camera movement would become proxy debates about the deeper contradictions defining the industry: contradictions between Americanism and internationalism, between confident commercialism and inquisitive experimentalism, between careful craft and the routines of mass production. When Maurice Kann worried that German angles were devolving into American pranks, he gave voice to deeper anxieties about the industry's status. This chapter examines the moving camera in the 1920s not just as a technical innovation but also as a figure of rapidly shifting aesthetic significance.

Tricks and Kicks

A quick survey of the preceding decades provides some useful context. During the 1900s, a camera might ride an elevator ascending to the top of the Eiffel Tower, observe the skyscrapers of New York from the vantage point of a boat on the Hudson, or travel by train around a Colorado mining town.[4] One company, Hale's Tours and Scenes of the World, even offered spectators the chance to sit in an exhibition space shaped like a railroad car. Watching the film gave viewers the imaginary experience of traveling through a landscape by rail. The experience was bodily as well; seats could be rigged to shake in the manner of a moving train.[5] In all of these films, the primary appeal was not an unfolding story but the cinema's capacity to represent a moving view.

The scholar of early cinema Tom Gunning has proposed an influential distinction between the cinema of attractions and the cinema of narrative integration. The former, which dominated film production until approximately 1907, offered spectators a range of "attractions"—exciting moments of spectacle such as the sight of an exotic location or the glimpse of a woman's ankle. A film from this period might include a story, but often it was just an excuse to string together a series of stunts, jokes, tricks, and other distractions. Later, narrative emerged as the dominant organizing principle, eventually culminating in the feature-length production that became Hollywood's major product after around 1915. As Gunning argues, we should think of this shift not as a gradual process of improvement, as if guided by a teleology of progress, but as a more fundamental shift in cinema's address toward its spectators. The cinema of attractions, with roots in the fairground and vaudeville, directly appealed to the spectator's sense of astonishment. The cinema of narrative integration worked indirectly, prioritizing the mediating layer of a linear story unfolding in a coherent fictional world.[6]

Billy Bitzer, who would later become famous as D. W. Griffith's leading cinematographer, executed some of the most astonishing camera moves of the "cinema of attractions" period. For his film *Panorama of the Brooklyn Bridge* (1903), Bitzer perched his camera on top of one of the bridge's towers. The camera pans from left to right, allowing the bridge to come into frame, pass across, and exit. This technique privileges the process of movement over the bridge itself, which occupies center screen for but a moment. The following year Bitzer photographed the Westinghouse factory from the vantage point of an industrial crane gliding over the floor. No one dominates the composition; the film instead honors industrial technology by celebrating a machine that is kept offscreen: the crane moving the camera. Another film from 1904 is even more impressive: Bitzer's *Interior New York Subway, 14th Street to 42nd Street* features a camera placed on one train, following another train as it winds through the shadows of a subway tunnel, all while illuminated by a third train running alongside on a parallel track.[7] The resulting images are mesmerizingly abstract; the photographed train becomes an animated square, growing and shrinking as the camera approaches and recedes (fig. 1.1a–b).

The appeal of these films lies in the display of what the camera can do. By contrast, the integrated film will suit the visual style to the needs of the narrative, sometimes favoring modest camerawork, sometimes taking advantage of the camera's sensory appeals to make the story itself more exciting.[8] *Suspense* (1913) concerns a terrified woman (played by codirector Lois Weber) who calls her husband to tell him that a knife-wielding thief is entering her home. The husband hops in someone else's car and goes to her rescue, pursued by a policeman. One shot looks over the husband's shoulder toward the front of the stolen car, showing the pursuit car in a rearview mirror. The policeman on the pursuit car lunges for the husband, but then the pursuit car loses its speed and recedes into the mirror's background. Although the shot is independently

1.1 In *Interior, New York Subway*, the camera follows a moving subway car.

interesting in the manner of an attraction, the composition intensifies the emotion that gives the film its title: suspense. In a suspenseful narrative, we look forward in time, fearing one outcome and hoping for another; a classic way of increasing suspense is to make the outcome we fear appear more likely.[9] In this film, the moving camera produces suspense because our experience of anticipation is linked directly to our perceptions of speed and space. The closer the policeman gets, the more our fears increase. By placing the camera on the cars and allowing us to see both vehicles at the same time, the filmmakers allow us to see the inch-by-inch shortening of the distance between the two cars, resulting in a moment-by-moment tightening of tension.

In this case, the narrative and the attraction mutually intensify one another: the more impressive the stunt, the more suspense we feel. However, the principles can be mutually limiting as well because the two approaches rely on different modes of address, with the attraction soliciting the viewer's attention directly and the narrative working through the mediating frame of a fictional world.[10] Consider the most famous series of moving-camera shots from this decade: the Babylon sequence in D. W. Griffith's film *Intolerance* (1916). Partly inspired by the Italian spectacular *Cabiria* (1913), Griffith and cinematographer Billy Bitzer photographed this sequence using an enormous elevator dolly. As Bitzer later described it, "The dolly was 150 feet high, about six feet square at the top and sixty feet wide at the bottom. It was mounted on six sets of four-wheeled railroad-car trucks and had an elevator in the center. . . . Twenty-five workers pushed it smoothly along the rails."[11] Although *Intolerance* is a narrative film of extraordinary ambition, these shots put the technology of movement on display. In the first Babylon scene, the camera starts out high above the set—a monument to decadence featuring sculptures of elephants, massive curved columns, and a stairway with a procession of Babylonians (fig. 1.2a). As the camera moves forward, Bitzer's contraption lowers it to the ground, arriving at an empty space between two rows of women with their arms upraised in a ceremonial pose (fig. 1.2b). The dolly is not moving toward a particular charac-ter so much as it is traveling through the set to let us know just how enormous it is. Similar to Bitzer's work during the previous decade, this shot requires a diffuse mode of attention: we must scan the frame to appreciate its overwhelm-ing accumulation of detail. To be sure, the extravagance of the technique expresses the decadence of Babylonian society. But that narrative function recedes in the context of the film's larger aim of astonishing the spectator with the spectacle of movement itself.

For all these impressive achievements, not everyone at the time agreed on the moving camera's value. When *Cabiria* inspired a brief vogue for the wandering dolly, as in Raoul Walsh's film *Regeneration* (1915), the reviewers for *Wid's Films and Film Folk* denounced the technique, calling it a "freak trick" and hoping that someone would destroy the dolly with a giant ax.[12] Barry Salt

1.2 In *Intolerance*, a massive elevator dolly allows the camera to survey the spectacular Babylon set.

reports that the "tracking shot craze" ended by 1917.[13] Most films from the late 1910s and the early 1920s feature very little camera movement—not even simple pans to follow a character walking from one side of the room to another. Instead, editing devices such as the point-of-view shot and the match-on-action show how various spaces are connected. In Henry King's *Tol'able David*, a huge hit in 1921, the climactic scene relies on the careful sequencing of stationary shots. When David walks slowly toward the house where the villains are threatening David's beloved, the camera shows the entire action in long shot. When the most menacing villain pushes David to the floor, a match-on-action cut shows the shove in one shot before cutting to David's fall in the next. But the end of the sequence introduces an important exception to the norm of stasis: when David speeds back to the town in his carriage, the film shifts toward dynamism, both by placing the camera on the vehicle itself and by photographing the carriage from a car moving alongside. Whereas the camera in *Intolerance* flaunts its freedom to move about in space, the camera in *Tol'able David* moves only when its subject is in a moving vehicle.

One way of interpreting this difference is to say that filmmakers renounced camera movement in the name of the "invisible" style. But this is not quite right: the films of the 1920s contain plenty of eye-catching compositions and effects, even when the camera remains stationary. Cinematographers were beginning to think of themselves as artists, and culturally ambitious filmmakers increasingly turned to pictorialism for inspiration, using gauzy filters and careful compositions to produce imagery reminiscent of art photography.[14] The most artful frames in Frances Marion's film *The Love Light* (1921) are stationary—not because the filmmakers were worried about distracting our attention from the story but because they did not want to distract our attention from the

elegantly silhouetted compositions. The moving camera lacked these painterly connotations; as such, it was more suited for action than for drama.

On some films, the separation of functions was so stark that the task was
delegated to a specialist: the Akeley operator. During the 1910s, the wildlife photographer Carl Akeley had invented a camera that allowed him to photograph
animals from a distance with a telephoto lens. The camera included a gyroscopic
mechanism that made it easier to pan and tilt smoothly, and the mechanism
was eventually incorporated into an Akeley tripod.[15] Another feature was the
camera's variable shutter; when opened up to 230 degrees, any onscreen movement would register with a slight blur. This might sound like a defect, but Akeley
operators believed that the blurriness enhanced the sense of speed. (By contrast, a smaller shutter opening would register a series of crisp, frozen stills.)
The Akeley camera became a default tool for chases, airplane sequences, and
horse races. Ira Hoke, an Akeley operator, admitted that the camera was not
suitable for everyday shooting; rather, it was "an auxiliary tool" for the purposes
of "speed portrayal." The break from ordinary practice was part of the appeal:
in Hoke's words, "The director of modern productions intersperses Akeley
scenes into the regular photographic action for the purpose of 'pepping up'
sequences which would otherwise drag."[16] The shots do not contribute to a film's
narrative so much as they compensate for its deficiencies. Alternatively, the
filmmakers might employ a dynamic shot to amplify a scene that is already
exciting. The chariot race in *Ben Hur* (1925) is both a dramatic and a visual high
point: dramatic because it is the culmination of the long-simmering feud
between the hero and the villain; visual because the race offers a rush of movement, photographed with a battery of forty-two cameras mounted on cars and
platforms, including an Akeley to follow the action up close.[17]

There was at least one genre where scenes of movement were the rule, not
the exception: slapstick comedy. In a scene from *The Extra Girl* (1923), Sue
(Mabel Normand) rides a carriage to the train station in order to escape her
family and start a career in Hollywood. As in many silent comedies, in this
scene undercranking produces an exhilarating sense of speed. Working with
an Akeley, the operator pans at a consistent rate, and the figures stay the same
size for the entire shot.[18] Even better, the background zips by because of the lens's
narrow angle of view: with a telephoto lens, shifting the camera one degree to
the left completely changes the background (fig. 1.3a–b). The exhilarating speed,
enjoyable in itself, gives us insight into Normand's daring character. Just watch
her smiling in delight.

The cinematographer Fred Jackman photographed several Mabel Normand
comedies when she worked at Mack Sennett Studios. In 1922, Jackman wrote
an article proposing increased specialization as a sign of the profession's matu-
rity. The distinguishing trait of the comedy cinematographer was technical
skill, relying on camera trickery to convince the viewer that the performer was

1.3 A telephoto lens photographs an action scene in *The Extra Girl*.

in real danger. Some of Jackman's examples were effects shots, such as multiple exposures, and some were moving-camera shots. Jackman was particularly impressed by a cameraman who asked his crew to strap him to the smokestack of a fire engine so he could manipulate the camera while the engine careened down a street. What brought these examples together was "kick," defined as thrill, excitement, or fright.[19] As in the cinema of attractions, in comedy telling a coherent story was less important than stringing together a series of emotional jolts.

But comedy was changing: over the course of the decade, the films of Mabel Normand, Harold Lloyd, Charlie Chaplin, and Buster Keaton featured more complex narratives, requiring greater integration between story and gag. Lloyd's director Sam Taylor explained, "Always the gag furthers the story. In fact, only when it fulfills this requirement as well as being funny, can any incident stay in one of our pictures."[20] Comedy cinematographers found themselves in a tough position: required to execute difficult trick shots but expected to enhance a film's dramatic appeal. An article by Lloyd cinematographer Walter Lundin in 1924 expressed a mixture of hope and apprehension. Lundin reluctantly agreed with Jackman that the comedy cinematographer's reputation rested on trick shots; the accompanying illustrations showed Lundin "crouching on a platform affixed to the front of an automobile preparatory to shooting Lloyd in dangerous 'chase' scenes." But Lundin went on to argue that the comedy cinematographer must know how to execute "atmospheric" shots to complement the new dramatic scenes.[21] Lundin's work on Taylor's film *Girl Shy* (1924) maintains a strict separation of styles: the romantic scenes employ stationary framings and hazy diffusion, whereas the action scenes feature an array of crisply focused trick shots, as when the camera races alongside a fire truck while

Lloyd's character, the Boy, hangs on to a spiraling hose. This separation hints at a connotation of cultural inferiority that had attached itself to the moving camera. Perfect for scenes of raucous comedy, the technique remained unsuited to the production of dramatic atmosphere, which benefitted from painterly prettiness.

In practice, Lundin and Taylor were not above stretching the principle of narrative integration to include a good gag. In *Girl Shy*, when the Boy takes over a trolley so he can get to a church and break up a wedding, he must climb on top to reconnect the car to the overhead electric line. Then the film cuts to a drunkard inside the trolley car; waking up, this bewildered sot is astonished to see that the trolley is speeding along its tracks without the benefit of a driver. The tippler's point-of-view shots are among the most thrilling in the film, playing off the contrast between the streetcar's cab in the foreground, which remains stationary, and the city's streets in the background, which spin left and right as the trolley winds along its tracks. Although the gag reinforces just how out of control this trolley is, it ultimately distracts our attention from the primary suspense line, whereby the Boy must maintain his balance atop the vehicle. The result is not suspense but shock: jolts of astonishment as the image whips this way, then that.

Another common moving-camera joke might be termed the "revelation gag." Here, the camera starts out by showing us a detail and then dollies back to put the detail in a larger context, thereby overturning our original assumptions about the scene. In Lloyd's *Safety Last* (1923), the comedian plays yet another man called "the Boy." One scene opens with a title card announcing that the Boy "is in great danger." The next shot shows the Boy with his clothes in disarray, suggesting that we are about to witness a fight scene. The camera dollies back to reveal that he is fending off a crowd of female shoppers at the department store where he works. Following the logic of surprise, the tight framing has pushed the spectator to make a false assumption, which is corrected when the camera dollies back to reveal a larger picture.[22]

A third convention could be called the "following gag." The camera tracks along with one character who is trailing another very closely. Variations appear in *From Hand to Mouth* (1919; the Boy walks behind a man to retrieve a handbag); *The Extra Girl* (Sue thinks that she is walking with a dog in a lion costume, but we see that the creature is a real lion); and *The General* (1926; two boys follow Johnny, and Johnny's beloved follows all three). The execution of the gag in *Sherlock Jr.* (1924) is particularly deft. The protagonist is an aspiring detective who reads a guidebook advising him to trail the primary suspect. Taking the advice very literally, he walks one step behind the suspect for several yards. When the suspect stops to pick up a cigarette, Keaton pulls up just in time—and the camera halts briefly to keep them in frame (fig. 1.4a). When they start moving again, so, too, does the camera (fig. 1.4b). The humor of the scene

1.4 *Sherlock, Jr.* stages a follow shot with perfect timing.

arises from the incongruity between the story situation of two characters who cannot predict each other's actions and the performance of two actors whose movements appear to be in perfect synchronization—with each other and with the camera. Visually, the camerawork offers a useful comparison with the carriage scene from *The Extra Girl*. In the Normand movie, the filmmakers photographed the carriage with a distant camera and a telephoto lens, producing a flat band of space. Here, the filmmakers use a shorter focal-length lens, and the camera is not panning but moving laterally alongside the actors, most likely from the back of a truck. The buildings in the background look smaller, and it takes a longer time for them to move onscreen and off. The sense of speed is thereby diminished (because the background buildings are not whipping by), but the sense of depth is enhanced (because we can see the differences in scale between foreground and background and because we can see a parallax effect as closer objects appear to move more quickly).[23] Depth makes the joke funnier: our awareness that space stretches far into the distance makes it all the more incongruous that Keaton's detective holds so close to the suspect.

The opposition between static drama and dynamic comedy was sufficiently well established by this time that King Vidor could satirize it just a few years later. *Show People* (1928), like *The Extra Girl*, tells the story of a woman (Marion Davies) who goes to Hollywood in the hope of becoming a movie star. At first, she appears in roughhouse comedies, but later she stars in pretentious dramas. One day she is filming a romance outdoors; suddenly a slapstick comedy troupe approaches and interrupts her work. *Show People* represents the two film crews very differently. The romantic drama crew employs two cameras, side by side, both on tripods. The stasis of the cameras echoes the inertia of the scene, which depicts two lovers leaning languorously against a tree.[24] By contrast, the comedy crew has placed its lone camera in the back of a moving automobile;

the car hurtles down the road while photographing a succession of comedians prancing along in goofy costumes. The target of Vidor's satire here is the drama, not the comedy. The painterly drama has lost touch with the essence of cinema: movement itself.

When Sam Taylor wrote his article about the increasing narrativization of slapstick comedy, it appeared in the June 27, 1925, issue of *Film Daily*. In the very next column, the newspaper ran a story about a trio of European directors who had just been hired by the Hollywood studios: the German F. W. Murnau, hired by Fox; the Danish Benjamin Christensen, hired by M-G-M; and the Swedish Victor Sjöstrom, also at M-G-M.[25] Other European talents would soon follow.[26] Led by Murnau, these artists would introduce to Hollywood new ways of moving the camera. Some of their contributions were technical, but their deeper intervention was cultural. No longer a slapstick trick, the moving camera became an expression of artistic ambition. Once, the moving camera's cultural status seemed too low. Soon, its cultural status would seem too high.

German Angles and the Problem of Americanization

After seeing *The Last Laugh* in a special screening in 1924, William Fox signed Murnau to a contract, announced a day before the film's official American premiere in January 1925.[27] The film was not a financial success in the United States, but critics and filmmakers admired it greatly. At the *New York Times*, Mordaunt Hall called it a "highly artistic film masterpiece."[28] *Film Daily* featured the import on its top-ten list for 1925.. In 1926, E. A. Dupont's film *Variety* found success at the box office, while winning even more critical praise: Hall declared it "the strongest and most inspiring drama that has ever been told by the evanescent shadows," and the movie topped the *Film Daily* top-ten list for the year.[29] Both films won attention for their camerawork—though *Variety*'s salacious subject matter didn't hurt. *The Last Laugh*'s unusual techniques reportedly "astounded" many Hollywood directors; reviewers celebrated *Variety*'s "remarkable photographic effects" and "unusual angles."[30] The trade journal *Variety* showed particular enthusiasm for Dupont's film, commenting favorably on its "freaking photography" while pronouncing it "a corking picture."[31] "Freaking" and "corking": this was a rare combination, mixing artistic innovation with commercial appeal.

Murnau and Dupont's mobile shots soon came to be classified as "angles." Along with the bird's-eye view and the superimposition, any technique that departed from the stationary eye-level norm could be considered an "angle."[32] In contrast to Hollywood films that evoked the haziness of pictorial photography, the angle-filled imports called to mind the cutting-edge experimentation of avant-garde painting. One early review of *Variety* noted that the film's style was "in the modernistic manner of *The Last Laugh*."[33] Other critics referred to Picasso and Cezanne.[34] These allusions to modernism suggest an opposition between experimentation and storytelling, but Murnau insisted that the angle was a dramatic tool: "By itself an interesting camera angle does not mean a thing. If it does not help to intensify the dramatic action of the scene it is not only useless, it is dangerous, because instead of helping the dramatic action, it detracts from it. But what should the camera angle be if not interesting? It should be dramatic."[35] The interesting angle distracts from the scene; the dramatic angle intensifies the scene.

Later admirers would celebrate the Germans' technical ingenuity, as in articles marveling at Freund's ability to operate a camera while riding a bicycle.[36] But technology cannot have been the only reason for the films' appeal; slapstick cinematographers had been devising creative tricks for years. The real innovation was aesthetic: *The Last Laugh* and *Variety* amplified drama by using the camera to represent subjective states. In 1925, a full year before Murnau arrived in Hollywood, *Film Daily* printed an article by him where he explained his interest in subjectivity: "In making *The Last Laugh* I took for my goal the realization of a motion picture that would show us not only the outer surfaces, but the mental processes of a character. . . . So much of the subjective is left out of motion pictures; there is so much violent action or situation, that I thought it would be an innovation, worth emulation in America, to try to make audiences FEEL WITH the main character, rather than at what was happening to him."[37] Murnau's rhetoric echoed the ideals of German expressionism, looking past the surface of things to expose a deeper layer underneath. By suggesting that American films might imitate the technique, he implicitly criticized the existing Hollywood style for its reliance on the clean representation of external actions. Critics quickly adopted Murnau's ideas. By the time *Variety* came out the following year, they had learned to look for signs of the subjective: *Film Daily* noted that the cinematographer Karl Freund "photographs emotion, sound, hate," while a high-toned review in the *New Republic* claimed that the film "touches on moods too fragile for words, too tenuous to imprison, distorted creations of the unconscious mind."[38]

Although the films do include point-of-view shots, whereby the camera directly represents what a character sees, Murnau and Dupont often accomplish something more radical: they express a character's subjective experience *without* looking through that character's eyes. Borrowing a term from Jean Mitry, we might call this approach the "semisubjective" mode, mixing together internal and external aspects.[39] Consider the celebrated sequence of the porter's drunken dream in *The Last Laugh*. Far from being unambiguously subjective, the scene works in a variety of modes. In one shot, Murnau places the film's star, Emil Jannings, on a rotating platform with the camera, and it appears that the porter is remaining still while the world spins by in the background (fig. 1.5a–b). This shot does not represent the porter's point of view: the porter is in the shot, and we observe him from the outside. Yet we also see the room spinning around him, as if the film were offering us an external and an internal view simultaneously. Later, the old porter dreams of having superhuman strength, tossing around a suitcase with one hand. With the camera strapped to his chest, Freund circled around the porter to show the astonished faces of the imagined onlookers.[40] Again, we can observe the porter's pomposity from the outside, even as the bumpy camera movement assures us that we are looking inside his drunken dreams.

According to Graham Petrie, E. A. Dupont initially planned to film *Variety* in a more conventional manner, but both producer Erich Pommer and cinematographer Karl Freund convinced him to follow the fluid example of *The Last Laugh*.[41] The resulting technique won praise for its ability to reach "into Jannings's mind" and portray "what he thinks," but again the film mixed together a range of modes, including the semisubjective.[42] *Variety* tells the story of Boss Huller, a trapeze artist (Jannings) who leaves his wife for the younger Berta-Marie (Lya De Putti), only to realize that she has fallen in love with the handsome Artinelli (Warwick Ward). During the film's last trapeze performance, Huller is swinging back and forth, wondering whether he should commit murder by letting Artinelli fall. Freund attaches the camera to Huller's swing, producing a semisubjective effect similar to the rotating platform shot from *The Last Laugh*: Huller appears to be perfectly still, but in the background we see the two lovers, oscillating up and down even though they are the ones standing still (fig. 1.6a–b). The resulting image expresses turmoil (by creating the dizzying effect of oscillation) and obsession (by showing the image of the two lovers passing through the center of the frame again and again).

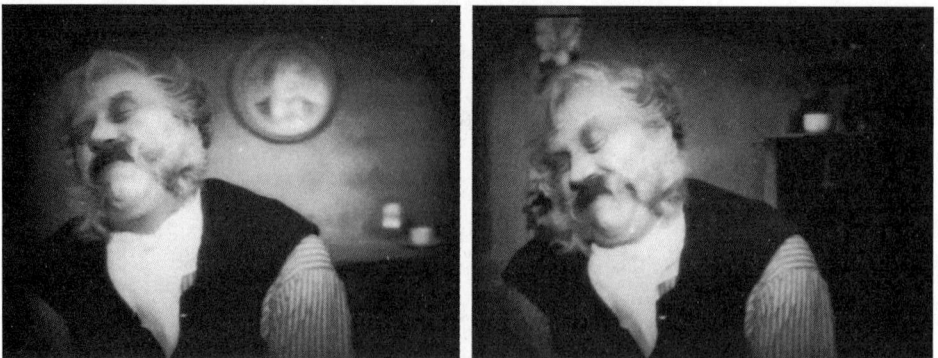

1.5 The world seems to be spinning around the porter in *The Last Laugh*.

1.6 *Variety* features an astonishing shot on a moving trapeze.

Several other sequences in both films follow the same principle, representing subjective experiences without depicting a character's optical point of view. In the celebrated trumpet shot in *The Last Laugh*, the camera, suspended from above, appears to track away from the musical instrument. (On set, the camera moved down toward the trumpet; the filmmakers reversed the direction by loading the film backward.) It is as if the camera has taken up the point of view of the sound itself, traveling from the trumpet up to the porter's ears.[43] Similarly, one of the key turning points in *Variety* occurs in a café: Huller realizes that Berta-Marie is cheating on him, and the camera spins in a circle. The spinning expresses Huller's emotions of overwhelming confusion without representing his literal point of view; he is not doing a pirouette in the middle of the café.

Murnau and Dupont also reimagined the vehicle shot. In *Variety*, the camera sits on a rotating Ferris wheel, representing the fairground as a site of overstimulation and chaotic energy. In *The Last Laugh*, the camera is in an elevator, descending toward a lobby packed with people walking to and fro. Although we might take the shot as the representation of a hotel patron's point of view, the real power of the shot comes from its ability to express the energy of the space itself. This hotel is a place of constant change, constant movement. Murnau lets us see that vitality by packing his compositions with contrast, playing the back-and-forth motion on the floor against the up-and-down motion of the elevator railing. Imagine the same scene photographed with a stationary camera in the lobby. This alternative would not offer the same degree of perceptual surprise. Both shots would show a hotel lobby with an elevator and a crowd of people, but the shot as given uses a motion-filled frame to represent the setting, allowing the energy of the former to express the vitality of the latter. Rather than representing character subjectivity, the shot energizes space.

Murnau and Dupont showed how to use the moving camera expressively, thereby offering an artistic alternative to slapstick trickery. In an editorial titled "What Does the Future Hold?" Maurice Kann enthused, "It seems certain the industry in America will turn to Germany to freshen jaded ideas to get a new slant on production."[44] But the response to the German films was not unanimously positive. As Jan-Christopher Horak explains, "There was a backlash against the 'German invasion' in America, even if it was confined to a few xenophobic articles in the industry trades."[45] Foster Goss, the editor of *American Cinematographer*, expressed offense at the idea that German filmmakers were doing anything new. After mentioning that Los Angeles audiences threw eggs at the screen during a viewing of *The Cabinet of Dr. Caligari* upon its local release in 1921, Goss offered a direct reply to Kann: "Which brings us to an article that appeared some time ago in the *Film Daily* lauding camera 'angles' as practiced in certain enumerated instances in German pictures. . . . It might be well for some writers to more carefully appraise the antiquated methods that they are prone to dress up in the clothes of novelty."[46] Goss's job was to advocate for cinematographers' interests, and the importation of talent from Germany represented a tangible threat to job security.

The objection to German innovations was not solely a matter of protectionism, however. A deeper source of tension concerned national identity itself. In an article in *Moving Picture World* in 1927, titled "Films from across the Sea," critic Charles Sewell conceded that German films with their "new camera tricks" had taken the lead in producing "high-brow pictures," but he wondered why those films did not made more money in the United States. He explained the discrepancy by pointing to "the basic difference in racial psychology." According to Sewell, "We [Americans] are optimistic and much prefer to gaze upon the brighter side of life. We are an energetic people and we want dash, vigor, vim, go, vitality, pep, action and we want our symbolism, our drama, our subtlety in such settings and in adopting the ideas of the foreign producers, our directors see that we get this."[47] Sewell's comments rested on a set of binary oppositions. German films were high culture; American films were mass culture. German films were pessimistic; American films were optimistic. German films were slow; American films were fast. Such claims were not unusual in the film criticism of the 1920s. As Peter Decherney points out, the British critic (and future Museum of Modern Art curator) Iris Barry routinely "asserted her ability to identify proper national traits through film," and she contrasted "slick and speedy" American productions with "ponderous" German ones.[48] Similarly, Graham Petrie has noted how fan magazines such as *Photoplay* contrasted hierarchical German values with supposedly more egalitarian American values.[49] Thomas Saunders explains that in Germany "the notion of incompatible national tastes or mentalities assumed axiomatic character."[50] These contrasts arose not from differences in economic strategy or even in filmmaking traditions but from more profound (in Sewell's word, "racial") differences between the two nations. Echoing the nativist, exclusionary discourse of the 1920s, Sewell stressed the differences between the two countries to the point that they appeared almost incompatible.

Other observers were cautiously optimistic. An article in *Moving Picture World* in 1926 featured an extended interview with Hermann Bing, a Murnau assistant who had come to Hollywood to prepare for the master's impending arrival. Bing appealed to a well-known metaphor of assimilation: "Hollywood is the melting pot of Cinemaland. Here are actors from every country, every race and every nook of the world, from the Esquimo of Alaska to the Black of Central Africa. Here Orientals mix with the Occident. . . . To this Cinema melting pot and its background, Murnau will bring the ideas and ideals of Central Europe, different entirely from those of America because of the psychic morbidity that has come into the depression that followed the war."[51] In spite of Bing's melting-pot cliché, he did not expect Murnau's cultural distinctiveness to dissolve away. Hollywood would benefit from Murnau's presence precisely because the German director would bring a distinctive point of view. Although noting that Murnau "dresses in American fashion," Bing assured the interviewer of Murnau's intention to make a film with subjective techniques and non-American subject matter.[52]

Murnau himself offered competing statements. On the one hand, he put forward a romantic vision of art, capable of communicating across borders: "An artist really cannot be classified by nationality. He is international and the thing which he creates is international."[53] On the other hand, he vowed to change his style to suit the needs of the American audience. According to Maurice Kann, Murnau "realized he was in America. A new world. He seemed to grasp that which serves to move this nation: speed, pep, initiative. And so, said he, he would shift from first to third speed that he might go forward with the procession."[54] The United States was a nation of speed; Murnau was willing to go fast.

If Kann is to be believed, Murnau made these statements on July 7, 1926. The occasion was a party at the Ritz thrown by William Fox in honor of the celebrated director. After signing with Fox in 1925, Murnau had remained in Germany to finish two more films at UFA, *Tartuffe* (1925) and *Faust* (1926), and now he was on his way to Los Angeles, where he would shoot his first Hollywood film. As Janet Bergstrom explains, "William Fox gave Murnau carte blanche to make the film of his dreams. This was unprecedented—all the studio's resources would be at his disposal."[55] The producer explained his motives plainly: Murnau's job was not to make "a freak picture" but to bring "new ideas to the making of American productions."[56] The resulting film proved too expensive to make a profit, but it ended up winning the first and only Academy Award for Unique and Artistic Picture, along with an Oscar for Charles Rosher and

Karl Struss's cinematography.[57] That picture was *Sunrise: A Song of Two Humans* (1927), and it would feature some of the most astonishing shots yet put on film.

Sunrise

A great deal was riding on *Sunrise*—not just Fox's investment but also Hollywood's ever-evolving identity as an industry both American and international. Would Murnau assimilate to the American style, devising unusual angles to add "kick" to the story? Or would the German director continue to explore the semisubjective realm with a style that had inspired critics to reach for comparisons to Cezanne and Picasso? Murnau had promised to make a film with American virtues: speed, pep, initiative. The finished film belies this promise: *Sunrise* is slow and serious, with characters notably lacking in drive. The story is about a rural couple, simply called the Man and the Wife (George O'Brien and Janet Gaynor). The evil Woman from the City (Margaret Livingston) convinces the Man to kill his wife in a staged boating accident. He cannot go through with the murder, and, overcome with guilt, he follows his wife to the city, where he slowly regains her trust. Whereas many Hollywood films emphasize external action, the conflict here is almost entirely internal: the Man must rediscover his love for his wife, and the Wife must recognize that his conversion is sincere. This minimal plot leaves ample room for emotional expression.

To tell this tale, Murnau used almost every cinematic device available, from set design and acting to lighting and camera movement. As in *The Last Laugh*, Murnau explored the ambiguous territory of the semisubjective. In one celebrated sequence, the Man walks through the marshes to visit with the Woman from the City. Cinematographers Rosher and Struss placed the camera on a platform suspended from tracks specially built into the studio's ceiling, using motors to aid the shot's operator, Struss, by lifting the camera platform up and down as it moved forward.[58] For all the shot's technical bravado, its real interest lies in its shifts from external to internal and back again. The camera starts out by following the Man from behind and then tracks with him in profile after he makes a turn to go through some trees (fig. 1.7a–b). Here, the mode is external but attached—we observe the Man from the outside, but we discover the space as he discovers it. When the Man approaches the lens (fig. 1.7c), the camera pans to the left and dollies forward, pushing through some branches to discover the Woman from the City (fig. 1.7d).[59] For a brief moment, it appears that the film has entered a subjective mode, representing what the Man sees through his own eyes. The Woman turns her head. Perhaps she will look directly at the camera, as if welcoming the Man's arrival—but, no, her gaze crosses past the lens, and the bored look on her face indicates that the Man has not yet arrived.

1.7 In *Sunrise*, the camera follows the Man as he walks through the marsh; later, the camera appears to look through his eyes.

First attached and then subjective, the mode becomes nonsubjective and non-attached, showing an event that the Man cannot see yet. A moment later the Woman looks offscreen again, this time recognizing that the Man is approaching. When he enters the screen from off-left, it is a further perceptual surprise: the last time we saw him, he was off-right. The Man and the Woman kiss, and the shot comes to an end. In a lecture in 1928, Struss described this shot in terms that reflect its ambiguity. His statement, "Here we move with the man and his thoughts," evoked a subjective interpretation of the image, but later he claimed, "We seem to be surreptitiously watching the love scenes," as if the camera had adopted the perspective of an unseen observer.[60]

Other shots extend this semisubjective approach. In *The Last Laugh*, Murnau had placed his camera on a rotating platform to create the effect of the world spinning around the porter. In *Sunrise*, Murnau designed an ingenious variation on this strategy, depicting the twists and turns of a trolley ride. The first part of the sequence was photographed on a trolley path built alongside Lake

Arrowhead; the rest was shot on another constructed line that circled into Rochus Gliese's enormous false-perspective city set on the Fox lot.[61] One shot shows the Wife huddling in the corner of the car. We can barely see her face, but the trolley veers right and then left, showing us tracks, a worker on a bicycle, a factory, and other images indicating that she is reaching the edge of the city (fig. 1.8a–b). The unpredictable swaying of the trolley expresses her emotional state—her terrified confusion about her husband's newly revealed capacity for violence and betrayal. Meanwhile, Murnau uses the trolley's movement to comment on the inevitability of modernity: these two peasants have no control over the trolley car, and they must stand by passively while the background changes from the countryside to the city, a change in landscape that will render their peasant lifestyle obsolete.

In her insightful analysis of the film, Caitlin McGrath has situated Murnau's shots within a longer tradition of camera movement stretching back to the cinema of attractions, as in Bitzer's subway film in 1904 (fig. 1.1).[62] Another proximate comparison is the trolley scene from *Girl Shy*. There, the Boy treats the world as a series of obstacles to be overcome, commandeering a trolley car to get to his destination as quickly as possible. In *Sunrise*, the movement of the trolley does little to advance the goals of either character, who are merely passengers on a journey they cannot control. In one sense, *Girl Shy* does a better job integrating story and shot: the action on the trolley serves to advance the protagonist's goal. In another sense, *Sunrise* is the more fully integrated of the two. *Girl Shy* briefly abandons the Boy to deliver a gag about the drunkard's confusion. *Sunrise* lingers on the passage of the trolley because its swaying motions serve to express the Wife's state of mind. Every swerve is expressive.

1.8 The Wife stands quietly on the trolley as the landscape changes behind her.

The latter film further develops its characterizati
pair of sequences showing the couple crossing the dan₍
sequence, the camera is on a dolly following the Wife (pı
as she walks from the trolley to the curb; halfway throug₍
grabs the Wife and walks with her the rest of the way. Severa₍
foreground and background, just missing the couple—and the
is crossing the street as well (fig. 1.9a–b). In the second sequence,
the Wife have reconciled, and they gaze into each other's eyes as the
busy street again (fig. 1.10a). They are utterly oblivious to the traffic, w₍
solves away to become a pastoral meadow, as if this peasant couple has
covered the country in the heart of the city (fig. 1.10b). Whereas the first sequ₍
unfolds in fast motion as if it were a slapstick stunt, the second sequence is
composite, using a traveling-matte effect that combines three distinct layers in
a single shot: a foreground layer with cars passing by closely; a background layer
dissolving from the city to the country; and a middle-ground layer showing the
lovers walking while the camera follows on a dolly. Each layer was shot separately, then printed onto a separate piece of film.[63]

This moment of joy does not mean that the film endorses the city and its
values of consumerism, pleasure, and distraction. The urban citizens constantly
remind the Man and the Wife that they are peasants; it is their acceptance of
this identity that allows them to reaffirm their values. When they kiss in the
middle of traffic, their love provides an escape from the modern city, even as
the traffic bears down upon them. The visual contrast between the bumping
dolly of the first sequence and the traveling matte of the second develops
the thematic shift. When the camera follows the Wife and the Man as they

1.9 The camera follows first the Wife as she begins to cross the street and then the Man
and the Wife as they scramble across it.

1.10 Later, a traveling matte shows the Man and the Wife in traffic; the urban background dissolves into a pastoral scene.

scramble across the street, their movements are so erratic that the couple never stays in the center of the frame. There is instead an oscillation from right to left as the couple jogs back and forth to escape the traffic. Later the traveling-matte effect locks the couple in the center of the frame, even though they are walking the whole time. The city around them buzzes with activity; the couple has become a symbol of stability.

Far from making a film with speed, pep, and initiative, Murnau tells a story criticizing those very values. Instead of delivering the occasional nonnarrative "kick," the moving camera expresses the characters' emotions while commenting on the ephemeral delights and the disorienting emptiness of modern life. The director's longtime booster Maurice Kann raved about the film, seeing it as the fulfillment of *The Last Laugh*'s promising experiments with the representation of subjectivity: "Murnau has succeeded in boring his camera lens into the very brain of his players and shows you in picture form the thoughts that surge through their heads."[64] Other critics commented on the film's internationalism—its hybrid mixture of European aesthetics with a Hollywood budget. Pare Lorentz—then a film critic, later an esteemed documentarian—thought that the German–American mixture was a failure. He praised the "breathtaking photography" and the "perfect" first fifteen minutes, but he argued that the extended sequence in the city contained too many gags, which had been added to entertain the "chocolate-sundae audience."[65] European artistry had given way to slapstick trickery. *Variety*'s critic wrote more favorably that the film was "made in this country, but produced after the best manner of the German school."[66] *Moving Picture World* noticed the film's "continental flavor," while commenting wryly on the association between national style and

cultural status: "Coming from abroad, this production would be hailed by critics as a triumph. Even with the American label they are forced to give it grudging
praise."[67] Whereas Lorentz denounced the film for including too many conces-
sions to the American audience, *Variety* and *World* positioned the film as a
fascinating hybrid, a European artwork made in Los Angeles.

In the end, *Sunrise* struggled at the box office, and Murnau's own career at
Fox took a downward turn.[68] He experienced less support and more constraints
on his remaining two films for the studio: the lost film *Four Devils* (1928) and
the smaller-scale film *City Girl* (1930), both designed as nondialogue pictures,
and both turned into part-talkies with added sequences not directed by Murnau.[69] But Murnau's impact was undeniable. As Janet Bergstrom reports, "[A]
sign of William Fox's appreciation of the artistic quality of Murnau's films was
that he encouraged his top directors to work in the same dark, visually expressive style."[70] She lists several examples of Fox films made in Murnau's style,
including *7th Heaven* (1927) and *Street Angel* (1928) by Frank Borzage, *Fazil*
(1928) by Howard Hawks, *The Red Dance* (1928) by Raoul Walsh, and *Mother
Machree* (1928) and *Four Sons* (1928) by John Ford. Other examples from the
studio might include *East Side, West Side* (1927) and *Frozen Justice* (1929) by
Allan Dwan as well as *Paid to Love* (1927) by Hawks and *Hangman's House* (1928)
by Ford.

Outside Fox Studios, there is evidence that the trend toward unusual angles
started well before *Sunrise* was released. In *The Eagle* (1925), the camera, suspended from a bridge stretched between two dollies, moves backward across a
table, appearing to pass through several solid objects along the way. Director
Clarence Brown explained, "We had prop boys putting candelabra in place just
before the camera picked them up."[71] An article in *Film Daily* in 1925 reports
that cinematographer J. Roy Hunt used a handheld gyroscopic camera, inspired
by *The Last Laugh*, to photograph *The Manicure Girl*, a lost film directed by
Frank Tuttle.[72] The following year Maurice Kann spotted the influence of *Variety* in two other Famous Players–Lasky films: Victor Fleming's *Mantrap* and
William Wellman's *You Never Know Women*. Kann even gave credit to the cinematographers: Jimmy (James Wong) Howe and Victor Milner, respectively.[73]
Less fortunate was Michael Curtiz, the Hungarian-born director beginning his
long career at Warner Bros. His American debut, *The Third Degree* (1926), earned
a skeptical review from Gilbert Seldes, who worried that directors were abusing the innovations of *Variety*.[74] *Photoplay* also denounced Curtiz's film, noting that it was "filled with German camera-angles that don't mean a thing."[75]
Another fan magazine complained, "The German films have caused our directors to become excited over the odd effects to be obtained by photographing
scenes from unusual angles."[76] An article in *Motion Picture Classic* declared that
camera angles were "the bunk" and blamed the critics for heaping praise
on European films when they employed the same "trick photography" that

Americans had been doing for years.[77] The critics gave voice to a widely shared worry. Hollywood studios had the resources to copy the latest techniques, either by hiring European personnel or by imitating their manner; what they needed to do was prove that they could use those techniques in a meaningful way.

Making Sense of the Mobile Frame

Mediating the impact of German cinema, trade journals summarized the thoughts of major figures, including Murnau, Dupont, Freund, and Pommer. Though we should be cautious about attributing the ideas to the filmmakers directly, the articles introduced several recurring themes that later practitioners would turn to for inspiration.

One theme was medium specificity. The German filmmakers worried that the cinema borrowed too many ideas from the other arts. "Our whole effort," Murnau claimed, "must be bent toward ridding motion pictures of all that does not belong to them."[78] Turning this negative prescription into a positive program, Murnau venerated movement itself: "The motion picture has too long copied its technique from the other arts. It is time that it be established as an individual form of expression. To achieve this end motion pictures must be actually motion pictures."[79] Karl Freund adopted identical rhetoric, urging that the accent be placed on the word *motion*: "It is necessary that the motion picture realize more fully it is a motion picture and consequently build up with those methods of expression that are only meant for such a medium."[80] Simply by panning or dollying the camera, a filmmaker put the medium's essence on display.

For all this enthusiasm about movement as a medium-specific trait, no one advocated moving the camera just to show off. As we have seen, Murnau insisted that good camerawork was "dramatic." Erich Pommer, who worked at Paramount for a year before returning to Germany in 1927, was more explicit: "People come to the theater to see a story revealed entertainingly. They do not come to see a batch of director's tricks."[81] The Germans purported to teach Hollywood filmmakers how to use the moving camera as a tool of drama, not as a trick.

While proposing dramatization as the prevailing purpose, these early theoretical statements pondered another problem—the problem of likeness. Should the camera move in personlike ways—panning modestly to mimic an observer's attention? Or should the camera move in ways that no person ever could—flying from here to there with superhuman mobility and speed? This problem would puzzle the theorists of camera movement for years to come. Both Dupont and Pommer argued that the camera should imitate the motion of a person, thereby setting certain restrictions on the technique. According to Dupont,

"Since the motion picture is nothing else but the reproduction of life and of the effects of life as watched by an unobtrusive observer, it is of the greatest importance that the spectator should become conscious as little as possible of the presence of the camera. The possibilities of the camera no doubt will always remain limited."[82] Dupont's producer, Pommer, expressed the same idea: "Make the camera view the scene as the natural spectator would see it."[83] Here, the two filmmakers echoed the contemporaneous ideas of Vsevolod Pudovkin, who developed a more systematic analogy between the camera and a hypothetical observer in his book *Film Technique* (1926).[84] All agreed that the filmmaker should draw an analogy between a camera and a person and then use that analogy to guide decisions about camera placement. Frankly, these sentiments sound strange coming from the makers of *Variety*, with its flamboyant fairground-ride aesthetic. But Pommer explained that the humanized camera could go to many strange places, but only as long as a person might go there, too: "I avoid all freakish shots. Here you will doubt me, perhaps, recalling those aerial sweeps from a flying trapeze in *Variety*. But consider this: those views were taken from the same vantage point as that of Emil Jannings, playing Boss, and of Lya de Putti, playing his wife [*sic*], both acrobats."[85] As long as a person could ride a trapeze, a trapeze was a suitable place to put the camera.

Critical discussion of Murnau was more conflicted, sometimes invoking the camera–person analogy to explain Murnau's movements, sometimes celebrating the filmmaker's ability to break free of that analogy. When Maurice Kann, the sympathetic editor of *Film Daily*, attempted to summarize Murnau's ideas, he offered a series of shifting similes: "The tripod must not be stationary. As the eye moves, so must the lens. Murnau would have the camera free as air. Perfection and the motion picture on its highest plane will come when the camera can be likened to a floating balloon: here, there and everywhere."[86] First, Kann compared the camera to a human observer, with the lens functioning as an eye. This optical analogy justified the use of camera movement, but it also presupposed a certain level of restriction because the human eye cannot see everything. Kann then shifted the metaphor from camera as eye to camera as air and then as balloon, implying that the camera should be liberated from all restrictions, floating from place to place with a freedom unavailable to any gravity-bound human. The Germans had referred to the new technique as the "unchained" camera; Kann offered a balloon metaphor to evoke the same idea.[87]

We might dismiss these contradictions as a bit of bad writing on Kann's part, but Murnau evoked similarly conflicting ideas elsewhere—and offered an intriguing resolution. In an article released during the publicity campaign for *Sunrise* in 1927, Murnau stated, "To me the camera represents the eye of a person, through whose mind one is watching the events on the screen. . . . It must whirl and peep and move from place to place as swiftly as thought itself, when it is necessary to exaggerate for the audience the idea or emotion that is uppermost in the mind of the character."[88] Starting with the camera–eye analogy, Murnau shifted to a new analogy: the camera as thought. Whereas the faculty of vision is subject to physical restrictions, the mind may jump around in time and space. The camera, he insisted in another article, "should be as mobile as possible to catch every possible mood."[89] Taking full advantage of the medium's powers, the go-anywhere camera enriched storytelling by amplifying subjective experiences.[90]

These snippets from the trade journals posed several questions that would recur in the debates on camera movement over the next several years. Is there an essence of cinema? Yes: movement itself. Can the moving camera tell a story? Yes: by expressing the characters' thoughts and emotions. Should the camera imitate a person? Yes . . . and no. Maybe the camera is similar to an eye or maybe to the human mind. Or maybe the camera should simply float freely, the better to fulfill the medium's potential.

To be sure, a few scattered comments in trade publications did not constitute a fully developed theory. But *Sunrise* made these debates tangible for every Hollywood practitioner. When the camera follows the Man across the marsh, it mimics his movements for a while, only to demonstrate its freedom to leave him behind. When the traffic-gnarled street dissolves away to become a peaceful meadow, the cinema becomes thought, representing the idealized fantasies of the Man and the Wife as they imagine themselves outside the city. When the trolley winds its way through the trees and into the city, the cinema becomes a transcendent art of movement. Each shot embodies a theoretical problem.

Prominent American film critics such as Gilbert Seldes and Alexander Bakshy picked up these themes. Even before the appearance of *The Last Laugh*, Seldes had defined "movement governed by light" as the essence of the cinema.[91] Three years later, in 1927, he argued that the German imports had shown how the moving camera could be used to "heighten interest" and "carry on narrative," and he worried that their Hollywood imitators appeared "to have no idea what the angles can be used for."[92] This argument neatly inverts our expectations about the two cinemas. It was the stylish Murnau and Dupont who employed angles to tell a story, and it was the Americans who moved the camera to make technology a spectacle.

Similarly, Bakshy appealed to medium specificity when he insisted that the art of cinema "must function in movement, i.e. through movement it must reveal its form and significance."[93] He listed the different kinds of movement available: the movement of characters and objects onscreen, the movement of the camera (both within shots via cinematography and between shots via editing), and the movements of the image itself, as when the picture expanded or diminished onscreen.[94] Taking medium specificity to its logical conclusion, Bakshy rejected any analogy between the camera and the spectator's eyes. "This is therefore a purely visual world," he wrote, "and moreover a world seen not by the human eye but by the camera—a much more powerful instrument for seeing detail, magnifying the image, and bringing distant objects into view than mankind has been endowed with."[95] Whereas the human eye was confined to the body, the camera could move anywhere. (Bakshy defined "movement" broadly enough to include editing as well as dollying. Both were forms of shifting the camera's viewpoint.) Nevertheless, Bakshy could not resist the urge to anthropomorphize the camera: "In watching a performance on the stage the spectator is governed by the actual conditions of space and time. Not so in the case of the movie spectator. Thanks to the moving camera he is able to view the scene from all kinds of angles, leaping from a long-distance view to a close-range inspection of every detail."[96] Rather than define the movie spectator as a person looking at pictures on a screen, Bakshy identified the eye of the spectator with the eye of camera, hurtling together through space.

Notice that the theory of the camera's personlike qualities cuts across some familiar distinctions, such as subjective versus objective and restricted range versus unrestricted range.[97] The camera that moves the way a person moves may be subjective (representing a character's moving point of view) or objective (moving in the manner of a human observer watching the characters from the outside). The camera that moves the way a person moves may be restricted (following one character from scene to scene) or unrestricted (shifting freely from character to character). Similarly, we should resist the temptation to define the go-anywhere camera, which breaks free from human restrictions to fly through the air, as an "omniscient" camera. Omniscience implies knowledge, which implies personhood, which is exactly what this particular variant of the unchained camera does not have. Rather than assume that the camera is always like a person, we may examine how camera movement constructed this analogy—and tore it down.

In practice, many Hollywood filmmakers of the late silent period embraced the go-anywhere ideal. In Clarence Brown's film A Woman of Affairs (1928), the camera dollies back and dissolves through a door as if by magic, echoing a moment in The Last Laugh when the camera appears to dissolve through glass. The effect is explicitly antianthropomorphic, relying on trickery to perform a movement that would be impossible for a person (or, indeed, for any physical being). Even more impressive were the era's "How did they do that?" shots, designed to leave spectators gasping in astonishment. In 7th Heaven, directed by Murnau's Fox colleague Frank Borzage, the two protagonists (Janet Gaynor and Charles Farrell) climb the stairs to reach an attic apartment on the seventh floor, and the camera follows them higher and higher until they reach their destination. Cinematographer Ernest Palmer credited art director Harry Oliver with the shot's design.[98] Photographs show an elevator constructed next to the unusually tall set.[99] Although the effect was achieved with the help of a hidden cut, stitching together two separate shots of a somewhat shorter stairway, the end result is a brilliant metaphor for spiritual transcendence, making us aware of the presence of a camera and then astonishing us with this machine's defiance of the laws of gravity. Elevating the camera gives form to Borzage's romantic themes.

Imitating *Sunrise*'s marsh shot, many filmmakers started dangling their cameras from ceilings, as if the camera could fly. King Vidor, who gushed that Murnau and Dupont had "freed the camera from its immobility," reported using "an overhead wire trolley" to photograph the famous office sequence in *The Crowd* (1928).[100] The film's protagonist, John Sims (James Murray), has moved to New York. After a quick city montage, the film cuts to a low-angle shot of an enormous skyscraper—actually, a miniature lying on the floor. The camera appears to crane up, up, impossibly up, toward one of the higher floors, where it approaches a window (fig. 1.11a). The film dissolves to an angle perched high above an enormous room filled with desks—so many desks that they took up "a complete, bare stage," according to Vidor.[101] The camera, suspended from above, tracks over the desks and locates the protagonist, toiling away at a boring job (fig. 1.11b). Even more than the stairway scene from *7th Heaven*, the shot rejects the ideal of human-scaled movements in favor of something more spectacular. Here the effect is deeply ironic, contrasting the camera's superhuman powers with the protagonist's very human failures. Just prior to this scene, John has professed his desire for greatness. The sheer impossibility of the shot mocks the grandeur of his dreams. When the camera's ascent turns into a descent, its sweeping view becoming a conventional medium shot, we realize the stark contrast between the camera's seeming ability to go anywhere and John's own fate, going nowhere.

1.11 In *The Crowd*, the camera scales the heights of a skyscraper and flies over a room full of office workers.

William Wellman's wartime drama *Wings* (1927) features several astonishing vehicle shots, with the camera bolted onto a diving airplane.[102] As impressive as these shots are, the camera's movements remain limited to those that a familiar machine might perform. But the film's Parisian café scene bewilders us with an unmanned flight. The camera, suspended from tracks in the ceiling, moves forward past five different couples at five different tables, finally locating Jack the pilot, getting drunk at a sixth table. Each table offers a quick sketch of the unconventional sexuality seen to be typical of Parisian life: a wealthy older woman with a younger man, two women holding hands (fig. 1.12a), a man and woman nervously looking about for fear that they are being watched. In each instance, it appears that the camera is going to bump into the characters, but the staging creates enough space for the camera to pass through, as when a woman tosses a drink into a man's face, causing the man to lean back just in time. The shot's very audacity serves to characterize the city of Paris, represented as the global capital of scandalous behavior. By moving down a sequence of tables, the shot creates an effect of seriality: each table is just one more manifestation of the Parisian spirit. When the camera finally arrives at the intoxicated Jack, he is shown to be one of the series (fig. 1.12b). Our upstanding American hero has become just as French as everyone else.[103]

Wellman subsequently regretted his "dizzying" Paris shot in *Wings*.[104] Perhaps the go-anywhere camera was too spectacular for everyday use. But setting up an absolute opposition—either narrative or spectacle—overlooks the possibility of a "both–and" solution. The gravity-defying shots in *7th Heaven*, *The Crowd*, and *Wings* astonish us with the camera's ability to go anywhere while contributing to narrative goals that are particular to each film: expressing romantic aspiration, evoking the feeling of working for a large corporation, and mocking a temporarily debauched protagonist, respectively.

1.12 In *Wings*, the camera flies through a Parisian café.

A more pressing problem with these shots was purely practical. The strategy of suspending the camera from above was ill suited to mass production: even a minor alteration might require the crew to remove the dangling platform and reorganize a set of tracks located dozens of feet above the studio floor. Other solutions from the late silent years proved to be equally short-lived, even if the results were sometimes spectacular. In *Quality Street* (1927), director Sidney Franklin moved across the set on roller skates while operating a Bell and Howell camera.[105] In Cecil B. DeMille's *The Godless Girl* (1928), a "traveling elevator cage" lifted the camera and crew during a *7th Heaven*–inspired stairway scene.[106] In William Wyler's *The Shakedown* (1929), a camera attached to an industrial crane looked down on the protagonist as he rode the hoist to the top of an oil derrick; the result recalled the trapeze shots from *Variety*. Some of these technologies were creative, even thrilling; they were also dangerous and difficult to duplicate.

Consider the impracticality of another technique: the ramp. Paul Fejos's film *The Last Performance* (1929) is a thriller about a talented but unloved magician who commits a murder. An early scene shows the tragic protagonist, Erik the Great, looking around the audience for a person to hypnotize. He settles on a group of wealthy spectators and military officers sitting in the box seats. When the patrons lock their eyes onto Erik, the film alternates between two matching movements: an apparent crane up toward the patrons and an apparent crane down toward Erik, staring directly into the camera (fig. 1.13a–b). Although these upward and downward movements look like crane shots, production photographs reveal that Hal Mohr's crew constructed a platform dolly and pulled the camera up and down a steeply sloping wooden board (fig. 1.14).[107] However inexpensive the lumber, such a solution posed potentially expensive problems in time management. Suppose Fejos decided that the camera should descend a thirty-five-degree slope instead of a thirty-degree slope or that the camera

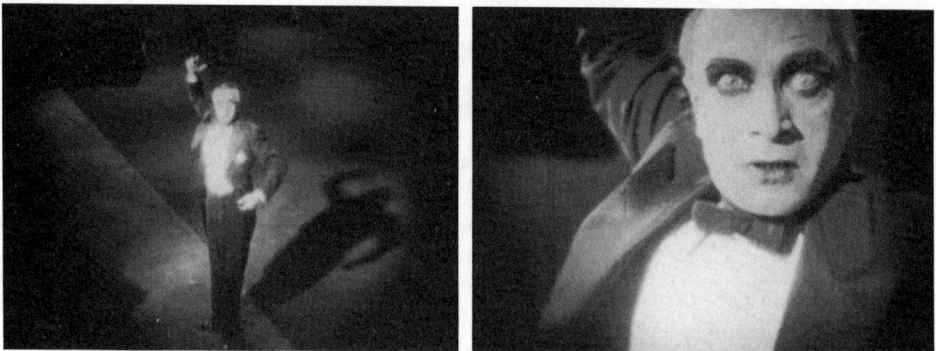

1.13 In *The Last Performance*, the camera descends toward Erik the Great.

1.14 A production photograph shows the camera sliding down a ramp. (Courtesy of the Academy of Motion Picture Arts and Sciences)

should travel twenty feet instead of fifteen? These simple changes might require a grip team to reconstruct the entire ramp, wasting valuable time. Fejos and Mohr eventually solved these problems by designing an enormous but comparatively efficient crane for their first sound film, *Broadway* (1929), discussed in the next chapter.

Murnau experimented with a crane on his film *Four Devils* (1928), a circus drama in the manner of *Variety*; one review noted that it married "Continental design" with "Yankee" sentimentalism.[108] As Janet Bergstrom explains in her careful account of the film's production, Fox Films originally released a nondialogue version of the film with a synchronized score in October 1928; later, the studio hired a separate crew to tack on some sound sequences, and this part-talkie version was released the following year.[109] Both versions are now lost, but it must have been a remarkable film indeed, featuring shots photographed with the "Go-Devil," a "gigantic apparatus" weighing twenty tons and including an arm that could rotate around a steel upright.[110] In one contemporary publication, quoted by Bergstrom, Murnau described a particularly ambitious shot: the camera "must gallop after the equestrienne, it must pick out the painted tears of the clown and jump from him to a high box to show the face of the rich lady thinking about the clown."[111] The Go-Devil gave form to the fantasy of omnipresence, as if the camera were empowered to go anywhere at any time.

In all of these examples, the camera was quite obviously a machine, capable of moving in ways an ordinary person cannot. But Murnau and his peers had proposed another way of thinking about the moving camera, theorizing the machine in anthropomorphic terms. Rather than push through walls or fly into the sky, this personlike camera could imitate the movements of a person—either a fictional character or an unseen observer.

In Hollywood's tales of action and romance, the representation of a character's point of view could be a powerful storytelling tool, establishing who wants what—or whom. In *Wild Orchids* (1929), a visiting businessman (Lewis Stone) introduces an Indonesian prince (Nils Asther) to his wife, Lillie (Greta Garbo). The film cuts to a dolly shot, moving into a close-up of Lillie. Although both men are walking toward her, the straight-line momentum marks the shot as a representation of the prince's point of view—specifically, his desiring gaze, tracking toward Lillie relentlessly. The subsequent shot represents Lillie's point of view: a stationary close-up of the prince, with Asther looking directly into the lens. The film has structured its point-of-view shots according to logics of gender and race. On the one hand, there is a clear contrast between the male gaze and the female gaze as the contrast between mobility and stasis echoes the film's larger themes about the hunter and the hunted. On the other hand, the film represents the Indonesian man's desire as inherently threatening. The rest of the film will work to neutralize this threat, reestablishing the white couple at the center.

A movement skeptic might argue that the camera was actually ill suited to the goals of representing a character's moving viewpoint. Not only is the camera's one-lens "vision" quite unlike binocular human sight, but its patterns of movement are also strangely inhuman. A straight-ahead tracking shot is too smooth; a bumpy dolly shot too jerky. A horror film might turn these seeming inconsistencies to advantage, exploiting the strangeness of camera movement to produce an uncanny effect, as in Universal's horror-comedy *The Cat and the Canary* (1927), directed by Paul Leni.[112] This film's point-of-view shots are eerily ambiguous. Early in the tale, a title card announces that a house may or may not be haunted by the ghost of old, wealthy Cyrus West. In the next shot, the camera, mounted on a dolly, moves around a corner and then down a hallway, panning left and right as it goes forward. The shot is disorienting—at first, we just see a pattern of vertical lines, and then this flat image opens up to a surprisingly deep space. The camera heads toward the end of the hall, but the panning movements make it seem as if it might duck into a side door; before that possibility is confirmed, the shot fades to black, leaving us permanently uncertain about where the camera was going. It is an unsettling shot, appropriate for a horror movie and specifically for a movie in which the idea of the unseen machine generates considerable fear. With its gothic architecture, the house may seem premodern, but it turns out that there are all sorts of gears and mechanisms behind these walls, allowing them to open up and reveal grasping hands and falling bodies. The house is an uncanny mixture of the human and the machine. The dolly shot evokes that same horrific blend, representing the not-quite-human perspective of a ghost who might not exist through the means of the not-quite-human movements of another being that is not supposed to exist in the fictional world: the large, lumbering camera.

A later scene develops this idea of the inhuman point of view. The family members are debating the contentious terms of a will. Above the table hangs a portrait of West, an angry old man with one disturbing eye open. When the portrait falls to the floor, we see a shot moving downward toward the table, representing the point of view of the painting—an inanimate object.[113] A few moments later the preternaturally serious maid walks over to pick up the portrait. The film cuts to a lateral dolly shot showing all of the other characters watching the maid's slow progress across the floor. All indications suggest that this is the maid's moving point of view, except for the fact that the maid is not looking in the direction of the family members. These two moving shots form a mirrored pair, both representing a not-quite-human point of view—in the first case because the subject is an eerily lifelike portrait, in the second case because the subject is an ominously machinelike person. The choices here seem perfectly suited to the tale being told, a tongue-in-cheek ghost story that encourages us to wonder whether its ghost is real or not. *The Cat and the Canary* comments on the uncanny nature of camerawork itself, ridiculing the oft-posed analogy between the camera and the human by representing the camera's eerie point of view as simultaneously human and inhuman.

Outside the horror genre, a film might use the moving camera to represent a character's subjective states in a nonliteral way. As we have seen, Murnau and Dupont explored the possibility of using the camera semisubjectively, as when a spinning movement evokes emotion (in *The Last Laugh*, drunken delight; in *Variety*, jealous rage) without suggesting that the character in question is whirling in space. Hollywood filmmakers seeking heightened emotional engagement adopted this more evocative approach to the point-of-view shot. In Clarence Badger's *It*, a Paramount production from 1927, Betty Lou (Clara Bow) goes to the Ritz in the hopes of finding her boss, the handsome Waltham (Antonio Moreno). When she sees him, the film cuts to Waltham, and the camera rapidly dollies in from a medium long shot to a medium close-up of his smiling face. The shot represents Betty Lou's point of view, but not in a literal way. Betty Lou stands still; her point of view hurtles forward. While representing what she sees, the shot conveys the desire that she feels. We can think of this figure as an "amplified" point-of-view shot, using the machine's power to zip through space to express a very human emotion.

Filmmakers of the period went to great lengths to build elaborate devices that could amplify ordinary human experiences. A production photograph from *Hotel Imperial* (1927) shows a device that looks almost—but not quite— like a modern crane, featuring an elevator dangling from an arm attached to a post (fig. 1.15). Alternatively, the elevator could be attached to an overhead track.[114] Paramount released *Hotel Imperial* in early 1927, after *Sunrise* had begun production but before it was released. Like Fox, Paramount had its eye on the European market: in addition to Scandinavian director Mauritz Stiller, the film's European crew included star Pola Negri and producer Erich Pommer. One scene offers another variation on the amplified point-of-view shot. Lieutenant Paul Almasy (James Hall) is pretending to be a hotel worker. While standing on the second floor, he leans forward to get a closer look at something below, and the film cuts to a high-angle shot of the partying soldiers. In the background, the Russian general Juschkiewisch (George Siegmann) enters the

1.15 The makers of *Hotel Imperial* built an awkward crane. (Courtesy of the Academy of Motion Picture Arts and Sciences and Marc Wanamaker/Bison Archives)

hotel, and the camera swoops down to isolate the threatening figure from the crowd. The subject onscreen is deeply human: a man focuses his attention on a threat. The scene offscreen was absurdly inhuman: cinematographer Bert Glennon, trapped in a cage, riding down an elevator suspended from the ceiling.

A third variation appeared in *Street Angel* (1928). The team behind *7th Heaven*—director Frank Borzage, cinematographer Ernest Palmer, and set designer Harry Oliver—used a crane, probably made of wood, to photograph this circus-themed drama.[115] According to Hervé Dumont, Murnau was so impressed with the film's camerawork that he hired Palmer and his colleague Paul Ivano to work on *Four Devils*.[116] In one scene, the impoverished Angela (Janet Gaynor) worries that she does not have enough money to help her gravely ill mother. She looks outside the window, and the camera dissolves to a high-angle shot craning down toward a streetwalker as she is approached by a john. The descending motion expresses Angela's fears that she may need to turn to prostitution to save her mother. Each amplified point-of-view shot in *It*, *Hotel Imperial*, and *Street Angel* expresses a different aspect of subjectivity: desire, attention, identification. In so doing, each shot expresses an ideology. As Laura Mulvey has argued, Hollywood films often use visual style to characterize the male as active and the female as passive.[117] The male gaze helps the man to accomplish his goal, as in *Hotel Imperial*, where the man seeks to control his environment by seeing everything first. Paul does not want to be the general; he wants to defeat him. In *Street Angel*, Angela experiences not the active gaze of confrontation but the passive gaze of identification; she fears that she will become the prostitute. In this context, the speed of *It*'s dolly is rather daring, characterizing Betty Lou's gaze as an active gaze, seeking out the object of her desire. Betty Lou herself is almost embarrassed at the directedness of her own gaze; after spotting Waltham, she shyly turns her head away . . . and then turns back again for another peek. In all three examples, the camera moves like a person, but each movement evokes different ideas depending on the context of the surrounding scene. Far from setting a restriction on the meanings of camera movement, the principle of mimicry expands the meanings of movement because each film expresses different ideas about what it is for a person to experience the story world.

In the Shadow of *Sunrise*

One way to approach the works of the late silent period is to use the films as proof of influence. The method is suspiciously easy; we see a late silent film with camera movement, and we say, "Murnau has done it again." Art historian Michael Baxandall has proposed a useful corrective to the "influence" idea. He writes, "If one says that X influenced Y it does seem that one is saying that X did something to Y rather than that Y did something to X. But in the consideration of good pictures and painters the second is always the more lively reality. . . . If we think of Y rather than X as the agent, the vocabulary is much richer and more attractively diversified."[118] The second artist, Y, might refer to X, copy X, distort X, paraphrase X, refine X, or tackle X, to list just a few alternatives. Crucially, the later artist is never entirely free, able to choose any option at will. The institutional and cultural contexts set limits and open up specific possibilities, as when a painter's workshop establishes the norm of copying the master very closely or when the culture of modernism encourages the sharp critique of old models.

Hollywood's own production culture encouraged filmmakers to adopt the most up-to-date technologies, both to maintain the industry's status as the most advanced in the world and to increase its capacity to tell emotionally engaging stories. Dynamic camerawork seemed ideally suited for appropriation. Yet important questions remained—not so much questions of technology or technique, but questions of cultural value. Could the German angles be Americanized? Was it possible to combine artistic ambition with slapstick kick? Could long-lingering passages of semisubjective technique help a filmmaker tell a fast-moving story? Rather than say that Murnau and Dupont's followers had fallen under their influence, we would do better to say that subsequent filmmakers appropriated their techniques purposefully to advance their own ideas about the nature of cinematic storytelling. Some films borrowed specific ideas from *Sunrise* while turning them into visual gags, thereby returning the mobile frame to its earlier American home in slapstick. Other films treated the dynamic style as something foreign, reserved for films with European subjects, often (but not exclusively) made by European-born directors. Still other films self-consciously exploited the techniques of European modernism to tell stories with urban settings in the United States, thereby claiming the moving camera as a technique for the critical representation of contemporary American life.

Mary Pickford's romantic comedy *My Best Girl* (1927) looks like the missing link between Harold Lloyd and F. W. Murnau. The film uses the moving camera to deliver slapstick-inspired jokes while expressing exuberant delight in the energy of the American city. As the film's producer and star, Pickford handpicked director Sam Taylor, who had helmed several Harold Lloyd comedies, including *Girl Shy*. Cinematographer Charles Rosher had been crafting Pickford's perfectly lit close-ups for years, but he had recently become one of Murnau's most important collaborators, spending a year in Germany observing the production of *Faust* (1926) and then seven months in the United States photographing *Sunrise* with Karl Struss. *My Best Girl* incorporates several visual ideas from *Sunrise*, reimagining them as slapstick gags. In one scene, Maggie (Pickford) and Joe (Buddy Rogers) cross a busy city street while looking playfully into each other's eyes. The two lovers remain utterly unaware of the traffic around them, which whizzes by, just missing them several times. The scene synthesizes the two crossing-the-street scenes from *Sunrise* (figs. 1.9 and 1.10), but the result is startlingly fresh. In Murnau's film, the city is terrifyingly dangerous, becoming safe only when the lovers imagine themselves elsewhere. By using a traveling matte to produce this magical effect of two lovers finding bliss in the city, Murnau hints at the idea's very impossibility. By contrast, Pickford and Rogers actually perform the stunt: both the actors and the camera cross the road, their movements perfectly timed to avoid the vehicles zipping past. The effect is a utopian image of the modern city as a perfectly balanced system, a place where humans and machines can thrive together. The British critic Robert Herring saw *My Best Girl* before *Sunrise*, and he went on to write a scathing review of Murnau's film, in part because he thought that *My Best Girl* did a better job using the camera to say something meaningful about the modern city![119]

Combining art with slapstick, another scene in *My Best Girl* manages to evoke both the meditative trolley shot from *Sunrise* and its manic cousin from *Girl Shy*. Maggie, sitting on the back of a truck, deliberately drops a package in the street to force Joe to chase after her to return the package. The gag is staged in depth, with the camera on the moving truck and pointing back toward Joe, who races toward Maggie in the foreground (fig. 1.16a). Joe eventually hops onto the truck bed, where he and Maggie exchange stories. The composition stages an image of romantic union against a moving background of buildings, streets, and trolley cars (fig. 1.16b).[120] Boldly rejecting the convention of setting romantic scenes against pretty pastoral backdrops (as in Pickford's earlier film *The Love Light*), *My Best Girl* situates romance right in the middle of the dynamic city. Similar to *Girl Shy*, Pickford's film uses a gag to depict the city in motion.[121] Similar to *Sunrise*, the truck scene uses the moving background to express the female protagonist's emotions. The emotions have changed—from the Wife's

1.16 Joe and Maggie share a romantic moment in the middle of the city in *My Best Girl*.

wounded confusion to Maggie's romantic exhilaration—but the idea of using a vehicle shot to externalize internal states remains the same.

My Best Girl Americanizes the German angle by resituating it within the slapstick tradition. John Ford's *Four Sons* tells a story set in both Germany and the United States, and the moving camera develops the film's themes about the losses and opportunities that Americanization might bring. Though William Fox encouraged Ford to work in Murnau's style, Ford did not need much prodding: one contemporary article quoted him as saying that *Sunrise* was the greatest film he had ever seen, unlikely to be surpassed in the next ten years.[122] Ford visited Germany in 1927, where he photographed unused footage with Karl Freund.[123] When Ford returned to the United States, he photographed several scenes for *Four Sons* on the leftover sets from *Sunrise*. Murnau's marsh became Ford's battle site, while Murnau's city set became Ford's New York.[124] Given that the American director would later abjure excessive motion, *Four Sons* may seem disappointingly derivative of the German approach.[125] In one scene, the camera pans to a soldier, who lifts a trumpet and points it directly at the moving camera, echoing the trumpet scene in *The Last Laugh*. A tricky two-floor elevator shot in *Four Sons* quotes its precursor's opening scene. Ford borrowed from *Variety*, too: one shot shows two lovers on a swing, seemingly still while the background swings up and down behind them in the manner of Dupont's film.

Though we might dismiss some of these shots as uncomplicated copies, a closer look at the film suggests that Ford used the moving camera to develop one of his characteristic themes: the theme of community and its passing. The story is about a German woman who loses three of her sons to World War I. In the end, she is reunited with her sole remaining son, who has moved to the United States.[126] A community is destroyed and then partially reconstituted, but we sense that the reconstitution will never diminish the overwhelming feeling of loss. The opening scene establishes the German town's sense of community. The camera follows a friendly postman as he greets several citizens during his morning walk through the town. With his flowing mustache and splendid uniform, the postman of *Four Sons* resembles the proud porter of *The Last Laugh*. In Murnau's film, the sense of community proves to be illusory; the porter's neighbors are quick to mock his fall from grace. In *Four Sons*, the neighborhood feeling is quite genuine: the postman's role is to bring the town together, and he plays this role with justified pride. The moving camera stresses the theme of connectedness. We see the postman amble down the street and offer a friendly greeting to every figure he meets along the way— young and old, civilian and police, human and canine. The camera takes it all in, uniting the community within the frame (fig. 1.17a–b). This optimistic opening serves to ground the sadness to come: war will change the postman's role irrevocably, requiring this man of friendly greetings to deliver one death notice after another.

1.17 In *Four Sons*, a postman greets the community on his way through town.

At the end of the film, the German mother must travel to the unfamiliar United States. Here we see another variation on the crossing-the-street shot, familiar from *Sunrise* and *My Best Girl*. A policeman helps the mother make it through the traffic, but there is none of the sense of magic we find in the film's predecessors, as when the Man and the Wife imagine themselves in the country or when Maggie and Joe escape death through the power of slapstick coincidence. Ford places his camera right in the street, dollying with the mother and policeman and keeping their figures in the stable center of the frame even as they walk through the jumble. The shot forms a thematic pair with the earlier shot of the postman, a relationship partly grounded in contrast: the sunny day versus the rainy night; the postman versus the policeman; the small German town versus the large American city; the warm welcomes exchanged between neighbors versus the casual glances passed among strangers. And yet there is a faint echo of the previous shot's sense of community, with a uniformed figure playing his role by helping to bring a family together. The echo is mildly comforting, even as its very faintness reminds us of how much has been lost. In this echo, we find Ford's characteristic attitude to tradition and modernity. He celebrates tradition while acknowledging how much of tradition must inevitably be destroyed by modernity—a modernity of warfare, urbanization, capitalism, and Americanization.

Indeed, the fact that the film is about Americanization adds another layer of meaning to Ford's decision to photograph the film in such a self-consciously "Germanic" style, with clear citations of Murnau and Dupont. By using the moving camera so boldly, Ford contributes to the assimilation of German angles into the Hollywood cinema, and yet he does not want us to forget where these angles came from and maybe wants us to wonder what is lost when one style becomes assimilated to another.

Fox Films was not the only company to encourage directors to work in the German style. Like William Fox, Carl Laemmle had been born in central Europe to a German Jewish family, and he worked to take advantage of his knowledge of the German market. It was Laemmle's company Universal that had released *The Last Laugh* in the United States—a release upstaged by Fox's signing of the director the previous day.[127] Universal opened a subsidiary production company in Germany in 1926, but Nazi brutality eventually forced Universal to close its doors in 1936. In the late silent period, the studio hired a number of talented European directors, including E. A. Dupont, the German expressionist Paul Leni, and the Hungarian-born independent filmmaker Paul Fejos (originally, Pál Fejös).[128] Though trade journals commented on Dupont's mastery of "strange camera effects,"[129] the director made only one film at Universal before moving to the United Kingdom, where he continued to develop his signature style on *Moulin Rouge* (1928) and *Piccadilly* (1929). He eventually returned to the United States and directed some undistinguished B-films.[130] By contrast, both Leni and Fejos had short but spectacular careers at Universal, where they took full advantage of the vogue for unusual angles.

Universal's transnational strategy could produce thrilling results. *The Man Who Laughs* (1928) was a carnival story with a hint of horror, evoking various German predecessors. At one point, Dupont was assigned to direct the project, but the task soon fell to Paul Leni.[131] Born in Stuttgart, Leni had designed sets for Dupont and other German directors in the 1910s and early 1920s. He then codirected the early *kammerspiel* film *Backstairs* (1921, with Leopold Jessner) from a script by Carl Mayer, who would write *The Last Laugh*. Leni's German expressionist classic *Waxworks* (1924) earned him a contract with Universal, where he directed *The Cat and the Canary* and other films in the mystery-horror genre before dying young in 1929.[132] Given this background, it is perhaps not surprising that the mobile shots in *The Man Who Laughs* owe a considerable debt to the example of *Variety*. The opening fairground montage features a shot with the camera in a spinning Ferris wheel, almost identical to a shot in Dupont's film. In the climactic scene, the victimized and deformed protagonist Gwynplaine (played by Conrad Veidt from *Waxworks*) dangles from a ledge. He looks at the crowd below, and the camera suddenly cranes down toward the ground, even though Gwynplaine is still holding on up above. The subjective shot represents Gwynplaine's fear of falling rather than the fall itself, and it closely resembles a moment on Dupont's film in which Huller imagines the death of the rival trapeze artist Antonelli. Both films use a descending camera to represent a fall that occurs only in the protagonist's mind. Movement represents thought.

The Man Who Laughs employs Germanic "angles" in such a way that their foreignness seems amplified. The story has a European setting. The director and the star had made their names in Germany. And the mobile shots evoke specific precedents from a celebrated German release. More broadly, the film could be seen as a continuation of pan-European trends in camera movement, as in Abel Gance's astonishing film *Napoléon* (1927). Another Universal release, *Lonesome* (1928) by Paul Fejos, took a different approach to Hollywood transnationalism. Here, a European-born director would evoke the styles of European modernism to present the story of a self-consciously typical American couple. In contrast to the preceding three examples—the slapstick-inflected style of *My Best Girl* (set in the United States), the Murnau-inflected style of *Four Sons* (set largely but not exclusively in Germany), and the Dupont-inflected style of *The Man Who Laughs* (set in Europe)—*Lonesome* would argue that modernism, for all its European connotations, might just be the right approach to represent the energy and alienation of the big American city.[133]

Like many films from the period, *Lonesome* contains a synchronized soundtrack and an awkward sequence with dialogue, but most of the film was shot silent. More than just a romance, *Lonesome* is a film about life in the contemporary city, where all actions are mediated by machines. Jim (Glenn Tryon) works in a factory; Mary (Barbara Kent) works at a switchboard. They travel around on buses and trains. In their leisure time, they ride on a roller coaster—a roller coaster that breaks down and separates them. In the end, a machine brings them back together again, as the sound of a record player motivates the surprise revelation that these two strangers have been neighbors in the same apartment building the whole time.

To tell this story of humans finding love in a world of machines, Fejos relied on the familiar technique of the vehicle shot, placing the camera on an elevated train, a bus, and a roller coaster. The vehicle shot had been around for decades, serving as an engaging attraction during the early 1900s, but *Lonesome*'s opening cites a more proximate source: the documentary *Berlin: Symphony of a Great City* (1927), directed by avant-garde filmmaker Walter Ruttmann and photographed by Karl Freund, the cinematographer who shot both *The Last Laugh* and *Variety*. *Berlin* takes the "symphony" idea very seriously, cutting together various images of movement in order to produce an abstract rhythm, as in an opening montage showing a train's arrival into the city. Similarly, *Lonesome* begins with the title "New York wakes up—The machinery of life begins to move," a phrase neatly establishing the contrast between the inorganic and the organic. After the title, the film's first shot takes the point of view of a camera perched on the front of an elevated train. Pointing up and to the right, the camera shows buildings zipping by in the foreground, while skyscrapers loom beyond. Then the camera pans to the left, revealing a perspectival image of the train tracks winding through the city. With its two distinct halves, this shot develops the dialectical logic established by the "machinery of life" metaphor. The first half of the shot is disorienting but exciting. The film has not established the existence of a train, and it is not obvious right away that we are riding along on an elevated train. The initial impression is instead a rush of movement as unfamiliar buildings whip past, one after the other. The second half of the shot provides the missing orientation: the sight of the train tracks confirms our suspicion that the camera is on a train, and the vanishing-point composition provides a stability that was lacking in the shot's opening blur. But this stability comes at a price as the second half of the image lacks the dynamic energy of the first. We have moved from the chaos of life to the order of the machine. The montage elaborates on these themes for another twenty-five seconds, superimposing various images (authoritarian traffic cops, lively jazz musicians) over shots of the city whirring by, while whistles and horns blare on the soundtrack. Even the open-minded Maurice Kann was a little shocked by Fejos's work; he called *Lonesome* "the most violent instance of the floating camera we have yet witnessed."[134]

Fejos once claimed that speed was the "prevailing, dominant motive" of America.[135] Faced with this culture of speed, he experimented with new forms of representation, as if Hollywood's existing forms were inadequate to the task of representing the complexity of American life. Through movement, *Lonesome* shows us what it feels like to live in the modern American city: confusing, yes, but also exciting; alienating, yes, but also romantic.

If we approach *My Best Girl*, *Four Sons*, *The Man Who Laughs*, and *Lonesome* from the standpoint of influence, then the four films end up looking very similar: all support the claim that Murnau influenced American cinema. But if we reverse the analysis, thinking about what the later filmmakers are doing with the earlier exemplars, then these films look very different indeed. *My Best Girl* adopts specific shots from *Sunrise* while avoiding their high cultural status; *Four Sons* uses self-consciously "Germanic" techniques to address the themes of assimilation and loss; *The Man Who Laughs* copies a successful German predecessor, increasing its appeal to the European market; and *Lonesome* reworks the established convention of the vehicle shot in light of *Berlin*'s abstract rhythms, thereby offering a quasi-modernist interpretation of its deliberately simple American story.

***

The German contribution to Hollywood cinema was not the technical task of moving the camera; rather, it was the daring proposal that the moving camera was more than a trick. Murnau and Dupont had championed movement as an essential component of the cinematic art. The Hollywood studios would soon take this art and turn it into a craft, based less on bursts of innovation and more on reliable systems of mass production. But Murnau's and Dupont's more abstract ideas—ideas about subjectivity, drama, and medium specificity—would linger for decades.

CHAPTER 2

PURPOSES AND PARALLELS

F. W. Murnau delighted in ad hoc solutions. He proposed impossible shots and challenged his crew to put those ideas onscreen, prompting Karl Freund to operate a camera on a bicycle and pushing the *Sunrise* team to lay down a mile of track for the trolley sequence.[1] These shots inspired more admiration than imitation: Hollywood cinematographers did not become master cyclists, and producers did not invest in their own trolley lines.[2] Instead, the studios invested in technologies that were reliable and repeatable. By 1934, Freund was working in Hollywood and declaring, "There is no doubt in my mind that the American method of filming motion pictures is by far ahead of the foreign method."[3] The modernist impulse to "make it new" had become the organized system of the modern corporation.

Now the camera was mobile. How could it be mobilized? Blessed with the world's best dollies and cranes, the filmmakers of the 1930s considered when to use the technology and why. Some filmmakers argued against camera movement on the grounds that it was too flamboyant. Because these counterarguments were rather loud, it is tempting to see "restraint" as the dominant trend of the era. Within film studies, it is common to draw a distinction between "motivated" camera moves, which follow figure movement, and "unmotivated" camera moves, which do not. Perhaps the era's filmmakers insisted on "motivation" in this narrow sense of the term.

However, I think it is more useful to see the call for restraint as only one trend among many and not necessarily the most important one. The easy availability of dollies and cranes encouraged filmmakers to think more deeply about the cinema's expressive possibilities, telling stories with irony, intensity, and emotion. The unobtrusive "follow shot" was indeed a convention of the era, but so was its opposite: the shot that moves freely to reveal what a character does not know. The discussions surrounding the mobile frame in the 1930s were genuine debates, entertaining a wide range of possibilities.

Rather than rely on the opposition between the unobtrusive and the flamboyant or between the motivated and the unmotivated, this chapter organizes its account by distinguishing between two kinds of claims that structured the decade's theoretical debates: means–end claims and analogical claims. Both the defenders and the critics of camera movement relied on means–end thinking, making sense of the moving camera in light of the purposes it might serve—from irony to immersion, from revelation to concealment, from sensory appeal to reflexive commentary. A means–end theory asks, "What can the camera do?"

By contrast, an analogical theory asks, "What is the camera like?" As in the silent period, many practitioners assumed that the camera should move like a person. But is the camera like a theater spectator, watching the action from afar? Or like a disembodied eye, moving magically throughout the scene? Should the camera's movements be restricted to those a person might perform? Or be expanded to include all the movements a viewer might imagine? Hollywood filmmakers never settled on a single coherent ideal. In some shots, the camera does not move like a person at all. When it does, it imitates a person in opportunistic, shifting ways. Parallels served purposes. By evoking an image of what the camera was like, a filmmaker made an implicit argument about what the camera could do.

This chapter tells a story of technologies transformed by ideas. The first section offers a quick overview of the era's new technologies of camera movement, starting with the transition to sound and ending in the late 1930s. The remaining sections take technology as a given, focusing instead on the resulting aesthetic debates.

Ice Boxes and Baby Carriages

When Hollywood filmmakers began recording synchronized sounds in the 1920s, first in a series of short subjects and eventually in feature-length films such as *The Jazz Singer* (1927), sound engineers faced the problem of isolating dialogue from the grinding clamor of the cameras. The Mitchell camera quickly replaced the noisy Bell and Howell as the industry's standard, but omnidirectional microphones still picked up too much sound.[4] For a few years, a common solution was to cloister the camera in a booth. According to one article in 1929, a booth was "a small, portable, sound-proof room into which camera and cameraman were locked while working. The scene was photographed through a large window of optically plane glass at the front of the booth, while entrance was through a door at the rear."[5] Though the booth was known as an "ice box," conditions inside were actually quite hot. Even worse, photographing a scene through glass made the resulting images look "mushy," and the booth's enormous size eliminated "any possible mobility."[6] Many filmmakers saw this period as a step backward in cinematic technique. In King Vidor's words, "cinematography had retrogressed to the nailed-down tripod of the early days."[7] Recalling a sound engineer's dictates, William Wyler complained, "I'd say, 'I want to move the camera during this shot,' and he'd say, 'Oh, you can't do that. That's crazy.'"[8]

The multicamera filmmaking that dominated the early sound years posed another obstacle to camera movement. Instead of cutting together several different soundtracks, a crew might record a single track while photographing the scene from multiple angles simultaneously. As Donald Crafton explains, "The goal was to furnish the film editor with complete coverage of the scene from one wide view—the so-called master shot—and a sufficient number of angles and focal lengths from which to fashion a smoothly cut sequence adhering to the established principles of continuity."[9] The end result might look very similar to a scene photographed in the single-camera style (or, in Crafton's terms, the multiple-take method), but the approach limited the crew's options for camera placement. By dollying in for a close-up, one camera might enter another camera's field of view, spoiling the latter's composition.

The brief period of multicamera filmmaking changed the way writers crafted their screenplays. A continuity script, or "continuity," was a document that described what the film would look like shot by shot, providing a detailed plan for the production crew to follow.[10] The silent era's continuities contain surprisingly detailed instructions regarding camera movement. For instance, Bess Meredyth's continuity for *A Woman of Affairs* is packed with moving-camera terms, such as "pull back slightly," "moving shot," "interesting camera shot," and "pam," spelled with an *m*. There is even a reference to a "Zum lens."[11]

Such detailed instructions became unnecessary when the screenwriter adopted the assumption that multicamera shooting would provide the editor with a variety of angles on any given line. Here are breakdowns from the scripts for three of director Clarence Brown's silent films: 327 shots for *Flesh and the Devil* (1926, continuity by Benjamin Glazer), 694 shots for *Trail of '98* (1928, continuity by Glazer and Waldemar Young), and 498 shots for *A Woman of Affairs*. Those numbers dipped considerably when Brown directed a trio of multiple-camera films with Greta Garbo: 107 shots for *Anna Christie* (1930, continuity by Frances Marion), 108 shots for *Romance* (1930, continuity by Edward Sheldon), and a mere 93 shots for *Inspiration* (1931, continuity by Gene Markey). Editing rates slowed down after the transition to sound, as Barry Salt and others have documented.[12] Meanwhile, multiple-camera shooting temporarily shut the screenwriter out of the process of visualizing the story. A dialogue revision for *Romance* contains the following note by screenwriter Edward Sheldon: "There is no attempt below to indicate camera angles or business, which will be supplied by Mr. Brown at his discretion."[13] Filmmakers soon returned to single-camera shooting as a norm, and screenwriters resumed the practice of breaking films down shot by shot. Taking three more Clarence Brown films as examples, we find the following breakdowns: 382 shots for *Night Flight* (1933, continuity by O. H. P. Garrett), 215 shots for *Chained* (1934, continuity by John Lee Mahin), and 286 shots for *Sadie McKee* (1934, continuity by John Meehan).[14] By indicating angles in their scripts, screenwriters reclaimed some of their lost authority over a film's visual design.

The early sound period of mushy, stationary photography was brief. Indeed, Barry Salt argues that "there was remarkably little discontinuity in the use of camera movement across the transition to sound in Hollywood."[15] Ambitious shots appear in several films from 1929—most famously in Rouben Mamoulian's *Applause* but also in such forgotten titles as *The Saturday Night Kid*, in which the camera dollies up and down the aisles of a department store, and *Street Girl*, RKO's debut film, in which the camera dollies backward underneath a stairway during a musical number. When in doubt, a filmmaker could photograph a difficult shot silent and edit it into a sound film. That same year, art director William Cameron Menzies designed a trio of films (*Alibi*, *Bulldog Drummond*, and *The Taming of the Shrew*), each featuring a bravura sequence in which the camera dollies forward through a deeply perspectival composition, as if immersing the spectator in a three-dimensional space.

Early filmmakers solved the mobility problem by placing the entire camera booth onto a wheeled chassis, but a more promising alternative was to dampen the noise of the camera with some sort of modestly sized covering.[16] Options that appeared in the early sound years included the Baby Booth, the Blimp, the Bungalow, the Hat, the Barney Google, and the Horse Blanket; *blimp* and *barney* soon became generic terms. Most of these covers were boxes made of aluminum, plywood, or yucca and lined with sponge, rubber, or felt.[17] Reducing the need to take the box off and on between shots, studio camera departments adorned the boxes with useful attachments. The Paramount Sound Blimp, known as the "Rolls Royce of Blimps," offered such luxuries as a follow-focus device, a lens shade, and a Lupe light bracket.[18]

Blimps could be quite heavy, especially when they were lined with lead. With a camera inside, the resulting monstrosity might weigh up to 260 pounds.[19] Although blimps grew smaller over the years, that first generation of lead-lined boxes prompted studios to replace their silent-era tripods, most of which could hold no more than 80 pounds.[20] They often replaced the tripods with dollies, which made it easier for camera crews to move the equipment from one spot to another between takes, even if the camera remained stationary during the actual filming.[21]

In addition to their practical benefits, cranes and dollies offered aesthetic opportunities. At Universal, director Paul Fejos and cinematographer Hal Mohr worked with the Consolidated Steel Corporation to build an enormous crane for the early-sound-era musical *Broadway* (1929). This massive device featured a thirty-one-foot-long steel girder attached to a fourteen-foot-tall cylindrical steel turret, which was mounted onto a six-wheeled truck chassis. A camera platform capable of holding three people rested at one end of the crane, counterbalanced by weights at the other end. Total weight: twenty-eight tons. Cost: $35,000.[22] Photographs of the "Broadway Boom" highlight its glorious modernity, its steel beams blending with the Cubistic design of *Broadway*'s nightclub set (fig. 2.1).

According to Mohr, "Paul wanted a piece of equipment that we could just make the camera do anything in the world with."[23] The rhetoric invokes the go-anywhere ideal of the late silent period; the film itself brilliantly exploits the tension between the human scaled and the mechanically marvelous. One sequence

2.1 Universal used an enormous crane to photograph *Broadway*. (Courtesy of the Academy of Motion Picture Arts and Sciences and Marc Wanamaker/Bison Archives)

begins on a close image of a dancer putting her makeup on in her dressing room (fig. 2.2a). The camera dollies back as the dancer joins her peers. Continuing backward, the camera reveals more and more space, and we learn that all of the dancers are attired in ridiculous, fabulous skyscraper costumes (fig. 2.2b). It is as if the camera itself were one of the dancers, milling about this way and that, gradually making its way through the exit. With the help of some hidden cuts, the camera even passes through some curtains, exactly like the dancers approaching the stage (fig. 2.2c). Then something astonishing happens: the singer begins his act, and the camera ascends to a great height, moving backward all the while (fig. 2.2d). Having established the pattern that the camera will imitate the human perspective, Fejos breaks the pattern, showing us exactly what a twenty-eight-ton crane with a counterweighted thirty-one-foot arm can do: fly sublimely above characters stuck to the ground.

The spectacle of this shot sets up the irony of a later one. After the club has closed for the night, workers set about the task of cleaning it for the next night. We see two women on their knees while they scrub the floor. Then the camera

2.2 *Broadway*'s camera precedes dancers exiting their dressing room; once onstage, the camera ascends to a spectacular height.

vaults up into the sky, looking down on the women from a great height. Previously, the dazzling acrobatics of the camerawork expressed the spectacle of the nightclub. Here, the camera's superhuman mobility comments on—and mocks—the very ideal of spectacle, suggesting that the Broadway Boom, like the nightclub itself, is a false luxury produced by labor kept hidden from view.[24]

Why would a cost-conscious studio such as Universal invest in such an extravagant purchase? As expensive as the crane was, the boom saved money over time. To see why, compare the crane shots in *Broadway* to the suspended-camera shots in Vidor's film *The Crowd* or to the cranelike ramp effects in another film by Fejos, *The Last Performance*, discussed in the previous chapter. Creating a custom-built track or ramp for each shot required a great deal of labor, as Lutz Bacher has explained.[25] The Broadway Boom and its successors were expensive to manufacture, but they allowed filmmakers to make minute adjustments relatively quickly, and they could be reused in film after film. The key to a successful crane lay in the counterweighting. On one side of the crane was the camera platform. On the other side was a set of weights—oftentimes blocks of lead placed in a bucket—which balanced out the weight of the camera and crew (assuming the length of the crane was taken into account). If the balance was just right, then a single member of the grip crew could lift the crane with a minimum of effort, even though the crane as a whole might weigh thousands of pounds. According to director Fritz Lang, Hollywood's technologies surpassed what was available in Germany before he fled that country in 1933. "The technical end was indescribably better" in Los Angeles, he said. "I remember for *M* [1931], my first talkie, I needed a boom. There was no boom. Nobody had ever heard about a boom in Germany." Lang went on to describe an improvised contraption in which some "heavy-bellied" men served as counterweights on a boom built with a twenty-foot two-by-four.[26]

Many Universal films of the 1930s feature remarkable camerawork courtesy of the Broadway Boom, from the battle sequences in Lewis Milestone's *All Quiet on the Western Front* (1930) to the experimentation scenes in James Whale's *The Bride of Frankenstein* (1935). Whale's *Show Boat* (1936) took full advantage of the Broadway Boom's mobility. When Paul Robeson sings "Ol' Man River," the camera arcs around the actor before moving in for a big close-up. Not just a formal innovation, the shot carries political meaning, radically insisting on giving Robeson the star treatment he deserves.

After the Broadway Boom, most subsequent cranes were smaller, albeit still greater than human scale. Paramount's crane was compared to a "swan" or a "giant bird."[27] At M-G-M, John Arnold, the longtime president of the American Society of Cinematographers (ASC), designed a crane made of Duralumin instead of steel, which reduced the weight to 3,300 pounds and the cost to $3,500.[28] In 1938, the trade journal *International Photographer* listed all of the cranes available throughout Hollywood, both from the studios and from rental houses: weights ranged from 2,000 to 9,000 pounds; maximum heights from nine and a half to forty-two feet.[29] By then, even Universal had supplemented its crane from 1929 with a more practical model made of Duralumin.[30] Cinematographer Mohr acknowledged that the original Broadway Boom was absurdly large: Universal needed to build a new studio just to accommodate it. But Mohr insisted that this large device, capable of swinging 360 degrees in any position, was more flexible than its smaller successors. These advantages aside, the crane was repurposed as a rigging device, reduced to hauling equipment up the scaffolding. Decades later, when Mohr came across the Broadway Boom in a junkyard on studio grounds, he almost wept.[31]

Other technologies were more modest in size. One option was the simple platform dolly: a horizontal surface with four wheels attached, providing a resting place for a standard tripod. More flexible were newly invented dolly devices such as the Rotambulator and the Velocilator. M-G-M's John Arnold took credit for the Rotambulator's design; Bell and Howell manufactured the device. This three-wheeled dolly featured a tall post on a rotating circular platform that the operator could control with foot pedals (fig. 2.3). For arcing shots, the operator would rotate the platform while the dolly grip maneuvered the third wheel. Although the camera could be positioned at various heights along the post, one contemporary critic noted that the original Rotambulator's lack of hydraulic vertical motion compared unfavorably with the Velocilator.[32] Engineers at Fox designed the latter dolly in 1933, and the independent equipment company Fearless manufactured the device for use across the industry. The Velocilator's contribution was an arm that functioned like a miniature boom (fig. 2.4). In 1936, a variation appeared featuring a turntable that allowed the arm to spin around 360 degrees, as on the Rotambulator. Victor Raby's version was known as the Raby; Fearless's version was known as the Panoram.[33] The four-wheeled Velocilator could run on pneumatic tires, or the crew could lay down tracks for an even smoother ride.

Dollies and cranes complemented one another, but they gave form to competing ideals. As we saw in the previous chapter, the early champions of camera movement pondered the tension between two different proposals: the cautious recommendation that the camera should move like a person versus the bold declaration that the camera should move in ways no human ever could. If the crane offered the filmmaker the chance to fly through the air, then the dolly kept movement to a human scale. Both the Rotambulator and the Velocilator offered maximum heights of less than seven feet. Whereas the Universal crane rested on a motor-driven chassis capable of moving twenty miles per hour, a dolly had to be pushed, working within the limits set by the dolly grip's strength and agility. Note that the generic term for the dolly throughout the decade was *perambulator*. In British English, that term is a synonym for *pram* or *stroller*, and some American cinematographers began using the term *baby carriage* as shorthand.[34] The camera–baby analogy was not new: Edgar Ulmer claims that

2.3 Cinematographer William Daniels and operator A. Lindsley Lane on the M-G-M Rotambulator. (Courtesy of the Academy of Motion Picture Arts and Sciences and Marc Wanamaker/Bison Archives)

he, Freund, and Murnau were walking down Kurfürstendam Boulevard in Berlin when they saw a woman pushing twins in a stroller, a sight that supposedly inspired Ulmer to suggest putting the camera on a dolly in *The Last Laugh*.[35] Whether true or not, Ulmer's story worked to personalize the technology, favoring relatability over spectacle.

2.4 The Velocilator featured a small boom arm that supported the camera. (Courtesy of the Academy of Motion Picture Arts and Sciences and Marc Wanamaker/Bison Archives).

Top M-G-M cinematographers such as William Daniels continued to use the Rotambulator for the rest of the decade, but it appears that the Velocilator was the more popular design across Hollywood.[36] A report noted in 1936, "The Fox–Fearless type of dolly, or Velocilator, has found its way into nearly all the larger studios because of its mobility and the ease with which it handles the heavier blimps."[37] Many studios developed their own variations on the Velocilator design. Warner Bros. produced a small-arm dolly in 1934; Paramount introduced a small-arm dolly in 1935; RKO developed its variation in 1937.[38] The small-arm dolly found such wide usage that it came to be known quite simply as a "dolly." Splitting the difference between the large crane and the small dolly, Paramount introduced the Baby Boom, a crane that was small enough to fit through a doorway.[39] Virgil Miller, the studio's Camera Department head, explained later, "No studio is complete without the highly specialized 'boom' of various sizes."[40]

Miller hosted an important meeting at Paramount in 1932, sponsored by the Academy of Motion Picture Arts and Sciences. There, he introduced such devices as the Baby Boom, the Paramount Blimp, and the Rotambulator to the industry at large.[41] Such meetings demonstrate the workings of an increasingly oligopolistic industry, as analyzed by David Bordwell, Janet Staiger, and

Kristin Thompson. In their book *The Classical Hollywood Cinema*, Bordwell notes that rather than wait for inspiration to strike some random inventor, "Hollywood had a network for the organized articulation of technical questions and the systematic search for answers."[42] As a result of such networks, the major studios soon owned equipment that allowed run-of-the-mill hacks to execute dolly shots that would have astonished the greatest filmmakers of the late silent period. Upon visiting M-G-M, a British producer expressed his admiration: "It is never a matter of 'You can't have the velocilator [*sic*] until so and so has finished with it.' You just order it and it's there."[43]

Watching the expert camerawork of the decade, we might forget how much craft went into getting the details just right. Particularly astonishing is the fact that crews were working with parallax viewfinders, not reflex viewfinders. Whereas a reflex viewfinder allows the operator to look through the lens of the camera during filming, a parallax viewfinder is a separate device attached to the outside of the camera and pointed toward the scene to approximate the view through the lens itself.[44] The trick is to angle the parallax viewfinder correctly. If the subject is five feet away, then the viewfinder must be angled sharply; if the subject is twenty feet away, then the viewfinder must be nearly parallel to the camera's body. The era's large soundproof blimps made the problem even more difficult because parallax is more severe the farther the viewfinder is from the lens. A good operator needed to anticipate the viewfinder's inaccuracies and compensate for them. In 1936, M-G-M Camera Department head John Arnold ensured greater accuracy by inventing a new follow-focus apparatus. With the aid of gears, the operator would change the focus on the lens and the viewfinder simultaneously while shifting the viewfinder's angle of view.[45] Arnold was so pleased with his device that he had it installed on all forty of M-G-M's cameras.

Diffusion presented another challenging technical problem. Most cinematographers photographed long shots with little or no diffusion, while employing heavier diffusion on the close shots, especially of women. What if the camera had to dolly from long shot to close-up? Rouben Mamoulian's film *Queen Christina* (1933) ends with such a shot; his crew employed a long piece of sliding glass to introduce the diffusion gradually over the course of the approach.[46] A few years later Columbia engineer Emil Oster worked with cinematographer Peverell Marley to design a variable-diffusion device, which would drop an open-edged piece of gauze into the camera's matte box during a dolly-in.[47]

Some innovations did not catch on right away. Zoom lenses had been used for a handful of silent films. Nick Hall cites *It* from 1927 as the first known example, though the relevant technology predates the cinema.[48] The zoom is not really a camera movement so much as it is a magnification of the image: zooming changes the focal length of the lens, shifting from wide angle to telephoto or vice versa. A couple years later Joseph Walker invented his own zoom lens, which he used on a number of Columbia productions. After the transition to sound, Bell and Howell marketed the Varo lens, and Otto Durholz invented another prototype.[49] Meanwhile, Paramount released a number of films featuring zooms (probably, as Hall suggests, relying on silent-era technology), including *Broken Lullaby* (1932), *Island of Lost Souls* (1932), and *Love Me Tonight* (1932). Although some hoped that the zoom would replace the cumbersome crane, the zoom never could fulfill that promise. A crane is capable of moving left, right, in, out, up, and down; the zoom has but two directions—in and out. The director Allan Dwan complained that early zoom lenses were too "bulky" and that they never offered the true "effect of movement."[50] With its technology of magnification, the zoom offered neither the personlike movement of the dolly nor the go-anywhere flexibility of the crane.

For outdoor shooting, most studios adopted custom-built camera cars, thereby rationalizing the old silent-era strategy of attaching a camera platform to the back of a car or truck.[51] For the Oscar-winning Western *Cimarron* (1931), RKO placed a twenty-three-foot-tall tower on top of an automobile chassis.[52] This mobile tower may have been impressive, but it was too top heavy to be practical. Perhaps fearing that the car might topple over, the filmmakers avoided moving the camera at the highest angles. Later camera cars were much sturdier, such as Warner's 1936 model, which offered four separate camera mounts (on a front platform, on a back platform, in the body, and atop the cab), eliminating the need for separate tripods. With a Lincoln motor upgraded to 135 horsepower, the car could drive up to seventy miles per hour.[53] It was known as an "insert car," and its primary purpose was to supply additional footage for montages and car chases.

Dangerous shots created a niche job for specialty cameramen, such as Elmer Dyer, who took out full-page ads in *American Cinematographer* to promote himself as an "aerial cinematographer" and "Akeley specialist."[54] But the most precarious jobs were soon swept aside by a major shift in Hollywood's filmmaking practice: the increasing reliance on special effects to execute moving-vehicle scenes. RKO effects specialist Vernon Walker explained that the transition to sound introduced new obstacles: "A scene to be taken within a trolley car would be practically impossible from the standpoint of recording sound. The extraneous noises, the transporting of sound equipment, the tying up of traffic in the desired location, and the expense involved make a suitable case for the use of process photography."[55] The change was cultural as much as it was technological: the freewheeling experimentation of silent-era effects work gave way to a more systematic and predictable approach, at least in theory. Recall that Fred Jackman once celebrated the slapstick cinematographer as a daredevil. By 1937, Jackman was the owner of his own effects firm, and he offered a more sober-minded account of the effects business, noting "the tremendous difference between the magic-working trick cameraman of a few years ago and the special-effects engineer of today. The former was merely an ingenious craftsman; his present-day successor is more nearly comparable to a production executive."[56] Youthful delight had given way to corporate efficiency.

Before the rise of rear-screen projection in the early 1930s, filmmakers often relied on traveling-matte systems, such as the Williams process, first patented in 1918.[57] An alternative approach known as the Dunning process was first patented in 1927; it manipulated complementary colors to produce a similar effect.[58] The science behind these processes demonstrated a sophisticated understanding of color theory and sensitometry, but the resulting images often contained visible flaws, as in the automobile shots in *Back Pay* (1930), where one can see a fringe separating the foreground from the background, indicating imperfectly aligned mattes.

Around 1932, rear-screen projection rendered the traveling matte obsolete, at least for the next few decades.[59] A secondary camera crew would photograph the moving backgrounds ahead of time; those backgrounds would be projected on a large screen behind the actors while they pretended to drive a car (or mount a horse or ski a slope or walk down a street). In one sequence in Frank Borzage's film *Man's Castle* (1933), Spencer Tracy and Loretta Young stand in front of a rear-projection screen depicting a crowded city street—but the people behind them look larger than the stars! More competently, a scene in *Mr. Deeds Goes to Town* (1936) shows the title character (Gary Cooper) on a train, pulling out of his beloved small town. Although Deeds looks crisp in the foreground, the small-town crowd looks hazy on the always-imperfect rear-projection screen. The effect is oddly expressive, enhancing our sense that Deeds's move to the city is severing his connection to small-town life. However obvious some of these effects might appear today, they represented a significant upgrade in efficiency. Paramount effects specialist Farciot Edouart listed several advantages: no danger to the actors; less concern about weather disrupting the schedule; more control over lighting. Rear-screen photography, he claimed, allowed crews to work under "completely controllable conditions," systematizing what once was unpredictable.[60] His list does not mention what was lost: the dizzying dynamism of the silent-era vehicle shot, with one machine precariously perched on another.[61]

Writing in 1978, Lutz Bacher argued, plausibly, that the camera-carriage technology of the early 1970s was much the same as the camera-carriage technology of 1929. Not until the Steadicam of 1976 did camera crews have to contend with a radically new technology.[62] Looking at the studios' preference for pliable but predictable tools, an observer might conclude that Murnau and Dupont's impact had been diminished or even annulled. Late-silent-era discussions of camera movement often used the language of modernism, invoking such ideals as subjectivity and medium specificity. The studios had taken these quasi-modernist ideas and turned them into the predictable techniques of a corporate film factory. Many European innovators of the 1920s were no longer working in Hollywood: Paul Leni and F. W. Murnau died young; Paul Fejos and Erich Pommer returned to Europe; Mauritz Stiller returned to Europe and then died young. Even some of Murnau's most devoted admirers, such as John Ford and Frank Borzage, were beginning to use the moving camera more conservatively. Innovations had been replaced by standards.

But what of Murnau's call to make the audience feel with the character? Of Karl Freund's plea for a medium-specific art of movement? Of Maurice Kann's hope for a camera that could move here, there, and everywhere? Did these ideas wither away like the pages of the trade papers where they first appeared? I think not. If anything, Murnau's and Pommer's and Dupont's ideas had assumed more lasting form, built into the steel tresses of the cranes and the rubber wheels of the dollies that could be found on the floors of every major studio in Hollywood. Silent-era filmmakers had longed for the day when the camera would be truly mobile. That day had arrived. Now filmmakers had to figure out what to do with their newfound powers.

When to Move and Why

As John Caldwell has explained, filmmakers share practices, but they also share ways of thinking and talking about the tools they use.[63] Far from assuring unanimity, the shared framework of a production culture sets the stage for lively aesthetic debates. Consider the year 1932, when the moving camera became a point of contention for many filmmakers. At least half-a-dozen films that year featured spectacular introductory shots, including *Young America*, directed by Frank Borzage; *Scarface*, by the usually restrained Howard Hawks; *Frisco Jenny*, by Wild Bill Wellman; *As You Desire Me*, by silent-era aesthete George Fitzmaurice; *Union Depot*, by the workmanlike Alfred E. Green; and *One Way Passage*, by the camera-drunk Tay Garnett. Yet the year also saw a significant backlash against the moving camera. The ASC hosted a meeting at Paramount Studios to discuss the problem. Summarizing the meeting, *American Cinematographer* complained that "directors in Hollywood have been practically going wild in an attempt to inject moving camera shots in their pictures."[64] The ASC's accusation was simple: many of the new dolly shots lacked purpose. Leading cinematographer John F. Seitz declared that filmmakers were "making moving shots with no reason."[65] Victor Milner denounced directors who designed difficult dolly shots to impress their colleagues and "with no other reason apparent."[66]

Reading this call for reason, we might assume that the cinematographers were attempting to enforce a simple rule, insisting that the camera should move only when a character moves. However, this narrow reading does not do justice to the nuances of the debates. An early champion of the moving camera was Rouben Mamoulian, who attended the ASC's meeting in 1932 and bravely defended the technique, arguing that effective angles "add power and punch to the scene."[67] The same year Mamoulian explained his philosophy of "angles" to *American Cinematographer*: "The director must know how to use his camera; when to use unusual angles—and why; when to move the camera—and why."[68] The appeal was to means–end thinking, justifying a technique in light of the purposes it might serve. Echoing an argument that Murnau had made a few years earlier, Mamoulian invoked the ideal of drama: "If they [camera movements] aid the dramatic progress of the picture, they are good, and must be used; if they hinder it, they must not be used."[69] With these passages in mind, there is no reason to believe that the only viable dramatic purpose of a dolly shot was to follow character movement.

Mamoulian's film *Applause* from 1929 is justly celebrated as the first all-talkie to feature significant use of the moving camera. Although shooting most of the film at Paramount's Long Island studio, the crew photographed several stunning scenes on location.[70] The film's advertising campaign appealed to the familiar "camera-as-person" model to help viewers make sense of the style: "His camera sweeps about, roving hither and yon, just as the eye would do in real life."[71] But the film belies this description. Rather than imitate the movements of a hypothetical observer, Mamoulian's camera is unapologetically rhetorical, framing pictorial compositions that comment on the characters—often at their expense. The story is about the burlesque dancer Kitty Darling (Helen Morgan), who tries to protect her daughter, April (Joan Peers), from the seamy world in which she lives. In one scene, Kitty's exploitative lover, Hitch, convinces her to write a letter to April, asking the daughter to join the family (fig. 2.5a). At the end of the scene, Kitty and Hitch walk toward a desk. Dollying with the characters, Mamoulian's camera rests on a very unusual composition: Kitty's face occupies the lower-right corner of the frame, but Hitch is now offscreen, his shadow looming large on the back wall (fig. 2.5b). The result is a piece of

2.5 In *Applause*, the framing emphasizes the symbolism of a shadow.

heavy-handed symbolism. The shadow tells us that Hitch is evil; Kitty's placement in the corner evokes her powerlessness. The film could have cut to this
composition, but the dolly-in announces the framing as a deliberate choice.
Knowing that the camera could be rolled back a few feet reinforces our awareness that the storyteller has chosen not to do so. Neither character is aware of
the symbolism; the spectator could hardly miss it.

We can think of this discrepancy in knowledge as a form of irony: the images
carry a meaning that is available to spectators while remaining unavailable to
the citizens of the fictional world. As V. F. Perkins has argued, some discrepancy in knowledge is inevitable in any film about a storyworld. Not only do we
notice things that the characters do not, but "each of them has a vast body of
knowledge that is not detailed for us."[72] Even if Kitty were to look up, notice
the shadow, and think, "It's like a symbol of his evil, domineering power," the
symbolism would mean something different to her because she is the one who
must suffer the consequences of Hitch's abuse. Ironic differences in knowledge
are not just occasional effects but permanent possibilities—possibilities Mamoulian is eager to exploit.

At the end of *Applause*, Kitty dies by suicide, and April, still ignorant of
Kitty's death, tries to take over her mother's role in the burlesque act. The film's
final shot stages a series of critical compositions. Escaping the clutches of Hitch,
April runs off the stage and into the arms of Tony, a naive sailor who has offered
to marry her and take her home to Wisconsin. The camera dollies back to show
us the two lovers embracing underneath a poster of Kitty. On the poster, Kitty
looks youthful, but we know what April does not: that Kitty is dead. The film
fades to black. Again, Mamoulian has used the dynamic frame to make ironic
comments. By running away from Hitch into the arms of Tony, April is rejecting the burlesque way of life and accepting a new domestic role; the panning
shot echoes her choice, moving Hitch offscreen and the sailor on. By bringing
Kitty's image back into the frame, the dolly ensures that we do not miss the
juxtaposition: the daughter accepting domesticity below, the mother performing sexuality up above. Only in death, the film suggests cynically, has Kitty succeeded as a mother.[73]

In later interviews, Mamoulian ungenerously took full credit for these innovations, insisting that he had to bully cinematographer George Folsey into
moving the camera.[74] The director brought the same sledgehammer approach
to his subsequent films, framing ironic compositions that his characters were
too oblivious to see. In *City Streets* (1931), the camera follows a gangster walking down the hall, but the framing remains loose enough to show the shadow
of a rival gangster trailing just behind him. The symbolism (shadow as impending death) is unknown to the characters but head thumpingly obvious to us. In
The Song of Songs (1933), the camera pans away from a disrobing Marlene Dietrich to frame various nude sculptures, thereby encouraging the spectator to

imagine Dietrich's nudity without showing it directly. Rather than imitating a hypothetical observer seeking the best possible view, the filmmaker selected what to reveal and what to conceal. In both films, irony evades censorship, keeping murder and sex off the screen but in our thoughts. The play of concealment and revelation is so brazen that the scenes mock the Motion Picture Production Code, prompting us to wonder at the arbitrary rules that made certain images acceptable and others censorable.

One of Mamoulian's most audacious experiments of the early sound period was *Dr. Jekyll and Mr. Hyde* (1932). The film opens with a three-and-a-half-minute sequence looking through the eyes of the doctor, played by Fredric March. First, we see Jekyll's hands playing an organ, the shadow of his head cast upon the sheet music (fig. 2.6a). Then a butler enters and speaks directly into the camera, as if talking to Jekyll himself. Rapid whip-pans and cuts suggest the doctor's rapid shifts of attention. Cinematographer Karl Struss had operated the camera during *Sunrise*'s complicated marsh sequence; here, working with operator George Clemens, he wheels the dolly in multiple directions.[75] Approaching a mirror, Jekyll turns to the right and looks at his own reflection (fig. 2.6b). In a clever trick, the mirror is actually a window, revealing March performing in a duplicate room on the other side.[76]

Does this sequence run counter to Mamoulian's preference for ironic detachment? In *Applause* and the other films, Mamoulian uses the camera to frame compositions that the characters cannot see; the movement ensures that we notice the director's wry composition. In *Dr. Jekyll*, Mamoulian uses an always-moving camera to show us exactly what the character does see. Yet ironic distance remains. Jekyll is not looking at a composition; he is looking at his hands, his butler, and his mirror. We are looking at carefully composed pictures of what Jekyll sees. The film asks us to interpret these images in ways

2.6 In *Dr. Jekyll and Mr. Hyde*, the camera imitates Jekyll's point of view.

that Jekyll cannot. The image of the mirror (or, rather, of a window that appears to be a mirror) comments on cinematic identification. Just as Jekyll seeks vicarious and illicit pleasures by becoming Mr. Hyde, the spectator seeks vicarious and sometimes illicit pleasures by identifying with fictional characters such as Jekyll/Hyde. With its split-personality story line, Robert Louis Stevenson's novel raised questions about the nature of the self; Mamoulian evokes those questions cinematically in this bewildering subjective sequence, asking us to identify with the protagonist's point of view while reminding us that we are only ever looking through the inhuman "eye" of a machine.

In comparison to the often bombastic Mamoulian, Ernst Lubitsch played games of concealment and revelation with greater wit. Gerald Mast described Lubitsch's technique as "an art of omission"; through composition and camerawork, "he consistently shows less than he might, implies more than he shows."[77] Rather than follow his characters neutrally, Lubitsch might dolly away from his characters or anticipate their movements or frame them in unusual ways—all to produce unusual compositions carrying ironic meanings. Lubitsch was explicit about his goals; he told his biographer, Herman Weinberg, "The camera should comment, insinuate, make an epigram or a *bon mot*, as well as tell a story. We're telling stories with pictures so we must try to make the pictures as expressive as we can."[78] The first sentence positions the ironic effect as a bonus, something added to the story. But the second sentence offers a different view: the ironic comment is synonymous with expressive storytelling.

In his early Hollywood films, such as *The Marriage Circle* (1924), Lubitsch rarely moved the camera, instead relying on eye-line matches and match-on-action cuts to stitch spaces together. He soon mastered the familiar silent-era comedy technique of the revelation gag.[79] *So This Is Paris* (1926) opens with a scene of a shirtless, turbaned man taking out a knife and stabbing a woman he has thrown onto a divan. It seems like the projectionist has made a mistake: Isn't this supposed to be a movie about Paris? Then the camera pans to the left, revealing a bearded man playing the piano. We realize that we have been in Paris all along, watching the rehearsal of a terrible play. Before the punch line, we know less than the characters; after the revelation, we know more because the absurdity of the juxtaposition is clear to us in a way the characters will never understand.

As Kristin Thompson points out, Lubitsch began to move the camera more freely after Murnau's arrival in Hollywood, as in his German-themed film *The Student Prince of Old Heidelberg* (1927).[80] By the early 1930s, camera movement had become a key component of Lubitsch's scene construction. In *Design for Living* (1933), photographed by Victor Milner, one scene shows Gilda (Miriam Hopkins) explaining to two men, George (Gary Cooper) and Tom (Fredric March), that she is in love with both and would prefer not to choose between them. Rather than giving each actor a close-up, Lubitsch employs a series of group shots, changing the composition to reflect the moment-by-moment progression of the scene. Table 2.1 describes two consecutive shots from this thirty-nine-shot scene: the thirty-third and the thirty-fourth.

When Gilda explains that social norms prevent a woman from trying out her options with the same sexual freedom as a man, the framing creates separate two-shots, as in 33a, 33b, and 33c; the separation echoes Gilda's monologue about the impossibility of a woman desiring two men at once. Lubitsch could have achieved a similar effect by editing together 2 two-shots, but the use of the moving camera places extra emphasis on Gilda's agency—*her* movement creates the pairs. At the end of this shot, Tom asks, "Which [one] do you want?" The film cuts to a single of George (34a), who stands up and joins the others in what is now a three-shot: George on the left, Tom on the right, and Gilda in the middle (34b). Gilda bows her head and admits, "Both." What could be more ordinary than a simple three-shot? But Lubitsch selects the right frame for the

TABLE 2.1 Two Consecutive Shots from a Longer Scene in *Design for Living* (1933)

Shot	Composition	Number of Characters in the Shot	Subsequent Camera Movement
33	a	Two: Gilda and Tom	Camera follows Gilda from Tom to George.
	b	Two: George and Gilda	Camera follows Gilda from George to Tom.
	c	Two: Gilda and Tom	
34	a	One: George	Camera follows George to Gilda and Tom.
	b	Three: George, Gilda, and Tom	Camera follows Gilda to George.
	c	Two: George and Gilda	Camera follows Gilda to Tom.
	d	Two: Gilda and Tom	Camera reframes as Gilda moves to the center.
	e	Three: George, Gilda, and Tom	

moment. The men are willing to contemplate the possibility of Gilda refusing to choose between them, and the three-shot emphasizes the unity of the group. Gilda then compares each man to a different style of hat; the composition moves from the three-shot (34b) into a two-shot with George (34c) and then to a two-shot with Tom (34d), eventually returning to the balanced three-shot as Gilda declares that both hats would be "so becoming" (34e). Camera operator William Mellor does great, velvety work here, in perfect coordination with Miriam Hopkins's every gesture as Gilda forms a pair with one man, a pair with another, and then a trio with both of them.[81] Again, we see a pictorial pattern—three, two, two, three—that echoes the subtext of the scene (figs. 2.7a–d). Although *Design for Living* was produced during the so-called pre-Code period, Lubitsch's film was still subject to Hollywood's self-regulation regime, then overseen by the Studio Relations Committee.[82] The committee required the filmmakers to establish that Gilda does not enjoy a sexual relationship with both men; rather, the three lovers agree to a platonic relationship until Gilda makes up her mind. Lubitsch uses the moving camera to hint at the censored content, highlighting Gilda's erotic agency by following her every move as she constitutes and reconstitutes intimate two-shots and three-shots with George and Tom.

2.7 In *Design for Living*, the composition shifts from three-shot to two-shot to two-shot to three-shot.

Throughout this scene, Lubitsch shows himself to be a master of the follow shot, timing the camera's movement to coincide with a character's. Elsewhere Lubitsch let his camera roam freely, as in his recurring window-to-window technique.[83] The camera, located outside a building, peers through a window to spy on a character. Then the camera cranes away from the window, eventually spotting another character in another room behind another window. Iterations of the window-to-window sequence appear in *Trouble in Paradise* (1932), *The Merry Widow* (1934), and *Angel* (1937)—not to mention in *Love Me Tonight* (1932), the romantic comedy that Mamoulian directed in a pastiche of Lubitsch's style. In *The Merry Widow*, roguish ladies' man Danilo (Maurice Chevalier) is preparing to meet the wealthy Madame Sonia (Jeanette Macdonald), and he begins to sing. The camera dollies away from Danilo and surveys the hotel from the outside. Craning past one window and then another (with the help of some dissolves and a miniature model), the camera locates Sonia's room and dollies laterally past four windows in a row: a curtained window, two windows opening up a view of Sonia with her attendants, and a final window revealing six gentlemen eavesdropping in the antechamber. At first, the sequence gestures toward romance, connecting our two lovers, as if by fate. But the closing image punctures the romantic mood by revealing that Danilo is just one ambitious suitor among many.

Surprisingly, both Mamoulian and Lubitsch endorsed the idea that camerawork should remain "invisible" to the spectator. In 1929, a trade journal article celebrating the innovative camerawork in *Applause* quoted Rouben Mamoulian saying, "I do not believe that the audience will be conscious of the camera movement."[84] This was a strange statement to make in the middle of a publicity campaign marketing the camerawork as a film's selling point. In 1933, Lubitsch stated flatly, "The moving camera is good only as long as it is unnoticeable."[85] One year later Lubitsch sent his camera flying from window to window to window to window in *The Merry Widow*. Perhaps Mamoulian's and Lubitsch's words were mere rhetoric, not reflective of their true intentions. Perhaps, given the nature of Hollywood publicity, they never spoke these words in the first place. But the contradiction may be more apparent than real. For many Hollywood filmmakers, saying that a technique was invisible was a way of saying that the technique was functional, with irony included as a perfectly permissible purpose.

If filmmakers who championed "invisibility" did not restrict themselves to follow shots, then the reverse is also true: the follow shot could be flamboyant. Lubitsch's Paramount colleague Josef von Sternberg would dolly laterally to keep Marlene Dietrich in the center of the frame, while surrounding the star with a riot of décor. As the camera dollied past, foreground objects would fly across the frame, turning a simple follow shot into a frenzy of movement. Examples can be found in the hospital scene in *Morocco* (1930, with palm trees and hanging lamps in the foreground); the street scene in *Shanghai Express* (1932, with dozens of extras in the foreground); the flophouse scene in *Blonde Venus* (1932, with silhouetted bars and beds in the foreground); and the postparty scene in *The Devil Is a Woman* (1935, with plants, wicker chairs, columns, and streamers in the foreground). The compositions are so complex that it is easy to lose sight of the film's star amid all this detail.

These examples suggest that Paramount allowed (and perhaps even encouraged) early-sound-era directors to test out what the moving camera could do. This brings us to the comments of Victor Milner, author of the essay "Let's Stop Abusing Camera Movement" (1935). A longtime cinematographer at Paramount, Milner had worked with both Mamoulian and Lubitsch. At the ASC's meeting in 1932, he argued articulately against excessive mobility. In his article three years later, he insisted that the only good dolly shot was one that was "virtually imperceptible" and "wholly subservient to the story."[86] Reading these comments, we might suppose that Milner was utterly opposed to the ironic camerawork that I have been describing here; a closer look at the essay, however, reveals that he was willing to endorse complex camerawork in the right contexts. While omitting reference to the overwrought Mamoulian, Milner showered praise on Lubitsch; it was Lubitsch, in fact, who was credited with devising shots that were "wholly subservient to the story." Milner's other favorite director, Cecil B. DeMille, was not averse to crane shots, either; publicity shots routinely showed him riding the boom.[87] When Milner offered specific examples of moving-camera shots that were effective, he described two scenes from *Cleopatra* (1934), the DeMille film that won Milner an Oscar. Neither example was a simple follow shot, "motivated" in the narrow sense of the term. Indeed, both were deeply ironic. In the first example, the camera starts out on a medium shot of Cleopatra (Claudette Colbert) and Marc Antony (Henry Wilcoxon), only to dolly back to reveal that the two lovers are seated in an enormous boat with dozens of bare-chested men rowing their oars and a muscular Egyptian banging a gong. The shot is both spectacular and ridiculous, poking fun at two powerful rulers striving for intimacy in the most grandiose surroundings. In the second example, a pair of lateral dollies passes from one group of gossipers to another. Starting out as a follow shot, the camera detaches itself from the final group of gossipers (fig. 2.8a) and prowls past some curtains to locate Brutus and his allies plotting Caesar's assassination (fig. 2.8b). Again, movement offers cynical commentary by showing us more than any one character could possibly see. The gossip seems even more inconsequential when contrasted with the world-changing action being plotted just a few feet away, and the implied comparison with gossipers undercuts Brutus's self-important posturing.

Milner saw no contradiction between the irony employed by Lubitsch and DeMille and the general mandate to make the camera "subservient" to the story.

2.8 In *Cleopatra*, the camera leaves a group of gossipers to locate Brutus plotting the murder of Caesar.

If this seems paradoxical, we should remember that storytelling involves more than just advancing the plot mechanically, step by step. As Douglas Pye writes, "Movies not only present a dramatic world but equally create and interpret it."[88] The telling expresses an attitude. Each of the ironic effects discussed here produces an emotional payoff: in *Applause*, a rising sense of dread that the despicable Hitch will continue to manipulate Kitty and begin to exploit her daughter; in *The Merry Widow*, the hope that Danilo and Sonia may fall in love, qualified by our awareness of the cynicism of the situation; in *Cleopatra*, the self-satisfied historical certainty that Brutus will murder Caesar, combined with the smirking realization that gossip-driven Roman society may be little different from our own.

If Milner was not mounting an argument against the ironic camera, then what exactly was he railing against? To put it simply, pointlessness. He despised shots that made no contribution to a film's larger goals. Nobody likes pointlessness, but cinematographers had a special objection against it: their crews had to lay the tracks, set the focus, and push the dollies. Without purpose, the cinematographer was merely following the whims of a mercurial director. With purpose, the cinematographer was the proud leader of a team, collaborating in the creation of a richly effective work of art. The motivated/unmotivated distinction does not capture the nuances of Milner's argument, which insisted on the primacy of storytelling while acknowledging that the camera might support the story in many ways, whether it follows figure movement or not.

Another easily misunderstood voice of skepticism was ASC member William Stull. In the early 1930s, Stull wrote short film reviews and technical articles for *American Cinematographer*, where he consistently chastened directors for their abuse of the moving camera, a flaw he found in Mamoulian's *The Song of Songs*, Lewis Milestone's *Rain* (1932), DeMille's *The Sign of the Cross* (1932), and Tay Garnett's *Prestige* (1932). At first glance, it appears that Stull was against camera movement *tout court*, but a closer look reveals surprising complications. Stull's specific critiques involved the timing of the shots in question: they occurred too early in each story. He pointed to Mamoulian's "misuse of the camera in the early sequences," to Milestone's decision to burden "the earlier sequences of the picture" with "an excess of perambulation," and to DeMille's overuse of the moving camera, "especially in the earlier sequences."[89] Stull's critique of *Prestige* was particularly sharp. "Throughout the first half of the picture, the camera is hardly stationary for a moment," Stull wrote. "This in itself is bad cinematics, but it is rendered far worse by the fact that it emasculates several legitimate moving shots occurring later, at the climax of the picture. Had the early part of the film been treated conventionally, these later moving shots would have served their dramatic purpose."[90] Stull's point was not that flamboyant camerawork was inherently bad; it was that flamboyant camerawork should be reserved for crucial moments. *Prestige* is, in fact, a bad film, telling a colonialist and patriarchal story about an elegant Frenchwoman, Therese (Ann Harding), who learns to support her husband, Andre (Melvyn Douglas), as he struggles to keep control of a penal colony in French Indochina. Early in the film, director Tay Garnett and cinematographer Lucien Andriot stage an audacious three-minute-long take. The camera follows Therese walking away from a window, arcs around a group of officers and their wives, follows a senior officer into the hallway, holds on a two-shot as the officer informs Andre that he has been transferred to Indochina, dollies backward to precede Andre as he joins Therese at the party, and then dollies in, out, and in again as Andre gives Therese the bad news. The camera reports indicate that this single shot took more than a day to stage, rehearse, and execute,[91] but the camerawork does little to amplify the scene's dramatic progression. Two crucial events happen in this scene: the senior officer tells Andre the news, and Andre, in turn, tells Therese. Neither moment stands out visually. The first happens in the middle of an extended two-shot composition, with no camera movement for emphasis. The second receives the benefit of an assertive dolly-in, but this gesture remains one movement among many. If anything, the visuals are at their most dynamic when the drama is least intense, as when the camera arcs around the irrelevant officers and their wives or when the camera travels through a doorway to follow a senior officer before we know why this man is important. Stull was correct: the filmmakers were showing off. By contrast, the camerawork is much more consequential in a later scene when Therese arrives at the outpost for the first time. As she enters the fort, she looks to the right, and the camera whip-pans to a guillotine, the pan masking an edit. Circling around, the camera shows a bunch of men powering a water wheel, a small group of solders on patrol, and a larger group of soldiers gambling. As if this 360-degree move were not flashy enough, a real elephant proceeds to lumber through the frame, passing between Therese and the still-moving camera! Like the first example, the shot is absurdly complicated, but the degree of dramatic justification is much higher here. Therese's surprise arrival is the crucial turning point in the story—a moment of peak dramatic intensity that merits a spike in visual intensity.[92] The camera participates in Therese's bewilderment, as if it were spinning around dizzily and discovering an unfamiliar space.

Rather than argue against all movement, Stull adopted a simple heuristic: keep the camera stationary in scenes of low intensity and move the camera liberally in scenes of high intensity. Consider his praise for the dolly and crane shots in *Grand Hotel* (1932), directed by Edmund Goulding and photographed by William Daniels. Stull called them "cameraman's trucking-shots" and insisted that "not one of them is used except for a legitimate dramatic purpose."[93] Upon reading this review, we might expect the camerawork to consist of modest follow shots, but the film belies this expectation at its most decisive moment. When a climactic murder is reported, the film cuts to a high-angle view of the telephone operators, and the camera cranes downward. Then the film cuts to another high-angle view of the hotel lobby, and the camera cranes upward. The editor of *Grand Hotel*, Blanche Sewell, championed the principle of efficiency: "Footage that doesn't mean a great deal to the story" should be eliminated, she wrote, no matter if it is "very fine photographically."[94] What legitimate dramatic purpose could these two cranes serve? Neither shot follows a character walking across the stage. Neither shot reveals a new piece of information. Neither shot represents a character's point of view. If my reading of Stull is correct, the purpose lies in the timing of the shots: they increase the visual intensity as the narrative reaches a culmination. The film's camera operator, A. Lindsley Lane, proposed just such a principle: the "restless mobile camera" should be reserved for scenes of high "dramatic intensity."[95] Indeed, the fact that the two cranes are not simple follow shots increases their effectiveness. A follow shot keeps a walking subject locked in the center of the frame. A dynamic crane shot is more intense because it puts the entire frame in motion.

This group of practical theorists approached the problem of camera movement as a problem of means and ends. They asked, "What purpose does the moving camera serve?" Their answers varied considerably, even when they counseled restraint. But there were other ways to frame the debate. Many practical theorists supplemented means–end thinking with analogical thinking, asking whether the camera should move like a person or not.

Problematizing the Point-of-View Shot

The camera–person analogy is so pervasive in Hollywood's discourse of camera movement that it is important to remember that the camera is in many ways quite unlike a person. The camera is a machine that takes pictures. Filmmakers organize these pictures into patterns. Rather than think of the camera–person analogy as a literal claim, we might think of it as a guide for the construction of patterns—temporary patterns that shift with the film's dynamic needs, with its range of narrative, nonnarrative, and extranarrative appeals. Analogical thinking complements means–end thinking. By anthropomorphizing the camera, the practical theorist tentatively commits to a set of creative choices, saying, "I am going to position the camera in personlike ways and avoid camerawork that seems overly machinelike." Behind each parallel lurks a purpose, from irony to immersion. As in the silent period, in later periods the idea that the camera might move like a person took different forms in the 1930s. Most literally, the camera's movements might represent a character's movements, as in a point-of-view shot. More loosely, the camera might mimic the movements of an observer—a hypothetical onlooker who watches the story unfold.

Let us start with the most literal form of the camera–person analogy: the point-of-view shot. Several films of the early 1930s experimented with the technique: *Dr. Jekyll*, of course, but also *Inspiration* (1931), *A Farewell to Arms* (1932), *Guilty as Hell* (1932), *The Sport Parade* (1932), *The Story of Temple Drake* (1933), and *The Kennel Murder Case* (1933). At first, we might suppose that the point-of-view shot serves an obvious function, encouraging identification by asking the spectator to see the world through a character's eyes. But the process of identification was never so simple. Some point-of-view shots encourage identification; some do not; and some ask us to confront the logic of identification itself. In Michael Curtiz's film *The Kennel Murder Case*, detective Philo Vance (William Powell) explains his theory of the murder, even though he has not yet identified the specific suspect. While Vance's explanation plays on the soundtrack, the camera represents the murderer's point of view, stalking through the house and looking for the victim. Cinematographer William Rees sells the trick by casting the man's shadow on a nearby wall. Notice that the primary purpose of the shot is to *block* identification. We do not know whose point of view is being represented, and the shot serves to conceal the murderer's identity.

Compare this example with the extended subjective sequence in Frank Borzage's film *A Farewell to Arms*, where the technique produces a rich feeling of empathy for the protagonist. Recently wounded, Frederic (Gary Cooper) is wheeled into a makeshift hospital in an Italian church. The camera adopts his point of view as he helplessly stares up at the ceiling. Heads pop into the frame occasionally to exchange dialogue with Frederic (fig. 2.9a), but for several seconds we simply watch the vaulted ceiling pass by, giving way to the inside of a dome (fig. 2.9b). Notice how the *lack* of information encourages identification with Frederic. He is unfamiliar with this new location, and so are we. He is desperate to know if he may meet his beloved Catherine (Helen Hayes) at this hospital, and so are we. Of course, we know that we are watching a film, so our

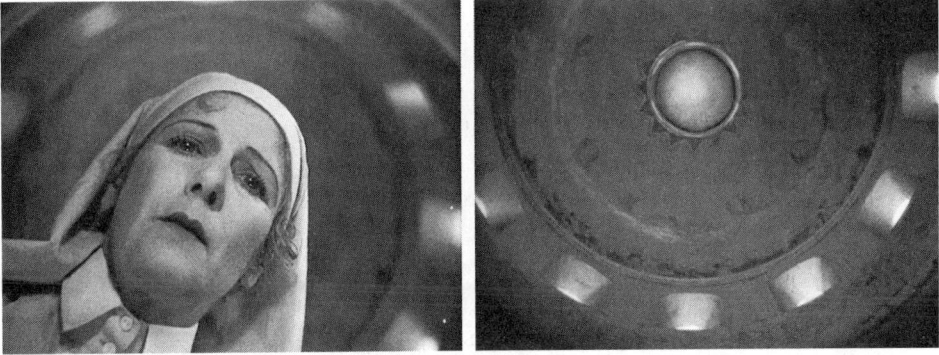

2.9 The camera represents the point of view of a patient in *A Farewell to Arms*.

identification can never be total. But the filmmakers produce an affinity between Frederic's exceedingly limited state of knowledge and the spectator's. Trapped inside Frederic's consciousness, the camera offers no reassuring information. Instead, it stares into the circle of the dome, beautiful but empty.

Turning the argument around, a filmmaker might foster identification by *refusing* to use a point-of-view shot, conspicuously detaching camera from character. Another scene from *A Farewell to Arms* shows a pregnant Catherine writing a letter describing her new apartment in Switzerland to her faraway lover, Frederic. As Catherine reads her letter aloud, the soundtrack plays her voice, describing the apartment in the most luxurious terms she can think of; meanwhile, the camera wanders about the apartment, isolating details that belie her words.[96] When Catherine says that the bed is "fit for an empress," the camera shows a bed that is small and Spartan; when she praises the "maroon velvet carpet, ankle deep," we see a rug that is wrinkled and tattered. As Catherine jokes about her dire circumstances, we are asked to share in her knowledge and emotions, without looking through her eyes.

Point-of-view plays a different role in the horror genre. As we saw in the previous chapter, silent-era horror films such as *The Cat and the Canary* featured "ambiguous" point-of-view shots, playing on the camera's machinelike qualities to produce a sense of the uncanny. This tradition continued into the 1930s, as in Roland West's *The Bat Whispers* (1930). Based on a play West had adapted once before (with minimal camera movement), this early sound film appeared in two versions: 35-millimeter and the still-rare widescreen format 65-millimeter. The story concerns a masked supervillain who terrorizes a house full of oddballs until he is exposed in a last-minute twist. Though the Bat turns out to be an ordinary human, for much of the film it appears that this disguised rogue has the gift of omnipresence, suddenly appearing where we least expect him.

The camera evokes this quasi-superpower by executing several dazzling dolly and crane shots, zipping through space and entering rooms as if by magic.[97] In one sequence, a shot of a round clock face dissolves to a graphically matched image of a round train wheel spinning on a track. Next, the camera dollies laterally past a cityscape, rendered in miniature, as if the train were dashing by. The film then dissolves to a shot representing the point of view of the train itself, speeding toward the sign of a sanitarium. So far the movements are rapid but not magical; they evoke the velocity of a rushing train. The next shot shifts the imagery toward a more supernatural register. As the camera careens toward a stately bank, the shadow of a bat envelops the facade, suggesting that the camera has been representing the moving point of view of the Bat himself all along. A final dissolve introduces an overhead view, looking over the Bat's shoulder as he peers through the window into the bank itself. Astonishingly, the camera cranes down as if passing through the glass of the skylight, quoting the moment in *The Last Laugh* when the camera dollies forward and dissolves through glass. Throughout this sequence, the film develops an extended comparison between the camera and the Bat: both have the power to fly through space, to climb walls, to peer through windows, to see without being seen. But the analogy does not humanize the camera so much as it renders it uncanny: like the Bat, the camera is eerily human and nonhuman at the same time.

Here, the film takes advantage of an obvious but important fact: the camera is not a person. When the camera dollies, it moves with a straight-ahead smoothness that seems alien to human motion. Most of the time, this smoothness is not a problem. Nobody requires the camera to move like a person because the camera simply is not a part of the fictional world. But what if a filmmaker does want to locate the camera's movements within the storyworld, as in a moving point-of-view shot? In *The Kennel Murder Case*, it could be argued that the camera does a poor job representing a character who is walking through a house; its movements are too strange, too inhuman. *The Bat Whispers* takes this strangeness and turns it into an asset, evoking the movement of some supernatural entity. Another early horror film, *Chandu the Magician* (1932), is even more explicit about the supernatural strangeness of the moving frame. In one scene, the protagonist (Edmund Lowe) and the Princess (Irene Ware) are looking into a crystal ball in order to spy on Roxor (Bela Lugosi), an evil genius who is building a death ray under the ruins of an old Egyptian temple. After a close-up of the crystal ball, a slow dissolve introduces a flurry of dynamic shots: toward the temple, through the doors, down a hallway, left, right, down another hallway, left again, down a third hallway, and down to reveal an overhead view of the maniac's laboratory. The camera's inhuman ability to fly through space evokes the crystal ball's mystical powers.

Although the vogue for subjective shots soon subsided, the camera–person analogy remained persistent. Many Hollywood filmmakers insisted that the camera should always move the way a person moves—not just in point-of-view shots, but in every shot. According to this line of thinking, the camera represented the eye of an unseen witness to the storyworld's action. But what sort of observer was this camera-eye to be? Like a criminal stalking through space? Like a powerless patient, wheeled around by others? Like a mysterious being endowed with quasi-superpowers? Or like an utterly ordinary person?

Camera as Observer

One famous advocate of the camera–person analogy was Howard Hawks. Early in his career, Hawks worked at Fox Films, where he indulged in camerawork tricky enough to compete with F. W. Murnau. Hawks later dismissed this frippery and switched to a simpler approach: "The best thing to do is to tell a story as though you're seeing it. Tell it from your eyes. Let the audience see exactly as they would if they were there. Just tell it normally. Most of the time, my camera stays on eye level now. Once in a while, I'll move the camera."[98] A person watching an event does not leap about in space; the way to stay focused on an event is to stand still and turn one's head. In *Bringing Up Baby* (1938), when Susan (Katharine Hepburn) tears David's coat, the camerawork seems effortless, panning to the right as David (Cary Grant) tries to walk away, then pausing when he hears the sound of the rip (fig. 2.10a–b). Hawks's personlike parallel is plausible: with the camera set at eye-level height, it is easy to imagine a human observer watching the scene, turning this way and then stopping, just to follow the action.

Edward Branigan has examined the language of anthropomorphism in film theory. On the one hand, he grants that there are deep reasons to describe the camera using analogies to human perception. On the other hand, he warns that

2.10 In *Bringing Up Baby*, the camera appears to watch the scene, as if it were an unobtrusive observer.

we should be wary about taking certain metaphors, such as the camera's "eye," too literally.[99] Aesthetic statements advance agendas. Hawks projects an image of himself as a no-nonsense craftsman, a regular guy who set aside his youthful attempts to compete with the artsy European Murnau. When cinematographers of the 1930s appealed to the camera–eye analogy, they did so to press their own demands, calling for directors to waste less time on labor-intensive dolly shots. Though plausible, such arguments were opportunistic. A filmmaker might argue that a dolly shot is strangely inhuman and accept the fade-out as the most natural thing in the world.

Indeed, filmmakers invoked the camera–person analogy to justify wildly divergent techniques, from the roving camera to the stationary one. In an interview for *International Photographer* in 1934, the German director Erik Charell, in Hollywood at the time to direct a musical for Fox Films, explained why he believed that camera movement was superior to editing as a storytelling technique: "Everybody knows that the motion picture camera is supposed to take the place of the spectator's eye and see what he sees. . . . If it is absolutely necessary to show a close-up of a player to emphasize a dramatic expression, then the camera should move in slowly, just as if the spectator should walk up to that player and look him in the eye. It should never leap about like a kangaroo."[100]

Charell argued that editing was too discontinuous to imitate human perception and recommended long-take camera movement as a more anthropomorphic alternative. Compare Charell's thoughts with those of cinematographer James Wong Howe, who made the case *against* excessive dollying the following year: "The camera should always be regarded as representing either the eye of the audience or, in rare instances, the eye of another player. Now the audience cannot move closer to the player in the theatre, and our scene has not showed any other player approaching him. Therefore if we must bring the audience's attention to the player's face, the natural thing to do is progress by direct cuts from the long-shot to the closer one."[101] Howe adopted the same premise as Charell—but drew the opposite conclusion! He agreed that the camera should behave like a person, but he insisted that editing, not camera movement, did a better job imitating the eye's shifts of attention. Such shifts in logic make one wonder to what extent the camera–person analogy was a serious proposal and to what extent it was a rhetorical flourish. At times, the analogy served as a handy trope to justify whatever technique the filmmaker was predisposed to defend.

Analogical thinking supported means–end thinking. By modeling the camera's movements on those a person might perform, the filmmaker aimed to accomplish a purpose. One oft-cited goal was immersion, allowing the viewer to experience a sense of entering the fictional world and seeing it from the position of the camera. Virgil Miller, who designed several cranes when he was head of Paramount's Camera Department, explained that good cinematography "leads an audience away from thoughts of mechanical and chemical processes to the story being told, making them forget they are watching projected light on a piece of cloth—they are thrilling to the action of real, live people doing what they themselves would like to be doing."[102] The engineer L. M. Dieterich applied the same logic of immersion to the specific problem of camera movement in 1932, proposing that "the closest possible imitation of natural sight" was the "underlying principle for the production of motion pictures."[103] Dieterich advised filmmakers to avoid certain techniques (blurry shots with jerky motion) and embrace others (cleanly photographed shots with smooth camera movement). For many theorists, restraint preserved the analogy between the camera and the eye of an observer. Illusionism compensated for the cinema's alienating machinelike qualities.

Echoing these arguments, subsequent film scholars have posited illusionism as one of the defining traits of the classical Hollywood cinema.[104] However, many of Hollywood's own practical theorists admitted that perfect illusionism was not possible—and perhaps not even desirable. The same Virgil Miller who claimed that audiences forgot the piece of illuminated cloth also longed for the silent-cinema days when cinematographers flashed "Corots, Rembrandts, Titians, Millets, and Raphaels" on the screen.[105] The same L. M. Dieterich who called for the "imitation of natural sight" admitted that the novelty of an unusual shot "is always a valuable screen asset" as long as the spectator enjoyed it.[106]

Filmmakers who endorsed the camera–person analogy often did so loosely, willing to abandon the idea in the face of shifting purposes. David Abel, the RKO cinematographer who photographed most of the Astaire–Rogers classics, once explained: "The lens represents a normal point of view, as of an audience witnessing a stage performance."[107] Fred Astaire, who choreographed the musical numbers, encouraged crews to employ long, flowing takes that preserved the integrity of the dances.[108] In practice, Abel's camera rarely adopted the perspective of a theater spectator quite so literally: such a camera would have recorded the dances from a low, unmoving angle. Instead, the camera remained at eye-level height, dollying left and right to keep Astaire and Rogers in the center of the frame, as if mimicking the shifting attention of an interested observer. The subservient camerawork looked easy, but one director explained, "Every time Fred and Ginger moved toward us, the camera had to go back, and every time they moved back, the camera went in. The head grip who was in charge of pushing this thing was a joy to watch."[109] In *Top Hat* (1935), Jerry (Astaire) sings "No Strings" to his friend Horace (Edward Everett Horton). The camerawork remains completely subordinate to Jerry's movements. When Jerry dances behind some chairs, the camera dollies in to follow; when Jerry spins to the right, a pan keeps him in frame.

But then the camera does something surprising. As Jerry pounds his feet on the floor, the camera dollies back and tilts downward to reveal a couch. After a dissolve, the camera continues its downward motion, as if passing through the floor (!), and cranes forward to disclose Dale (Ginger Rogers), sitting up in her bed and looking skeptically at the ceiling. Jerry's tap dancing has awoken Dale, and she is not pleased. Rather than insist that the camera is imitating a human observer who can dissolve through a floor, we might say more simply that the filmmakers have abandoned the fiction that the camera is a personlike observer of the scene. When it suits the needs of the film, the camera imitates a person. When it doesn't, the anthropomorphic fiction is dropped.

The musicals of Astaire and Rogers contrast with those of Busby Berkeley, the choreographer responsible for *42nd Street* (1933), *Gold Diggers of 1933*, and other Depression-era extravaganzas. In an Astaire–Rogers film, the musical numbers are integrated with the plot, as when Jerry's loud tap dancing sets up the meet-cute with Dale. In a Berkeley film, the musical numbers might be crammed together at the end of the film, after most of the story lines have been resolved. Released of its storytelling burdens, the camera is free to sustain other goals. Cinematographer Sol Polito, who photographed several numbers for Berkeley, reported that one of the major functions of his camerawork was to allow the spectator "to admire the perfection of form of the dancers." The camera does not look so much as it ogles. Polito explained his philosophy by offering a variant of the camera-as-person analogy. "The function of the camera," he stated, "can be compared to a pair of opera-glasses in the hands of a member of a theatre-audience."[110] Like Abel, Polito compared the camera to a theater spectator; unlike Abel, Polito equipped his hypothetical viewer with opera glasses, thereby suggesting that the cinema amplified the spectator's powers of vision.

Even this expanded analogy does not come close to accounting for the delirious camera positions that Berkeley actually employed. Totally rejecting the theatrical aesthetic of the earliest sound films, Berkeley brazenly places his camera directly above his kaleidoscopic chorus girls—or under them when they are swimming in a pool. In one outrageous shot in *42nd Street*, the camera dollies through the legs of a dozen chorus girls, eventually locating Dick Powell and Toby Wing, who smile directly at the audience (fig. 2.11a–b). Making a mockery of Polito's opera-glasses analogy, Berkeley's dance celebrates the cinema's capacity to offer views that no theater spectator could ever expect to see. When Howard Hawks said, "Tell it from your eyes," he meant that the filmmaker should restrain the movement of the camera, keeping it at eye level, pointing it only where a human observer might look. If Berkeley's camera is an eye—a leering, objectifying eye—then it is a disembodied eye, freed from earthly restrictions.

But the camera–person analogy remained tenacious. In 1935, M-G-M camera operator A. Lindsley Lane contributed three articles to *American Cinematographer*; his middle article set out a working theory of the camera as an ideal observer. The title of the article was significant: "The Camera's Omniscient Eye."

2.11 The camera dollies through the legs of chorus girls in *42nd Street*.

Although the concept of "omniscience" solved some theoretical problems, it also introduced new ones. Lane defined omniscience as a sense of "all-seeingness" whereby the film "stimulates, through correct choice of subject-matter and set-up, the sense within the percipient of 'being at the most vital part of the experience—at the most advantageous point of perception' throughout the picture."[111] With his insistence that the camera could see, Lane appealed to the anthropomorphic idea that the camera is an eye, modeled on the figure of an observer. But the camera is not just any ordinary observer. A person watching a chain of events might miss crucial details; witnesses do not always know where to look. Lane complemented the camera–eye analogy with an appeal to the medium-specific ideal of spatial freedom: this particular eye can go anywhere, as if the spectator has the power to move instantly to the optimum viewing position. "For each instant of the picture's duration," he wrote, "there is but one best point of perception for the camera lens."[112] One point at a time—the job of the filmmakers was to figure out where that "best" point was and to put the camera there every possible moment. Such an aesthetic need not rely on extravagant crane shots in the manner of a Busby Berkeley film. Lane explicitly stated that "cinematographic effects" had been "over-stressed."[113] His "ideal observer" argument instead provided a justification for the unobtrusive classical scene construction that dominated Hollywood filmmaking in the 1930s and beyond. A few years after Lane wrote this article, he operated the camera on *Marie Antoinette* (1938), working as usual for cinematographer William Daniels. In one scene, a worried Louis (Robert Morley) waits to see the extinguishing of a candle—the official symbol that his father has died and that Louis himself is now king of France. The title character (Norma Shearer) enters, hoping to tell her husband that she would like to return to Austria. Before she gets a chance, the candle is extinguished, and she realizes that her fate will be tied to

Louis's forever. The director, W. S. Van Dyke, was famously efficient; by my count, the scene contains eighteen shots and nine setups. After panning to follow Louis and Marie Antoinette in the master, the camera remains stationary (apart from a few barely perceptible reframes) during the shot-reverse-shot sequence that occupies the middle portion of the scene. One might wonder why a camera operator such as Lindsley Lane would advocate a style that left him with so little to do. In fact, Lane and Daniels believed that the camera crew should control the audience's attention via focus pulling, not dollying. An article celebrating their work stated, "With Lane, Daniels worked out a technique of always having his camera focused on the point of interest." As Daniels himself explained, "If Miss Shearer walks to a window and looks out, the focus switches to the object she is watching. This changing of focus is accomplished in a split second. Its object is to keep the attention of the audience centered on the point of action."[114] Lane and Daniels were evidently taking advantage of John Arnold's M-G-M focusing device. For the crucial moment when the candle is extinguished, a wider angle shows Louis on the left and Marie Antoinette on the right, both sharp. The candle is several yards away in the center of the frame. When Marie Antoinette turns her head, the focus shifts to the candle. The timing is impeccable: assistant William Riley pulls in perfect synch with Shearer's performance. No dollying required.

Here we see many of the traits of the classical Hollywood style at its most canonical: the camerawork appears to be omniscient, illusionistic, invisible, personlike, and subordinate to storytelling. Lane explicitly endorsed every one of these ideas in "The Camera's Omniscient Eye." Film scholars subsequently identified the "best angle" ideal as a defining feature of Hollywood storytelling. According to Robert B. Ray, Hollywood films offered their viewers a particular contract: "At any given moment in a movie, the audience was to be given the optimum vantage point on what was occurring onscreen. Anything important would not only be shown, but shown from the best angle."[115] Marilyn Fabe explains why this variant of classicism was so appealing: "As spectators identified with an omniscient point of view, gazing at people to whom we are invisible and about whom we have superior knowledge, we experience the feeling of having a power, perspective and knowledge that we lack in life."[116] The scene from *Marie Antoinette* relies heavily on this sense of superior knowledge. Not only do we peek into the private chambers of the king and queen; we know their fates better than they do.

But Lane's theory and practice were more complicated than this one article could suggest. "The Camera's Omniscient Eye" was just one article in a three-part series. In other passages in the series, he abandoned the analogy of the ideal observer in favor of blunt rhetorical thinking: the control of the frame is a tool for "elimination and suggestion," for "selection, synthesis, and emphasis."[117] Far from insisting that the camera operator keep the subject in the center of the frame at all times, he celebrated the operator's power to turn the picture edge into a "live element," activating the spectator's imagination by keeping crucial details offscreen, not on.[118] Far from demanding that figure movement should motivate camera movement, he argued that the follow shot was overused and that the visual "crescendo" was underused.[119] (Recall the crane as crescendo in *Grand Hotel*, also photographed by Daniels and operated by Lane.) Even the sample scene from *Marie Antoinette* mixes registers. During the middle of the scene, the camerawork is restrained, subtly directing our attention to the protagonist's shifting emotions. But the filmmakers cap the scene with a moment of ironic commentary à la Mamoulian. The final shot positions the new queen on the right side of the frame, with the king on the left. Then the camera dollies in to reframe the queen in a symbolic composition, her face locked between two candles. The symbolism is trite but effective: as Marie Antoinette realizes that her new responsibilities will prevent her from returning to Austria, the composition evokes the image of a prison. The filmmakers have abandoned illusionism in favor of heavy-handed irony.

We might think of this as a moment of uncharacteristically forceful narration, allowing the filmmaker to peek out from behind the observer's mask. But the filmmaker's control of the frame is a given, in evidence all along. It is the personlike observer who comes and goes. Indeed, an insistence on the figure of the "all-seeing eye" may blind us to a deeper logic of Hollywood framing, grounded in the play of revelation and concealment.

The Controlled Frame

The term *omniscience* is sometimes associated with David Bordwell's work on classical Hollywood narration, but he has offered a clear warning that the word may be misleading: "In any particular narrative we don't really know everything in godlike fashion. The narration is presented as omniscient in principle: it could give us access to everything, but it doesn't."[120] Douglas Pye is even more skeptical of the term. Referring to films that switch freely from character to character, Pye writes, "It is tempting to refer to such modes of narration as 'omniscient,' but the term is misleading in its implication that there are no limits set to our access."[121] My own view is that the metaphor of omniscience distracts us from the cinema's ever-unfolding play of disclosures, especially when we seek to understand why the camera moves. The camera may fly freely or inch ahead humbly, but it always frames a limited view of the storyworld.

In a well-told story, the decision to withhold information may be just as advantageous as the decision to reveal it. Consider a crucial scene in John Ford's film *Wee Willie Winkie* (1937). Cinematographer Arthur Miller favored the Raby dolly, employing a small boom arm in the manner of a Velocilator.[122] This device allowed his crew to make minute adjustments to the frame, controlling each composition with pinpoint precision. Late in the film, Sergeant MacDuff (Victor McLaglan) lies dying in a hospital bed, and Priscilla (Shirley Temple) sings "Auld Lang Syne" to comfort him. At first, the camera rests slightly below both characters' eye level; MacDuff's body dominates the composition (fig. 2.12a). As Priscilla finishes her song, the camera dollies in and booms up a few inches. Now the only visible part of MacDuff's body is his hand in the corner. MacDuff lets go of the flowers, and we understand that he has died (fig. 2.12b). The camera pans to follow Priscilla as she leaves the room in the mistaken belief that MacDuff has fallen asleep. A soldier takes Priscilla's hand and walks with her offscreen. Instead of following her, the camera remains stationary, racking focus to the bagpipe player mourning in the background. Priscilla runs back onscreen to tell the bagpipe player not to cry; the shadow of the other soldier decorates the back wall (fig. 2.12c). Priscilla exits the shot for good, and the tearful musician stands to play a funereal tune. Finally, the camera pans and dollies back, giving us another look at MacDuff's hands in the foreground while offering an occluded view of the bagpipe player behind the screen (fig. 2.12d). To say

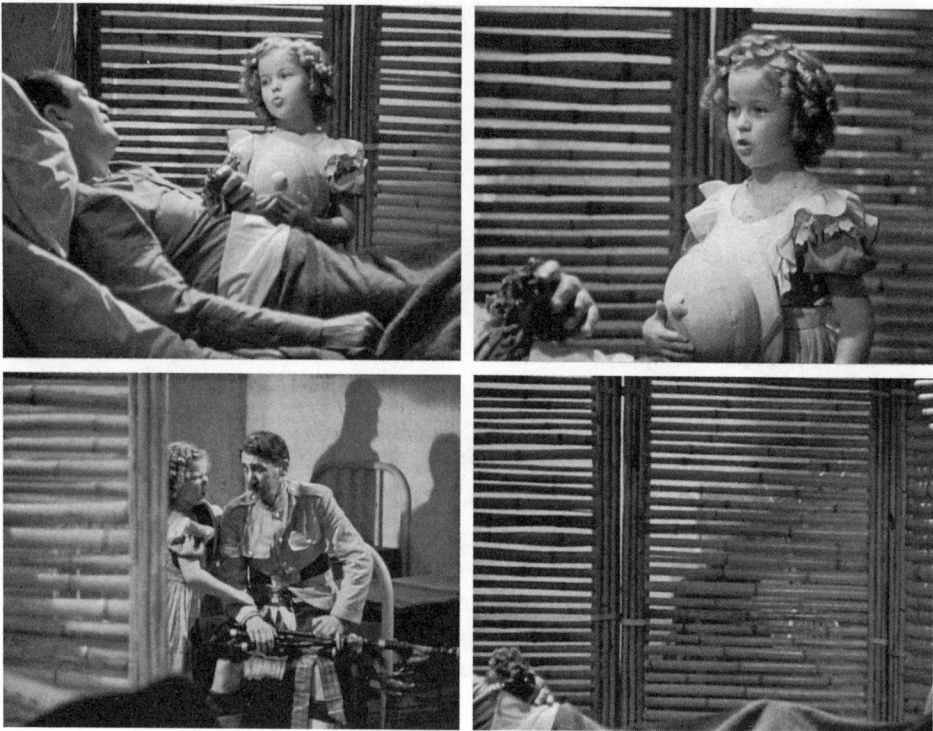

2.12 In *Wee Willie Winkie*, Priscilla sings to MacDuff as he dies.

that every move has a purpose is to underestimate the elegance of the design, for every move has at least two purposes. The dolly–boom movement toward Priscilla emphasizes Shirley Temple's adorableness while isolating MacDuff's hand discreetly as he passes away. The pan to the right follows Priscilla's movement while revealing the bagpipe player in tears. The pan to the left follows the bagpipe player's exit while revealing MacDuff's hand once again. The end result is an eloquent commentary on vision and knowledge: Priscilla has seen MacDuff's death, but she does not know what it means. Our own vision remains limited, just a succession of partial views: a hand releasing some flowers, the shadow of a soldier on the back wall, a bagpipe player standing behind a screen. But, for all these limitations, we are asked to comprehend the significance of these images with an adult wisdom that Priscilla at this moment does not possess.

The eminent narratologist Meir Sternberg once wrote that understanding a narrative "entails an interplay between the one sequence's flow of development and the other's flow of disclosures—between the two great sources of narrative change, in the world itself and in our knowledge about it, respectively."[123] In *Wee Willie Winkie*, the flow of developments takes place in the storyworld: MacDuff passes from life to death. The flow of disclosures takes place onscreen: a sequence of framed pictures shows MacDuff's hand, conceals it, and then reveals it once more.[124]

Suppose Ford and his colleagues had handled this scene slightly differently, keeping the camera stationary with MacDuff's face in the foreground from beginning to end. From the standpoint of the storyworld, the results would be largely the same: life, then death. From the standpoint of the pictorial sequencing, the results would be very different indeed, losing the scene's gentle emphasis on Priscilla's failure to realize what is happening. Whether the camera moves or not, all cinematic storytelling requires the filmmaker to make choices about revelation and concealment. The moving camera makes these choices visible: acts of exclusion unfolding in time.

In *Wee Willie Winkie*, the camera's exclusions echo the protagonist's state of ignorance. Alternatively, the camera might adopt a more informative perspective, consistently providing the necessary clues to allow the spectator to anticipate what is going to happen next. Such a camera comes close to the "all-seeing" ideal that is associated with Hollywood storytelling more generally, but even here the metaphor of omniscience remains imperfect. Consider another death scene, this one in the film *Angels with Dirty Faces* (1938). Three gangsters—Mac (George Bancroft), James (Humphrey Bogart), and Rocky (James Cagney)—listen to a radio address by Jerry (Pat O'Brien), a priest who promises to go after the gangs. The boss, Mac, expresses his desire to kill Jerry, but Rocky defends the priest, an old friend. What follows is a series of escalating deceptions: James, a corrupt lawyer, pretends to convince Mac to go easy, who pretends to agree. Rocky pretends that he is satisfied, and he pretends to leave. After eavesdropping on the exchange between Mac and James, Rocky steps out and shoots them to protect Father Jerry and himself. Working with cinematographer Sol Polito, director Michael Curtiz photographed the scene from several angles, favoring cutting rather than camera movement. For much of the scene, Curtiz's technique is highly informative: we see all the characters, and we see right through their attempts at pretense. Whether mobile or stationary, the camera always seems to be in the right place at the right time. When James dishonestly tells Mac that they should not kill the priest, a simple over-the-shoulder close-up shows James winking at Mac, a detail that Rocky is not supposed to see. When the street-smart Rocky catches onto James's lies anyway, a close-up single lets us see Rocky's knowing smile, which the other two gangsters are too busy to notice.

Then the strategy shifts—away from the all-seeing eye. When Rocky steps out of the back room to confront his boss, the film cuts to a medium long shot of Mac, hastily raising his own gun to protect himself (fig. 2.13a). Surprisingly, the camera whip-pans to the right, dollying in toward a nearby mirror, which reflects the image of Rocky firing away (fig. 2.13b). Is this really the "best" view of the action—the view that an allegedly omniscient observer might provide? If the goal is maximum clarity, then the answer is "no." Instead, the filmmakers have sacrificed clarity in exchange for a rich cluster of effects. Hollywood's Production Code regulated depictions of violence, and the dolly toward the mirror allows the film to represent the murder indirectly, without showing the bullets striking Mac's body. The mirror serves as a handy symbol of Rocky's duality: Cagney's character is both good and bad, and his decision to commit murder is both right (he is protecting a priest) and wrong (it is still murder). Meanwhile, the rapid speed of the whip-pan adds visual intensity to the scene,

2.13 In *Angels with Dirty Faces*, the camera pans and dollies toward a reflection to show a murder obliquely.

amplifying the emotional intensity of the murder. While obeying the letter of the Production Code, the filmmakers twist its spirit, using dynamic camerawork to characterize the killing as exciting, making the murderous Rocky more heroic.[125]

Here, we can explain the whip-pan not by appealing to a global principle of omniscience but by considering the effects that the filmmakers are trying to achieve. In the first half of the scene, the filmmakers are striving for a particular effect—allowing the spectators to understand everyone's hidden motivations. Cutting from one ideally placed angle to another is a means to an end, helping us spot the nuances of every facial expression, whether the characters notice them or not. Then the filmmakers adopt a new trio of goals: depicting a murder within the boundaries of the Code, offering symbolic commentary on Rocky's dual personality, and marking a dramatic turning point with a spike in visual intensity. The impression of knowing everything we need to know is not an end in itself but a temporary effect that can be built up and torn down, depending on the ever-shifting dramatic needs of the film at hand.

The Production Code gave filmmakers a good reason to favor oblique storytelling strategies, both in scenes of violence and in scenes of sexuality. But the point applies more broadly: storytelling inevitably involves the play of information. Bound by a frame, the cinema discloses some details but not others. I think this statement is true of narrative filmmaking in general, but it is a point that the filmmakers of the 1930s were especially eager to explore, as the newly available moving camera heightened their awareness of the craft of framing. To be sure, a filmmaker can reveal or conceal a detail in many ways: by cutting to a close-up, by having the actor walk offscreen, by ending a scene sooner than we expect. The moving camera was just one option among many, and it had no special powers in the art of disclosure. What it did have was the ability to make the play of revelation and concealment unusually salient. When the frame moves from left to right, a part of the storyworld glides offscreen, and another part of the world slides onscreen. When the frame moves forward, a part of the storyworld becomes more visible, and another part of the world disappears. To watch a dolly shot is to see the cinema's selectivity in action.

One filmmaker who thought deeply about this problem was Fritz Lang, who remarked, "My way of shooting is through disciplined selection."[126] Commenting on camera movement specifically, he explained that a director should give the dolly grip a specific reason for every movement: "If he doesn't understand why, he may go too far or he may not go far enough."[127] A celebrated scene in Lang's film *You Only Live Once* (1937) comments on its own flow of disclosures with a remarkable degree of reflexivity, using camera movement to expose the filmmaker's power to lead—and mislead—the audience. As we await the outcome of a trial, the film dissolves to a headline, announcing that the protagonist Taylor (Henry Fonda) has been freed (fig. 2.14a). The camera pans to the left, disclosing an alternate headline, announcing that the jury is deadlocked (fig. 2.14b); then the camera dollies back to reveal that a newspaper editor is considering three possible headlines (fig. 2.14c). Finally, the camera dollies in toward the third headline, pronouncing Taylor guilty (fig. 2.14d). The effect is satirical, mocking the sensationalizing conventions of journalism. (In the photographs accompanying the headlines, Taylor looks handsome in the first, neutral in the second, and menacing in the third.) At the same time, the shot mocks the sensationalism of cinematic storytelling itself, showing that our every assumption is subject to the film's control. The filmmaker's seeming omnipotence does not provide the spectator with a feeling of omniscience. If anything, our awareness of the shifting frame heightens our awareness of our own ignorance.[128]

The idea that the camera is always a tool of selection does not imply that the camera never imitates a person. Rather, the camera imitates a person provisionally, to produce specific effects. Lang himself claimed to be interested in producing a strong identification between spectators and characters. He said, "The audience has been projected into the position of the actors, seeing with their eyes, thinking with their brains, expressing their emotional reactions . . . and the camera is the instrument of this major liberation."[129] In practice, Lang

2.14 *You Only Live Once* manipulates information to mock the conventions of journalism.

devised perverse variations on the point-of-view shot, encouraging acts of identification and criticizing identification at the same time. *Fury* (1936) features
one of the most disturbing point-of-view shots ever put on film. A lynch mob
is approaching a jail, and we see a full shot of innocent victim Joe Wilson (Spencer Tracy) looking through the bars of his cell. The next shot shows the mob's
point of view: the camera cranes slowly forward, inching closer and closer
toward the jail. Lang explained his purpose clearly: "I roll the camera forward
as a man would walk and thus approach the jail. The audience becomes the
mob."[130] Notice the shift from the individual ("a man") to the group ("the mob").
The shot does not represent any single person's point of view; rather, it represents the inexorable point of view of the lynch mob itself. The effect is a horrific sense of the uncanny. The crowd has many people, each with a unique point
of view, and yet the single eye of the camera has fused those perspectives
together. Showing Wilson's glance first prepares us to identify with his point
of view—the perspective of the persecuted victim. But then we are forced to
look through the collective eye of the horde. In so doing, Lang challenges spectators to confront their own willingness to identify with the lynch mob—and
to confront the cinema's frightening power to fuse together a crowd's emotions.

The example returns to the camera–person analogy by situating it within
the larger perspective of means–end thinking. Rather than look for the all-
seeing eye everywhere, we may ask how each film develops temporary analogies
to produce temporary effects, always shifting as the narrative unfolds. Looking to filmmakers' theoretical statements, we find support for this more mal-
leable proposal in an unlikely place—the writings of Lindsley Lane. Recall
that "The Camera's Omniscient Eye" was one entry in a three-part series. In
the other two entries, Lane sketched an alternative to his own "ideal observer"
theory. Though barely fleshed out, this alternative may represent Lane's most
useful contribution to Hollywood's working theories of the moving camera. I
call this alternative the "theory of the participatory camera." Rejecting the figure of the disembodied eye, the participatory camera adopts the emotional,
engaged observer as its model.

The Participatory Camera

In his article "Rhythmic Flow—Mental and Visual," Lane described a scene
from Sidney Franklin's film *The Barretts of Wimpole Street* (1934). The poet Elizabeth Barrett (Norma Shearer), an invalid, is resting on a couch with her dog,
while her siblings are doing their best to cheer her up. Her sister Henrietta
(Maureen O'Sullivan) begins to dance for joy. After a cut to Elizabeth, the film
returns to a closer view of dancing Henrietta; the camera pans left with her
as she spins past a lamp (fig. 2.15a). So far the shot is a routine follow shot,

panning with a character in motion. Then Henrietta circles back to the right, but the camera—unexpectedly—continues panning to the left (fig. 2.15b–c). For a moment, we see nothing but the background blurring by, until the camera comes to rest on a tight medium close-up of the Barrett girls' domineering father (Charles Laughton), who is appalled to see Elizabeth, Henrietta, and the others enjoying themselves (fig. 2.15d). The example demonstrates the principles of emphasis and elimination that Lane mentioned elsewhere (stressing the looming presence of the father while conspicuously excluding everyone else), but Lane's description goes further, anthropomorphizing the camera by describing it not as an ideal observer but as an engaged participant. After panning with Henrietta across the room, the camera "continues on irresponsibly and gayly [*sic*] toward the door and bumps abruptly into the scowling and elder Barrett just entering the room."[131] Lane's language endows the camera with human traits—not just the faculty of perception but also emotions, for the machine is behaving "irresponsibly and gayly." Continuing in this anthropomorphizing vein, the passage explains, "The camera has taken unto itself the children's stolen joy, participating with them in it through Henrietta's dancing, and has been caught unawares and checked up with frightening abruptness by

2.15 In *The Barretts of Wimpole Street*, the camera pans away from Henrietta and discovers the threatening form of Mr. Barrett.

the ever-threatening menace."[132] Evoking joy and surprise, this camera is not an omniscient eye at all: it loses sight of Henrietta dancing, and it is a split second late in discovering Mr. Barrett, who is already angry and already a little shockingly close to the camera when he appears. The movement produces an effect of empathy: the pan away from Henrietta echoes her delight (or perhaps Elizabeth's vicarious enjoyment of Henrietta's bodily freedom), just as the abrupt stop mimics the surprise that Elizabeth, Henrietta, and the others feel when they recognize Mr. Barrett's intrusion. Revealing Mr. Barrett's presence several seconds before any of the characters notice him, the participatory camera shares in the characters' emotions not by representing their perceptions, but by imitating their affective gestures.[133]

Filmmakers appealed to analogies to make sense of the tools they used. Thinking of the camera as a participant provided the crew with a simple heuristic guiding the design of dolly shots: move the camera to mimic a character's emotionally charged actions. As with other analogies, it was theoretically possible to deploy the participatory camera from beginning to end, but a more likely strategy was to adopt the metaphor as a temporary pattern, either adopted or abandoned depending on the desired effect.

Two examples discussed in chapter 1—*The Last Laugh*'s drunken-porter shot and *Variety*'s trapeze shot—provided powerful models. In each, a character appears in stasis as the world spins around in the background. In the former, the spinning is psychological (the porter is not really turning); in the latter, the spinning is real (the trapeze is actually swinging up and down). Both shots use the spinning to express the character's emotional state even though the camera is not looking through the character's eyes. Murnau's *City Girl* featured another memorable prototype. The young farmer Lem (Charles Farrell) has brought the title character Kate (Mary Duncan) home to meet his family. Her city life was oppressive; in the end, country life will prove just as cruel.[134] But the moment when Lem shows Kate the fields for the first time is a moment of joy; it is as if Kate has never seen such wide-open spaces. Playfully she runs through the fields; Lem catches up to her and kisses her; after an imperceptible jump cut, she runs away again, still laughing; they kiss a second time and fall backward into the wheat. Rapidly tracking alongside Kate, the camera appears to share her delight. Murnau's camera is unchained, indeed; never before has the machine seemed so free.

A skeptic might say that this example is just a follow shot, tracking along with characters in motion. But look more closely. Follow shots take many forms—fast or slow, deep or flat, simple or complex—and their meanings are ever shifting. Compare the exuberance of *City Girl*'s follow shot to the control of a follow shot from *Les misérables* (1935). Master cinematographer Gregg Toland was nothing if not precise; that same year he had invented an attachment to the Velocilator dolly to give the camera operator the power to make minute adjustments to the frame.[135] Inspector Javert is just beginning to figure out that the mayor might be his old nemesis Jean Valjean. Deep in thought, Javert walks down a hallway, passing through an area of shadow into an illuminated space; the shift from darkness to brightness symbolizes his emerging understanding. Actor Charles Laughton, operator Bert Shipham, and the anonymous dolly grip work together in perfect synch, ensuring that the actor remains in a tight shoulders-up composition from beginning to end.[136] The concluding composition is eerily symmetrical, with Javert in the center and two policemen balancing each other in the soft-focus background. If the camera were one centimeter to the right or left, the symmetry would be destroyed. The camerawork's precision mirrors Javert's exactitude.

The participatory camera observes a character from the outside while expressing something about the character's internal states. The French film historian and theorist Jean Mitry argued that Hollywood films of the late 1930s came to rely more and more on this two-pronged strategy, which he called the "semi-subjective image." The concept was broad enough to include moving shots and certain kinds of stationary shots. For Mitry, the crystallizing film was William Wyler's *Jezebel* (1938), which he praised as "a landmark in the history of cinema ignored by most contemporary critics." In one scene, Julie (Bette Davis) is preparing to meet her beloved Pres (Henry Fonda), who has been away for a year. Mitry describes the camerawork: "We see her arranging flowers and changing round the ornaments, flitting about, altering everything with feverish activity. The camera, framing her in midshot, follows her everywhere. She stops, moves, turns, spins around in a sequence of short tracking shots punctuated with various pans." The film does not quite match Mitry's description, but the lesson he draws is instructive. The camera observes Julie from the outside and yet moves in ways that express her state of mind. Mitry continues, "The agitation of the camera movements, prompted by the nervousness of her movements, conveys her agitation to the audience, which thereby experiences the same feelings of impatience and irritation and shares in her emotion."[137] The argument here is that a point-of-view shot would have been *less* effective emotionally because it would have denied us the opportunity to scrutinize the character's face. The outside view is essential, allowing us to understand the situation. Only when we understand the situation can we imagine how we might feel and project those feelings onto the character.

Like Lane's participatory camera, Mitry's semisubjective image mimics the movements of a fully embodied character, not the movements of a disembodied, all-seeing eye. As feminist scholars have pointed out, Hollywood's theory of the ideal observer constructs a viewing position that is implicitly male, offering spectators the opportunity to experience a sense of power by identifying with a commanding gaze.[138] But the participatory camera may be gendered differently. The camera may mimic a dancing teenager (*The Barretts of Wimpole*

Street), a policeman in thought (*Les misérables*), or a couple in love (*City Girl*). Some of these characters are powerful, and some are weak, but they are never all-seeing because they are embodied characters living in a world of limitations. To be sure, this does not mean that the participatory camera is necessarily a more progressive concept than the admittedly problematic ideal observer. When Lane compares the camerawork in *The Barretts of Wimpole Street* to Henrietta's behavior, he repeatedly uses terms that are culturally coded as feminine: the camera appears irresponsible and frightened. Similarly, when Mitry argues that the camera is imitating Susie in *Jezebel*, he describes her behavior as flitting about with impatience and irritation. Both define the camera's emotional expressivity by relying on cultural tropes of femininity as impetuous and unpredictable. The participatory camera is just as much an ideological construct as the all-seeing one.

Nevertheless, the participatory camera offers a refreshing alternative to the ideal observer because it is more varied and flexible. According to the theory of the all-seeing camera, there is but one correct place for the camera to occupy at every conceivable moment. The participatory camera is different, imitating this character and then that one, evoking one emotion and then another. Hollywood characters are constrained by ideologies of gender and race and class, but those constraints admit some degree of play—a degree of play that the moving camera can explore.

Consider the newspaper genre, with its hard-drinking hacks and its fast-talking dames. At its best, the genre offers multiple masculinities and multiple femininities, cuing different kinds of camera movement. Here are two newsmen and three newswomen, all distinct. In Lewis Milestone's film *The Front Page* (1931), manipulative editor Walter Burns (Adolphe Menjou) strides through the newsroom while a colleague tries to talk to him (fig. 2.16a–b). Unlike the beleaguered colleague, the confident camera has no trouble keeping up with the speedy, self-centered Burns. The effect of swiftness is not as easy to achieve as it looks. A tightly coordinated follow shot might actually create the impression of stasis by keeping the character fixed within the center of the frame. Milestone solves this problem by placing a row of desks in the foreground. Close to the camera, the desks fly across the frame, enhancing the impression of breakneck velocity. Like Burns, the camera seems quick, determined, and indifferent to anything that is not its subject.

The Murder Man (1935) shows another recurring masculine type in the newspaper film: the weary reporter. Exhausted crime journalist Steve (Spencer Tracy) enters the newsroom. The camera, in a position behind Steve, dollies forward as he saunters down the aisle, panning left as a woman gives him a message, panning right as a man repeats the same message, panning left as another woman hands him a piece of paper, and panning right as Steve crumples up the paper and tosses it playfully at his friend Mary. Steve is the weariest of weary

2.16 The dolly moves quickly to keep up with Walter Burns in *The Front Page*.

reporters—we eventually learn that he committed the murder he is supposed to be investigating. He ignores the first few people he talks to, and the camera echoes his unconcern, panning indolently toward the other reporters and then panning away before they can register, settling on a stable composition only when Steve stops to flirt with Mary. Again, the camera mimics a male gaze, but this gaze seems defeated, wandering back and forth, lacking in agency.

Newswomen figure differently. In *Dance, Fools, Dance* (1931), one sequence shows a series of reporters writing about the murder of a colleague. The camera dollies down a row of four desks. The first reporter is writing a story about the killing; the second is writing about the resulting dragnet. The third desk is empty; it belongs to the victim. The fourth desk belongs to Bonnie (Joan Crawford), typing the obituary. Showing more of the space than any one character can see, the camera makes a double-edged ironic comment. On the one hand, Bonnie is a fully integrated member of the newsroom, hard at work like everyone else. On the other hand, the sequence suggests that she retains her difference. The two male reporters are writing hard-boiled stuff ("cold-blooded killing," "dragnet"), but Bonnie's obituary is suffused with emotion ("popular," "beloved"). After introducing this contrast, the scene shifts toward the participatory mode. A medium shot shows Bonnie typing away; she looks to her right, and the camera pans to reveal the unused typewriter at the desk beside her; the pan quickly returns to Bonnie, who bites her lip and gets back to work. By panning one way and back again, the camera echoes Bonnie's momentary hesitation, characterizing her gaze in tragic terms: desiring to see, but with no object.

In contrast to the uncertain Bonnie, the protagonist of *Front Page Woman* (1935) is driven to succeed. Disappointingly, the film's introduction of this dynamic character is quite passive. She is the only woman in a tightly packed newsroom, and the staging works to emphasize just how out of place she is. In one shot, Ellen (Bette Davis) is barely visible in the background, blocked by a man lighting a cigarette. The camera pans to follow another man carrying a typewriter and then rests on two men discussing their discomfort with an upcoming execution. Another reporter enters, and the camera dollies right to follow him as he hangs up his coat and speaks with some men playing cards. When the man sits down, we get our first clear view of Ellen, sitting apart from the men while she eats a sandwich. The film then cuts in to a close-up to give us a better view of the anxiety she is trying to conceal. The restless camera has taken its cues from the bustling of the men, and now the film isolates the lone woman by photographing her in a different style: a glamorously lit, stationary medium close-up. Following the logic of so many Hollywood films, as analyzed by Laura Mulvey, the men move through a three-dimensional space, whereas the woman is trapped in two-dimensional stasis.[139]

If the introduction of Ellen is remarkably timid, then the introduction of Hildy Johnson (Rosalind Russell) in Hawks's film *His Girl Friday* (1940) is exhilaratingly modern. In her first sequence, Hildy strides through the newsroom (fig. 2.17a–b), just as Walter Burns does in Milestone's earlier version of the same story. Menjou had played Walter as a scoundrel, so single-minded that he barely acknowledges his colleagues; as played by Rosalind Russell, Hildy's demeanor is congenial but no less confident. When the film cuts to a moving point-of-view shot, the camera dollies past a pair of men and a pair of women; a subtle pan keeps the figures at the center of the frame for a brief moment, just enough to suggest that Hildy acknowledges them with friendly respect, but not so long as to suggest that she is anything less than focused on her goal. When the camera is not looking through Hildy's eyes, it participates with her movements, flying through the office briskly and smoothly. One can almost sense the camera crew catching their breath as they ride along.

2.17 Hildy Johnson strides across the newsroom in *His Girl Friday*.

Taking its cue from character, the participatory camera moves the way a person moves. Its model is not a person in the abstract, but a person in the moment—a person with goals, desires, and limitations. The participatory camera need not offer the best view of the scene in the manner of the ideal observer. Instead, it offers a view of the scene that is emotional, engaging, and embodied.

* * *

At the start of the 1930s, camera carriages were awkward and experimental. By the end of the decade, the moving camera had become a symbol of Hollywood's technological sophistication. In 1937, camera engineer Emil Oster stated that "modern directorial technique" favors camera movement.[140] Two years later cinematographer Lee Garmes noted, "Modern production technique calls for an incredible amount of 'dollying.'"[141] In 1941, John Arnold casually referred to the "popularization of the modern moving-camera technic."[142] Whether they celebrated this development or not, they all agreed: the moving camera was here to stay.

The challenge was to move the camera with purpose. Skeptics had proposed a dwindling list of acceptable purposes, such as following a character across a room or introducing a scene. In this chapter, I have argued that the skeptics did not always win the day. The most curious fact about the ASC's meeting in 1932 to curtail camera movement is this one: the night ended with a screening of two German films, Walter Ruttmann's *Berlin: Symphony of a Great City* (1927) and Erik Charell's *The Congress Dances* (1932). The former is an avant-garde documentary photographed by Karl Freund, the latter a musical packed with extravagant camera movements. Perhaps the goal was to warn participants about what not to do, but I have to wonder if the screening ended up having the opposite effect, showing a whole generation of filmmakers the power of movement.

CHAPTER 3

DYNAMISM, SERIALITY, AND CONVERGENCE

I n 1933, William Stull wrote that studios had adopted new perambulators to make the "moving camera scenes required by modern technique."[1] Here, the word *modern* appears in its descriptive sense, meaning "up-to-date" or "conforming to contemporary standards." But Hollywood filmmakers had not forgotten the exhilarating days of *Sunrise, Lonesome,* and *The Crowd* in the late 1920s, when the moving camera might be "modern" in a deeper sense of the word, expressing the perils, joys, and anxieties of contemporary life.

Films of the 1930s and early 1940s deployed this visual resource to analyze three distinct facets of the current culture: dynamism, seriality, and convergence. This was not the moving camera's only function or even its most important one, but it is a function that tells us a great deal about cinematography as a vehicle for ideas. Each facet could be represented in a positive or negative way. First, the literal dynamism of the moving-camera shot might express the metaphorical dynamism of the big city as a place of energy and overstimulation. Films working in a celebratory mode presented this dynamism as vitality, whereas more critical films characterized the same quality as chaos. Second, a filmmaker might dolly down a serial array of objects—such as a row of desks in an office or a shelf of consumer goods in a department store—in order to emphasize the quality of sameness. As with dynamism, the representation of seriality could be positive or negative, championing the abundance of the American economy or denouncing the meaningless repetition of mass production. Third, the camera might show how specific spaces, such as apartment buildings and train stations, brought previously unconnected characters together. This convergence produced the positive meaning of genuine community or the negative meaning of mere contiguity. Contemporary American life was multifaceted—chaotic and orderly, disparate and interconnected—and the moving camera proved to be a valuable tool for filmmakers looking to capture that complexity.

Iconography and Style

Hollywood produced films about a wide range of subjects—ancient Rome, the Old West, the French Revolution—and the moving camera could express ideas in any genre. There was no necessary connection between the moving camera and the theme of American modernity. A pan might reveal a bucolic countryside as well as a vaulting cityscape. A crane might follow a horse as well as a race car. Films set in the past used expressive camerawork all the time—see, for instance, the first appearance of John Wayne's character Ringo Kid in *Stagecoach* (1939). It is one of the great introductions in all of cinema: the dolly's movement is exhilaratingly fast, and Wayne has never looked better. The moment is so exciting that the glaring technical error—a loss of focus midway through the shot—actually helps the scene. We meet the Kid, and then he goes blurry, and then—heroically—he comes back into focus, an imperfection becoming perfection once again. The energy here expresses admiration for a valiant past.

As noted in the introduction, the Proteus principle reminds us that the same pattern may produce different effects. I start here with the premise that there is no inevitable link between style and meaning—not between movement and modernity and not between the dolly and John Wayne. That does not mean that all meaningful techniques remain equally available to filmmakers at all times. By studying a given production culture, a historian may discover localized norms. One of Hollywood's enduring subjects was contemporary American life, with its nightclubs and its tenements, its shopgirls and its elevators. Filmmakers watched each other's works, and they picked up strategies for recurring settings and situations: interesting ways to shoot a train station, exciting ways to shoot a city street, funny ways to shoot a factory. They learned that the moving camera had the power to convey attitudes and ideas about consumer capitalism, about changing gender norms, or about the conflict between the rural and the urban.

Rather than make an argument about all Hollywood films, I want to explain how filmmakers used the moving camera to characterize contemporary American life in three very particular ways—as dynamic, serial, and convergent. A few more distinctions will clarify the target of my claims. Imagine five categories, each one a subset of the one preceding. First, we have Hollywood films as a whole, from the rugged Western to the modern musical. Within this vast category, there exists a subset: Hollywood films that represent contemporary American life. A film in this subset might deploy its iconography in a relatively neutral way, depicting a few cars and apartment buildings to indicate that its story is set in New York City in 1932. Within this subset there exists another, more interesting category. In addition to telling a story that happens to be set in the contemporary world, a film might craft its iconography to convey specific themes: for instance, by using cars and apartment buildings to make an incisive comment about urban life, perhaps delighting in the sense of speed or criticizing the anonymity of apartments. Broadly speaking, these films are "about" American modernity in a way that the larger subset of films is not; they treat contemporary life as a theme. An even narrower class of films includes those that use stylistic strategies to develop their themes—for instance, by using montage to represent the city as chaotic or by using art deco sets to represent upper-class life as elegant and desirable. Here, camera movement holds no privileged place. A static film might comment on contemporary American life in countless ways. The last subset is the narrowest of all, comprising films that use camera movement specifically, rather than montage or some other device, to develop themes about modern life, perhaps by tilting up to skyscrapers to capture their scale or by dollying through factories to depict their repetitive structures. Such films use camera style to express ideas. This claim need not require that the moving camera inevitably carries these meanings. It only asserts that the thematically rich characterization of modern life was one recurring function of camera movement. A skeptic might suppose that this last category of films formed a small cluster of one-off examples. The aim of this chapter is to prove to the contrary that this category was large, diverse, and interconnected, encompassing such distinct works as Street Scene (1931), Gold Diggers of 1933, The Grapes of Wrath (1940), and The Human Comedy (1943). These films are distinct, but they all use the moving camera to say something meaningful about contemporary American life.

Several film scholars have examined the modernity of the cinema in general and the modernity of Hollywood cinema in particular. Miriam Bratu Hansen has argued that commercial cinemas around the world constitute a form of "vernacular modernism," offering spectators the opportunity to engage with the excitements and traumas of modernity.[2] In some passages of this article on the form, this concept appears to be very broad indeed, stretching to include all of Hollywood cinema. Elsewhere, Hansen insists that vernacular modernism must be defined more narrowly to retain its usefulness.[3] Defending this narrower definition, Daniel Morgan has argued helpfully that the concept should be grounded in criticism, taking a close look at the shifting meanings of modernity in individual films.[4] Others, such as Charlie Keil, have rejected the concept of vernacular modernism altogether, especially as applied to Hollywood, because it fails to explain American cinema's transition to the set of coherent storytelling practices associated with the classical Hollywood cinema.[5]

My own approach is to shift attention away from the rather broad concept of "modernity" and toward the concrete problems that filmmakers faced when they addressed a trio of more localized themes, which I call dynamism, seriality, and convergence. Working within a historical poetics framework, I continue to assume that Hollywood filmmakers valued emotionally engaging storytelling as a guiding ideal. At the same time, I argue that they used stylistic devices, including camera movement, to celebrate and criticize aspects of American society that seemed distinctly modern. These two claims are compatible. In the right context, they are mutually reinforcing. When telling a story with themes of dynamism, seriality, and convergence, even the most classical filmmaker had to ask: How might the moving camera help me tell this particular story with its particular themes?

To be sure, there is nothing radical about the claim that Hollywood made films about contemporary American life, just as there is nothing surprising about the claim that Hollywood made films about life in ancient Rome or the Old West. The challenge is to show that Hollywood filmmakers tackled these stories with a set of shared visual strategies, going beyond one-off examples. Consider two films, both from M-G-M. In *Emma* (1932), Marie Dressler plays a rural woman who experiences the unfamiliar environment of a big-city train station. When her kindly but absent-minded employer (and future husband) Mr. Smith drops a ball of yarn, Emma must rewind it while enduring the stares of several onlookers as she walks through the station. Working with cinematographer Oliver Marsh and camera operator Eddie Fitzgerald, director Clarence Brown photographs the bulk of the gag in a single shot, dollying with Dressler as she passes from one waiting room to another (fig. 3.1a–b).[6] The scene obeys the familiar norms of Hollywood storytelling: Emma follows her goal of retrieving the yarn, and the camera follows her. But the camera accomplishes two functions at once. While following Emma, it offers an evocative image of a modern train station, packed with strangers: some notice Emma; some do not; some register onscreen for a significant moment while the dolly pauses on its way; and some appear as just a blur while the dolly passes imperviously by. Brown could have used match-on-action cuts to represent Emma crossing the floor, or he could have used point-of-view structures to emphasize her focus on the yarn; instead, the lateral dolly makes the scene a series of surprises as the size of the crowd and the depth of the space change moment by moment.[7] Elsewhere, *Emma* generates much of its comedy in contrasting the old and new; its most outrageous comedic set piece involves Marie Dressler spinning upside down while her character attempts to operate a mechanical flight simulator. In the train station, the visual humor arises from the contrast between Emma's singular focus on the unraveled yarn and the casual disregard of the crowd that surrounds her.

3.1 The camera dollies with Marie Dressler as she winds a ball of yarn in *Emma*.

3.2 In *The Clock*, the camera follows a soldier through Penn Station.

This strategy of moving the camera to express the energy of a train station was so effective that other filmmakers used it, too. In 1945, M-G-M, the same studio that had released *Emma* thirteen years earlier, released *The Clock*, a romance directed by Vincente Minnelli. After a brief introductory montage, a dissolve takes us inside the large Penn Station set. Joe (Robert Walker), a corporal on leave, is in the middle ground, walking from right to left. The camera follows him, but at first it is difficult to pick Joe out from the crowd (fig. 3.2a). Joe eventually approaches two separate men to ask for suggestions about what to see in New York. Now the camera moves closer, framing Joe from the knees up for the duration of the shot (fig. 3.2b). The sense of chaotic motion remains. The camera is distant enough to allow the occasional extra to pass by in the foreground, and the background remains vibrant, showing people moving up and down the stairs and escalators. (In this way, the film does narrative work, preparing us for the meet-cute, as Judy Garland's character, Alice, will bump into Joe a few minutes later next to the escalator.) Like *Emma*, *The Clock* shows a character from a small town trying to navigate a modern train station. Like Clarence Brown, Minnelli uses the moving camera to follow his overwhelmed protagonist through the crowd, evoking the dynamism of the station itself.

Neither example is meant to imply that Hollywood filmmakers always dollied during train station scenes or that they dollied only in train stations or even that they were more likely to dolly in train stations. My claim is not about statistical correlations, but about meanings in contexts. In these two films, with these two stories, and with these two characters, the camera's movement contributes to the characterization of the train station as a vast, confusing, fascinating space. The claim is not so big as to take in all of Hollywood, but it is not so small as to treat each film as sui generis. Instead, the claim proposes that Hollywood filmmakers *shared* themes and motifs, drawing on overlapping contexts: professional, technological, ideological, economic, artistic.

Striking a balance between the microlevel history of one-time examples and the macrolevel history of cinema as a generalized manifestation of modernity, a history of themes and motifs tracks how filmmakers developed a shared iconography of contemporary American life—and a shared stylistics to represent that iconography expressively. Unlike avant-garde filmmakers, commercially oriented Hollywood filmmakers were not under cultural pressure to innovate at all times; they valued proven techniques they could use again and again. But Hollywood was not like an automobile factory: each film was different (however minor some generic variations might be), and so each film called for unique treatment.[8] The variability of the visual motif allowed the filmmaker to start with a familiar formula and then alter it to suit the theme at hand. Even old studio hands who kept their minds on the most hard-headed practical concerns—What is this scene about? What equipment do I have available? How have other filmmakers photographed similar situations?—might represent contemporary American life in expressive ways.[9]

The next three sections consider how Hollywood filmmakers deployed the moving camera to address the themes of dynamism, seriality, and convergence. Each theme produced at least one distinctive motif—one distinctive way of deploying the moving camera to represent the theme expressively. The final two sections extend the argument by explaining how Hollywood filmmakers used these shared strategies to address the dynamism, seriality, and convergence of two inescapable events: the Great Depression and World War II.

Dynamism: Movement and Montage

According to Kristen Whissel, many American films of the early twentieth century worked to "shape and define a sense of the national specificity of the

American experience of modernity" by representing the figure in traffic—with the term *traffic* encompassing both street traffic and more general patterns of circulation.[10] Late-silent-era filmmakers extended this fascination for the figure in traffic, as seen in a trio of films discussed in chapter 1: *Sunrise, My Best Girl,* and *Four Sons.* Each film encapsulates its tale of a character confronting the big city with the image of a person walking precariously through a knot of cars. Significantly, the camera crosses the street (or appears to cross it with the help of special effects) alongside the characters, as if participating in their experience. The movement of the camera thereby intensifies the energy and chaos.

A hypothesis seems irresistible: the dynamism of the camera expresses the dynamism of the city. The challenge is to pitch the proposal at the right level of generality—not so broad as to encompass all films and not so narrow as to treat the matter as a set of unique examples. My solution is to look for concrete repetitions whereby certain visual strategies became familiar options (or even clichés) without becoming mandatory. The crossing-the-street shot was one such option—a recognizable, repeatable motif that remained available to filmmakers throughout the 1930s and beyond. Having experimented with the idea in *The Last Laugh* and *Sunrise,* Murnau offered a fresh take on the technique in *City Girl,* giving it new shades of meaning.[11] The film's depiction of the city woman is more sympathetic than it is in *Sunrise,* but its representation of the city itself is more despairing. Scenes of the waitress Kate (Mary Duncan) in her apartment evoke a sense of loneliness reminiscent of Edward Hopper paintings such as *Night Windows* (1928). Scenes of naive farmer Lem (Charles Farrell) walking on the city streets evoke a different kind of loneliness—the solitude felt in the midst of an overwhelming crowd. One scene shows Lem standing on a curb and reading a newspaper (fig. 3.3a). The camera dollies backward into

3.3 In *City Girl,* an urban crowd overwhelms a farmer.

the street, and an automobile drives by, passing through the space that the camera had just traversed. Two more cars drive past, and then pedestrians swarm into the crosswalk. Lem, who once dominated the foreground of the image, is now barely visible in the background, on the right edge of the frame (fig. 3.3b). Unlike the traveling-matte effect of *Sunrise*, which keeps the lovers locked in the center of the frame, *City Girl*'s chaotic jumble of motion makes the individual human irrelevant. One might tell the same story by cutting across the street to a cluttered long shot of Lem, but the dolly allows us to see the spatial transformation as it happens. We struggle to keep Lem in view as the composition shifts him from the center to the periphery, allowing the urban world to break through the barrier of the frame and engulf our hero.

Charlie Keil has warned against the temptation to equate all dynamic sequences with modernity, "as such a move risks diluting the specific qualities of modernity to the point where any instance of rapid movement onscreen serves as modernity's functional equivalent."[12] With this in mind, a skeptic might concede that Murnau's sequence is about modernity—the film is called *City Girl*, after all—while arguing sensibly that we cannot generalize from one shot to Hollywood as a whole. However, I do think there is a middle ground where a strategy becomes a shared resource rather than just a one-off example. Variations on the crossing-the-street shot can be found in *Street Scene* (1931, a passing car almost mows down an earnest man reading his book); in *Hallelujah, I'm a Bum* (1933, a despairing woman barely notices the cars whizzing in front of her); in *The Whole Town's Talking* (1935, a meek office worker who has been mistaken for a gangster scrambles through heavy city traffic); in *Ninotchka* (1939, a man and a woman meet by chance on a traffic island); in *Foreign Correspondent* (1940, an assassin pushes the hero into a street as a car zips past); in *Lady in the Dark* (1944, in Technicolor a woman walks through a busy city street as bright-yellow cabs drive by); and in *Fallen Angel* (1945, the camera spins around 360 degrees to reveal action on both sides of a busy street). Indeed, the motif would remain available for decades; witness the variations in Otto Preminger's *The Man with the Golden Arm* (1955) and Vincente Minnelli's *Bells Are Ringing* (1960). The repetitions here go beyond the level of content to include the level of style. All of these films stage the action with the camera dollying or craning through the street. The resulting scenes are doubly dynamic, mixing figure motion with camera movement.

The fact that the motif was optional does not make it any less meaningful. The dynamism works thematically by characterizing the city as indifferent to the individual's concerns, but each film modifies the motif to suit the themes of the particular story. *Hallelujah, I'm a Bum* reworks a sad scene from *My Best Girl*, thereby suggesting that the figure of the woman in traffic is particularly poignant. *The Whole Town's Talking* reworks the first crossing-the-street shot from *Sunrise*, thereby amplifying the sense of urban danger. Some of the most thoughtful mutations appear in the works of Frank Borzage, as in *Bad Girl* (1931), *Big City* (1937), and *Three Comrades* (1938). In *History Is Made at Night* (1937), Borzage reworks the moment in *Sunrise* when the city dissolves away to become a meadow. Charles Boyer's character Paul knows that he must return to France to face a murder charge, but he and his beloved, Irene (Jean Arthur), face the temptation of escape. They walk across the street to take a closer look at a Tahiti poster in the window of a travel office. The camera follows them across the street, moving steadily forward even as a car enters its path, almost hitting Paul and Irene. When they arrive safely to the other side, the film cuts to Paul's point of view, dollying in toward the picture of Tahiti. As in *Sunrise*, an image of urban danger gives way to an illusory image of escape. The city emerges as dynamic and complex—and as a threat to the harmony of the couple.

Another way to represent the dynamism of the city was through a recurring technique that we might call the "manic city montage." Such montages rely on rapid editing, superimpositions, and camera movement to represent the city as an explosion of energy, exciting but overwhelming. These montages take advantage of special-effects technologies such as optical printing and rear-screen projection. Examples appear in *Delicious* (1931, a climactic scene unfolds to the music of George Gershwin); in Chaplin's *Modern Times* (1936, a burst of chaotic urban imagery serves as the punch line to a joke about the Tramp's failed attempts to relax); in *Three Smart Girls* (1936, a New York City montage features a boat, two cars, and a tilt up to a skyscraper), and in *Hollywood Hotel* (1937, the cacophony of the city dissolves into the delirium of Hollywood itself). Shed of its utopian impulses, the montage would later become a staple of film noir, as in *Murder, My Sweet* (1944), where a series of slow optical-printer zooms evokes the anxious atmosphere of Los Angeles at night. One of the best manic city montages appears in Mervyn LeRoy's film *Big City Blues* (1932). The protagonist Bud (Eric Linden) is a naive country boy who moves to the city. Upon his arrival, the filmmakers position Bud and his suitcases on a treadmill in front of a rear-screen projection. The background footage is gloriously dynamic, more like a city symphony than a realistic effect (fig. 3.4a). The canted frame pans left and right, causing skyscrapers to dance and whirl (fig. 3.4b). As in *Berlin: Symphony of a Great City*, we see a throng of elevated trains rambling through the city. As in Dziga Vertov's *The Man with the Movie Camera* (1929), a split-screen effect juxtaposes images canted in opposite directions. Though our hero is destined for disillusionment, *Big City Blues* encourages us to share his initial feelings of wonderment, using the manic city montage to represent the city as a place of exuberant vitality.

The montage in *Big City Blues* clearly draws on precursors from European modernism, but the movie as a whole is very far from the avant-garde. To see why, compare this montage with a superficially similar sequence in the Dadaist

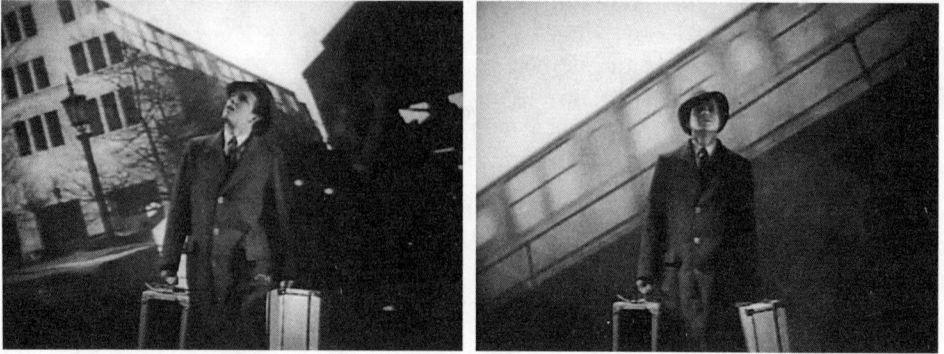

3.4 A montage in *Big City Blues* evokes the conventions of the city symphony.

classic *Entr'acte* (1924). In René Clair's film, the camera rocks unpredictably while photographing the city of Paris from the top of a tall building. A paper boat appears superimposed over the image, as if the swaying city were a sea upon which a ship might sail. The water imagery connects the sequence to the previous scene, showing two rooftop chess players doused by a stream of water; meanwhile, the whirling of the camera connects to another recurring image, showing a tutu-wearing ballet dancer jumping up and down. Neither of these links counts as a narrative connection; indeed, there is no thread of action that can help us make sense of *Entr'acte*'s provocatively irrational sequence of events. By contrast, the montage in *Big City Blues* shows its protagonist overwhelmed by the city, and the rest of the film's narrative will show just how dangerous his naïveté can be. The sequence's narrativity and its representation of American modernity are mutually informing. Bud's wide-eyed wonder cues us to read the canted angles as confusing; the jumbled montage primes us to expect the city to turn on Bud eventually. The two functions—telling Bud's story and expressing the city's dynamic chaos—amplify one another.

Hollywood's most prominent montage practitioner, Slavko Vorkapich, was also an innovative theorist. Like Murnau, Vorkapich championed movement as a medium-specific trait: "Here we have found the key to the understanding of our new medium. Motion is what makes it different from photography or painting."[13] Vorkapich situated the perception of movement within a larger theory of human psychology, resting on the (perhaps dubious) distinction between the optical and the mental. "Look at the screen only optically," he wrote, "regardless of what the picture represents. If you look at it optically only, that is, with your eyes alone, and not with your minds, what will you see— different grades of light and darkness, spread over the surface of the screen."[14] Returning to *Big City Blues*, one might describe figure 3.4b in this way: a man carries his suitcases through the city, while an elevated train passes by. Or one might describe the same image this way: a dark gray blob bumps up and down in the center of the image, while a series of rectangles swooshes by, following a diagonal line from the left side of the screen to the top. This second description treats the screen as a two-dimensional surface with shadows moving across it, not as a shifting picture of a stable world.

Vorkapich called for the coordination of these two aspects. Whether employing photography or animation, the cinema displays patterns of light and shadow, patterns that we see with our eyes even as we recognize with our minds what those patterns depict. The trick is to manipulate the optical patterns so they produce emotions appropriate to the subject. Vorkapich's primary example is the hotel scene in *The Last Laugh*, with its camera descending in an elevator and then moving across the busy lobby: "Optically speaking, rhythmically moving and changing patterns on the screen were pleasing and intriguing to the eye; mentally speaking, the picture gave a living, pulsating impression of a hotel. The atmosphere was expressed in terms of motion."[15] Even if we were to ignore the hotel, we would get the impression of dynamism from the formal pattern of movement alone. This abstract dynamism intensifies our reaction to the subject matter itself—the hotel—because the film's energy perfectly expresses the feeling of this lively, modern space.

Like a film score, the ever-changing pattern of light and shadow on the screen should produce a series of moods suited to the subject: "Different motions have different emotional values."[16] With his emphasis on medium specificity and abstraction, Vorkapich developed a theory with clear roots in European modernism, but he made that theory palatable to Hollywood by explaining how a dynamic image might contribute to an overriding goal—evoking feelings.[17] The subjects could be contemporary, as in *The Last Laugh*, but they need not be. Indeed, Vorkapich applied his technique to a wide range of subjects and settings, from cities (*Manhattan Cocktail*, 1928) to parties (*Sweepings*, 1933), from Mexico (*Viva Villa!*, 1934) to China (*The Good Earth*, 1937).

Other thinkers picked up Vorkapich's ideas, pondering how editing and camera movement might work together to produce intensified effects. In 1934, *American Cinematographer* published a fascinating article by Harry Perry, a special-effects cinematographer. Perry asked his readers to imagine a montage showing the following sequence of images: a snail, a baby, a man walking, a bicyclist, a family sedan, and a racing car. The principle was simple: onscreen movement increased visual intensity. Even with shots of identical length, "the increasingly dynamic subjects will make the shots seem to get shorter and shorter, building up to a definite cinematic climax." Next, Perry asked his readers to imagine the same sequence with shorter and shorter shot lengths: "The result will be a bewildering crescendo of speed." Finally, he proposed adding camera movement to the mix, recommending "5 feet of a follow-shot of the family car crossing the screen, followed by 4 feet of an Akeley-shot of the racer. Next, about 2 feet of the original 'dolly-shot' of the walking man; 1 foot of the running-shot of the cyclist; a dozen frames of the running-shot of the family car, and finish with eight frames of the racer."[18] Like Vorkapich, Perry argued that films created patterns of visual intensities. Long takes, slow figure movement, and stationary framing reduced intensity; shorter takes, rapid figure movement, and dynamic framing increased it.

Even if we dismiss the writings of Vorkapich and Perry as marginal to Hollywood practice, the films of Lewis Milestone are hard to ignore. Milestone won his second Best Director Oscar for his work on *All Quiet on the Western Front* (1930), one of the most admired films of the early sound period. Born in Russia (present-day Moldova), Milestone was familiar with montage theory. He also admired Murnau's films, which taught him to appreciate the value of an unusual angle.[19] Taking full advantage of Universal's Broadway Boom, *All Quiet*'s battle sequences combine the dynamic camerawork of Murnau with the rapid editing of montage.[20] In one scene, a stationary shot of a German soldier firing a machine gun (fig. 3.5a) is intercut with a shot traveling from left to right, showing one soldier after another being felled by brutal gunfire (fig. 3.5b). The result is a graphic pattern of alternation: stasis, motion, stasis, motion. Vorkapich had argued that an abstract pattern could imitate the atmosphere of a hotel; Milestone designed an abstract pattern that could imitate the workings of a machine gun, with rapid but unbearably systematic motion. The lateral motion of the Broadway Boom makes the scene even more horrifying, suggesting that the movement might go on indefinitely, showing us one more death in the series and then another as quickly as bullets can pass through a gun.

3.5 *All Quiet on the Western Front* intercuts a stationary shot of a machine gun with a lateral movement past dying men.

Milestone continued to experiment with dynamic montage, as in *The Front Page* (1931), where lateral dolly shots of ringing telephones are intercut with arcing shots of busy reporters, and in *Rain* (1932), where stationary shots of raindrops build in intensity, culminating in a shot moving away from a downpour. The Proteus principle still applies: meaning changes depending on the context. Dynamic montage evokes the natural energy of rainfall just as well as it expresses the nervous tension of the newsroom. Indeed, *All Quiet on the Western Front* illustrates the flip side of the Proteus principle: the same technique may express two different meanings. The gunfire montage suggests dynamism—the shocking speed of the machine gun—but it also suggests the reverse—the horrible predictability of battle. The lateral movement suggests that the killing may extend forever.

Tom Gunning has argued that we should consider modernity from both perspectives: not only as a culture of energy and shock but also as a culture of hyperrationalism, dedicated to constructing new industrial and bureaucratic systems.[21] Hyperstimulus was just one aspect of modernity and not always the most important one. The city, the factory, the office building, and the department store may be exciting, but they can also be something else—repetitive, controlled, as monotonous as a machine gun. Certain stories made the theme of hyperrationalism unusually salient. What strategies did filmmakers use to express this set of themes?

Seriality: One Thing After Another

To evoke the idea of stultifying sameness, many filmmakers used a technique I call the "seriality shot." A quick look at a canonical French example offers an introduction to the technique. After setting aside the anarchist experimentation of *Entr'acte*, René Clair became one of the most admired filmmakers in the world with his innovative early sound films *Sous les toits de Paris* (1930) and *Le million* (1931). Insisting that "the cinema must remain visual at all costs," Clair rejected the filmed-theater model in favor of the creative juxtaposition of sound and image.[22] After the release of his film *À nous la liberté* in 1931, American trade journals commented favorably on his visual style. *Variety* pronounced the film "more Germanic than many German films."[23]

In the opening shot, the camera dollies from right to left, revealing one toy horse after another (fig. 3.6a). On the twelfth horse, the camera reverses its direction, tilting up to reveal uniformed prisoners manufacturing these toys (fig. 3.6b). The camera eventually rests on one prisoner, Émile (Henri Marchand), who looks up and winks at his friend. Both the toys and the prisoners form a series: a set of similar subjects lined up one after the other. Rather than represent this grouping in long shot, Clair has heightened the sense of repetition

3.6 The camera reveals a series of toys and prisoners in the French classic *À nous la liberté*.

by employing a lateral tracking shot. The camera moves down the row, allowing some members of the series to pass offscreen and new members to emerge. This movement captures the continuity of the series, while suggesting that the chain of repetitions extends beyond the depicted space. Juxtaposing serial toys with serial prisoners, Clair introduces the film's thesis visually, condemning the carceral conformity of modern life, with its systems of mass production and mass social control. Modernity means monotony.

Crucially, the scene's redundancy is not absolute. As the camera dollies from one toy horse to the next, the subtle differences among horses shows that each successive toy is slightly more finished than its predecessor. Once the camera reverses course, the repetition heightens our awareness that the men are by no means identical: they have different numbers, different heights, and different degrees of dedication to their work. When the camera rests on Émile, the effect is not just to mark this character as one of the series but also to introduce a character who will remain resolutely an individual. In a single shot, Clair has raised questions that we might pose about any seriality shot. Does the film represent seriality as a form of absolute repetition, or does the film hint at the underlying diversity of the series? Is the series a closed set, or might it go on indefinitely? Does the protagonist stand apart from the series or merge into it?

In 1936, Charlie Chaplin reworked Clair's assembly-line gag for the brilliant factory sequence in *Modern Times*. Though Chaplin soon found himself embroiled in a lawsuit for stealing Clair's idea, the revised camerawork produces a very different effect. After panning with a worker who is crossing the factory set, the camera reveals two men hammering onto a tool as plates speed by on the assembly line. In contrast to Clair's smooth tracking shot, Chaplin's camera starts and stops, picking up a worker during its initial pan and then resting on a stable composition that allows us to compare the two hammering men with one another. Chaplin cast two actors who look comically dissimilar: one is a small man with gray hair and a relatively neat appearance, and the other is a large mustached man with stains on his sleeveless undershirt. The repetitiveness of the assembly line contrasts with the idiosyncrasy of the men operating it. Next, the walking worker continues to pass through the background of the shot; the camera pans to follow him and introduces the Tramp, whose small size contrasts amusingly with the burliness of the man in the undershirt. The Tramp's appearance marks him as an individual, even as his gestures look shockingly mechanical. For the rest of the shot, the camerawork continues to develop this dialectic between the human and the machine. When the Tramp is at his most machinelike, ratcheting repetitively, his human form dominates the stable composition. But when the Tramp acts like a person, raising his arms to scratch his armpits or argue with the foreman, then the camera pans to follow the assembly line itself, temporarily letting the factory's mechanical motion dictate the pace. If Clair's relentless camera movement suggests that the logic of the series dangerously overwhelms individual differences, then Chaplin's more sporadic camerawork constantly reminds us of the presence of the human within the mechanical.

Already in 1927, two eminent historians had identified seriality as one of the defining features of contemporary American culture: "In all the land save in out-of-the-way places, there could be found none but machine-made objects, duplicated by the ton, impersonal, standardized according to patterns adapted to fingers of steel."[24] Just as many Hollywood films of the period represented American society as exciting and unpredictable and free, many others took a more critical view, mocking the mindless repetitions of the machine age. The crossing-the-street shot and the manic city montage allowed filmmakers to address the vitality of the modern city. The seriality shot gave filmmakers an equally flexible resource to represent the cultures of mass production, mass consumption, and mass destruction. Whether telling a story about an office, a prison, a war, or a department store, a filmmaker might send a camera down a row of people or objects, allowing some members of the series to pass offscreen and other members to enter anew. This argument need not assume any necessary correlations between subject and technique. One might dolly down a row of horses in a Western just as easily as one might dolly down an assembly line in a factory film. The meanings of seriality change with the context.

The prison genre proved to be a perfect showcase for the seriality technique, as in George Hill's *The Big House* (1930). The main protagonist of the film is Morgan (Chester Morris), a criminal who wants to go straight, even as he remains loyal to his volatile prison buddy Butch (Wallace Beery). They clash with Kent, a weak snitch played by Robert Montgomery. Screenwriter Frances Marion won an Oscar for her work on *The Big House*; a few years later she authored a textbook insisting that a plot must focus on one or two characters to intensify the spectator's emotional engagement with the story.[25] Her commitment to solid plot construction poses an interesting challenge in the prison genre: it is hard to make a character stand out from the crowd when the crowd is shaped like a lineup. How do you represent characters as individuals while acknowledging that they are living under a regime mandating strict conformity? A scene showing the prisoners singing a hymn provides one possible answer, employing a serial composition to highlight the pairing of Morgan and Butch while suggesting that the contemptible Kent is barely worthy of notice. The shot begins on Morgan and Butch as Butch looks around suspiciously. Then the camera dollies to the right, moving past several prisoners and passing right by Kent, who slides in and out of the frame, never coming into focus. Robert Montgomery is one of the film's stars, and the camera skips by him as if he were an extra! When the camera reaches the end of the row, it reverses direction, dollying impassively by Kent a second time before settling on another stable composition favoring Morgan and Butch. The one-minute shot privileges the two prison buddies in various ways: they are in focus, they appear at the beginning and end of the shot, and they are afforded the dignity of a stable frame. While they sing along with everyone else, their wandering eyes remind us that these tough guys are individuals pursuing a goal. By contrast, pretty-boy Kent is trying to merge unobtrusively into the series, and the camera treats him with disdain, not even bothering to slow down or to rack focus while passing over him two separate times.

Normally, it would be bad business to merge the star with the series; however, a serial array may serve as a useful contrast, providing a background against which the star may shine. An excerpt from Lenore Coffee's screenplay for *Possessed* (1931) illustrates this principle. The scene in question did not make it into the finished film, but Coffee's description is remarkably precise. The film would open on a brief montage introducing a factory. Next, we would see a "revolving table, around which are seated seven girls with an empty place for an eighth. The camera is in the center of this table which revolves so rapidly that the faces of the girls are a whirling blur. This movement slows down as the dissolve comes in until it reaches normal speed. We then see that these are factory girls seated around this revolving table on which are the paper box lids and fancy covering papers." A blur would become a series. Eventually, "the camera moving with the revolving table comes to Marian next who makes no contribution to the conversation. We feel instantly that this girl is different—dressed like the others—working like the others—but with an arresting quality about her."[26] The ensuing story will be about this girl who is different—the one who stands apart from the series. Seriality sets up the star.

We might expect the office film to be more hopeful than the factory film, but this space proved equally susceptible to serialization. In the United States, corporations had been growing larger and more bureaucratized since the nine-teenth century. As the historian Nikil Saval explains, "Clerical workers, no longer enjoying the easy rapport with their two or three fellow workers and their bosses, were now massed together in highly regimented rows, to mimic—for lack of another precedent—the factory floor."[27] Even before the Great Depres-sion began, King Vidor had mocked the factory-like seriality of the modern office in *The Crowd*. The film's original treatment had made the theme of seri-ality explicit, calling for "100 desks all alike" and "100 clerks all alike watching the clock."[28] Many subsequent films owed a debt to *The Crowd*. At least one film, *The Easiest Way* (1931), copied the film quite literally, borrowing *The Crowd*'s celebrated skyscraper shot apparently by striking its own shot from the same negative. Ernst Lubitsch adapted imagery from Vidor's film while adding a fresh interpretation. In his contribution to the compendium film *If I Had a Million* (1932), a wide shot introduces an open-plan office space with four long rows of desks. The camera dollies to the left, following a man crossing through the bull-pen. But then the camera pans away from the anonymous man and begins to dolly forward down the center aisle, loosely following another anonymous man in the distance. Passing a few desks, the camera pans to the right and frames a medium shot of Phineas Lambert, the sullen bureaucrat played by Charles Laughton. This pencil pusher soon learns that he has won a million dollars. He walks up the stairs, passes through several doors, arrives at the office of the pres-ident, and blows the president a raspberry. Lubitsch uses multiple stationary shots to represent Lambert walking from office to office, thereby emphasizing how the separation of spaces reflects corporate hierarchy. But the opening shot is a smooth camera move, suggesting the lack of hierarchy at the lower levels where the anonymous drudges do their work. If anything, Lubitsch has taken the office motif from *The Crowd* and made it more despairing. Vidor's camera appeared to seek out the protagonist with single-minded determination; Lubitsch's camera appears to pick Lambert out at random, first following one man, then following another man, and then turning its focus to Lambert, who appears no more special than anyone else. This Depression-era short offers a remarkably despairing view of capitalism. There is little room at the top and a lot of room at the bottom, and only dumb luck can allow someone like Lam-bert to move from the bottom to the top.

The theme of upward mobility plays out differently in office films about women. For men like John Sims and Phineas Lambert, the office is a place where careers go to die. For women, offices carry a different set of cultural meanings. Commenting on office life in the early twentieth century, Saval writes, "Now all the lowly work was increasingly taken up by women; the pay for these jobs was also degraded (and degrading); and there was never a question that women would be able to move up the company ladder in the way men could. . . . Yet the office offered a sense of freedom to many women that shouldn't be underestimated."[29] Films of the 1930s express this ambivalence in many ways, from narrative to camerawork. Some films, such as *Employees' Entrance* (1933), show male bosses exploiting the women who work for them. Other films, such as *Baby Face* (1933), show strong and shrewd women using sex to gain power, securing promotions by having affairs with easily duped men. The latter film rewrites the skyscraper shot in an ingenious way. Whenever Barbara Stanwyck's character, Lily, initiates an affair, the film shows us the office building from the outside, and the camera moves from window to window, craning up a few floors to suggest Lily's rise in status. As film scholar Gwendolyn Audrey Foster writes, "Lily is embodied by the modern skyscraper; it is in turn emblematic of her hardening process, her quick-change class-passing from a woman trapped with trampy, old-fashioned clothing and hair to the dazzling, bleached blonde, Deco-gowned modern woman she becomes."[30] The skyscraper's seriality—all those identical floors—comes to represent the repetitiveness of Lily's actions. Off-screen, the American office typically consigned women to dead-end jobs, while men were more likely to receive steady promotions. *If I Had a Million* and *Baby Face* invert this picture, suggesting that men have only a lottery winner's chance of escaping the horizontal space of the office bullpen, whereas a woman like Lily can move vertically from job to job.

Factory films and office films explicitly associated seriality with the work cultures of modern capitalism. Meanwhile, the spread of department stores and other chains had encouraged Americans to think of consumption as another "mass" activity.[31] To evoke this figure of mass consumption, the camera might dolly down a row of pricey items or truck along a series of storefronts. One of the most cynical representations of the culture of consumption appeared at the end of the decade in *The Women* (1939), directed by George Cukor from a screenplay by Clare Boothe Luce. The opening sequence introduces a series of rooms in a salon. Each room offers a different service: a mud bath, a massage, and what is now known as a spin class. According to Cukor, "That was a stunt: to go through every known beauty operation that a woman can go through at Elizabeth Arden's, and do it in one shot."[32] Cukor's description is not entirely accurate; the sequence comprises ten separate shots, linked together with cuts and wipes. Most of the transitions are quite smooth, and the effect is to give the impression of seamlessness, as if the camera were traveling from room to room. At first glance, the sequence may not appear to be about seriality at all. We see different beauty treatments (high tech and low tech), different ages (young and old), different classes (wealthy clients and working-class employees), and different races (most of the women are white; one employee is African American). But the movement of the camera, always flowing from right to left, works to unite all of these differences under the heading of femininity, associated with an easily satirized search for beauty. No men appear in the film, but the implicit contrast with masculinity is striking. A film might represent a man in a serial formation when he is in a dead-end job or in the military or in prison, but a woman joins a serial formation in her leisure time. The mass culture of consumption offers women no escape from seriality.

Perhaps the most famous seriality shots of the decade appear in Busby Berkeley's musical numbers. With over-the-top absurdity, Berkeley mocks American capitalism's commodification of female beauty by pushing the commodification to delirious extremes. The serial movement is an essential component of this reflexive critique. In the opening scene of *Gold Diggers of 1933*, a close-up shows Fay (Ginger Rogers) singing "We're in the Money." After a cut, the camera dollies to the right to reveal another blond woman. Initially covering her face with a giant coin, the chorus girl swings the coin aside and smiles brightly to the camera (fig. 3.7a). The pattern is repeated several times, each time introducing another pretty face, until the camera reaches the end of the line, where, to our surprise, Fay reappears (fig. 3.7b). The seriality of the composition suggests that any woman can be exchanged for any other, just like pocket change. The fact that the women are not identical adds to the film's critique, suggesting how capitalism manipulates small differences to create the appearance of desirable variety in the midst of ceaseless repetition. Berkeley designed countless variations on this same-but-different motif, as in the "Tunnel of Pulchritude" number in *Dames* (1934), where dozens of women are arranged to form a rectangular corridor. The camera travels down the middle of this corridor—while rotating 360 degrees! Cinematographer George Barnes's crew had to design a special mount to allow camera operator Warren Lynch to complete this rotation.[33] The effect is so abstract that it barely seems to be about female beauty at all; whatever beauty is on display has been created entirely by the serial patterning of the choreography and camerawork.

3.7 The camera finds Ginger Rogers at the end of a chorus line in *Gold Diggers of 1933*.

Referring to a proto-Berkeley dance troupe known as the Tiller Girls, Siegfried Kracauer wrote, "The masses organized in these movements come from offices and factories."[34] The rigorous repetition of such images expresses the deeper logic of modern capitalism, which aspires to maximum interchangeability, whereby any worker can be replaced by any other. Perhaps it is implausible to suppose that spectators watching women jumping through waterfalls were thinking about the workings of capitalism—but this is exactly why we should consider Berkeley's musical numbers in the contexts of the films as a whole. The story portions of *Gold Diggers of 1933*, *Footlight Parade* (1933), and *Dames* explicitly depict women struggling to survive in an economy that considers them expendable. The dancers are not just abstractions; they are workers. When the musical numbers are viewed in isolation, Kracauer's comments may seem like a stretch. When the musical numbers are viewed as the culmination of a narrative trajectory, it becomes easier to see Berkeley's pictorial abstraction as a satire of a newly dehumanized culture of work.

Convergence: Tales of Contiguity

In Faith Baldwin's office novel *Skyscraper* (1931), a protagonist rides the subway to work. Inside this subway is "an amorphous mass of human beings; a mass which, upon reaching the platform, resolved itself into separately moving, breathing, sometimes thinking, atoms." The subway crowd brings together people who are "closely allied physically, but strangers."[35] In this passage, Baldwin captures something important about modern spaces: they produce provisional connections among the otherwise unconnected. Subways, apartment buildings, streets, ships, and cities—all of these spaces may fuse strangers together, sometimes for just a moment, sometimes for the rest of their lives.

Stories set in such spaces of convergence presented interesting problems for Hollywood filmmakers, who normally favored tightly plotted stories about one or two protagonists. As David Bordwell has shown, the film of Vicki Baum's novel *Grand Hotel* (1932) sparked a vogue for "network narratives," using a specific location to link disparate characters who become entangled in each other's lives.[36] When M-G-M adapted Faith Baldwin's novel *Skyscraper* as *Skyscraper Souls* (1932), the filmmakers explicitly appealed to the not-yet-released film *Grand Hotel* as a model. In a meeting with producer Bernard Hyman and writer Edith Fitzgerald, director Edgar Selwyn stated, "You are telling the story of a building and everything that is going on, the different stories, which at the end do blend together. You take *Grand Hotel*—they are all separate stories. They do gradually touch on each other."[37] The conversation quickly turned to a disagreement about film technique. Fitzgerald argued that *Grand Hotel* introduced its various story lines by cutting from one person to another in an opening telephone sequence. Hyman disagreed, stating that *Grand Hotel* used camera movement to shift from one story to another, following a character in one story line and then switching to the next: "They never made any wild cuts. . . . It was fluid."[38] Fitzgerald was correct: the telephone scene did, in fact, rely on cuts. (Perhaps Hyman was thinking about the lobby sequence, which used wide shots and panning movements to include multiple characters in the frame.) The discussion hinted at a general principle: in a tale of convergence, a moving camera can show how a particular space has joined two or more characters, even when those characters have had no previous connection with one another.

The opening scene of *Skyscraper Souls* adheres to this principle, favoring movement over cuts. After a dissolve, the camera follows Sarah (Verree Teasdale), walking from left to right. She collides with Tom (Norman Foster) and apologizes (fig. 3.8a). The camera then follows Tom as he bumps into a much larger man, who refuses to apologize (fig. 3.8b). A moment later Tom drops a nickel, leans over to look for it, and rudely grabs the ankle of Lynn (Margaret O'Sullivan), who has accidently stepped on the coin. The ankle grabbing makes for an excruciating meet-cute, but the scene does an effective job of introducing three of the film's main characters while suggesting that their respective meetings are largely matters of chance. As Merrill Schleier explains, "The lobby is rendered as a space where bosses meet secretaries and office boys alike, prior to conforming to the class and gender stratification in the office above."[39] The moving camera evokes a sense of fluidity, with minor encounters emerging from the crowd and then dissolving right back into it.

A prototypical convergence shot is one in which camera movement links two or more characters who inhabit the same space even though they are not (yet) connected by the plot. The causal chain may connect the characters eventually, or the characters might go off in different directions. Either way, the point of

3.8 *Skyscraper Souls* depicts the office building lobby as a space of unexpected encounters.

the shot is to show that it is the space itself, not some previously established plan, that has brought these characters together. The technique works by depicting *contiguity* and *simultaneity*. Cutting from one character to another might show that two characters are in the same place, but it would not have the same power to show us the spatial relationships so directly. The dolly shows us: this character is here, that one is there, and this is exactly how close here is to there, right now. Space enables fortuitous encounters.

The interest of the convergence shot extends beyond the narratological; the shot carries social significance as well. Describing some key aspects of American modernity, Kristen Whissel has written, "Members of different classes, ethnicities, nationalities, and races who fifty years earlier might only have encountered one another in public spaces suddenly found themselves sharing— and often struggling over—housing, transportation, labor, amusements, local politics, and city sidewalks."[40] Whissel extends her arguments about "traffic" well beyond the literal representation of cars and intersections, adding the exchange of bodies across various modern networks.

Grand Hotel and its imitators suggested that chance encounters were particularly likely in certain characteristically modern spaces, such as lobbies, train stations, and city streets. William K. Howard's film *Transatlantic* (1931) beat *Grand Hotel* to the box office by setting a similar story on a boat.[41] In the opening scene of *Transatlantic*, cinematographer James Wong Howe and operator Dave Ragin execute several spectacular crane and dolly shots.[42] The sequence does the work of classical storytelling—giving us information about the personalities of several major and minor characters—while evoking that fleeting quality that strikes so many critics as indelibly modern.[43] The opening shot of Alfred Green's film *Union Depot* (1932) (*Grand Hotel* in a train station) is even more delirious, taking full advantage of the crane's heightened mobility. Rather than establish plot points, the elaborate camerawork establishes a breezy, cynical tone by stringing together a series of ethnic jokes. *Union Depot* is often offensive, but its mobile frame pictures a complex, multiethnic America in a way that the homogeneous *Transatlantic* does not even attempt.

Of course, there is nothing inherently modern about convergence, in the cinema or otherwise. Cecil B. DeMille's film *The Crusades* (1935), set in medieval times, uses a town square to introduce three sets of characters who do not yet know each other; Victor Milner's camera cranes from one group to the next, emphasizing their incipient convergence. Nor is the idea unique to American subjects; many films with non-American subjects use convergence to connote otherness. Jules Furthman's screenplay for *Morocco* (1930) makes the strategy explicit, calling for a "moving shot" to depict a group of passengers on a ship approaching the harbor: "We see Greeks, Armenians, Turks, Spaniards, Italians, Senegals, Arabs, Moors, a band of gypsies [sic], a sleek Chinaman [sic] in European clothes, a couple of smart-looking French colonial officers, a shabby young Swede, a shabby old Englishman, all standing at the rail and staring at the land with the strange look of those who have wandered far."[44] Most of the characters depicted here will play no role in the story. Their function is to mark the location as cosmopolitan and exotic—cosmopolitan enough to serve as the backdrop to a story about two outsiders (played by American Gary Cooper and Paramount's new import from Germany, Marlene Dietrich) and exotic enough to motivate the inclusion of as much Orientalist imagery as the director, Josef von Sternberg, could pack into a frame. Following the same logic, the M-G-M film editor Basil Wrangell once wrote that the best way to introduce a hypothetical sequence in Shanghai would be to show "the amazingly cosmopolitan crowds in the Foreign Quarter."[45] By using racial diversity as the signifier of the exotic, Wrangell tacitly acknowledged the segregation of many American spaces.

Discussing such atmospheric sequences, Wrangell posed an important practical problem: "The background can't be allowed to leap forward and stop the story; so how do we arrange it? In general, we establish our atmospheric background at the beginning of a sequence, and then let it flow along as a natural undercurrent behind the action."[46] Instead of taking away from the story, an atmospheric convergence shot should give us a better understanding of the characters and their situations, thereby allowing the story to proceed. Consider an extraordinary shot from *Algiers* (1938). Art director Alexander Toluboff designed an elaborate Casbah set with narrow corridors and uneven ground. Because it would have been impossible to lay tracks down on this unusual surface, cinematographer James Wong Howe worked with dolly grip Buz Gibson and camera operator Arthur Arling to design an elaborate rigging system that would suspend the camera from an overhead railing.[47] In one scene, the French criminal Pépé le Moko (Charles Boyer) sits on his window ledge and sings a song. The camera wanders away from Pépé to reveal his neighbors, who listen to the song with obvious enjoyment. The choreography is astonishing. The camera moves backward, tilts up to show a woman dancing behind a barred window, tilts down to a reveal some more dancing neighbors, pans left and right while continuing its backward movement, sweeps left and right even more broadly to take in more of the crowd, and then dollies back slowly, eventually revealing Slimane (Joseph Calleia), a detective who has been trying to capture Pépé for years. This last image provides an immediate narrative payoff: Slimane is keeping an eye on Pépé. Meanwhile, the shot characterizes the neighborhood as a heterogeneous but thriving community: heterogeneous because casting and costuming create the impression of a chaotic mixture of races, genders, and faiths and thriving because the camera movement sites this diverse grouping in a shared space. However ebullient, the strangeness of the shot subtly undercuts Pépé's utopian hope for community amid colonization. At one point, the camera sweeps past a man wearing a fez and eating a banana to reveal a man wearing a fedora and playing with a ball-and-cup toy. The jarring nature of these contrasts suggests that the sense of happy unity may be less organic than it appears. In the end, Pépé will leave his community and die.

Even films that locate convergence in exotic locations were subject to Hollywood's official restrictions and tacit norms regulating the depiction of race on American screens. The musical *Footlight Parade* culminates in one of Busby Berkeley's most spectacular numbers, "Shanghai Lil." James Cagney plays an American sailor looking for his onetime love, Shanghai Lil, played by Ruby Keeler wearing "yellowface" makeup. In one shot, Cagney's sailor enters a bar, and the camera dollies left to right, revealing a series of patrons talking about Lil. At the end of the shot, the camera whip-pans to the right, picking up the sailor again as he exits. Formally, the shot is similar to the previously described seriality shot from the number "We're in the Money"; the camera starts on one subject (Cagney), moves down the line to reveal one face after another, and then surprises us by returning to the original subject. Functionally, the emphasis has shifted from gendered seriality to racial and ethnic convergence. The scene depicts various racial and ethnic groups: white American sailors, black colonial soldiers, a Jewish man in a tuxedo, a Chinese man wearing glasses. It is significant (and appalling) that most of the Asian women are played by white performers wearing makeup. *Footlight Parade* was released in 1933, the year before Hollywood tightened its system of self-regulation, and "Shanghai Lil" hints at the forbidden theme of miscegenation but does so ambiguously, suggesting the possibility of a sexual relationship between Cagney's sailor and Keeler's Lil and yet reminding us that the possibility is entirely fictional, enacted by white actors playing white dancers performing made-up roles on a stage. The shot may gesture toward convergence, but the racist use of yellowface makeup renders the sequence much less transgressive than it otherwise would be, suggesting that the mixture of races is more apparent than real.

Where does convergence happen? "Shanghai Lil" locates convergence in a flagrantly fictional elsewhere. Berkeley's title number in *42nd Street* (1933) locates convergence in the heart of New York City. After Ruby Keeler performs one of her quirky taps, we see a series of connective cranes, expertly photographed by the same team that shot *Union Depot*.[48] In one shot, the camera cranes down toward a salon next door to a hotel. Outside the hotel, the doorman and a wealthy woman dance separately; inside the salon, a man rubs a woman's face to the beat; outside the salon, a mismatched couple walks hand in hand. In just a few seconds, the shot has offered a series of juxtapositions: a working-class African American man and a wealthy white woman; a male salon employee at work and a female client at leisure; an unusually tall man and an unusually short woman. When the camera cranes from one dancer to the next, the point is not to show that causality connects the dancers; rather, it is to show that urban space creates the most unexpected pairings.

A film might extol convergence or condemn it. Rouben Mamoulian's *Love Me Tonight* (1932) celebrates the mixing of the modern city—in this case, Paris. When Maurice (Maurice Chevalier) sings "How Are You?" to everyone in town, the camera dollies joyously along, its energy amplified by occasional zooms. *Gone with the Wind* (Victor Fleming, 1939) rejects convergence, as in a bluntly racist scene showing Scarlett (Vivien Leigh) disgusted by the mixture of races in post–Civil War Atlanta, where the shot's commotion signifies chaos rather than freedom. James Whale's *Show Boat* (1936) represents convergence in the American South with more complexity. In one early scene, after the boat pulls into town, a shot dollying along a crowd of white extras cuts into a very similar shot dollying along a crowd of African American extras, which cuts into a dolly shot following two (apparently) white performers (played by Helen Morgan and Donald Cook). Although the cuts enforce rigid segregation between the two crowds, with whites massed together in one shot and African Americans massed in another, the flowing movement across the cut hints at the forbidden idea that they might be linked together. Indeed, we later learn that Julie, one of the performers, is of mixed race. The local authorities force Julie and her husband to leave town, and the camera, mounted on the Broadway Boom, cranes up from the scene of their departure to find Joe (Paul Robeson), watching in sympathy (fig. 3.9a–b). The segregation of the cut has become the convergence of the crane.[49]

Though convergence might happen anywhere, the massing of strangers side by side was a salient aspect of the modern city, made all the more significant in the United States because such configurations brought to the fore the long-standing conflict between democratic ideals and segregated reality. In 1938, urban theorist Louis Wirth wrote, "Cities generally, and American cities in particular, comprise a motley of peoples and cultures of highly differentiated

3.9 In *Show Boat*, a boom shot connects two expelled performers with Joe.

modes of life between which there often is only the faintest communication, the greatest indifference, the broadest tolerance, occasionally bitter strife, but always the sharpest contrast." Wirth argued that "heterogeneity" was one of the defining factors of urbanism, along with population and density.[50] Twenty-two years later Lewis Mumford argued with characteristic eloquence that the function of the city "is to permit—indeed, to encourage—the greatest possible number of meetings, encounters, challenges, between varied persons and groups."[51] More recently, in her history of American downtowns Alison Isenberg has examined the competing pressures that shaped the urban center in the twentieth century: "In the divided city (microcosm of a divided nation), the downtown has served as a potential place of interaction and negotiation of difference—a place of community gathering as well as all kinds of conflict. A dominant theme of twentieth-century urban life was the division of the city and the emergence of a world inhabited by separate races, classes, genders, and ethnic groups, but the democratic ideal of the downtown has optimistically suggested otherwise."[52] The hope that downtown might serve as a site of community emerged as an inspiring but occasionally troubling ideal—troubling not just because the hope has so often gone unrealized but also because the very definition of "community" might serve as a means of exclusion, for all its seeming inclusivity. These are the sorts of ambivalences that the Hollywood city film might address—or conspicuously ignore.

Mervyn LeRoy's film *Two Seconds* (1932) turns the convergent space of an American downtown into a joke. In his autobiography, the director explained that he was proud to have learned about "real people" while working as a newsboy in San Francisco as a child: "I met the cops and the whores and the reporters and the bartenders and the Chinese and the fishermen and the shopkeepers."[53] The same glib tone characterizes the city scenes in *Two Seconds*, set in New York. An early scene shows the protagonist, a shy construction worker (Edward G. Robinson), out on the town with his more sociable friend Bud (Preston Foster). Bud spots two women on the street and walks over to introduce himself, passing a chop suey restaurant along the way. As the camera follows Bud, an Asian American man enters the frame and walks alongside him, exiting the frame only after Bud arrives at the women. Normally, when the camera follows one person, other characters who enter the frame will walk at a different pace, to ensure that the primary character remains uncontested in the center of the frame. Here, Bud and the unnamed man walk at the same pace, and the result is a curious "double" follow shot, as if the camera were following two people at the same time even though the two men have nothing to do with each other besides contiguity. The resulting shot asks us to laugh at an incongruous juxtaposition, contrasting the two men in terms of age, height, and outfit, but above all in terms of race. The film makes a joke of downtown as a space of convergence. Isn't it funny, the shot asks, that the city should bring such different people together?

Another site of convergence was the apartment building; its architecture put different people side by side. *Sunnyside Up*, David Butler's early-sound-era musical from 1929, provided a powerful prototype. Technologically, the Fox Films production owed a clear debt to the studio's late silent masterpieces. As Jakob Isak Nielsen explains, cinematographer Ernest Palmer had collaborated with both Borzage and Murnau; the film's art director Harry Oliver was the same craftsman who designed the prototype crane for *Street Angel* (1928).[54] *Sunnyside Up* introduces a tenement neighborhood in a single shot lasting more than three minutes. After pushing through the middle of a game of street baseball, the camera cranes up to introduce one tiny apartment after another, each the scene of a comic vignette, such as a crying child getting a soup-bowl haircut and an older woman angry with her husband for reading the salacious *Police Gazette*. Without cutting, the camera crosses the street and shows an apartment on the other side, featuring an Italian American man ineptly asserting authority over his wife as she threatens him with a rolling pin. The joke marks the tenement as a space of ethnic heterogeneity, in contrast to the homogeneity that will characterize the film's other primary location: upper-crust Long Island.

Commenting on the history of tenements, the urban historian Larry Ford explains, "In the nineteenth century, most tenements and apartments had been built specifically for one race." During the 1920s, a boom in office and department store construction led to more demand for workers, and "apartment buildings evolved to provide a variety of housing for a variety of people."[55] But racial discrimination persisted (and persists). Offscreen, segregated housing policies excluded African Americans from many buildings. Onscreen patterns of segregation were just as rigid, if not more so. Instead of showing a desegregated and ethnically mixed space, *Sunnyside Up*'s opening sequence gestures obliquely toward the city's heterogeneity by showing a wide variety of ages: we see young children, teenagers, a young couple in love, a middle-aged policeman, and more. Age stands in for unrepresented forms of diversity. More abstractly, Butler's film gestures toward the ideal of inclusive diversity through its form. Imagine the same scene as a simple seriality shot, moving methodically down the row; the emphasis would be on the sameness of the apartment dwellers. Instead, the camera's motion is filled with surprises: down the street, panning to the right, craning up, tracking backward, swinging across the street, craning back down, and tracking backward once again. The unpredictability of the camera's movements mirrors the unpredictability of the neighborhood. In spite of the crying children and abusive spouses, the sequence presents the tenement positively, as a site of uninhibited emotion.[56]

With its complex camerawork and staccato montage, King Vidor's film *Street Scene* would become one of the defining city films of the period. As in the play from 1929 on which it was based, the film's story takes place entirely on the street in front of a New York brownstone. Elmer Rice, the author of the original play, explained, "I conceived the house as the real protagonist of the drama . . . which integrated and gave a kind of dramatic unity to the sprawling and unrelated lives of the multitudinous characters."[57] The apartment building is simultaneously a place of convergence and alienation, allowing different groups of people to live together while their lives remain unconnected. Even among the major characters, there is little sense of community in Rice's play: one of the first characters we meet is Mrs. Jones, a bigot who spouts anti-Polish and anti-Semitic views; another character, Mr. Maurrant, is a vicious nativist who expresses particular hostility toward Mr. Kaplan, a Jewish Communist.[58] Rice evokes the theme of disconnection by employing an unusually large cast, featuring two dozen speaking parts and several additional characters who wander past the building and are never seen again. The converging fates of the principals are set against the nonconverging fates of the bit characters. For the film version, Vidor resolved to keep the play's single setting while maintaining visual interest with an ever-changing style: "We would never repeat a camera set up twice. If the setting couldn't change, the camera would."[59] Like the play, *Street Scene* distributes attention across its very large cast. One shot presents nine characters, including Steve Sankey (Russell Hopton) and Anna Maurrant (Estelle Taylor). The scene has already hinted at what will turn out to be a crucial plot point: Steve and Anna are having an affair. But Vidor's preferred camera technique—call it the follow-and-switch—forces us to situate Steve and Anna in a larger context (see table 3.1).

Over the course of forty-seven seconds, the camera pans to follow four separate characters: Steve (crucial to the plot), a woman with a stroller (a bit part of no consequence to the story), Mrs. Cushing (a minor speaking part), and Mrs. Jones (an important secondary character). By following both the principals

TABLE 3.1 The "Follow-and-Switch" Technique in *Street Scene* (1931)

Composition	Camera follows . . .	. . . as she or he walks past . . .
1	Steve	Mr. Kaplan, Anna, Mr. Jones, Mrs. Fiorentino, Mrs. Jones, and the woman with the stroller
2	Woman with the stroller	Mrs. Jones, Mrs. Fiorentino, Mr. Jones, Miss Cushing, and Anna
3	Mrs. Cushing	Anna, Mr. Jones, Mrs. Fiorentino, and Mrs. Jones
4	Mrs. Jones	Mrs. Fiorentino, Mr. Jones, and Anna

and the extras, Vidor evokes the sense of contingency that was one of the play's signature features, as if the melodramatic central story line were not intrinsically more important than random events. The neighborhood itself appears to be the product of contingency: not an organic unit but a set of disparate people thrown together with no sense of shared purpose.

Although *Street Scene* came out in 1931, it was written before the start of the Great Depression. The next section considers how the Depression forced filmmakers to rethink the themes of dynamism, seriality, and convergence.

Stasis and Movement in the Great Depression

The Great Depression was a tricky subject for Hollywood filmmakers. Directors knew how to tell stories about individuals, but they did not necessarily know how to tell stories about the masses. Screenwriters knew how to link together cause and effect, but they did not necessarily know how to explain that a person's suffering was caused by the breakdown of an abstract economic system. Actors knew how to play a goal-driven protagonist, but they did not necessarily know how to characterize a person in utter despair, with no objective and no power to achieve change.

Perhaps because studio filmmakers were constrained by professional norms, some of the most famous American movies about the Great Depression were not Hollywood productions at all. The U.S. government sponsored *The Plow That Broke the Plains* (1936) and *The River* (1938), produced by documentarian Pare Lorentz. A recurring theme in both films is the convergence of the American economy. Plains and rivers stretch across several states, and they ultimately affect the lives of everyone in the country. By making the case that agriculture is a national problem ("From as far west as Idaho . . . from as far east as Pennsylvania"), these documentaries endorse national solutions, such as the Tennessee Valley Authority. The films rely visually on maps and montage to express this theme of connectedness, showing diagrams of the plains and cutting from one river to the next, from the Monongahela to the Red to the Ohio to the Yazoo.

In Hollywood, some filmmakers dodged the crisis by making films that ignored the Great Depression entirely, offering escapist fantasies instead. Other filmmakers tackled the issues while working within a resolutely classical mode, showing can-do protagonists surmounting every obstacle. Still others exploited a creative tension between competing forces. They told stories about goal-oriented individuals, as usual, but they used camerawork to characterize the enormity of the Depression. In the best of these examples, the filmmakers managed to make their stories more emotionally compelling precisely by showing how their directed protagonists might falter against the crisis's inevitable limits on human agency.

William Wellman's maternal melodrama *Frisco Jenny* (1932) portrays the San Francisco earthquake of 1906—a natural disaster that serves as a clear metaphor for the devastation of the Great Depression. One moment the city is thriving; the next moment everything has collapsed. In one scene, the protagonist, Jenny Sandoval (Ruth Chatterton), walks through a makeshift camp set up for displaced survivors of the quake. The camera dollies backward, preceding Jenny as she walks ahead; when she turns her head to the left, the camera pans to show a group of African Americans gathered by a tent and then pans back to pick up Jenny as she continues through the camp. We have seen the earthquake level buildings, but here the impact of the catastrophe is represented as a different kind of leveling, destroying distinctions of race and class. The movement presents the shot semisubjectively, as if the camera were momentarily adopting Jenny's point of view, encouraging the audience to share her sense of estrangement.

Stories of the Depression often deployed the moving camera to introduce new twists on the themes of dynamism, seriality, and convergence: dynamism because a dizzying dolly or crane might express a sense of overwhelming chaos; seriality because the camera might suggest that the Depression has "mass-produced" poverty; convergence because a judicious pan might reveal the forced intersection of strangers. Nobody was required to use the moving camera to evoke these ideas, but the dolly and crane emerged as eloquent options. Even Busby Berkeley's musical numbers addressed the Depression, most notably "Forgotten Man" in *Gold Diggers of 1933*. After Carol (Joan Blondell) finishes her torch song, the film cuts to a down-on-his-luck man walking around a corner (fig. 3.10a). Then the camera cranes up to reveal African American singer Etta Moten as a war widow singing the chorus (fig. 3.10b). Moten sits on the window sill of a lonely room; soon, the camera cranes away to show another war widow in the same apartment building (fig. 3.10c) and then down again to show a third apartment, occupied by an older woman in mourning (fig. 3.10d). Recalling the window-to-window sequence of *Sunnyside Up*, we can see how the craning movement in *Gold Diggers of 1933* serves to unite the African American Moten with two white women, the pain in Moten's voice giving expression to their suffering. War and poverty have brought these women together. But the camera movement separates as much as it unites: the apartment's rooms are far apart, isolating each woman within her respective window frame.

The specific argument of the song is to insist that the government fulfill its obligations to World War I veterans; more broadly, the musical number calls for New Deal–style government programs to address widespread unemployment directly. Later we see a group of men receiving sandwiches in a breadline, and the camera dollies down the row to show a dozen men, hungry but still proud. Whereas the women of "We're in the Money" are presented as near-identical copies, the breadline shot foregrounds individual differences: some

3.10 Etta Moten sings "Forgotten Man" in *Gold Diggers of 1933*.

of the men are movie-star handsome, but some are not; some are tall, but some are short; some grasp their lapels to ward off the cold, but some share a cigarette. Significantly, the shot's emphasis on difference does not extend to racial difference: all of the men appear to be white. In his recent history of the Great Depression, historian Ira Katznelson has argued that our admiration for the very real accomplishments of the New Deal must be qualified by a recognition of its troubling racial politics: many of its programs were sold as measures to get white men back on their feet, even as national politicians agreed to let southern Democrats extend the oppressions of Jim Crow.[60] The "Forgotten Man" number offers a similarly contradictory ideology, at times suggesting that poverty is a problem for all races, at times suggesting that the solution should be aimed at one group in particular: white men.

These reservations apply even more strongly to one of the era's boldest Depression-themed films, King Vidor's *Our Daily Bread* (1934). A sequel to Vidor's late-silent-era classic *The Crowd*, the film shows John and Mary becoming farmers. The earlier film showed cameras flying up skyscrapers; the later one is photographed in a sober style, using editing rather than camera movement to structure most of its scenes. Nevertheless, even the simplest dollies retain significance. John (Tom Keene) hopes to hire a wide range of skilled men to work together on a collective farm. He interviews the applicants one by one, and the camera follows him as he walks down the line, revealing a barber, a cigar salesman, a high-class pants presser, a plumber, a carpenter, a violinist, and a stonemason. John scoffs at the men with fussy trades and praises the men with the most practical skills, but it is clear that he respects any man who is willing to work. The cinematography visually reinforces this theme of unity amid diversity, linking the men together by including them in a single shot. Significantly, Vidor uses a different treatment for an angry man who insists on driving the tractor. Rather than dollying to include this divisive figure in the long take, the film cuts to him directly, following the familiar (but contextually dependent) idea that the moving camera unites where the cut divides. Though Our Daily Bread's communal impulse was unusual and even brave, the film's theme of inclusion was quite limited, encompassing occupational differences between white men while excluding women and other races altogether.

In all of these examples, the filmmakers try to understand the Great Depression from the perspective of the poor and the struggling. Quite a few Hollywood films approached the Great Depression very differently—by taking the side of the wealthy. For instance, Frank Capra's American Madness (1932) shows a banker facing a run on his bank. The film depicts its protagonist as an honorable individual struggling against the crowd's unreasonable behavior. During the bank run, the camera dollies down a row of patrons as panic mounts. Two men in ties agree, "We're a lot of suckers." A sophisticated woman exchanges complaints with a wiseguy. She says, "Outrageous." He replies, "It's worse than that, lady. It's lousy." The image is not a follow shot, timed to one person's movement; rather, the camera switches from one pairing to the next, emphasizing convergence. Normally, these characters would have nothing to do with each other, but the crisis of the economy has brought them here together. Even worse, the crisis is turning these individuals into a mass. Left alone, no one would withdraw his or her money, but each person who makes a withdrawal induces others to do the same. A moment later the protagonist, Dickson (Walter Huston), arrives to offer reassurance that the bank will not run out of money. Unlike the previous example, the shot of Dickson is a follow shot, keeping the goal-directed banker in the center of the composition.

Another bank-themed drama, Prosperity (1932), features variations on the same two techniques, centering protagonists while sweeping past crowds. Marie Dressler plays Maggie, who owns a small-town bank. When a panic begins, Maggie walks through the lobby to reassure her depositors; the camera moves laterally from left to right to follow Maggie, just as Capra's camera follows Dickson. The movement keeps Dressler in the center of the frame, echoing the reassuring order that she brings to the crowd. In the next scene, we learn that Maggie's callow son has invested the bank's bonds in a get-rich-quick scheme. When the film cuts back to the lobby, the panic has taken on a new sense of desperation. Now the camera dollies laterally from right to left very rapidly, turning the crowd into a blur. As in *American Madness*, a pair of shots has depicted the contrast between the individual agency of a responsible banker and the near anarchy of a panicking crowd, attaching the camera to figure movement in the former case and allowing the camera to roam freely in the latter. The result articulates a distinctly conservative ideological attitude to the Depression, placing the blame on a few unscrupulous criminals and a lot of irrational everyday people, while upholding the virtues of small-market capitalism by depicting the local banker as a figure of folksy wisdom.

Cultural historians such as Warren Susman and Lawrence Levine remind us that the culture of the 1930s was multifaceted: although millions confronted unemployment and scarcity, millions more continued to enjoy the ongoing transition to a culture of mass consumption.[61] A series of films set in department stores depicted these contrasting cultures, highlighting the bounty of consumer capitalism even in the middle of economic despair. An exuberant scene in *Sweepings* uses a lateral tracking shot to reveal consumers pressing against the counter during a manic sale event, associating visual dynamism with over-the-top abundance. (Ironically, this representation of pre-Depression consumer frenzy resembles the chaotic depiction of a bank panic: capitalism at its most energetic compared with capitalism at its worst.) In a much more somber scene in *Employees' Entrance*, the cold-hearted store manager, Anderson (Warren William), refuses to rehire Higgins (Charles Sellon), who has served the company for decades. The camera follows Higgins as he walks in despair across the storeroom floor, revealing one refrigerator after another. The contrast between the devastation on Higgins's face and the commerce on display utters a silent rebuke to Anderson's heartlessness.

Clarence Brown's department store drama *Looking Forward* (1933) reworks both ideas, first celebrating the store's abundance and then using that abundance as counterpoint to the firing of a loyal employee. Lewis Stone plays Service, the benevolent owner of a once-great but now struggling store in London. Early in the film, Service is riding in an elevator with Benton, a kind but unambitious accountant played by Lionel Barrymore. Rather than rely on rear projection, the filmmakers stage the scene in a real elevator, which opens up onto four separate floors, allowing extras to walk on and off.[62] The unity of this proto-Wellesian shot, displaying all four floors in wide-angle deep focus without a cut, comes to symbolize the unity of the company, pictured as an organic whole in which the boss and the employees share a single purpose, signaled by the owner's none-too-subtle name: Service. The concept of "service" extends to ownership itself; Service is a man who feels an obligation to treat his employees with paternal care. Under pressure from his colleagues, Service later betrays that obligation and fires the obsolete Benton, who leaves his boss's office and descends mutely on the escalator. The ascending elevator shot depicted the company as a family, with friendly interactions among employees great and small—everyone moved up together. The escalator shot shows Benton moving down, all alone, with the vast expanse of the store stretching off into the distance, signifying an opulence that mocks Benton's misery.

Although all three of these films offer criticisms of consumer capitalism, they end up endorsing that system. Indeed, Hollywood released a number of films about businessmen in the early 1930s, many promoting an ugly toughen-up ideology to the right of Herbert Hoover's, calling on the businessman to exercise leadership in the face of economic crisis even if it meant firing loyal employees. The businessman in such films may be benevolent, as in *Looking Forward* or *The Working Man* (1933), or rapacious, as in *Employees' Entrance* or *Skyscraper Souls*, but it is up to him to fix the economy, New Deal or no New Deal. We may be outraged when Higgins commits suicide in *Employees' Entrance*, but the predatory Anderson ends up saving the company from a class of villains even lower than the businessman: big-city bankers. We may be disappointed when Service fires Benton in *Looking Forward*, but the firing turns out to be the best thing to happen to both men. These films address the ideological challenges of the Great Depression by telling stories of failing stores, and they end up suggesting that the Depression will turn out to be a great opportunity, punishing the complacent and restoring the self-made ideal. This was an audacious—and appalling—argument to make when millions of people were facing the direst poverty.[63]

In *Dancing in the Dark*, a history of literature and film during the Depression, Morris Dickstein writes, "The Depression not only challenged America's economy and its political system, but also undermined the central myths and beliefs on which the system was founded." In particular, he points out that the 1930s were "the first period in which the phrase 'the American Dream' was commonly used, just when its premise of limitless opportunity and economic abundance seemed suddenly in doubt."[64] Similarly, these department store films raise doubts about the viability of the American Dream only to quash those doubts. Clarence Brown, the director of *Looking Forward*, described himself as a "red hot conservative," proud to make films about "the great American dream." But he freely admitted that the rags-to-riches story was an "impossible dream," offering little more than a thread of hope.[65]

If films such as *Sweepings* and *Looking Forward* depict seriality in order to reassure us that the economy that once produced abundance can do so again, then a more critical film such as Fritz Lang's *You and Me* (1938) questions whether abundance is a worthy ideal at all. Set to a musical score by Kurl Weill, the opening montage features a narrator proclaiming, "Whatever you see that you really want, you may have, provided you buy it. You'd like to live a life of luxury, wearing ermine wraps, a bracelet perhaps, or this sparkling gem. Remember they cannot belong to you, until you pay for them!" American capitalism, the film charges, turns everything into a commodity, precisely by stimulating desires that most people cannot possibly fulfill. Listening to this sardonic critique, we see serial images of the commodities described. A lateral tracking shot past some tableware dissolves to another tracking shot past coats and still another past jewelry, the seriality of one shot flowing into the seriality of the next, as if the consumer culture were so abundant that it will flow forever beyond the frame. Like the voiceover ("You'd like to live a life of luxury"), these sparkling images are presented to us directly, inciting our own desires. Yet the tracking shot avers that our desires can never be attained. Each consumer object moves offscreen just as quickly as it moved on.

In his book *Hollywood Modernism*, Saverio Giovacchini argues that many filmmakers of the 1930s, especially those on the left, embraced the ideals of "democratic modernism." Intellectuals, artists, and filmmakers of the period turned away from the excessive experimentation with form that characterized high modernism in favor of a broadly realist aesthetic that appealed to the masses by telling narratives of "the people."[66] I close this consideration of the Great Depression on film with two sequences about "the people": *The Grapes of Wrath* (1940) and *City for Conquest* (1940). Though both examples use the moving camera to comment on the abstract ideal of "the people," they represent that ideal in very different ways.

The ending of John Ford's film *The Grapes of Wrath* is justly famous, depicting Ma Joad (Jane Darwell) as she delivers her monologue: "We'll go on forever, Pa, 'cause we're the people." But the film's depiction of the people is not nearly as hopeful as these stirring words suggest. An earlier scene shows the Joads' truck pulling into a camp for migrant workers; cinematographer Gregg Toland described the shot as "a long travel shot through the sordid streets of a Hooverville."[67] As the heavily laden truck pushes ahead, wary onlookers step out of the way, and new migrants step into the frame, each one as leery as the last. Film critic Otis Ferguson mentioned this shot in his review: "The camera manages the whole story of the Okie camp as it moves down shack after shack, face after face, silent, hostile, and defeated."[68] Note the evocation of seriality: "shack after shack," "face after face." For readers of the novel, the shot's seriality may recall the rhythmic repetitions of Steinbeck's prose.[69]

Stylistically, the shot recalls the introduction of the neighborhood in Ford's earlier film *Four Sons*, discussed in chapter 1. In both, the camera enters a moderately shallow area and then moves to the right, revealing a corridor-like space for the camera to explore. But the meanings differ. In *Four Sons*, the postman ambles through town to connect the members of the community. In *The Grapes of Wrath*, the shot lacks a unifying center, and we see an assemblage of people who are still too shaken from the catastrophe to bond together in a meaningful way. Toland's wide-angle lens emphasizes the distance between the figures, visible in the prominent differences in scale between foreground and background. Most of the migrants walk in pairs or groups, but these clusters remain isolated from each other. A man and woman walk offscreen right (fig. 3.11a), then a woman with her children walks offscreen left (fig. 3.11b), and then two women hold for a beat before walking offscreen left (fig. 3.11c). No one remains onscreen for long. The camera even dollies past characters who will become important later, such as the man whose reasonable protest against corrupt labor-recruiting practices leads to an eruption of police violence (fig. 3.11d). With relentless movement, the transience of the composition echoes the transience of the characters, who know that they will never see their homes again. A more despairing picture of "the people" could hardly be imagined.

By contrast, the opening of *City for Conquest* is gloriously exuberant—a celebration of the theme of convergence. The film was written by the leftist screenwriter (and future blacklist victim) John Wexley and directed by Anatole Litvak, a Jewish European émigré who had directed the landmark anti-Nazi film *Confessions of a Nazi Spy* the previous year. As the film begins, a puzzled policeman (Ward Bond) harasses a loquacious homeless man called Old Timer (Frank Craven), who responds by offering a paean to New York City: "They come by the thousands, every which way: by water, by wheel, by foot, by ferry, by tunnel, by tube. Over, across, and under the river . . . from all over the nation,

3.11 In *The Grapes of Wrath*, a shifting composition represents a transient community.

from every nation on the globe. Seven million people, divided by a river and joined by bridges." Old Timer soon turns out to be a bit of a con artist, but here he is represented as a source of true wisdom. And his insight is that people who might have nothing in common can still come together to form a community: a city. Divided by a river and joined by bridges—the city connects people together, but it does not and should not form them into a homogeneous mass. The sequence visually echoes Old Timer's words through Litvak's use of camera movement. The camera initially frames a simple two-shot of the policeman and the homeless man, standing against a rear-projected cityscape (fig. 3.12a). Suddenly, a third man enters the frame, moving from right to left (fig. 3.12b). The camera rack focuses to the foreground and pans to the left, following the man as he takes our attention away from the character who is speaking. It is a shocking illustration of the very principle that Old Timer is propounding: New York is a city of strangers, and that is its strength. This third man is unknown to the policeman and to Old Timer, and he will prove irrelevant to the plot, but, as in *Street Scene*, the film finds him sufficiently worthy of attention to follow, even in the middle of another man's speech. After following the third man for just a second, the film dissolves to a manic city montage, a cacophony of canted

3.12 In *City for Conquest*, the camera pans to follow a random stranger; this movement initiates a lively montage.

angles, cityscapes, and crowd shots (fig. 3.12c–d). The montage is chaotic—and thrilling. Convergence has become dynamism: the source of New York's energy is its ability to draw strangers together. The rest of the film is comparatively bleak, proposing boxing as a metaphor for capitalism: a ruthless sport that leaves everyone injured. This exuberant opening offers the humanistic celebration of "the people" as an alternative.

Together, *The Grapes of Wrath* and *City for Conquest* demonstrate that the moving camera had become a remarkably flexible tool by the end of the 1930s, capable of expressing a wide range of meanings: dynamism and chaos, seriality and convergence, celebration and critique. The U.S. entry into World War II would bring the Great Depression to an end, but the ideas explored here would remain as relevant as ever.

The Moving Camera at War

During the preproduction of *Casablanca* (1942), a Warner Bros. memo noted that the play was an obvious imitation of *Grand Hotel*, the paradigmatic tale of convergence.[70] Everybody comes to Rick's: refugees and their Nazi persecutors; soldiers, policemen, and civilians; Europeans, Americans, and even a few Moroccans. Like the Great Depression, World War II gave new salience to the theme of convergence.[71]

In the combat genre, countless films represented the army, the navy, and the marines as collections of strangers who learn to work together. At the end of *Destination Tokyo* (1943), the camera dollies past eight sailors, each one rhapsodizing about a different desire: getting drunk on cider, listening to Dinah Shore records, or eating green vegetables. The dialogue reveals that these men were originally unknown to each other—men from different parts of the country, with competing ideas of the good life. But the camera movement qualifies this point in two ways: first, by suggesting that these disparate men have come together to form a group; second, by suggesting that joining the group has not compromised their individuality. The sailors remain individuals with specific desires, even as their shared experiences have made them comfortable sharing their desires with each other. As if to underscore this delicate balance of singularity and solidarity, the dolly presents the first four men in two-shots and the next four men in singles (fig. 3.13a–b). The two-shots suggest that the men are speaking to each other, but the singles suggest that each man is also speaking to himself.

Call this start-and-stop technique the "person-to-person motif." The camera moves from one person to the next, encouraging us to notice their differences and appreciate their similarities. The shot produces its meaning by creating an impression of sampling. These eight men with their eight desires stand in for

3.13 At the end of *Destination Tokyo*, the camera dollies along a row of returning sailors.

many more men with many more desires. To understand that the film is offering us a part to stand for a larger whole, we must appreciate that the view is fragmentary—a representative selection from a population too big to see. The person-to-person shot was a variation on the convergence technique, placing special emphasis on the moments when the camera holds on individualized compositions. By using a part to represent a whole, the person-to-person shot does ideological work. As "America, the Beautiful" plays on the soundtrack, *Destination Tokyo* celebrates the diversity of the United States while setting sharp limits on the nature of that diversity. Most of the men are nicknamed in accordance with jobs or traits: Cookie (the cook), Pills (the pharmacist), and Wolf (the womanizer). All of the men are white. The diversity on display is the diversity of desire: for food, for women, for cultural experiences. The dolly's gesture of unification even excludes the officers, who are represented in a separate stationary shot.

Offscreen, many citizens were struggling for deeper forms of diversity. African American soldiers spoke of fighting for a double victory, defeating racism abroad and at home.[72] Many of the New Dealers who ran the Office of War Information (OWI) shared their objections to segregation, and they encouraged filmmakers to represent the armed forces as unified but multiple, offering the nation and the world a more inspiring (if inaccurate) image. The OWI even produced a manual outlining norms that it expected Hollywood to follow. As the historians Clayton Koppes and Gregory Black explain, "The multi-ethnic platoon, 'using names of foreign extraction' (what American names were not of foreign extraction?) and showing occasional black officers, would strengthen the impression of national unity."[73] The goal was to represent the war as a "people's war," in which everyone had a stake.[74] These interventions occasionally backfired. Filmmakers routinely ignored the OWI's pleas to tone down anti-Japanese racism, and many filmmakers avoided racial stereotypes by "writing out" African American characters altogether.[75] Nevertheless, the multiethnic platoon came to be a defining convention of the combat genre.

Jeanine Basinger describes *Bataan* (1943) as the seminal combat movie, showing a "collection of misfits" who become "a coherent fighting group."[76] Just as importantly, *Bataan* provided a model for how the moving camera might structure the multiethnic platoon's visual representation. The director, Tay Garnett, had been an exponent of camera movement for more than a decade, most notably in early sound films such as *Prestige* and *One Way Passage* (both 1932). In *Bataan*, Sergeant Bill Dane (Robert Taylor) finds himself leading a ragtag group of men. One scene shows Dane asking each man to introduce himself; in order, he meets Purckett, Salazar, Hardy, Ramirez, Epps, Matowski, Malloy, Feingold, and Todd.[77] Each interview underscores the film's guiding theme that the group's heterogeneity—different ethnicities, different ranks, different services— will be a source of strength, not a problem. Epps (Kenneth Spencer), an African American soldier, already shares a working relationship and friendship with a white soldier from Pittsburgh, Matowski (Barry Nelson). As Elizabeth Reich explains, *Bataan*'s visible multiculturalism works to obscure the imperialism of the long-standing U.S. presence in the Philippines.[78] A Filipino scout's patriotism is signaled by his name: Yankee Salazar (Alex Havier).

While recognizing the group's diversity, Dane learns that two white men will present the biggest trouble spots. The good-hearted Purckett (Robert Walker) seems out of place because he is a member of the navy, not the army; the cold-hearted Todd (Lloyd Nolan) is even more worrisome because he is the only one who treats the sergeant with dangerous disrespect. (We later learn that "Todd" is a fake name and that he has a history with Dane.) The scene visually uses the moving camera to develop the theme of unity, while relying on shot-reverse-shot to single out Dane, Purckett, and Todd. The centerpiece of the scene is a ninety-second dolly shot, looking over Dane's shoulder as he walks down the line. The camera does not glide past each soldier in the manner of a seriality shot; instead, it stops every time Dane stops, granting each individual the attention he deserves. Although formally similar to a follow shot, keeping pace with Dane as he walks down the line, the shot functions primarily as a person-to-person shot, introducing one man and then the next. Crucially, the variable framing refuses to isolate each man from the group (see table 3.2).

Dane speaks to each man one by one, but the camera groups the men into successive pairs: Purckett and Salazar, Salazar and Hardy, Hardy and Ramirez, and so on down the line. An exception to the pattern comes at the end; the suspicious Todd is the only one without a pairing. The imagery foreshadows the upcoming story: Dane will have the hardest time incorporating Todd into the group. At the same time, the film elevates the stories of Dane, Purckett, and Todd above the rest. Purckett's interview comes first, handled in shot-reverse-shot. No

TABLE 3.2 Single Shot Progressing Through Several Different Groupings, *Bataan* (1943)

Composition	In Conversation	Clearly Visible	Shot-Reverse-Shot?
1	Dane and Purckett	Purckett and Salazar	Yes
2	Dane and Salazar	Salazar and Hardy	No
3	Dane and Hardy	Hardy and Ramirez	No
4	Dane and Ramirez	Ramirez and Epps	No
5	Dane, Epps, and Matowski	Epps and Matowski	No
6	Dane and Matowski	Matowski and Malloy	No
7	Dane and Malloy	Malloy and Feingold	No
8	Dane and Feingold	Feingold and Todd	No
9	Dane and Todd	Todd	Yes

other man is given the same shot-reverse-shot treatment—until the camera reaches the last man in line, Todd. In spite of its celebration of the multiethnic platoon, the scene gives special priority to the three protagonists, all of whom are white, and Epps is singled out as the only soldier to cede the conversation to another speaker. The shot's hierarchical pattern qualifies its theme of convergence.

Bataan uses the person-to-person technique to examine short-term convergence: war throws men from different parts of the world together, but just for a moment. Alternatively, a film might use smaller movements to suggest a deeper bond between soldiers. In *Guadalcanal Diary* (1943), the camera pans over a huge group of marines resting on the deck of a ship. Charles Clarke's deep-focus photography renders the scene with exceptional clarity, allowing each man to register as an individual. Then the film individualizes further by cutting to closer views. Potts (William Bendix), a guy from Brooklyn, boasts about the Dodgers; the camera pans to Alvarez (Anthony Quinn), who is remembering Conchita and Lolita in Laredo. The roles are stereotypical, but the effect of intimacy is extraordinary: the shirtless Alvarez rests his head on

Potts's chest, while Potts's arm rests casually behind Alvarez's back. After a cut to another character, the film returns to Alvarez and reverses its earlier movement, tilting from Alvarez back to Potts. Instead of craning from marine to marine to marine, the film has pared the person-to-person shot to an absolute minimum, simply panning from one man to another, later panning back again, suggesting a bond that is so intimate it is almost erotic.

The person-to-person shot may be contrasted with two related techniques: the seriality shot and the montage of faces. A seriality shot moves relentlessly down the line; a montage of faces cuts from one individual to another. The person-to-person shot finds healthy variation within a group. The camera may move in a straight line, or it may crane unpredictably, but the shot gives us enough time to appreciate at least a few of its subjects as individuals. We see this person and then that one, not just a series of interchangeable parts. Like the seriality shot, the person-to-person shot unites a group within a single shot; like the montage of faces, the person-to-person shot pauses to allow individual details to register.

The visual meanings of seriality changed during the 1940s, especially in documentaries that worked to associate homogeneity with the Axis powers. In Frank Capra's film *Prelude to War* (1942), a long montage of the Japanese, Italian, and German armies on parade creates the impression of overwhelming sameness, as if distinct soldiers have formed a soulless mass. The images, borrowed from Leni Riefenstahl's *Triumph of the Will* (1934) and other propaganda films, are nearly abstract, drained of individualized figures, whether the camera moves or not. A later montage in the same film shows a series of "Man on the Street" interviews with American citizens, most of whom still want to stay out of war. Although the montage ridicules the American isolationists, Capra's one-by-one strategy treats them as individuals with their own opinions, in sharp contrast to the highly serialized footage of the Germany army.

For fiction filmmakers, the aesthetic problem of representing seriality had become a deeply ethical one. Those with the courage to address the Nazi threat had to balance the obligation to represent individual victims with the equally pressing obligation to recognize the overwhelming scale of the Nazis' crimes. Fred Zinnemann's *The Seventh Cross* (1944) approached the problem with unusual care, subtly admitting its own compromises. As Vincent Brook has explained, the film (set during the 1930s) was the first Hollywood production to represent a concentration camp.[79] Concerned about an anti-Semitic backlash, M-G-M executives were reluctant to depict Jewish victims of the camps. So the film instead tells the story of seven men who escape from the camp; only one is Jewish. Although the film's director, Zinnemann, a Jewish émigré from Austria, lost his own parents to the Holocaust, he explicitly aimed to make a film that expressed a lingering hope that good might be found among the German people. Right on the cover of his shooting script, Zinnemann wrote, "This is about the dignity of human beings."[80]

Faced with this responsibility, *The Seventh Cross* takes an experimental approach. Early on, Zinnemann considered shooting the film through the protagonist's eyes, using "first person camera."[81] The finished film employs an even more unusual device—voiceover narration by a character who is dead.[82] In the opening scene, the camera dollies past a row of seven wooden crosses, and we hear the voice of actor Ray Collins. Collins had played the role of an already-dead narrator the previous year in M-G-M's film *The Human Comedy*. Here, the narrator, Wallau, projects wisdom—a wisdom deepened by an acknowledgment of his own inadequacy to the task before him. He says, "When all the stories of what happened in Europe have been told, as of course they never can be, *The Seventh Cross* will be remembered as the story of a few little people who proved there is something in the human soul that sets men above the animals." With these words, Jewish screenwriter Helen Deutsch introduces a crucial note of humility, admitting that all the stories "never can be" told. In support of this theme, the camerawork develops a contrast between the seen and unseen. The film opens on a single cross: a piece of wood nailed to a tree. Then the camera begins to dolly away, revealing a second cross and then a third, all the way up to the seventh cross. The bodies of victims hang from two of the crosses; the clothes of absent victims hang from four others. At the end of the shot, the camera dollies in toward the seventh cross, its emptiness standing for the one surviving escapee. In light of the voiceover, the image is rich with meaning. The shot's seriality, revealing one cross after another, gestures to the vastness of the camp's crimes, as if the series could extend forever. And yet the film visually represents its own failure to grasp this vastness. As the camera dollies to the left, it angles to the right, framing a comprehensive view that could take in all or most of the crosses. But the space is increasingly enshrouded in fog, preventing us from seeing all seven crosses at once. The more the camera moves, the more it loses sight of the first few crosses, obscured in haze. Only after offering this (failed) comprehensive view does the camera dolly in toward the seventh cross, cutting all the other crosses off from view. In so doing, the film implicitly criticizes its own narrative strategy. *The Seventh Cross* will tell the story of the concentration camps by focusing on one particular victim: George Heisler, the conscientious German who escaped. But the design of the dolly shot implicitly admits an uncomfortable truth: telling this story (of an escapee, explicitly identified as non-Jewish) inevitably obscures the other stories that the film is not telling (of the Jewish victims, unable to escape).

A familiar motif in the military film, the person-to-person shot proved to be equally useful in representations of the home front, as in *The Human Comedy* and *The Clock*. The former film was based on William Saroyan's original story, also released as a novel in the same year, 1943. Set in a fictional town called Ithaca, with a protagonist named Homer, Saroyan's novel returns again and again to the theme of returning. When soldiers visit the town, the experience is both like and unlike the experience of going home. Even the townspeople, recent immigrants in a still unfamiliar country, must ponder the meaning of home: "There they were, in Ithaca, California, probably seven thousand miles from what had been for centuries their home in the world. Naturally, there was a loneliness in each of them, but no one could know for sure that the same loneliness might not be in them had they been seven thousand miles away, back home."[83] Loneliness separates, but it also unites; the soldiers and the townspeople learn to share their loneliness together. In the end, the central Macaulay family loses a son to the war but welcomes home another solider—an orphan who is looking for a home. To evoke these sentimental themes, director Clarence Brown stages several variations on the person-to-person shot, sometimes placing more emphasis on separation, sometimes shading the emphasis toward unity. In one beautiful scene, three soldiers, accompanied by two women they have just met, enter a telegraph office and dictate messages to their loved ones. As Willie (Frank Morgan), the kindly manager of the telegraph office, reads each message in turn, the camera dollies back, framing ever more inclusive views of the group: we see three people as Willie recites a young soldier's vulnerable message to Chicago (fig. 3.14a), five people as Willie reads a more confident message to New Jersey, and all six people as Willie reads a joking message to Texas (fig. 3.14b). Rather than moving incessantly, the camera rests on three distinct compositions, giving us the time to listen to each message in turn. The final composition strikes an exquisite balance. On the left, we see the three soldiers and the two women. Differences in costume reinforce differences in gender: the men wear uniforms, while the women wear transparent raincoats. At the same time, youth unites the five figures, visually contrasted with the solitary older figure on the right. Meanwhile, focus allows Willie to cross the

3.14 In *The Human Comedy*, the camera dollies back to include the entire group at a telegraph office.

divide: he is in focus throughout the shot, and he shares that focus with each soldier as he speaks that man's words aloud. The scene would not convey the same meanings in deep focus; we would lose the sense of temporary but meaningful connection formed between Willie and each man. Nor would the scene convey the same meanings with cuts to smaller groupings; we would lose the sense of inclusion that comes from seeing the space enlarge before our eyes. The camera's movement echoes Willie's own, making room to welcome the public yet private messages of all who enter the telegraph office.

A later scene in *The Human Comedy* takes place on a military transport train. Sounding very much like a Capra documentary, Ray Collins's voiceover narration explains that the train holds "American boys—kids from big cities and from little towns, from farms and from offices, from rich families and from poor families. Kids brilliant and swift in spirit, and kids slow and steady. These are the Americans." The camera wanders down the aisle, looking left and then right and then left again, drawing our attention to one group of soldiers and then another. Some are having a conversation; one is writing in a diary; a few others are playing cards. The camera's complex movement—panning laterally while dollying forward—echoes the complexity of the group. The voiceover emphasizes geographic and economic diversity, but the image also gestures toward another kind of diversity. Most of the soldiers are white, but a few are Asian American—a gesture of inclusion that stands out in comparison to many combat films with their all-white platoons, though it may ring hollow in light of the fact that more than a hundred thousand Japanese Americans, many from Saroyan's California, had by this point been interned in camps throughout the West.[84]

A third scene makes a more explicit attempt to correlate American identity with ethnic diversity via another variation on the person-to-person shot. Diana (Marsha Hunt) and her boyfriend Tom (James Craig) drive through a park where various cultural groups are enjoying a celebration. In the corresponding scene in the book, Tom gives a speech: "Americans! Greeks, Serbs, Poles, Russians, Mexicans, Armenians, Germans, Negroes, Swedes, Spaniards, Basques, Portuguese, Italians, Jews, French, English, Scotch, Irish. You name it. That's who we are."[85] The film cuts the list down to five: Greeks, Mexicans, Armenians, Russians, and Swedes. Howard Estabrook's screenplay recommended shooting each dance separately, but Brown staged the sequence in a single long take.[86] Tom and Diana drive past each dance; the camera car follows along laterally. The bright exterior lighting allows cinematographer Harry Stradling to photograph the scene in deep focus, juxtaposing Tom and Diana in the lower foreground with the vividly costumed dancers in the upper background (fig. 3.15a–b). Sound and image strike a theme of unity through difference. "America" plays on the soundtrack throughout, but individual pieces of cultural music come to the fore as Tom and Diana approach. The laterally moving

3.15 Later in *The Human Comedy*, two characters drive through a park and comment on the nation's ethnic diversity.

camera treats each group as a separate entity, with its own dances, its own costume design, and its own music, suggesting that each group's ethnic identity has been carefully preserved, not melted away. But the scene's hierarchical structure qualifies its celebration of cultural uniqueness. Tom's voice dominates the soundtrack, just as the image of the car dominates the composition from beginning to end. Formally, the shot resembles the lineup shot in *Bataan*. There, the camera moves from person to person while following Sergeant Dane down the line. Here, the camera moves from group to group while following Tom and Diana down the line. Both shots celebrate the ethnic diversity of the group— and both shots undercut that celebration by giving special priority to the white man in the foreground, one granted authority by virtue of his rank, the other by virtue of his status as the scene's primary speaker.

My final example stresses the complex continuity of this tradition, stretching from the early sound era to the wartime period and beyond. During the 1930s, the train station served as a site of convergence, bringing strangers together in films such as *Emma* and *Union Depot*. The home-front film retained these meanings and intensified them, making the train station a privileged space for the representation of the nation. The era's best train station movie, Vincente Minnelli's *The Clock*, featured one of the era's richest person-to-person shots. A contributor to *The Screen Writer* complained that Minnelli sacrificed character to camerawork, but critic James Agee favorably compared Minnelli's "boom-happy" film to *The Last Laugh*.[87] The original story outline for the film, written by Paul Gallico and Pauline Gallico, placed special emphasis on the theme of unexpected connections: while telling the story of one couple, the film would tell the story of many others characters encountered along the way.[88]

The film's screenplay, by Robert Nathan and Joseph Schrank, called for special handling of the departure scene. Instead of cutting to the protagonists right away, the film would show "a series of little farewells, as the camera passes through the crowd at the station, searching for Joe and Alice."[89] In the finished film, the camera, mounted on a crane, moves past a series of vignettes, proceeding briskly enough to evoke the screenplay's sense of a "series" but slowly enough to allow individual details to register as a medley of distinctive voices plays on the soundtrack ("You take good care of your mother," "Good-bye, darling, I love you," "Oh, God bless you"). As in a neorealist film, the effect is to suggest that the film's story has been selected at random. The camera could follow this couple or that one. Each story would be just as ordinary as this one—and just as important. Of course, this selected-at-random quality is just a construction. No one will be shocked when the camera lands on Joe and Alice; amid the jumble of details, they are the ones who best fit the Hollywood mold: young, white, and played by appealing Hollywood stars. But the camerawork produces a mild surprise out of a predictable situation by withholding information for so long. The initial lateral movement through the crowd lasts for a full thirty seconds before Joe and Alice appear (fig. 3.16a). Then the camera changes direction, craning in diagonally as one last couple steps away to reveal Alice adjusting Joe's tie (fig. 3.16b). An act of selection feels like a moment of discovery. By situating each person within a larger sequence, the person-to-person shot allows Hollywood filmmakers to tell individual stories while gesturing toward other stories inevitably left untold.

This shot is very different from the train station shot in *Emma*, made thirteen years earlier. A follow shot has become a person-to-person shot; broad comedy has become sentimental drama. And yet these scenes share two closely

3.16 In *The Clock*, the camera searches through a crowd before locating the central couple.

related underlying ideas: the train station is a space that brings strangers together, and the moving camera is the right tool to evoke this feeling of convergence with energy and empathy.

* * *

Although there was no necessary link between a theme and a technique, the meanings of specific motifs accumulated over time. Working in the same industry, filmmakers engaged in an ongoing dialogue about how best to represent recurring situations. This chapter has examined how filmmakers devised a set of strategies to better characterize one oft-represented subject: contemporary American life. That culture was multifaceted, and so were the films. The moving camera proved to be a valuable tool because it could represent the many competing aspects of modern life—not just its dynamism but also its seriality and its convergence.

CHAPTER 4

CONSTRUCTING SCENES WITH THE CAMERA

The previous chapters analyzed a series of films made in the shadow of *Sunrise* (1927). While F. W. Murnau continued to set a powerful example, the 1940s saw the arrival or ascendance of new figures who would shape the history of the moving camera just as surely: the upstart Orson Welles, the British import Alfred Hitchcock, and European émigrés such as Otto Preminger and Max Ophuls. These new exemplars reinvigorated long-standing debates, such as the problem of balancing subjective and objective technique (the topic of chapter 5) and the problem of balancing revelation with concealment (the topic of chapter 6).

The present chapter focuses on the first few years of the decade, arguing that several of the era's filmmakers embraced alternative methods of scene construction, with significant consequences for how the industry perceived the craft of directing. For years, Hollywood's predominant method of scene construction relied on master-and-coverage technique. Shooting a great deal of footage allowed producers and editors to reshape scenes in postproduction. When Hitchcock arrived in Hollywood in 1939, he became a vocal advocate for "cutting in the camera"—that is, planning films ahead of time and shooting footage that could be assembled only one way. Several directors exiled from the German film industry also preferred this approach. Meanwhile, Orson Welles and other filmmakers explored an alternative that placed even more emphasis on a director's on-set decisions: the long take. The resulting experiments with scene construction did not represent a sudden break—all three methods had been available for years—but rather a gradual shift in the day-to-day balance of power within the studio walls.

No Hollywood filmmaker insisted on using one method of scene construction all the time; a film might employ master-and-coverage technique in one sequence and cutting-in-the-camera technique the next. But the choice was never neutral. Each method of scene construction placed more or less weight on the authorial contributions by producers, editors, directors, cinematographers, and grips. The first section of this chapter offers a quick overview of Hollywood's division of labor, listing various roles contributing to the art of camera movement, from the screenwriter to the director to the cinematographer to the grip.[1] The emphasis here is on the studio system's collaborative power.[2] The second section compares three methods of scene construction—master and coverage, cutting in the camera, and the long take. Each one offered different opportunities for camera movement; at the same time, each one encouraged certain forms of collaboration and discouraged others. The third section turns to the decade's discourse of camera movement, which attempted to resolve some of the emerging contradictions. Some observers upheld the dolly shot as an inspiring example of Hollywood's collaborative artistry, requiring high-paid stars to coordinate their craft with workaday grips. Others explained Welles's and Hitchcock's virtuosic shots in proto-auteurist terms, defining camerawork as a privileged technique for those looking to put a personal stamp on a film. Either way, it was clear that the reworking of the craft of scene construction required a renegotiation of the studio system's balance of power.

The Moving Camera from Script to Screen

Who moved the camera? The answer seems simple: the dolly grip. But the dolly grip was one component of a much larger system—a system that stretched all the way from preproduction to the studio floor and into the editing room. Many people must contribute if the camera is to move an inch.

One important contributor rarely set foot on the set itself: the screenwriter. As we saw in chapter 2, scripts provided blueprints for production crews to follow. Veteran screenwriter Frances Marion explained that the craft required "considerable knowledge of screen photography."[3] Some writers preferred terse instructions, leaving camera decisions entirely to the discretion of on-set crew, but others used vivid language to evoke specific visual ideas. For instance, Casey Robinson's screenplay for *Now, Voyager* (1942) contains precise instructions for a scene when Charlotte (Bette Davis) attends a concert with her fiancé, Elliot (John Loder), and her true love, Jerry (Paul Henreid): "CLOSE TRUCKING SHOT slowly moving in to Elliot, then continuing to include Charlotte, then continuing to go past

Elliot and include Charlotte and Jerry. The orchestra is playing. Elliot is seated on the aisle. As camera goes past him and Charlotte, we see that he is holding her hand."[4] Robinson advises a technique (the trucking shot), a speed (slow), and an order of presentation (first Elliot, then Charlotte and Jerry).

Directors and cinematographers had mixed feelings about these in-script contributions. *Now, Voyager*'s director, Irving Rapper, told an interviewer, "I always followed the scripts I was given to the letter,"[5] but it is clear that he took liberties with Robinson's instructions regarding camerawork. In this scene in the finished film, the camera starts on the orchestra conductor before craning down to reveal Elliot, Charlotte, and Jerry seated in the front row. Rapper looked to the script for ideas, not for specific instructions. Director Fritz Lang insisted that he had the ultimate authority to decide on camera placement, but he remained open to screenwriters' suggestions: "I say, 'Write everything in—I can always scratch it out.'"[6] Cinematographer Gregg Toland was less fair-minded; he claimed that directors and cinematographers "over the years have developed a method of reading scripts so they do not see these directions at all."[7] As far as Toland was concerned, the screenwriters' contributions to production were minimal. The crucial decisions—lens length, camera height, dolly speed—were worked out on the set, not on the page.

But the continuity script was more than just a set of friendly suggestions. Producers used continuity scripts to guide their decisions about budgeting and scheduling, while daily production reports kept crews on task.[8] For every day of shooting, the second assistant director would submit a record to the producer, listing which cast members were called, what time they showed up, and when the first shot of the day was photographed. Many of these reports listed "script scenes" and "setups." Suppose that a script called for four separate shots ("script scenes") to complete a scene: a long shot, a close-up, and two medium shots. Now suppose that the crew photographed the long shot and close-up as written but combined the two medium shots into one dolly shot following a character walking across the room. The daily production report would credit the crew with three setups on that day. More importantly, the report would credit the crew with all four script scenes, meaning that they covered the material in the script, even if they deviated from the script's exact instructions. Modifying or supplementing the script was completely normal: the production reports for RKO's *The Devil and Daniel Webster* (1941) credited the crew with all 116 script scenes, while noting that they photographed 717 setups; at Warners, the reports for *Passage to Marseille* (1944) gave credit for 400 script scenes, covered with 816 setups; on United Artists' *Sleep, My Love* (1948), 207 script scenes yielded 490 setups.[9] These numbers show that production crews had the freedom to modify a screenplay's instructions as long as they covered (or received permission to eliminate) every script scene on the list.

For days in which the filming was progressing unusually slowly, the assistant director might supply an explanation, letting the producer know whether an intervention was necessary or not. When the crew of Welles's film *The Magnificent Ambersons* (1942) spent the bulk of a long day filming a difficult stairway scene, the production report explained, "Lining up crane shot to 10:30 a.m. Rehearsed from 10:30 a.m. to 1:00 p.m. with crane. Relight 2:00 p.m. to 2:50 p.m."[10] The crew was in fact still on schedule because the mobile long take had made it possible to cover many pages in one day, but notes like this one provided a paper trail in case it might be necessary to remove a cinematographer later on. By the end of production, Harry Wild had replaced the dilatory Stanley Cortez.

Another way for the producer to control camera movement was through the budget. A cost-conscious production manager could refuse to allocate a studio asset, such as a crane or dolly, to a particular crew. Rick Jewell reports that RKO considered this approach in the late 1930s during a period when the studio prioritized B-film productions.[11] Over at low-budget Monogram Pictures, studio bosses tried to prevent director Joseph H. Lewis from using a dolly, but Lewis fought back. "I became so incensed," he said, "that I made up my mind we were going to have a dolly shot: so I had the camera taken off the tripod and mounted on the back of a grip truck and we drove the truck and recorded with the motor going and everything; they had to dub later on. I said, 'Don't ever refuse me a dolly again.'"[12] Lewis insisted that the right to dolly was the absolute prerogative of the director.[13] He took the studio's attempt to limit that right as an assault on his authority.

In response to the charge that camera movement was inefficient from a production standpoint, the champions of the technique argued that a well-designed dolly shot saved money. An article in *American Cinematographer* explained: "Camera movement is usually thought of as an 'expensive' element, since moving camera shots take more time to set up, rehearse, and film. This seeming extravagance is, however, balanced by the fact that it is often possible to lace together by means of camera movement as many as five scenes that would otherwise require separate setups."[14] Whether this argument was persuasive or not, most major studios allowed ample usage of the technique. Indeed, the dolly became a routine piece of equipment on movies with high or even moderate budgets. Consulting the existing budget documents for films from a number of different studios and production companies—such as Warner's *Torrid Zone* (1940), Columbia's *The More the Merrier* (1943), and Paramount's *Double Indemnity* (1944)—reveals that budgeters rarely bothered to list a specific cost for a dolly (although *Double Indemnity* did set aside $300 for a boom).[15] The fact that these films do, in fact, contain dozens of dolly shots suggests that budgeters ignored the dolly's costs because it was a routine expense—just part of the package made available to every crew every day.

Without careful preparation, an art director's designs might inadvertently hinder camera movement: a poorly placed piece of furniture might get in the way of a pan; a narrow doorway might prevent the dolly from entering a room; a low ceiling might make it impossible to crane. The most elaborate movements required art directors to construct sets with "wild" walls, which could move out of the way to make room for a passing crane. Some directors worked with their art directors to develop storyboards—drawings of each shot. In extreme cases, storyboards would transfer authority from the director to the art director, as often happened with William Cameron Menzies, who had been drawing storyboards since the late 1920s. In 1939, he designed the look of *Gone with the Wind*, and producer David O. Selznick granted him a new title: production designer. Over the next few years, Menzies enjoyed a fruitful collaboration with director Sam Wood, who gave Menzies free reign to design his trademark compositions, scattering actors toward all the corners of the frame.[16] Cinematographer James Wong Howe worked with Menzies and Wood on *Kings Row* (1942). Though impressed, Howe acknowledged that his own role was circumscribed in the process because he could photograph each set from one angle only.[17] Once an admirer of Murnau's mobile camerawork, Menzies had come to favor stationary frames, which gave him even more power to pack each frame with carefully composed details.[18]

Menzies's artistry was exceptional, but more commercial filmmakers also discovered the benefits of preplanning. At Paramount, cinematographer Victor Milner had been calling for preproduction meetings for years.[19] In the early 1940s, he finally got his wish when producer-director Cecil B. DeMille began the practice of asking the art director to sketch storyboards after consultations with the cinematographer, the costume designer, the assistant director, and the special-effects team.[20] These preproduction meetings facilitated budgeting and scheduling, and the resulting storyboards made shooting days more efficient.

Once on set, top directors such as George Cukor carefully guarded their authority over camerawork, even as they ceded authority to cinematographers on matters of lighting.[21] John Huston explained, "Lighting is almost completely up to the cameraman," but "the set-up is something else."[22] Clarence Brown said that he arrived at his "final determination of camera angles and/or moving shots" in rehearsals just prior to shooting.[23] John Ford acknowledged that he worked with the screenwriter on dialogue and situations, but he insisted that he devised the "shooting arrangements" himself.[24]

In this same interview, though, Ford rejected the idea that the director was the author of the film. He instead argued that the director was more like an architect, always working within a set of limitations. A building must be a specific size and shape to fulfill its purpose within a terrain. Similarly, a director must design a work that fulfills its purpose within a commercial context. Max Ophuls compared the role of the director to that of a choir leader. Insisting that a film has no single creator, he believed it was his job to "awaken the creative drive in each person."[25] Other directors took a more megalomaniacal view of their own authority. Frank Capra spoke of his "one man, one vision" philosophy, promoting the quasi-auteurist idea that films were better when one person—the director—oversaw preproduction, production, and postproduction.[26] Writing in 1953, King Vidor bemoaned the "sameness" of recent films; he claimed that "the power of individual expression alone will restore the motion picture to its predominant state."[27] It seems that Vidor had internalized the extreme individualist ideology of *The Fountainhead*, which he had directed in 1949.[28]

As long as the cinematographers retained the freedom to light the scene, most of them were happy to concede to the director's authority over matters of composition. As William Clothier explained, "It's stupid to fight with directors. If John Ford told me to put the camera upside-down, I'd put the camera upside-down."[29] Karl Struss acknowledged the director's authority with a metaphor: "He was the captain and I was the first lieutenant."[30] Joseph Ruttenberg used the same military analogy to describe Fritz Lang's working method: "He had sketches of every scene in the film, from the angle he thought the camera should be. Well, OK. The director is the captain and you don't argue with the captain. Discuss it perhaps, but not argue."[31] Ruttenberg was so willing to acquiesce to Lang that the director actually complained; apparently, Lang preferred having a knockdown argument from time to time. Cinematographer Hal Mohr offered a harsher assessment of Lang's controlling tendencies: "He had the faculty of riding the camera dolly. He had to watch through the finder; he'd hold the operator to one side while he'd be looking through. Hell, an operator has to have complete control of the camera while a scene is being shot."[32] Significantly, Mohr was defending not his own authority but the authority of his camera operator. In Hollywood's hierarchical system, the director could give orders to the cinematographer, and the cinematographer could give orders to the camera operator, but the camera operator should not have relinquished control of the apparatus itself. Among major cinematographers, only Gregg Toland went on record denying the director's absolute authority over camerawork. He conceded that directors sometimes had good ideas, but he insisted that it was the cinematographer "who must determine whether those ideas are workable."[33]

The cinematographer supervised three separate crews: the electrical crew, the grip crew, and the camera crew. The electricians, led by the gaffer, would set up and operate the lamps. The grips modified the lighting by placing gobos and silks in front of the lamps; because of their mechanical skills, grips also assumed the responsibility of operating the dolly and crane during and between shots. When the floor was not perfectly flat, grips would lay tracks and balance them with carefully placed wedges. The camera crew consisted of the operator (sometimes known as the "second cameraman," not to be confused with the second-unit cinematographer) and the assistants, responsible for loading the film and setting focus. Even the simplest tracking shot required the collaboration of at least three practitioners: the dolly grip, who pushed the dolly with delicate timing; the camera operator, who reframed the camera to maintain a balanced composition over the course of the shot; and the first assistant, who executed focus pulls by adjusting the lens in accordance with the dolly's distance from the subject.

For the era under discussion, most of these expert practitioners remain largely unknown because operators, assistants, and grips worked without screen credit. Production documents such as budgets and camera reports can fill some of the gaps, and we occasionally find due credit given in *American Cinematographer* and *International Photographer*. A few operators later became famous after they received promotions, as when Arthur Miller's former operator Joseph LaShelle won the Best Cinematography Oscar for *Laura* (1944), just a year after operating on Miller's Oscar winner *The Song of Bernadette*.[34] Such cases remained exceptional; anonymity was the rule.

It is worthwhile to pause and admire the artistry of these hidden practitioners in the grip and camera crews. The best teams made complicated shots look effortless. Consider a shot from John Huston's film *The Maltese Falcon* (1941). Arthur Edeson served as cinematographer. The camera operator was Michael Joyce, a longtime Warner Bros. employee whose career stretched back to the Busby Berkeley films of the 1930s. Wally Meinardus pulled focus. E. F. Dexter was (possibly) the dolly grip.[35] In one scene, Sam Spade (Humphrey Bogart) is walking along a busy street when Wilmer (Elisha Cook Jr.) begins to follow him. After the initial fade-in, Spade steps into the center of the shot. The camera moves back and pans to the right, revealing Wilmer in the background (fig. 4.1a).

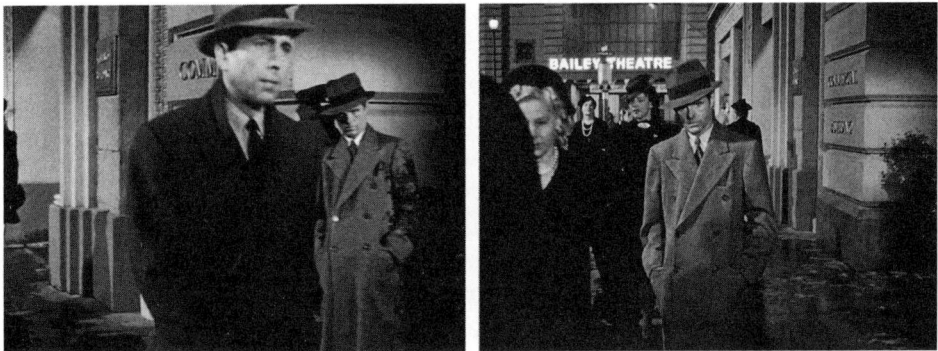

4.1 A seemingly simple shot in *The Maltese Falcon* required careful coordination.

Spade exits the frame, leaving Wilmer in the center. The camera continues moving back, but now it pans to the left to follow the slowly advancing Wilmer (fig. 4.1b). There is nothing flashy here—no five-minute dolly, no crane through the ceiling, just a slow move with some small-scale pans—but the shot works, developing an instant contrast between Spade and Wilmer. Spade walks with brisk confidence, whereas Wilmer, a wannabe tough guy, follows along more slowly. The camera moves relatively quickly—but not quickly enough to keep up with Spade, who steps closer to the camera before exiting the frame entirely. By contrast, the camera has no trouble holding the slow-moving Wilmer in the center of the frame. In a neat irony, the man who is being watched escapes our gaze, while the man doing the watching proves easy to target. Executing this shot, the dolly grip shows a deft touch, moving back with Spade, slowing down almost (but not quite) to a stop, and then moving back with Wilmer. The assistant's hand is equally sure, keeping Spade in focus, letting him go soft, racking to Wilmer, and maintaining the focus on Wilmer when he starts to move. And Joyce's operating is flawless. Just look at the shift when the pan right becomes a pan left—it is so smooth it is barely perceptible.

The collaboration we see here, among grip, operator, assistant, and actors, is very different from the collaboration between the director and the screenwriter or between the director and the art director. The work of preproduction is mental, verbal, and visual. The work of production is bodily. The actors move their arms and legs and torsos, and the grip and operator move theirs. Each must anticipate the others' gestures, like dancers in an ensemble. The Hollywood studio system relied on preproduction planning in order to rationalize production, but the process of filmmaking ultimately came down to craftspeople working together in the moment. One type of collaboration was corporate; the other was corporeal.

Producers rarely stepped on set, but they monitored each film's progress by watching dailies and specifying instructions via detailed memos. In some cases, a producer might complain that a crew was not moving the camera enough, as when Hal Wallis urged director Raoul Walsh, "Let's try to get some composition, and some moving shots, and some interesting stuff in the picture."[36] In other cases, a producer might complain that a crew was moving the camera too much, as when Wallis's boss Jack Warner advised director Michael Curtiz, "If you will stop all that superfluous roaming camera, Mike, you will make a great picture."[37] On B-films, directors enjoyed some freedom from producers' interference as long as they worked within their tight schedules.[38]

A daring director might ignore an executive's memo, but producers retained a powerful advantage: final cut. Under the producer's supervision, the editor had the responsibility of taking the footage from production and putting it together to form a scene. When a producer was displeased with an indulgent long take, he or she might order an additional day of shooting to provide the editor with a needed close-up. Some editors appreciated camera movement. Margaret Booth, head of the Editing Department at M-G-M, argued that "a good picture has an underlying rhythmic beat, almost like music." When the rhythm was too slow, a judicious panning shot would "infuse new life and action into a film."[39] Other editors held the opposite opinion: far from speeding up a film, a lumbering dolly shot dragged everything down. I. J. Wilkinson and W. H. Hamilton, two leading editors at RKO, complained: "With regard to camera movements—pans, dolly, zoom shots, etc., I do not know why most of these are used, as they can only slow up the action. For instance, the scene showing a character entering a room, crossing to the opposite side, when made with a dolly, has to follow the character every foot of the way, and is naturally quite dull."[40] Flatly rejecting the familiar technique of dollying in or out to establish the space, Wilkinson and Hamilton confined camera movement to action scenes. Such aesthetic debates masked an underlying struggle for authority. Many editors preferred to work without dolly shots because such shots provided fewer opportunities to cut.

Even in this quick sketch of the Hollywood production process, we can see that the work of camera movement was widely distributed. A producer might suggest a shot to a screenwriter, who might write it into the continuity, which might be revised on the fly by the director, who might give instructions to the cinematographer, who might reword those instructions to the dolly grip, who might execute the shot with a surprisingly rapid pace, which might suit the rhythmic requirements of the editor, who might show the rough cut to the producer, who might wonder who the hell suggested the shot in the first place. Many brilliant shots never made it off the cutting-room floor—or off the continuity's pages. But the division of labor facilitated the use of the moving camera by assigning specific tasks to highly skilled workers. Far from limiting filmmakers' ability to create complicated shots, the studio system enabled filmmakers to mass-produce them.

Methods of Scene Construction

In 1942, cinematographer John Boyle noted, "A good percentage of shots are made from dollies these days."[41] No great burst of technological innovation produced the decade's fluid style. If anything, the relevant cause was the exact opposite—professional crews mastering tools that they already had. At Twentieth Century-Fox, Joseph LaShelle and his former boss Arthur Miller continued to favor the descendants of the Velocilator, such as the Raby dolly.[42] Another Velocilator variant, the Houston-Fearless Panoram, remained in use into the 1950s.[43] At Universal, the Broadway Boom was still sending the camera skyward, as was its replacement, the Universal crane of 1937. At M-G-M, John

Arnold introduced a new crane in 1939, featuring an arm so well balanced that a grip could swing it with the touch of a finger.[44] Drawing on Arnold's earlier invention, the Rotambulator, the new crane could rotate around its base. This "rotating" crane soon became known as the "Ro crane" and eventually assumed the name "RO Crane."[45] Photographs show Arnold himself seated behind the camera, dangling from an arm that swoops and shimmers with art deco panache (fig. 4.2). He continued to tinker with the device for years, adding electronic controls and a motor in 1948 and then adapting the crane for Technicolor in 1952, just in time for *Singin' in the Rain*.[46] When M-G-M cinematographer Joseph Ruttenberg shot a film in the United Kingdom, the Elstree studio built him a replica of the RO Crane.[47]

Improved follow focus enhanced camera mobility. Technicolor cameras, with their large, heavy blimps, required remote focusing via a self-synchronizing control, which allowed the assistant to stand several feet away.[48] After shooting *Goldwyn Follies* (1938) in Technicolor, Gregg Toland adapted the idea of the remote control for use with any camera.[49] Engineers continued to tinker with follow-focus technologies for years.[50] Meanwhile, Toland gained fame for his contributions to an alternative approach: deep-focus photography. Taking

4.2 John Arnold shows off his latest invention, the RO Crane. (Courtesy of the Academy of Motion Picture Arts and Sciences)

advantage of superspeed emulsions, antiglare lens coatings, and improved arc lamps, Toland began shooting scenes with wide-angle lenses set to very small apertures, turning the camera into a "universal-focus" instrument.[51] Deep-focus photography allowed Toland's directors to design intricate compositions without camera movement, but it also allowed them to execute dolly shots without worrying about a loss of focus.

Although these technologies enabled the era's increasingly fluid camerawork, filmmakers continued to insist that the camera should move for a purpose, and they used the technology to solve the perennial problem of scene construction. For a simple conversation scene, each crew faced three major alternatives: master and coverage, cutting in the camera, and the long take. My examples focus on the early 1940s, but it is important to remember that all three systems had been around for years. Each system offered advantages and disadvantages for camera movement, and each system subtly altered Hollywood's division of labor.

Master and Coverage

Suppose a production team has been tasked with a scene showing two characters, each of whom speaks three lines of dialogue, for a total of six lines. The crew might start out the day by shooting the entire scene in a long shot, showing both characters speaking all of their respective lines. Then they might move the camera to an angle favoring the first character and photograph the entire scene again. Then the crew might move the camera to an angle favoring the second character and photograph the entire scene a third time. The editor now has choices. For any line of dialogue, the editor can select one of three possible angles: the long shot (known as a "master") or the shots favoring individual characters (known as "coverage" or "protection").

But the crew might go about shooting this scene in a different way. They might shoot the first line of dialogue from one position (perhaps a long shot), the second line of dialogue from another position (a medium shot of the second speaker), the third line from another (a medium shot of the first speaker), the fourth from still another (a close shot of the second speaker), the fifth from one more angle (an even closer shot of the first speaker), and the final line from yet another (say, a high-angle shot of the entire space). Now the editor has far less control than before. For each line, only one angle is available.

The distinction between these two approaches is not absolute, but the contrast was recognized within the industry. In 1937, film editor Maurice Pivar explained, "Some directors safeguard themselves by overshooting their pictures; that is, they shoot scenes from many different angles, for protection. Other directors, being more familiar with cutting pictures, cut most of their scenes in the camera."[52] John Huston also avoided overshooting; he called his more parsimonious approach "editing in the camera."[53] Rouben Mamoulian refused to allow Darryl F. Zanuck to edit his film; he explained, "I shot to cut."[54] The difference in approach reflects a different way of thinking about the craft of filmmaking. The director who shoots a master with extensive coverage plans to construct the scene after production, in the editing room—or to allow the producer to do the same. The director who cuts in the camera does the mental work of scene construction before shooting, either in preproduction meetings or in a burst of inspiration on set.[55] As Timothy Barnard explains, the French term *découpage* draws a similar distinction, albeit with different nuances: "*Découpage* involves the filmmaker, in tandem with the scriptwriter, cinematographer and other personnel (depending on one's attribution of film authorship and the production model and circumstances in play), deciding on the film's treatment before and during the film shoot."[56] The phrase *cutting in the camera* is admittedly awkward, but I will continue to use it because it had currency in the studio system. Indeed, the awkwardness is instructive. By defining the act of shooting as a kind of usurpation, as if filmmakers were cutting the wrong way, the term evokes the practice's contested status.

Though cutting-in-the-camera principles would grow more popular over the course of the decade, several major directors of the 1940s continued to prefer the master-and-coverage approach, including Frank Capra, George Stevens, and Mervyn LeRoy. LeRoy explained his working method in the following terms: "When a master scene has been shot, the director goes back for pickup shots showing the character, or characters, at different angles."[57] Shooting in this way could be quite tedious because the crew would need to film the same scene again and again. Capra's famously meticulous method was described as "mechanical," aiming for "full coverage of angles, from master shot to individuals."[58] When filming the close-ups, Capra would sometimes replay the sound from the master so that his actors could duplicate their own performances faithfully.[59] To secure even more footage, he sometimes employed a technique from the early sound days, filming key scenes with multiple cameras, as in the filibuster scene in *Mr. Smith Goes to Washington* (1939).[60] Whether filming with one camera or a dozen of them, the master-and-coverage filmmaker aimed to "overshoot" the film, producing extra footage to consider in postproduction. Why go to all this trouble? In an American Film Institute interview, Capra explained that he was closely involved in editing, and he appreciated the opportunity to structure a scene in postproduction: "I overshot purposefully so as to have some leeway." Capra then turned to George Stevens Jr., a leader of the American Film Institute's program. "His dad was the master of shooting for cutting," Capra clarified. "George Stevens made all his pictures in the cutting room; he had enough film. A fellow like Jack Ford was never interested in editing a film, so he would shoot it so that it could be edited in only one way. He had no leeway. I allowed enough leeway so that we could maneuver with the film."[61]

Significantly, Capra believed that his approach came closer to his proto-auteurist ideal of "one man, one vision." His regular screenwriter, Robert Riskin, could write master scenes without bothering to break them down into smaller units. Capra personally supervised the editing process, reshaping the footage to get the pacing and performances he wanted. By putting in the extra time, Capra ensured that he had an active hand in preproduction, production, and postproduction. Less-celebrated directors were unable to participate in postproduction. When filming stopped, they inevitably ceded control to editors and producers.

In principle, the distinction between the master-and-coverage and cutting-in-the-camera approaches had little to do with camera movement. One could employ either approach with or without dollies and cranes. In practice, however, each approach facilitated certain kinds of movement while discouraging others. A scene in George Stevens's comedy *The More the Merrier* demonstrates the affordances of the master-and-coverage approach. Set in Washington, DC, during the wartime housing shortage, the film is about a woman, Connie (Jean Arthur), who finds herself renting apartment space to two men: the young and handsome Joe (Joel McCrea) and the old and wily Benjamin Dingle (Charles Coburn). Stevens already had a history of shooting extensive coverage. (On *Gunga Din*, his crew shot 1,185 setups.[62]) As edited, *The More the Merrier*'s four-minute breakfast scene consists of twenty-eight shots, photographed from twelve different angles. In table 4.1, numbers represent shots, and letters represent setups.

The scene is never confusing, but there are so many angles that some of the shot transitions violate the 180-degree rule. Note that there was a good practical reason why Stevens did not move the camera until the end of the scene. Movement would have restricted the editor's options, thereby nullifying a key advantage of master-and-coverage technique. Consider Connie. At any time, editor Otto Meyer had the ability to choose from at least four options: the master, showing Connie, Joe, and Dingle (setup B; fig. 4.3a); another three-shot, positioning Connie between the two men (setup I; fig. 4.3d); a two-shot, pairing Connie with Joe in the foreground (setup E; fig. 4.3c); and a medium close-up of Connie (setup C; fig. 4.3b).[63] Now suppose that Stevens and his crew had decided to replace these four options with one shot: a slow dolly-in toward Connie, starting as a three-shot, becoming a two-shot, and ending as a single. The one shot might have emphasized her reactions effectively, but it would have restricted the editor's choices, eliminating the possibility of cutting to the closer view early in the scene (prior to the hypothetical dolly-in) or to the distant view later in the scene (after the hypothetical dolly-in). With stationary coverage, all four views remained available to the editor at all times.

TABLE 4.1 A Highly Edited Scene in *The More the Merrier* (1943)

Shot	Setup	Characters	Camera Movement
1	A	Connie	
2	B	Connie, Joe, Dingle	Minor reframe
3	C	Connie, closer than setup A	
4	D	Joe, with Connie in the foreground	
5	E	Connie, with Joe in the foreground	
6	D	Joe, with Connie in the foreground	
7	F	Dingle	
8	C	Connie, closer than setup A	
9	G	Joe and Dingle, past Connie's right shoulder	
10	E	Connie, with Joe in the foreground	
11	H	Joe and Dingle, past Connie's left shoulder	
12	C	Connie, closer than setup A	
13	G	Joe and Dingle, past Connie's right shoulder	
14	I	Connie, with Dingle and Joe in the foreground	
15	B	Connie, Joe, Dingle	
16	I	Connie, with Dingle and Joe in the foreground	
17	G	Joe and Dingle, past Connie's right shoulder	
18	I	Connie, with Dingle and Joe in the foreground	
19	F	Dingle	
20	B	Connie, Joe, Dingle	

Shot	Setup	Characters	Camera Movement
21	I	Connie, with Dingle and Joe in the foreground	
22	B	Connie, Joe, Dingle; Connie stands	Minor reframe
23	J	Connie, standing up	
24	K	Joe	
25	J	Connie, standing up	
26	K	Joe	
27	J	Connie, standing up	
28	L	Joe and Dingle, through the window; switch to Connie, seen through another window	Pan, dolly back, and boom down

4.3 The editor may choose from four separate angles of Connie in *The More the Merrier*.

The one dolly appears at the end of the scene (setup L). Joe and Dingle have been mocking Connie's fiancé, and she leaves in frustration when they start whooping and yelling. The camera, now positioned outside the kitchen, dollies back, pans to the right, and booms down, looking through another window to show Connie walking down the steps. She looks back toward the kitchen and smiles. As with many supposedly "unmotivated" movements, the point of the shot is to offer viewers privileged knowledge, revealing that Connie enjoys their boyish antics. Panning from one window to the other clarifies the spatial relationships, thereby emphasizing that we are seeing a side of Connie's personality that she is keeping hidden from both men.

Stevens complemented his complicated coverage with simple blocking, calling on all three actors to remain seated for the bulk of the scene. Other directors favored more intricate blocking, which required a significant modification to the master-and-coverage approach. Mervyn LeRoy's gangster romance *Johnny Eager* (1941) employs a version of the technique we might call "walk-talk-repeat."[64] The camera follows the characters as they enter a room. Then the camera remains stationary as the characters deliver their dialogue. When the characters walk to a different part of the room, the pattern repeats: moving to follow the walk, remaining stationary to cover the talk. The scene in question represents a battle of wits between Johnny (Robert Taylor) and the lawyer Farrell (Edward Arnold); Johnny wins. Notice the alternation of movement and stasis. Movement: Farrell enters, and the camera pans to follow. Stasis: shot-reverse-shot for the first few lines. Movement: the camera pans to follow Johnny as he calmly sits on the couch. Stasis: shot-reverse-shot for the next few lines. Movement: Johnny walks away, forcing Farrell—and the camera—to follow. Stasis: close-up shot-reverse-shot as Johnny wins the argument. A burst of movement: Farrell walks away; Johnny walks after him; Farrell leaves; Jeff (Van Heflin) enters the room. Finally, stasis: shot-reverse-shot as Jeff ruefully pours himself a drink. All of the blocking is meaningful. Johnny, in control from beginning to end, forces Farrell to follow him around, first to the couch and then to the other side of the room. After Farrell has conceded his defeat, Johnny flips the pattern and follows Farrell—precisely to mock Farrell with his own magnanimity. The angry intensity of the Johnny–Farrell interaction, building up to a volley of tight close-ups, contrasts with the sad dissolution of the Jeff–Johnny interaction. Jeff is clearly in love with Johnny, but there is nothing he can do about it. His side-by-side exchange with Johnny is given no shot-reverse-shot treatment; his more distant exchange is.

LeRoy and his crew stretched the idea of the fluid master to the breaking point, adding so much blocking (into the room, to the couch, toward the bar, to the door) that it would have been nearly impossible to capture all of it in a single shot, so they instead broke the scene down into smaller units. Each unit became a miniature master-and-coverage scene, with a two-shot and a shot-reverse-shot pair; the filmmakers then laced the scenes together with follow shots as the actors moved from position to position. The blocking set the pattern for the scene, but the editor retained the freedom to cut during dialogue exchanges.

Cutting in the Camera

Compared to the master-and-coverage approach, the cutting-in-the-camera approach enabled filmmakers to photograph a scene from a wider array of camera angles, albeit within the limitations imposed by the 180-degree system. Pushed to an extreme, each line of dialogue—each significant moment—could be awarded its own unique composition. Those compositions might be mobile, or they might be stationary, but in principle there was no reason not to move the camera every time as long as the movement made an impact.

David Bordwell has examined similar approaches in other cinema traditions, such as the "piecemeal *découpage*" of Japanese cinema and the "segment shooting" techniques of Hong Kong.[65] While the efficient master-and-coverage style was well suited to Hollywood's system of mass production, plenty of studio filmmakers incorporated cutting-in-the-camera principles into their works. During the 1930s, the style held particular appeal for visually oriented directors who had trained in Europe, such as Ernst Lubitsch, Michael Curtiz, and William Dieterle.[66] As early as 1929, Lubitsch was criticizing multicamera technique in favor of shooting "one angle of a scene at a time—and making it good!"[67] A later profile of the director reported that he had every scene "cut in his mind so there is little time lost [and] practically no waste footage."[68] The three-person scene from *Design for Living*, discussed in chapter 2, relied largely on the in-camera approach; twenty-seven separate setup produced the scene's thirty-nine shots. By the 1940s, Lubitsch had modified his approach, favoring longer shots with ensemble groupings.[69] Meanwhile, a new generation of filmmakers had arrived from Europe, this time in exile from Nazi persecution. As Vincent Brook explains, many of the Jewish émigré directors—including Fritz Lang, Robert Siodmak, Edgar Ulmer, and Curtis Bernhardt—also used cutting in the camera.[70]

Whereas Frank Capra argued that shooting extensive coverage gave the director more control by allowing him to reshape the film in editing, directors who were unable or unwilling to spend months in the editing room argued that cutting in the camera was the best way to maintain directorial control over the image because it prevented editors and studio bosses from tinkering with their work. Howard Hawks told an interviewer: "I hate the editing. . . . When I started out in this profession, the producers were all afraid that I made a film too short because I didn't give them enough film for editing. And I said, 'I don't want you to make the movie in the cutting room, I want to make it myself on the set, and if that doesn't suit you, too bad.'"[71]

Similarly, the editor turned director Robert Parrish explained that John Ford "very seldom shot more than one take; he used very little film, and was always under schedule or under budget. So, by and large, the film that the editor would get almost *had* to go into the picture."[72] Decision-making authority moved out of the editing room and into the mind of the director. Producers sometimes fought back. In 1936, Hal Wallis wrote yet another stinging memo to Michael Curtiz: "Are you trying to cut in the camera and pick out just those portions of the scene that you want to play in closeup? . . . I want you to shoot the entire scene in close-ups so that we can cut it the way we want."[73] At M-G-M, producer Irving Thalberg ordered reshoots to secure shots he needed in editing; his onetime protégé David O. Selznick adopted similar tactics.[74]

On set, some cinematographers preferred cutting in the camera because it allowed them to fine-tune each image. Lee Garmes claimed that the famously dictatorial Josef von Sternberg was actually "the easiest director to work with" precisely because he shot his scenes piecemeal, treating each line or gesture separately, to be lit with precision.[75] During the war, cinematographers advocated shooting fewer setups as a means of economizing on limited film-stock budgets.[76] Gregg Toland reportedly taught Orson Welles to cut in the camera, with minimal coverage.[77] Welles later abjured the approach, finding it "too Germanic."[78]

Perhaps the most famous champion of cutting in the camera was Alfred Hitchcock. Even before he arrived in Hollywood, Hitchcock had developed a rigorous and systematic philosophy of directing, relying on extensive preproduction to plan each sequence ahead of time, shot by shot. In an article he wrote in 1937, he explained, "I like to have a film complete in my mind before I go to the floor."[79] Hitchcock acknowledged that the process was a collaborative one. His wife, Alma Reville, was a screenwriter and editor, and they often did the planning together: "With the help of my wife, who does the technical continuity, I plan out a script very carefully, hoping to follow it exactly, all the way through, when shooting starts. In fact, this working on the script is the real making of the film, for me."[80] In Hollywood, Hitchcock continued to boast about both of these practices: planning each production ahead of time and then shooting each scene bit by bit. Widely publicized, the approach became part of his public persona. Even before Hitchcock had completed a single American film, an article in *LIFE* magazine contrasted him with the Russian director Sergei Eisenstein, noting that Hitchcock "shoots little that audiences will not later see."[81] A profile by Lewis Jacobs in 1941 noted that Hitchcock designed each shot during preproduction with the help of Reville and Joan Harrison, his secretary.[82] (Harrison soon became a successful writer-producer on films by Hitchcock, Lang, and others.) Discussing *Foreign Correspondent* from 1940, Jacobs was particularly impressed with Hitchcock's commitment to "piece-by-piece construction." Whereas the "academic director would have shot the scene in its entirety, a master shot, two medium shots and perhaps a close-up," Hitchcock, Jacobs observed, photographed a large number of short shots, with the result that the film was "edited before it was photographed."[83] All the editor had to do was trim the shots and join them together. As one editor explained, "There's no such thing as editing on a Hitchcock picture."[84] Hitchcock's producer, the master micromanager David O. Selznick, was not pleased to be left out of the process; he supposedly told his star director, "I can't get on with this goddam jigsaw cutting of yours."[85]

As Bill Krohn has argued, the public picture of Hitchcock as a master planner was partly a myth, albeit a myth Hitchcock encouraged: "Temperamentally uncomfortable with the chaotic element of film making, Hitchcock aspired to eliminate it. . . . But chaos was a frequent collaborator in his productions."[86] Hitchcock may have started his productions with detailed plans, but he remained willing to make changes when a better idea appeared. Nevertheless, Krohn acknowledges that Hitchcock's approach remained alien to the logic of coverage.[87] Whether Hitchcock gave himself alternate takes to work with or not, he approached filmmaking as a matter of putting pieces together.

For Hitchcock, piece-by-piece construction was perfectly compatible with camera movement. A scene from Hitchcock's first American film, *Rebecca* (1940), demonstrates Hitchcock's philosophy in action, dollying several times to shape a scene cut largely in-camera. Maxim de Winter (Laurence Olivier) tells Mrs. Van Hopper (Florence Bates) that he has become engaged to Mrs. Van Hopper's traveling companion, the unnamed protagonist played by Joan Fontaine. Mrs. Van Hopper pretends to be pleased, but her behavior toward her companion goes from patronizing to insulting. In the abstract, the scene represents a typical assignment for a Hollywood film crew—three minutes, three characters, one room. A Capra or a Stevens might have filmed the scene from stationary angles, enabling the editor to select from a range of singles, two-shots, and three-shots. Hitchcock's version also features a range of groupings, but two traits are worth noting. First, most of the angles are unique, covering one portion of action and never used again. The completed scene contains fourteen shots—from ten distinct setups (table 4.2). Second, several of the shots feature camera movement, not just for minor reframes, but for major regroupings, turning three-shots into two-shots or two-shots into singles.

The fourth shot (setup D) is particularly dynamic. It begins as a three-shot, with Maxim on the left, Mrs. Van Hopper in the middle, and Fontaine's character on the right (fig. 4.4a). No one character dominates the frame. But then Mrs. Van Hopper turns to her former companion and starts giving her instructions. As she does so, the camera dollies in, turning the three-shot into a two-shot, echoing Mrs. Van Hopper's attempt to exclude Maxim and resume her

TABLE 4.2 Several Regroupings Across Several Setups, *Rebecca* (1940)

Shot	Setup	Number of Characters in the Shot	Subsequent Camera Movement
1	A	One: protagonist	
		Two: protagonist and Max	Pan to follow protagonist and Max
		Three: Max, Van Hopper, and protagonist	
2	B	Three: Max, Van Hopper, and protagonist	Dolly in to Van Hopper
		One and a half: Van Hopper and Max's shoulder	
3	C	One and a half: protagonist and Van Hopper's shoulder	
4	D	Three: Max, Van Hopper, and protagonist	Dolly in to exclude Max
		Two: Van Hopper and protagonist	Pan to follow protagonist
		Three: Max, protagonist, and Van Hopper	
5	E	One and a half: Van Hopper and Max's shoulder	
6	D	Three: Max, protagonist, and Van Hopper	Reframe after Max exits
		Two: protagonist and Van Hopper	Reframe after protagonist exits
		One: Van Hopper	
7	F	Two: protagonist and Van Hopper	Dolly in as Van Hopper approaches
8	G	One: Van Hopper	
9	H	One: protagonist	

Shot	Setup	Number of Characters in the Shot	Subsequent Camera Movement
10	I	Two: protagonist and Van Hopper	Pan to follow Van Hopper
		One: Van Hopper	Continue following Van Hopper
		One and a half: Van Hopper's reflection (and her shoulder)	
11	H	One: protagonist	
12	I	One and a half: Van Hopper's reflection and her shoulder	Reframe as Van Hopper turns
		One: Van Hopper	
13	H	One: protagonist	Pan to follow protagonist
14	J	One and a half: Van Hopper and her partial reflection	Pan to follow Van Hopper
		One: Van Hopper	Continue following Van Hopper
		One and a half: Van Hopper and protagonist's shoulder	Reframe as Van Hopper exits
		One: protagonist	Dolly out

4.4 The regrouping marks the stages of an unfolding power struggle in *Rebecca*.

role as the primary force in her companion's life (fig. 4.4b). When Fontaine's character attempts to comply with Mrs. Van Hopper's instructions, Maxim stops her, and the protagonist soon finds herself in the middle of a reconstituted three-shot, positioned between Maxim on the left and Mrs. Van Hopper on the right. Once standing outside the awkward exchange between Maxim and Mrs. Van Hopper, the protagonist is now right in the middle of it. Cutting from a three-shot to a two-shot to a three-shot would produce a similar sequence of framings, but without the sense of spatial relationships shifting in time—a process of temporal unfolding that heightens our awareness of a power struggle developing moment by moment.

At the end of the scene (setup J), Mrs. Van Hopper walks from the mirror to the door and turns to give her former companion one last look. "Mrs. De Winter," she sneers. The camera dollies back and booms down slightly to frame a full shot of the future Mrs. De Winter. Now she is utterly alone, looking small and thin in the center of an expanding frame. Throughout, the camera's movements have made dramatic change visible, transforming one composition into another. Look at the chart: a three-shot becomes a two-shot, and then it becomes a reconstituted three-shot. A two-shot becomes a single, and then it becomes a mirror shot. The frame is not just mobile; it is protean.

The cutting-in-the-camera method did not mandate camera movement. By the 1940s, both Ford and Hawks had abandoned the flashy camera movements of their late-silent-era years in favor of careful blocking within relatively stationary frames. Nevertheless, I think it is fair to say that camera movement was an affordance of the bit-by-bit approach—an enabled option. A dolly-driven director could design quick little moves to emphasize each moment without worrying about whether the resulting composition would remain useful for the rest of the scene. Consider a famous scene from *Casablanca*, directed by Michael Curtiz, working with the expert camera team from *The Maltese Falcon*.[88] Curtiz had been cutting in the camera for years, even in the face of Wallis's stinging memos. Here, the director deploys the method to amplify a double-barreled plot twist. The scene depicts Rick (Humphrey Bogart) giving the letters of transit to Victor (Paul Henreid). When Captain Renault (Claude Rains) steps out to arrest Victor, Ilsa (Ingrid Bergman) is shocked—but then Rick pulls a gun on Renault. On the level of the story, the scene delivers a great double switch. Oh, no, Rick is betraying Victor and Ilsa! But wait—he is actually helping them! Each twist gets its own burst of movement. After Renault steps forward, the film cuts to a close-up of Ilsa (fig. 4.5a). Immediately, the camera follows Ilsa as she moves past Rick into a three-shot with Victor, Ilsa, and Rick (fig. 4.5b). This changing composition carries thematic significance: after Rick's (apparent) betrayal, Ilsa moves from Rick's side of the room to Victor's. Now she occupies a position between the two men, leaning closer to the one she admires and away from the one she loves. Curtiz had a reputation for cutting *on* the movement.[89]

4.5 As a plot twist unfolds in *Casablanca*, the composition changes quickly.

Notice how the movement begins a split second after the cut, swooping into a new composition before we can get our bearings. Rick's decision disorients Ilsa; we participate in her disorientation. A few moments later, the second twist occurs, represented with another dynamic burst. Renault looks down; cut to the gun in Rick's hand; tilt up to reveal Rick's determined face. Again, the shot holds thematic meaning, repeating and varying an earlier scene when Ilsa pulled a gun on Rick. But the quick-change composition also works expressively, creating a feeling of visual astonishment that amplifies the emotional feeling of the double twist.

Hollywood publicity touted Lubitsch's and Hitchcock's careful preplanning, thereby marketing their artistry by equating the craft of direction with the task of deciding where to put the camera. Behind the scenes, producers grudgingly acknowledged that the approach could save time and money when executed with skill. Indeed, Selznick was not opposed to the practice, in spite of his alleged remark about "jigsaw cutting." Recall that it was Selznick who elevated William Cameron Menzies to the role of production designer for *Gone with the Wind*. The producer asked Menzies to draw each shot ahead of time as a way of controlling costs on his gargantuan production. Selznick later told Hitchcock that "cutting the film with your camera" was desirable as long as the director produced more setups per day.[90] Meanwhile, *Gone with the Wind, Rebecca, How Green Was My Valley* (1941), and *Casablanca* all won Best Picture Academy Awards, suggesting that cutting in the camera was quite compatible with Hollywood ideals.

Indeed, when we look past the big-name directors, we find many films from the early 1940s that adopted the approach, even at conservative studios such as M-G-M. The quirky thriller *Grand Central Murder* (1942) provides a good demonstration of how an otherwise uninspired director could construct scenes in-camera. The director, S. Sylvan Simon, was no Hitchcock. He was not even a Michael Curtiz. He was just a competent M-G-M employee with a good cinematographer (George Folsey), a professional Hollywood crew, and the best equipment John Arnold had to offer. In one scene, Inspector Gunther (Sam Levene), an overmatched detective, interviews various suspects; the smug protagonist Rocky (Van Heflin) takes over the questioning. Whereas *Casablanca*

TABLE 4.3 Several Regroupings Across Several Setups, *Grand Central Murder* (1942)

Shot	Number of Characters Whose Faces Are Clearly Visible	Subsequent Camera Movement
1	One: Frank	Dolly out to include Gunther
	Two: Gunther and Frank	Dolly out to include Rocky and Sue
	Four: Gunther, Frank, Rocky, and Sue	Dolly in toward Gunther and Frank
	Two: Gunther and Frank	Pan past Rocky and Sue; boom up to Turk
	One: Turk	
2	None: focus on gun in Gunther's pocket	Dolly out and tilt up to Gunther, Pearl, Baby, and Frank
	Four: Gunther, Pearl, Baby, Frank	Rack focus to Pearl; later, boom to follow Gunther
	Three: Rocky, Gunther, McAdams	Reframe to include Frank
	Four: Frank, Rocky, Gunther, McAdams	Dolly in to reframe after Frank exits
	Three: Rocky, Gunther, and McAdams	Reframe after McAdams exits
	Two: Rocky and Gunther	Pan to follow Rocky
	One: Rocky	
3	One: Gunther	Pan to follow Gunther

Shot	Number of Characters Whose Faces Are Clearly Visible	Subsequent Camera Movement
	Two: Gunther and Rocky	Dolly to follow Rocky
	Two: Rocky and Gunther	
4	One: Frank	
5	One: Baby	
6	One: Turk	
7	One: Pearl	
8	One: Paul	
9	One: David	
10	Two: Rocky and Gunther (continues shot 3)	Pan to follow Rocky
	One: Rocky	Pan and rack focus to Paul, Roger, Constance, David
	Four: Paul, Roger, Constance, David	
11	One: Constance	Dolly out to include Roger and Gunther
	Three: Roger, Constance, and Gunther	Dolly in to Constance
	One: Constance	

gains its energy from quick little moves, the scene in *Grand Central Murder* develops a different rhythm: three relatively long takes, followed by a burst of montage, leading to two more longer takes. Following the logic of cutting in the camera, almost every shot is unique: ten setups, eleven shots (table 4.3). Aside from the quick montage, each shot features multiple camera stops.

The anonymous assistant cameraman did amazing work, executing more than half-a-dozen focus pulls in the second shot alone: focusing on the gun in

4.6 During an interrogation in *Grand Central Murder*, the camera moves from suspect to suspect.

Gunther's pocket, switching to Rocky and Frank (Tom Conway) in the foreground (fig. 4.6a), switching to Pearl (Connie Gilchrist) and Baby (Betty Wells) in the background (fig. 4.6b), switching to Gunther as he stands up, remaining on Gunther as he gives orders to a colleague, remaining on Gunther as the camera dollies in (fig. 4.6c), switching to Rocky as he steps forward (fig. 4.6d), and remaining on Rocky as he walks into a single on the right—all in one shot! Visually, the fluid style expresses what it feels like to watch a mystery. Maybe that person did it . . . or that one . . . or that one. As our minds jump from suspect to suspect, the camera jumps from composition to composition, favoring one suspect and then another.

If a diverting M-G-M thriller could employ cutting-in-the-camera principles, then the approach was not a radical challenge to studio practices. It only seemed radical in the realm of ideas. For directors such as Hawks and Huston, cutting in the camera evoked rebellion and unconventionality. In later years, filmmakers who cut in the camera remembered the practice with pride, as proof of their ability to wrest control away from producers.

The long take represented a different challenge to the existing balance of power. In theory, the technique offered directors even more control, holding forth the promise of keeping the producers' meddling out of the process altogether. In practice, the technique relied heavily on one of the studio system's greatest strengths—its stable of highly trained, collaborative craft workers.

The Long Take

The celebrated long takes of the 1940s had many precursors. During the transition-to-sound period, filmmakers used the long take as an alternative to multicamera filmmaking. Rouben Mamoulian's *Applause* featured a four-minute-long take, the camera dollying in and out to mimic the patterns of continuity editing. After the return to single-camera filmmaking, the long take remained a viable option, as in the films of Edmund Goulding, John Stahl, and George Cukor.[91] The results could be understated, as in a fluidly staged three-minute scene in *The Magnificent Obsession* (1935), or wildly overstated, as in a spectacular six-minute musical number in *The Great Ziegfeld* (1936).[92] The technique proved to be particularly useful when filmmakers wanted to capture the depth and intensity of a star performance, as in a five-minute shot of Paul Muni delivering an impassioned monologue in *The Life of Émile Zola* (1937).

If we now think of the long take as a distinctive device of the 1940s, then *Citizen Kane* gets a great deal of the credit. Orson Welles did not invent the technique, but his film offered a powerful model for what the long take could achieve. Indeed, the film offered several models. Some scenes employed the long take as an extension of cutting-in-the-camera principles, unfolding discrete compositions over time; others employed the long take as a more radical alternative, challenging spectators to make sense of a complex spatial array. At one extreme, the moving camera might switch from one character to another, breaking the scene into a sequence of legible compositions. At the other extreme, the camera might remain resolutely still, relying on deep focus to register several layers of action from foreground to background. As an example of the former, consider the eighty-second scene when Susan (Dorothy Comingore) meets Kane (Welles) for the first time. Recovering from a toothache, Susan laughs at the sight of Kane after a passing carriage has splattered him with muddy water. The camera's movement weaves together a series of discrete compositions, tilting from a puddle to the drug store (fig. 4.7a), craning past the carriage toward the laughing Susan (fig. 4.7b), panning to reveal the drenched figure of Kane (fig. 4.7c), dollying in to show a tense exchange, and dollying in again as Kane's tone softens (fig. 4.7d). One could imagine the same scene cut together in-camera. A puddle. A carriage. A woman laughing. A drenched man. Such a sequence would tell the same story, but movement adds a new dimensionality to the scene, showing separation gradually transforming into unity. The pan divides the two figures into separate frames, while letting us know just

4.7 In *Citizen Kane*, the camera cranes, pans, and dollies to frame several discrete compositions in a single shot.

how far apart they are: Susan over here, Kane over there. Later, the dolly-in gives added emphasis to the characters' movements: the curious Susan walking past and away from Kane; the confident Kane stepping toward Susan.[93]

The puddle scene follows the familiar logic of Hollywood scene construction, moving forward step by step, as in the unfolding interrogation of *Grand Central Murder*. Elsewhere, *Citizen Kane* models a very different approach to the long take, exploiting the resources of deep-focus cinematography to such a degree that extensive camera movement became unnecessary. The results look completely unlike cutting in the camera, not just because there are no cuts but also because the resulting scene refuses to employ a sequence of different angles. When Bernstein (Everett Sloane), Thatcher (George Coulouris), and Kane discuss a legal document, the action unfolds over the course of a single 140-second shot. As in the previous example, the staging follows a pattern of gradual revelation: first we see Bernstein; then we see Bernstein and Thatcher; and then we see Bernstein, Thatcher, and Kane. But these revelations are the product of the characters' movements, not the camera's. Thatcher appears when Bernstein lowers the document, and Kane appears when he steps into the shot from behind Bernstein (fig. 4.8a–b). The camera's movements are simply minor reframes,

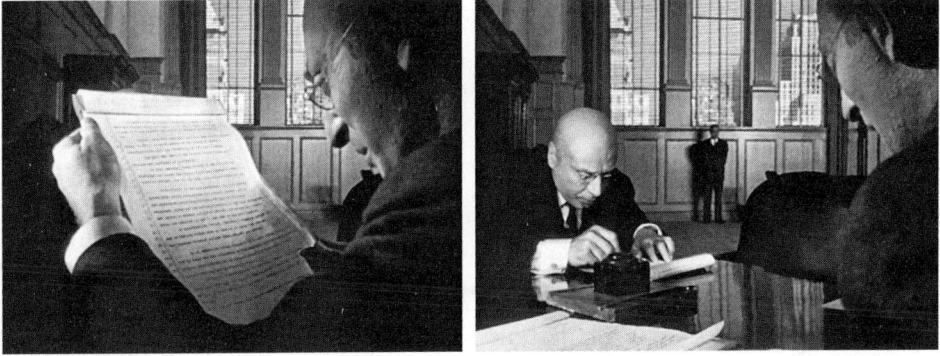

4.8 In another scene in *Citizen Kane*, the camera barely moves, recording the action in tremendous depth.

panning to the right in order to center Kane when he enters and tilting up when he approaches the foreground. Instead of laying out the scene as a series of angles, the deep staging fits everything in the same frame, requiring the spectator to notice several things at once: Bernstein's defeated posture, Thatcher's slightly shaking hands, Kane's slow gait.

The difference is partly technical: Thatcher's scene employs greater depth of field. But the difference is also conceptual: Thatcher's scene makes more demands on the spectator. Discussing the film's long takes, cinematographer Gregg Toland proposed a relevant distinction. In an article published in 1941, he explained that he and Welles sought to avoid "direct cuts" whenever possible. In some scenes, they would "pan or dolly from one angle to another," thereby creating a sequence of angles along the lines of traditional continuity construction. But the scenes featuring the deepest focus were different. Here, "important action might take place simultaneously in widely separated points in extreme foreground and background."[94] The key word in Toland's account is *simultaneously*. In place of the familiar sequence of angles, a deep-focus shot confronts the spectator with multiple events at the same time. The difference is a matter of control. Should the frame dictate the spectator's attention or offer the spectator a measure of freedom? In one contemporary article, Welles pointed out that most filmmakers used shallow focus to direct attention, and he claimed that he used deep staging to accomplish the same goal.[95] But another article in 1941 made the opposite point, suggesting that the pan–focus technique gave each spectator "the privilege of looking at any part of the screen, as in the theater."[96]

The French critic André Bazin was particularly impressed with Welles's stationary staging in depth, both in *Citizen Kane* and in its successor, *The*

Magnificent Ambersons: "Welles quite often reinforces the maintenance of this dramatic unity by refusing to use camera movements that would in fact reestablish, by a succession of new framings, a hypothetical breakdown into shots."[97] With this reading in mind, the puddle scene seems relatively conventional. The camera simply moves from one well-placed angle to the next, like cutting in the camera without the cuts. The real innovation lies in the second example, which forces us to take in the entire composition—Bernstein, Thatcher, Kane, the documents, the window, the blinds, the reflections on the table—all at once rather than in sequence.

Like Murnau's film *Sunrise*, *Citizen Kane* became a textbook with many lessons. Only a few filmmakers drew the lesson that Bazin saw so presciently: the lesson that deep-focus photography could challenge a spectator's perceptual limits. William Wyler took full advantage of Gregg Toland's skills to design complex shots with multiple points of interest, as in *The Little Foxes* (1941) and *The Best Years of Our Lives* (1946). According to Wyler, this approach "lets the spectator look from one to the other character at his own will, do his own cutting."[98] But most filmmakers were reluctant to grant so much freedom to the spectator. Rather than use the long take to force spectators to find meaning in an array of ambiguous details, they saw the long take as a substitute for cutting in the camera—another way to produce a sequence of meaningful compositions without relinquishing too much authority to editors. For instance, the director Joseph H. Lewis devised a long take for the climactic scene of his low-budget thriller *Secrets of a Co-ed* (1942). He later explained his reasoning to Peter Bogdanovich: "I decided to shoot the entire courtroom sequence as one shot. We rehearsed till about three o'clock in the afternoon—and then made the take. And in those ten minutes you saw close-ups, long shots, medium shots, over-the-shoulder shots, you name it; the camera was moving constantly."[99] In fact, Lewis exaggerated the complexity of the shot, which lasts six minutes rather than ten, simply craning in on a lawyer (Otto Kruger) and panning to follow him as he delivers a closing argument that becomes a confession. But Lewis's exaggerations are instructive. He described the process of shooting a long take as if he were cutting in the camera, creating a sequence of angles, from close-ups to long shots, in the manner of a conventional scene. Indeed, the long take's value to Lewis was not so much formal as it was institutional. By staging a long take, a director could usurp even more power from the producer. When Bogdanovich asked Lewis if he shot coverage, Lewis replied, "Protection! Oh, heavens, no. A man must have courage."[100] If Lewis learned anything from Welles, it was not that the long take could confront the spectator with a world of ambiguity but that the long take served as the ultimate expression of a maverick director's rebellion against the system. Welles indulged in the same hypermasculine rhetoric: "A long-playing full shot is what separates the men from the boys. Anybody can make movies with a pair of scissors and a two-inch lens."[101]

Lutz Bacher has explained how long-take filmmaking rebalanced the division of labor in Hollywood and other industries.[102] In preproduction, writers had to decide (in collaboration with producers, directors, and others) how much detail to include in each script. These decisions would have consequences for the work of assistant directors, who sought to keep the crew on schedule, shooting a certain number of pages per day. On set, directors had to learn how to inspire or bully the crew into executing complicated maneuvers. From the standpoint of the producer, the real trouble came in postproduction. According to Bacher, "Mobile long takes do not lend themselves to manipulations of content in post-production. Hence producers who insist on such interference are apt to be hostile to them."[103] Depending on the schedule and the budget, producers often overruled their directors, demanding additional footage that could be used to break up an overly long take. Welles suffered this indignity several times. In one scene in *The Magnificent Ambersons*, the camera follows George and Lucy as they walk down the street. Lucy (Anne Baxter) rebukes George (Tim Holt) by remaining polite to him even as he pleads with her to show some sort of emotional response. The long take heightens our awareness of time as Lucy determinedly maintains her cordial facade for one full minute and then another and then another. When RKO recut the film, editor Robert Wise preserved most of Welles's long take, but he inserted one ill-fitting close-up of Anne Baxter holding back tears as George walks away. For many critics, the extra shot cheapens a brilliant scene not just because its dewy softness does not match the appearance of the long take but also because the image of Lucy crying alters the character's intentions, as if she were keeping up her facade for George's benefit alone.[104]

Such examples support the popular image of the rebellious director shooting long takes to ward off studio interference, sometimes unsuccessfully. But we should resist the temptation to anoint every long-take director as a defiant auteur. For all its connotations of bravado, the long take remained compatible with studio filmmaking at the highest levels—a technique that took full advantage of each studio's pool of skills. The demands on the crew were high for the long take; one missed focus pull, and they might need to shoot the entire scene over again.

Ultraconventional M-G-M produced plenty of films using the long-take approach, as in Minnelli's and Cukor's works. The musical *For Me and My Gal* (1942) contains several remarkable examples. Director Busby Berkeley, famous for his outrageous musical numbers at Warner Bros. in the 1930s, had become a skillful dramatic director by the early 1940s. In one three-minute scene, Jimmy (George Murphy) tells his vaudeville partner Jo (Judy Garland) that he would like to leave their act; we know that he is making a sacrifice for her benefit, allowing her to form a new act with the caddish but talented Harry (Gene Kelly). Berkeley stages the entire scene as a two-shot, keeping both characters in frame at all times (table 4.4).

TABLE 4.4 **Single Shot Capturing Several Variations on the Two-Shot in** *For Me and My Gal* (1942)

Composition	Jo: Placement—Scale—Position	Jimmy: Placement—Scale—Position
1	Left—Full Shot—Standing	Right—Medium Long Shot—Seated
2	Left—Full Shot—Standing	Right—Medium Long Shot—Standing
3	Left—Medium Shot—Standing	Right—Medium Shot—Seated
4	Right—Medium Long Shot—Standing	Left—Medium Long Shot—Standing
5	Left—Medium Long Shot—Standing	Right—Medium Long Shot—Standing
6	Left—Medium Long Shot—Standing	Right—Medium Shot—Seated
7	Left—Medium Shot—Standing	Right—Medium Shot—Seated
8	Left—Medium Close-Up—Standing	Right—Medium Close-Up—Standing

In lesser hands, the staging would be monotonous, but Berkeley's two-shot takes many shifting forms over the course of three minutes: Jimmy seated in the foreground as Jo enters in the background (fig. 4.9a); Jimmy and Jo with their backs turned away from each other; Jo standing close to Jimmy but turning her shoulder slightly away; Jo turning her back on Jimmy; Jo, keeping her back turned, as she pretends to be busy; Jimmy turning his back on Jo as he pretends to be casual; and, most devastating of all, Jo pondering her future with Harry even as Jimmy holds her in his arms (fig. 4.9b). The top-notch camera crew, led by William Daniels, did outstanding work. Notice the subtle booming movement, probably executed with the RO Crane, and the carefully judged depth of field. The camera starts relatively low, at Jimmy's eye level when he is seated; in imperceptible stages, it booms upward over the course of the scene,

4.9 In *For Me and My Gal*, the shot begins in separation and ends in proximity.

ending between the actors' eye levels when they are standing. The focus is deep enough to carry both actors when photographed in medium long shot but shallow enough to create separation between the foreground and background when the actors appear in medium close-up.

This scene from *For Me and My Gal* occupies a middle position between the two alternatives suggested by *Citizen Kane*. Like the Bernstein–Thatcher–Kane shot, the composition is relatively consistent, holding on a two-shot instead of breaking the scene into alternating singles. As in the puddle scene, the camera in the Jo–Jimmy scene moves several times to give structure to the unfolding drama. The technique establishes a meaningful pattern that will pay off dramatically in a later scene. Jo soon finds herself in the same situation as Jimmy: she must pretend to Harry that she wants to leave the act so Harry may become the star he always wanted to be. Harry behaves selfishly at first, but he ends up staying with Jo and kissing her for the first time. This later scene is a clear repetition of the first—with the significant variation that the exchange leads not to a separation but to a deepening of the partnership in question. The filmmakers repeat the long-take strategy for the first half of the scene, thereby underlining the point that the Jo–Harry interaction is a recurrence of the Jo–Jimmy interaction, only to switch to a shot-reverse-shot strategy for the second half of the scene, thereby reminding us that the Jo–Harry interaction ends differently, with romance.

Who decided where the camera should go? The question may be turned around. Following a particular system of camera placement changed who got to make creative decisions in the first place. Even more than cutting in the camera, the long take became a symbol of directorial daring. This mythology was not entirely false; the technique did alter the balance of power, minimizing the contributions an editor or producer might make in postproduction. However, the mythology obscured as much as it revealed: the long take represented collaborative filmmaking at its best, synthesizing the director's commands, the actors' expressions, the cinematographer's ingenuity, and the practical expertise of countless grips whose work remained without credit.

Theorizing the Fluid Camera

By the middle of the decade, industry observers had spotted a trend. Not only were many Hollywood filmmakers moving the camera more fluidly, but they also seemed to be doing so more purposefully. The films of Welles, Hitchcock, Preminger, and others inspired new debates about the contributions that the moving camera might make to Hollywood storytelling. On one level, these debates addressed familiar aesthetic questions: When should the camera move, and why? At a deeper lever, the debates addressed questions of power. Some observers, such as the *American Cinematographer* writer Herb Lightman, insisted on a collaborative model of authorship; others, such as the *Hollywood Quarterly* contributor Irving Pichel, pointed out patterns of camerawork to bolster the claim that the director should be the primary decision maker. These debates about the director's control over the camera were also debates about the camera's control over the spectator. The mobile camera offered a fantasy of total control, directing the spectator's gaze with pinpoint precision. Yet the era's fluid camerawork inspired another ideal: the ideal of understatement. Perhaps the best moves were not the strongest ones, but the gentlest.

In 1941, the film critic Otis Ferguson once visited the set of *The Little Foxes*, directed by William Wyler and photographed by Gregg Toland. Although the film is now famous for its deep-focus photography, Ferguson was most impressed by the labor involved in shooting coverage. "It is hard to realize," he wrote, "what tedious and backbreaking work goes into the actual shooting of any Class A picture." Staging, lighting, and photographing a single shot was challenging enough, but Hollywood crews had to do it again and again. The repetition derived from the logic of scene construction: "That many scenes are shot first from one side, then from another, then from above, etc., is the elemental fact needed for the camera to keep shifting to its highest point of emphasis and interest."[105] Echoing the theories of A. Lindsley Lane in the mid-1930s, Ferguson assumed that good camerawork offered the most interesting angle at all times.

The same year, 1941, the young director Garson Kanin expressed a similar idea, stating with wonderful cogency that a spectator should experience a film as if watching "a sequence of events viewed from the most advantageous position."[106] Unlike Ferguson, who delighted in the image of a collaborative team, Kanin explicitly argued that creating this sequence was the director's primary task.[107] He explained: "[The director's] main job lies not so much in directing the actor as in directing the audience—or more particularly in directing the audience's attention and the audience's emotions. You want the audience to think and to feel a certain thing at a certain time. That is necessary to gain the desired effect. The film director can do that, can absolutely control the attention, the focus of the audience."[108] Kanin theorized direction in the most forceful terms. By pointing the camera, the filmmaker took hold of the spectator's attention.[109] A film did not just represent a series of events; it represented those events from a series of shifting angles. The challenge was to find the most advantageous angle at every possible moment.

Kanin reportedly had an "abhorrence of moving the camera," in part because he believed that camera movement was a threat to Hollywood's prevailing ethic of invisibility. "Nothing is gained," he told Lewis Jacobs, "by calling the picturegoer's attention to the fact that he is watching a deliberately staged piece of film."[110] More speculatively, the theory of the advantageous angle could be interpreted as holding a bias toward the cut as the ideal transition from one view to the next. If the advantageous angle for this moment is a long shot and the advantageous angle for the next moment is a close-up, why bother dollying from one to the other, passing through all those not-so-advantageous angles in between? With a straight cut, the advantageous appears instantaneously.

Against this background, Herb Lightman's mid-decade article "The Fluid Camera" represented a major intervention. Not only did Lightman offer a robust defense of the moving camera, but he also did so by appealing to familiar principles of sequential storytelling: "Often it is found that a series of consecutive compositions can be embodied in one scene and connected by well-motivated camera movement. The resulting scene (which otherwise would have been staged as a series of choppy scenes) becomes a fluid continuity of changing compositions."[111] Following current usage, Lightman used the term *scene* as a synonym for *shot*. A crew should plan out the sequence of framings ahead of time, with long shots and close-ups and everything in between. Then, instead of shooting all of these pieces separately, the crew should combine several shots into longer units. The result would shift fluidly from composition to composition, as in the scenes from *Rebecca* and *Grand Central Murder*. Pushed to the extreme, the fluid-camera approach could turn every scene into a long take—not a deep-focus stationary take, as in *Citizen Kane*'s Bernstein–Thatcher–Kane scene, but a long take that followed the sequential logic of traditional scene construction, as in that movie's puddle scene. In Lightman's telling, the fluid camera had already become a major convention of Hollywood filmmaking. His examples included several recent Oscar winners: *How Green Was My Valley, Casablanca, The Song of Bernadette, Laura, Gaslight* (1944), and *The Lost Weekend* (1945).[112]

Like Kanin, Lightman assumed that the art of cinematic storytelling was inherently sequential, shifting from one advantageous angle to the next. Unlike

Kanin, Lightman believed that the moving camera could deliver the sequence of compositions more effectively. To bolster his case, Lightman appealed to the camera–person analogy that had structured Hollywood's practical theories for decades. Starting his essay with the truism that the "camera is the 'eye' of the audience," he took the analogy to its logical conclusion, arguing, "If the spectator were actually present in the situation depicted upon the screen, he would not just stand in one place and restrain his eye from moving about in an effort to follow the action. Rather, he would move around."[113] According to this reasoning, the camera should move from one salient detail to another because an observer would move from one salient detail to another. Anticipating the charge that the movement of an industrial contraption was too mechanical to represent such an observer, Lightman turned the objection around on the skeptic. It was editing, he argued, that was alienating, totally unlike human perception. The moving camera accomplished the same goals in a more human way: "Thus the audience's attention is held without mechanical interruption to the subject-matter of the scene."[114]

As a contributor to *American Cinematographer*, Lightman was understandably reluctant to give all the credit for the fluid camera to directors. He praised Alfred Hitchcock on the grounds that Hitchcock was a "cameraman's director" whose "touch" left ample room for cinematographers to engage in self-expression.[115] Discussing the work of cinematographer Joseph LaShelle, Lightman barely mentioned director Otto Preminger at all. He instead presented LaShelle as the leader of a tightly knit team, inspiring operators and assistants to achieve the perfect coordination that a smooth dolly shot required. Arguing that the moving camera had become a signature element of LaShelle's personal style, Lightman noted that the cinematographer "has a particular genius for breaking a scene down into various forceful compositions and joining these different 'points of view' together through smooth camera movement."[116] Preminger's subsequent career suggests that Lightman did not give him enough credit. The producer-director enjoyed productive relationships with several cinematographers, and he mastered cutting in the camera as well as the long take. By the 1960s, Preminger had developed his own philosophy of the fluid camera: "Every cut interrupts the flow of storytelling."[117]

However we apportion the credit, an example from *Laura* demonstrates fluidity in action. In a ninety-second shot, acid-tongued Waldo (Clifton Webb) criticizes Laura (Gene Tierney) for falling in love with the working-class detective who is investigating a murder plot. During the first half of the shot, Waldo paces back and forth, attempting to anger Laura, who sits calmly drinking her tea. In the background stands a clock, which will turn out to be a vital clue. Working with a small-arm dolly (probably the Raby), the operator follows Waldo's movements, reframing to include Laura when Waldo approaches her, reframing again to exclude her when he walks away. In this way, the camera participates in Waldo's anxiety, shifting in and out, up and down, and left and right as he walks this way and that (fig. 4.10a–b). After Waldo tells Laura that she always gets hurt by men, Laura stands up and turns her back on Waldo, assuring him pointedly that no man will ever hurt her again. In contrast to the agitation of the first half, the camerawork here is controlled, panning with Laura to form a balanced two-shot; the camera's poise echoes Laura's own (fig. 4.10c). In the final stage of the shot, Waldo approaches Laura and turns her around so she must listen to him talk about his jealousy. On Waldo's movement, the camera dollies in rapidly, shifting from a medium long shot to a tight close-up of Waldo facing Laura (fig. 4.10d). The speed of the dolly is surprising, echoing the implied violence behind Waldo's refusal to allow Laura to turn away. One could imagine the same series of actions depicted in a series of shots, but this alternate version would lack the expressivity of the fluid version, where the camera's motions mimic both characters' shifting emotions: Waldo's agitation, then Laura's composure, then Waldo's aggression.

One month before Lightman produced his article on the fluid camera, the actor-director Irving Pichel published another major discussion of the moving camera, "Seeing with the Camera," in the highbrow journal *Hollywood*

4.10 In *Laura*, the camera follows Waldo, then pans to follow Laura, and then dollies in as Waldo approaches.

Quarterly. Pichel's theory differed from Lightman's on several counts. Whereas Lightman gushed enthusiastically about camera movement, Pichel proceeded cautiously. Whereas Lightman praised the camera crew, Pichel privileged directors. Whereas Lightman favored the rhetoric of power and control, Pichel argued that directors could adopt a wide range of personas, from the all-powerful force to the gentle guide.

Rejecting talk of fluidity as vacuous, Pichel believed that it was the uninspired, workmanlike director who "justifies movement of the camera as the pursuit of 'fluidity.'" Standing apart from the hacks, a few directors, such as Ford, Lubitsch, and Welles, had proven that it was possible to use the camera more systematically. Pichel's great insight was that their systems varied. Some moved the camera often; others hardly at all. Either way, the key was to develop a rigorous approach toward the camera–eye analogy: "Whose eye do we conceive the camera to be? And how is it to be used? The answer to the second question will be provided by our answer to the first."[118] Reversing the standard view that parallels should serve purposes, Pichel argued that parallels should take priority. It did not matter if the director endorsed the camera–person analogy or rejected it as long as the director had a coherent philosophy. For instance, John Ford used the camera as if it were an ordinary human observer: "He rarely causes the camera to move, thus permitting the spectator to orient himself in a stable world." Such an approach required restrictions on camera placement; at all times, the camera was to occupy "feasible human viewpoints." Alternatively, Ernst Lubitsch treated his camera as if it were an omniscient but personable storyteller—a "gentle guide" who said to the spectator, "'Let me show you what I saw.'"[119] The resulting camera was partly anthropomorphic, bearing a distinctive personality, and partly unlike a person, seeming to know more than the average human observer. Lubitsch's "omniscience" implied the need to choose from a limitless array of possible view. Far from feeling "all-knowing," the spectator remained subject to the director's play of concealment and revelation. Orson Welles went even farther in this direction. His camera was totally liberated from constraints, able to fly anywhere at any time, shedding its personlike qualities altogether. As Pichel explained, "It is not conceived of as having a personality of its own, but as being simply an instrument in the hands of the director, capable of highly flexible expressiveness, as a violin is played when played upon by a virtuoso."[120] Instead of comparing the ultramobile camera to a person, Pichel compared it to radar: a superhuman technology that could locate the distant and unseen. Such a camera was omnidirectional but not really omniscient—because omniscience implied a knowledge that this inhuman machine clearly lacked.

With his audacious mix of metaphors for the camera—guide, virtuoso, observer, radar—Pichel subtly altered the rhetoric of camera movement. Contemporaneous theorists framed the problem using the language of domination:

Kanin insisted that the director's job was to "control" the audience's attention; Lightman argued that the audience's attention must be "held" on the subject; Joseph LaShelle said that cinematic storytelling should be "forceful"; Hitchcock warned that the director should never lose "power over the audience."[121] By moving or cutting to a new angle, the filmmaker was grabbing spectators and pushing them into the action. Against this background, Pichel's proposals offered a fresh alternative. Reimagining the metaphor of control, Pichel posited a spectrum of possibilities. At one end of the spectrum was the camera as instrument, a tool entirely subject to the director's powers. At the other end of the spectrum stood the camera as observer, offering spectators the chance to look at the world for themselves. In the vast middle range was the camera as guide. Here, the language of power and control yielded to a new ideal: gentleness. A guide does not grab; a guide points. A guide does not block everything else from view; a guide says calmly, "Look here."

On one level, Pichel's rhetoric calls to mind André Bazin, who also pondered the ways a filmmaker might guide our eyes with more or less force. However, Pichel classified his examples very differently. Bazin was impressed by Welles's use of relatively stationary long takes, which offered freedom to the spectator, especially in comparison to Hollywood's traditional methods of scene construction. Commenting on the four-minute kitchen scene in *The Magnificent Ambersons*, Bazin observed, "The camera obstinately refuses to come to our assistance, to guide us in the perception of an action that we feel is gaining momentum, even though we don't know when or where it will erupt."[122] This "refusal to move the camera" produced an effect of "counter-emphasis" that Bazin compared to the rhetorical figure litotes, or understatement.[123] For Pichel, the most striking thing about Welles's technique was not his deep-focus cinematography or his long takes or his use of understatement. Rather, it was Welles's roaming camera, which belonged to the other side of the spectrum, the side of domination. When the camera flies freely, its apparent liberation paradoxically demonstrates the director's omnipotence—and therefore the spectator's powerlessness. Pichel grouped Welles not with Wyler but rather with Busby Berkeley and Josef von Sternberg, two masters of delirium.

My point is not to say that Bazin was right and Pichel was wrong or vice versa; it is to show that filmmakers and critics could look at *Citizen Kane* and see different things. For Pichel, the film's most astonishing shots offered new ideas about what the moving camera could do, exploring the go-anywhere ideal so thoroughly that the camera lost its personlike qualities altogether. He noted that Welles's camera "goes where no human eye could possibly go."[124] Many of the film's most virtuosic shots were executed with a combination of camera movement and special effects, amplifying the camera's seemingly magical powers. As the first opera performance in *Citizen Kane* begins, the camera climbs up to reveal two stagehands passing judgment on Susan's execrable singing.

A crane executed the movements at the beginning and end of the shot; Linwood Dunn executed the middle portion on his optical printer.[125] The camera's ascent initially seems majestic, expressing the grandeur of opera. And yet the point of the shot is to undercut that sense of splendor. The higher the camera goes, the more it reveals the ugly machinery of the theater, settling on two stagehands who see right through the opera's pretense of artistry. In another virtuoso sequence, the camera appears to crane through a neon sign and dissolve through a skylight, all in the midst of a thunderstorm.[126] An article in *Hollywood Quarterly* singled out this shot as a conspicuous flaw—an example of Welles's taste for "sheer filmic exhibitionism."[127] In Welles's defense, such conspicuous virtuosity had plenty of precursors—from the "How did they do that?" shots of the late silent period to the through-the-window acrobatics of Curtiz and Hitchcock.[128] Even better, Welles's flamboyance made a thematic point. The camera's virtuosity stands in ironic contrast to Susan's sordid surroundings, just as its power to go anywhere stands in ironic contrast to Thompson's permanent failure to learn anything useful.

At the end of *Citizen Kane*, Thompson and his colleagues have just abandoned the search for Rosebud, and the film dissolves to a vast pile of junky treasures (fig. 4.11a). After craning past a series of discarded objects for a full fifty seconds, the camera finally settles on a composition featuring the doll from Susan's bedroom and the sled from Kane's childhood (fig. 4.11b). The latter, of course, is Rosebud. The craning movement offers us privileged knowledge while subtly undercutting any feelings of authority we might gain. When the identity of Rosebud is revealed, we have learned something important, but this moment of insight comes after we have been exposed to an array of objects that will remain forever meaningless. The shot's seriality emphasizes the scale of our ignorance. No matter how far the camera travels, the accumulation of permanently unfamiliar trinkets will always exceed the boundaries of the frame.

4.11   A crane shot ends with a view of Charles Foster Kane's childhood sled.

If *Kane* provided one model for the moving camera—technically complex, free of restrictions, ironic—then the film that beat it for the Best Picture Academy Award for 1941 provided another. In *How Green Was My Valley*, the camerawork is beautiful but restrained, allowing actors to perform in space. The director John Ford later explained his reticence: "I don't like to have the audience interested in the camera. The camera movement disturbs them."[129] Irving Pichel himself was a contributor to *How Green Was My Valley*—he provided the voiceover—and he seemed to prefer Ford's approach, noting that the director's penchant for stationary camerawork gave the occasional moving shots "uncommon effectiveness and meaning."[130] Carefully chosen movements offered gentle commentary rather than overwhelming control.

In a celebrated scene in Ford's film, the just-married Angharad (Maureen O'Hara) steps into a carriage with her stuffy husband. The carriage rides away, opening up a view to the background, where her true love, the minister Mr. Gruffydd (Walter Pidgeon), steps out to watch her departure from a distance (fig. 4.12a–b). We have seen the anxiety in Angharad's face; now we see the anguish in Gruffydd's posture. The thirty-five-second shot starts with a fairly complicated maneuver, arcing around the back of the carriage, but the most significant movement is the one that the camera does not make. When the carriage drives away, the camera does not crane in toward the minister to emphasize his expression. There is not even a cut. Instead, the camera remains far away, the film's reticence echoing the minister's own, the camera's distance underlining his separation from Angharad. According to cinematographer Arthur Miller, Ford had reasoned, "If I make a close-up, someone will want to use it."[131] As in the Rosebud shot, we are given a piece of privileged knowledge: we see the minister's suffering, and we see that all of the other wedding guests

4.12 In *How Green Was My Valley*, the camera remains discreetly distant from the minister.

have failed to see it. But Ford offers us this privileged information in a way that preserves the minister's privacy.

It is sometimes speculated that Arthur Miller beat Gregg Toland for the Best Cinematography Oscar for 1941 because Miller offered a more moderate version of the deep-focus technique that Toland had pushed to such extremes, as if the voters preferred Miller's restraint because his technique was closer to Hollywood's existing norms. However, it should be noted that there is nothing conventional about the restraint shown here. Hollywood filmmakers valued efficiency, but they also valued emotional expression. Cutting to a closer view, craning to a closer view, dollying to a closer view—all would have been customary options in a scene of such suffering. By representing an emotional turning point so tactfully, Ford and his collaborators were breaking the rules, not following them.

Borrowing the term that Bazin applied to Welles in his gentler moments, we might describe the rhetorical effect here as a form of understatement. In negative terms, understatement is a refusal of emphasis. A scene depicts a crucial detail in the storyworld, but the filmmaker refuses to play up that detail with any of the standard devices in the Hollywood tool kit—the cut to the close-up, the stinger on the music track, the dolly-in. In more positive terms, we might say that the understated filmmaker stages the scene in a way that is both complex and balanced—complex because the film offers us multiple points of interest and balanced because those multiple points are presented in a relatively level hierarchy. In this scene from *How Green Was My Valley*, there are multiple points of interest—the minister, of course, but also the guests, the gravestones, the mountain, and the beautiful tree rippling in the wind. The composition ensures that we notice the minister, positioned near the center of the frame in near silhouette against the haze, but the hierarchy remains balanced, and there are good reasons to notice the other details, too. The guests are closer and well lit, and the tree takes up half the frame.

To be sure, Pichel overdrew his opposition between Ford and Welles; Ford could be forceful, and Welles could be muted. The striking thing was the act of classification itself. Lightman lumped Ford and Welles together as embodiments of the trend toward fluidity. Pichel lumped Ford with Leo McCarey and bunched Welles with von Sternberg. In so doing, both theorists used the act of classification to teach their readers an important lesson about Hollywood filmmaking: even in the heart of the studio system, there was no one way to shoot a scene.

* * *

The innovative films of the early 1940s did not fundamentally change Hollywood's methods of scene construction; cutting in the camera and the long take had been familiar options for years. But the heightened visibility of these two alternatives in the early 1940s made an outsize impact on the industry's self-perception, opening up the possibility that a director might use the camera to evade a producer's control. The result was a curious paradox. The studio system had enabled the decade's increasingly complex camerawork by producing a set of highly trained workers who had mastered a difficult craft. Yet the more accomplished the camerawork, the more a film seemed to be the product of a single storytelling voice—a voice that came to be associated more and more with the figure of the director. The camera was increasingly fluid; so was the industry's balance of power.

Like *Sunrise*, films such as *Citizen Kane*, *Rebecca*, and *Laura* served as exemplars for future filmmakers to imitate, revise, or reject. They attracted attention because they revived long-standing puzzles, such as the problem of balancing subjectivity with objectivity and the problem of balancing revelation with concealment. I turn to these problems in the next two chapters.

CHAPTER 5

BETWEEN SUBJECTIVE AND OBJECTIVE

I n 1949, the longtime Twentieth Century-Fox cinematographer Charles G. Clarke gave a speech at the George Eastman House in Rochester. "Upon being assigned to a new production," he explained, "the Director of Photography carefully studies the script and plots the style of photography most appropriate to the story."[1] The Hollywood style was multiple; different stories called for different styles. While screenwriters spent the 1940s experimenting with alternative narrative techniques, such as flashbacks, dreams, and voiceovers, filmmakers explored an equally wide range of camera techniques. The period that produced the flowing cranes of *Letter from an Unknown Woman* (1948) also produced the enervating bumpiness of *Body and Soul* (1947); the period that produced the point-of-view shots of *Lady in the Lake* (1947) also produced the cool detachment of *Where the Sidewalk Ends* (1950).

To explain these trends, filmmakers and critics appealed to a familiar binary opposition: either the camerawork was subjective, as in a point-of-view shot, or the camerawork was objective, as in almost everything else. The simultaneous rise of the semidocumentary trend and the point-of-view craze had made the distinction seem more relevant than ever. However, a closer look at the era's films suggests that the opposition between subjective and objective was never as obvious as it appeared. Far from splitting their approaches into two clearly defined modes, filmmakers problematized the distinction in various ways: using documentary techniques to represent emotionally intense fictional situations, designing subjective sequences to display the camera's mechanical powers, and exploring the many forms that an allegedly objective style might take. No camera could record the world impartially, and none could duplicate human perception perfectly. The interest lay in between.

The first section of this chapter shows how the brief vogue for point-of-view technique in 1947 was the culmination of a long-term interest in using the moving camera to represent character perceptions. The second section borrows terms from narrative theory to argue that camerawork may express subjective states even when the film in question does not employ point-of-view shots per se. The third section turns to films on the "objective" side of the spectrum, ranging from the sympathetic camerawork of Max Ophuls to the detached style of Otto Preminger. The final section considers how filmmakers adapted the quasi-objective techniques of documentary filmmaking to various genres, such as the war film, the boxing film, and the crime film. The chapter proceeds roughly from the subjective to the objective, but the argument throughout is that the categories were never absolute. Even in the most extreme cases, the modes remain partial and provisional, shifting in time as each story unfolds.

You Are the Camera!

Perhaps the strangest trend of the postwar period was the point-of-view craze, appearing most notably in the noir duo *Lady in the Lake* and *Dark Passage* (1947). Whereas the contemporaneous semidocumentary created an impression of objectivity through restraint, these psychological thrillers used a highly mobile camera to represent characters' perceptual experiences. Although benefitting from wartime technologies, this seemingly short-lived trend had a much longer history. In the 1920s, European émigrés had shown the power of subjective and semisubjective techniques, as in *Sunrise* and *The Cat and the Canary*. In the 1930s, moving point-of-view shots appeared in several Hollywood films, from thrillers such as *Dr. Jekyll and Mr. Hyde* to romantic dramas such as *A Farewell to Arms*. As the 1940s began, two talented newcomers, Orson Welles and Alfred Hitchcock, reintroduced the problem of subjectivity—and reimagined how the problem could be solved.[2]

According to Robert Carringer, Welles spent several months (and a considerable sum of money) preparing *Heart of Darkness* as his first project for RKO. The studio abandoned the project when Welles proved unable to cut the budget down to a reasonable figure.[3] Part of the problem was Welles's desire to photograph the film using an innovative first-person technique. This technique would have allowed him to play both Marlow and Kurtz—the former in voiceover, the latter onscreen.

The Welles archive contains an intriguing document that spells out the logic behind Welles's approach: "The camera has to function not only as a mechanical recording device but as a character. The actors have to play to the camera (which is Marlowe [*sic*]) just as if it were a human being and not a collection of lenses, cogs and film."[4] The director would rehearse his actors carefully to allow them to perform unusually long takes—in one case, lasting up to twelve minutes. Elsewhere, the crew would use invisible feather wipes to create the impression of a film without cuts, as if unfolding in a single extended shot. To ensure smoothness, the operator would execute most of the film's movements with a gyroscopic camera: "This last is necessary because the camera, as Marlowe [*sic*], has to move around the rooms and even sit down and stand up. With cameras now in use . . . a feeling of terrible stiffness, a mechanical effect, is noted. With the gyroscopic camera held in the hands of the cameraman himself a more casual effect is produced."[5] During the silent period, Karl Freund had strapped a camera to his chest and stabilized its movements. *Heart of Darkness* looked both back to this silent-era technique and ahead, several decades, to the Steadicam.

The screenplay laid out Welles's intentions even more clearly. Instead of starting the story of Marlow and Kurtz right away, the film would begin with a series of short scenes, training spectators to understand the bizarre experience they were about to have. In the first scene, the camera would represent the point of view of a bird in a cage. Welles (playing himself) would look into the camera and ask the bird to sing. Then he would take out a gun and fire at the camera, as if killing the bird. Fade out. As James Naremore explains, this unrealized scene used the point-of-view shot to enact a complex fantasy of power.[6] The script imagined the director as all-powerful, in control of everything the spectator might see, and indeed capable of "killing" the spectator by cutting to black. And yet this fantasy of power had its limits. In the imagined scenario, Welles kills the bird when it refuses to sing. It was as if the first-time filmmaker were doubting his ability to manipulate the spectator.

The screenplay's second scene offered another variation on the same fantasy. Now, the camera would represent the point of view of a death-row inmate. Welles would play the warden, leading the prisoner-camera-spectator to an execution. Again, Welles equated the director's power to control the spectator's viewpoint with the power to take life. Addressing his spectators in the second person, Welles explicitly asked them to identify with the camera: "That's you. You're the camera. The camera is your eye."[7] But this fusion of the spectator with the camera was not even remotely empowering. To identify with the camera was to give your vision to someone else—the all-powerful director who could place the camera anywhere in the storyworld or cut you off from sight entirely.

The screenplay proceeded to develop Conrad's central story but using the camera to represent Marlow's point of view: "CAMERA LOWERS as Marlow sits down . . . RISING as Marlow rises."[8] Carringer explains that RKO script supervisor Amalia Kent supplied the script's detailed terminology.[9] The screenplay even described a trick that had been used in the early 1930s, casting a shadow on the wall to indicate Marlow's presence, as in *Inspiration* and *The Kennel Murder Case*. But the screenplay's commitment to the point-of-view principle was not absolute. During a particularly meditative passage, the camera was to crane up into the sky and look down on the harbor and jungle in miniature. At the end of Marlow's journey, the camera was to reverse this motion, returning with inhuman speed from the jungle to the harbor. In this way, sequences of first-person perception would alternate with sequences of go-anywhere virtuosity.

After the cancellation of *Heart of Darkness*, Welles explored the camera's inhuman mobility in *Citizen Kane*, most notoriously in the film's through-the-skylight shots. The following year, 1942, Welles returned to the problem of the point-of-view shot, planning another subjective sequence that failed to make it to the screen, at least in the form he originally intended. The scene in question is the montage of the decaying city when George (Tim Holt) walks home for the last time in *The Magnificent Ambersons*. Although the montage in the finished film is remarkable, the screenplay's handling of the sequence was revolutionary. The script's instructions read, "George is walking slowly up the street away from camera. CAMERA FOLLOWS, MOVING FASTER than he does until it is so close that his body creates a dark screen for a DISSOLVE."[10] The idea here was to show the camera entering George's body, as if camera and character had merged. The script continued, "In a SLOW MOVING SHOT we see the following (with a sort of slight dissolve or wipe from one scene to the other, but retaining a moving-forward speed) for the camera, which is now George, is slowly walking along the street and we are seeing what George sees."[11] In most films, the point-of-view shot performs a simple explanatory function, letting us know who sees what. One may understand the relevant information without "becoming" the character. Welles takes the point-of-view idea further, asking us to imagine what it would be like to get inside someone else's head.

Walking down the street, George would encounter some youngsters in a car. Then the camera would adopt the car's point of view, driving away from a humiliated George. Such a scene would have symbolized George's defeat, his human point of view replaced with a machine's point of view. Soon the camera would become George again, approaching his body and dissolving into it. The camera as George would enter the house and look around slowly: "MOVING SHOT as CAMERA WANDERS SLOWLY about the dismantled house—past the bare reception room; the dining room which contains only a kitchen table and two kitchen chairs; up the stairs, close to the smooth walnut railing of the balustrade."[12] Soliciting an extended and intense experience of imaginary identification, the scene would build tremendous empathy for George, right at the moment when he is to receive his long-awaited comeuppance. Evidence suggests that Welles and his crew actually photographed this sequence. After replacing Stanley Cortez with RKO cinematographer Harry Wild, Welles asked Cortez to shoot additional footage—including material photographed in the Amberson home with a camera but no cast members.[13] An RKO press release later alluded to the scene of George wandering around the house ("As he enters the door, the camera becomes Holt") and explained that the crew experimented with the handheld camera: "To accomplish the feat, a standard camera was strapped to a husky assistant cameraman, and with lights and sound equipment being carried also, the camera made its circuit of the house."[14] Apparently, the footage was unusable, and Welles scrapped it even before RKO mandated its own savage cuts.[15] The effect of merging the camera with George's body does not appear in the cutting continuity of the 131-minute version of *The Magnificent Ambersons*.[16]

We will never know if a version of the film following the script would have been more or less powerful than the version we have. We do know that the existing montage is extraordinary.[17] On the soundtrack, Orson Welles reads words taken almost verbatim from the book by Booth Tarkington: "The town was growing and changing. It was heaving up in the middle incredibly. It was spreading incredibly. And as it heaved and spread, it befouled itself and darkened its sky." The corresponding passage in the novel blames recent waves of migration and immigration for the decline in the city's once genteel atmosphere.[18] Rejecting this racist explanation, Welles's film instead develops the idea that the city is an organism that has grown so big that it threatens to destroy itself. The montage shows a series of buildings, dissolving one on top of the other. We could interpret these shots as representations of George's point of view or as Welles's commentary on urban decay or both. Graphic contrasts enhance the impression of disorder. The first shot shows a building with a cylindrically shaped corner (fig. 5.1a). A slow dissolve replaces this cylinder with another—the cylinder of an industrial silo. The first shot also introduces a diagonal line pattern, as power lines swoop from the upper right to the lower left. A later image flips this diagonal pattern around, showing power lines swooping from the upper left to the lower right (fig. 5.1b). As a whole, the montage brings to fruition Slavko Vorkapich's idea that a film's graphic patterns should express the feeling of a film's subject. Here, a visual cacophony expresses the bewildering chaos of the changing city. The montage consists of around a dozen shots; the camera moves in each one. We never see George onscreen, suggesting that this muddled city has already erased his presence. Indeed, the sequence shows no people at all, as if the horrible growth of the city were proceeding of its own accord, untethered to human needs.

Like Welles, Alfred Hitchcock explored the shifting territory between the restrictive point-of-view shot and the roaming but selective external camera. In writings and interviews, Hitchcock expressed two competing attitudes toward the point-of-view shot. On the one hand, he argued, "Subjective technique,

5.1 In *The Magnificent Ambersons*, a montage represents a walk through the city.

putting the audience in the mind of the character is, to me, the purest form of the cinema."[19] On the other hand, he acknowledged that extended point-of-view sequences were counterproductive: "The eye must look at the character."[20] When the camera becomes a character, the film denies the spectator the opportunity to look at the character's own face. Paradoxically, an overreliance on point-of-view shots weakens a film's emotional impact. For Hitchcock, Kuleshovian montage provided the best solution: show the character's face, show what the character sees, and then show the character's face again. In this way, the filmmaker may represent a character's point of view while allowing the spectator to register the character's emotional reactions.

Hitchcock's first American film, *Rebecca*, showed that by 1940 he was already aware of these tensions, developing a persistent contrast between imaginative freedom (as when Joan Fontaine's dreaming protagonist imagines herself passing through the iron gate at Manderley) and lived constraint (as when the protagonist finds her moving point of view blocked by the housekeeper, Mrs. Danvers). Later Hitchcock films developed further variations on the same basic structure. What if the camera is looking through the eyes of a villain? What if the camera is nearly looking through a character's eyes—but not quite? What if the camera is looking through one person's eyes—and then through another's?[21] A brief exchange in *Shadow of a Doubt* (1943) illustrates the figure's capacity for moral complexity. Young Charlie (Teresa Wright) has learned that her uncle, also named Charlie (Joseph Cotten), is a murderer. She decides to wear an incriminating ring to let him know that she knows the truth. As she walks down the stairs, Uncle Charlie recognizes the ring (fig. 5.2a). The film cuts to a medium shot of Young Charlie, and the camera dollies in to isolate the ring on her finger (figs. 5.2b–c). Like the amplified point-of-view shots discussed in chapter 1, the camera movement represents Uncle Charlie's subjective

5.2 In *Shadow of a Doubt*, the camera's movement represents the focusing of Uncle Charlie's attention.

experience without representing his optical experience. Uncle Charlie stands still, but the rapid movement suggests that he is focusing his attention on the incriminating ring. Meanwhile, the distant-to-close movement gives us a brief glimpse of Young Charlie's expression, looking intently toward Uncle Charlie to see if her provocative accessory has registered its intended meaning. When the film cuts back to a stationary image of Uncle Charlie's expression (fig. 5.2d), what was once an unmediated shot of Uncle Charlie has become an image of what Young Charlie sees—again, not from her exact position in space but in a manner that echoes her intense focus on her uncle's reactions. Instead of representing the entire moment of recognition from Uncle Charlie's point of view, the film has maintained its strategy of doubling the two characters: showing what Uncle Charlie sees (not quite through his eyes), then showing what Young Charlie sees (not quite through her eyes). The resulting orientation is complex. As the film's protagonist, Young Charlie is the primary vehicle for our sympathies. When repressed fear and anger appear on Uncle Charlie's face, the effect is thrilling (because her plan is working) and worrisome (because she may be in danger). At the same time, Uncle Charlie is not a typical villain. He is the most sophisticated person in town, and Young Charlie has spent much of the film admiring him. The look of fear on his face may provoke a glimmer of sympathy for him, too, even as the look of anger reminds us that the recipient of that sympathy remains a threat.

Hitchcock explored the power of the point-of-view shot more explicitly in *Spellbound* (1945), a thriller about psychoanalysis—indeed, about subjectivity itself. The film features a spectacular closing shot, representing the point of view of a murderous psychiatrist, Dr. Murchison (Leo G. Carroll), who points a gun at his colleague Dr. Petersen (Ingrid Bergman). After she talks the madman out of killing her, Murchison turns the gun around and points it at the camera— that is, at himself (fig. 5.3a–b). The gun fires in a burst of red, and the film ends. Because cinematographer George Barnes was unwilling to photograph the scene in Tolandesque deep focus, the crew constructed an enormous model hand and gun, which wheels around to face the camera.[22] The strangeness of the scene is only partly attributable to the huge sculpted hand with its neatly trimmed fingernails; the scene mixes together contradictory emotional appeals. The point-of-view shot asks us to imagine being in Murchison's position; we must understand why he decides to let Petersen go and why he decides to kill himself instead. But the scene works as the culmination of a suspense story only if our sympathies remain with Petersen. She is the one facing the threat, and she is the one who solves the problem. When the gun fires, the moment may spark feelings of fear as we imagine being the target, but the real effect is one of triumph, celebrating Petersen's victory. Indeed, this very split may be the point of the shot. A film about fragmented subjectivity ends with a shot that fragments our own experiences.

5.3 At the end of *Spellbound*, the camera represents a murderer's point of view as he commits suicide.

Critics quickly noticed Hitchcock's skill with the point-of-view shot. James Agee thought that Hitchcock was unique: "One would think that the use of the camera subjectively—that is, as one of the characters—would, for many years, have been as basic a movie device as the close-up, but few people try it, and Hitchcock is nearly the only living man I can think of who knows just when and how to."[23] Others placed Hitchcock at the forefront of a broader trend. In 1946, the prolific Herb Lightman noted a recent turn toward "the subjective camera." His key examples included two Hitchcock films (*Lifeboat*, 1944, and *Spellbound*) and an adaptation of an earlier Hitchcock film (John Brahm's *The Lodger*, 1944). The article proposed a simple opposition between objective and subjective: "Usually, the camera maintains the role of a detached observer of the story. . . . Occasionally, however, the camera steps out of its role as casual observer and becomes a participant in the story. In so doing it assumes the point of view of one of the characters."[24] The purpose of the subjective camera was emotional engagement. Ideally, a spectator would identify with a character and share that character's experience: "The subjective approach, when well executed, tends to bring the audience into the picture. It is allowed to see part of the action as it appears to one of the characters, and it will subconsciously experience the same reactions he does."[25] Lightman qualified his bold claims by insisting that the subjective camera should be used as an occasional effect only. This restriction initially seems puzzling. If a Hollywood filmmaker aims to increase a film's emotional appeal, and the subjective camera is capable of heightening emotional response, then why shouldn't a Hollywood filmmaker use the technique all the time? Given Lightman's preference for discomfiting examples, a plausible answer may be that most films do not require subjective shots because their stories carry an obvious emotional appeal already. When watching a romantic comedy, we do not need extra encouragement to identify with the protagonist, who is usually charming and attractive. But when we are watching a disturbing mystery, a point-of-view shot may be more useful precisely because identification is more difficult to achieve. The subjective shot asks us to imagine something that is hard to imagine, such as killing or being killed. Regarding the ending of *Spellbound*, Lightman observed, "Audiences viewing it become participants in expected murder (vicariously, of course), and then become victims of a suicide." Switching to the murder scene in *The Lodger*, he enthused, "The killer had not been shown, and yet the audience had had the unique jolting experience of having directly participated in a murder."[26] Lightman advised using the subjective shot sparingly not because it was inherently arty but because its primary purpose was delivering an unexpected jolt, forcing us to imagine what it would be like to do something shocking.

Scholar Susan Smith has argued that Hitchcock developed three distinct kinds of suspense, which she calls "vicarious," "shared," and "direct." With vicarious suspense, the spectator experiences anxiety on behalf of a character precisely because the spectator has crucial knowledge that the character does not. With shared suspense, the spectator identifies with the character more closely because both are fully aware that the character is in danger. With direct suspense, a film's subjective techniques encourage spectators to imagine, at least momentarily, that they themselves are in danger.[27] *Spellbound* puts us in a peculiar position, asking us to imagine being Dr. Murchison, a killer and an eventual suicide victim, while experiencing shared suspense with the wholly sympathetic Dr. Petersen, a character who knows full well that she is in danger. Rather than align our imaginations with our morality, the sequence pulls the spectator in different directions at once, toward the likable Dr. Petersen and toward the criminal Dr. Murchison.

Like Hitchcock, John Brahm used subjective camerawork to provoke morally uncomfortable emotions, asking us to identify with characters committing horrible crimes. In the opening scene to *Hangover Square* (1945), the "objective" camera introduces a busy city square. A hurdy-gurdy plays an unsettling tune, and the camera cranes up past a gas lamp toward an antiques shop. In the apartment above the shop, a large man is attacking the shop's owner. Then, shockingly, the camera appears to *become* the large man, advancing toward the old antiques dealer. In defense, the dealer picks up a stray object and strikes his attacker (the camera). After a hidden cut, the large man's hand enters the frame, stabs the dealer, grabs a gas lamp, and throws it onto the body, which catches horribly on fire. Only then do we see the face of the large man, later identified as Bone, played by Laird Cregar. Although the scene is set in the past, the film makes an oblique reference to the Holocaust, showing the brutal murder of a character whose costume identifies him as Jewish. Brahm, himself a Jewish émigré who began his career in Germany, used this bizarre opening to raise troubling questions about the nature of cinematic technique.[28] By preventing us from seeing Bone's face, the framing directs our sympathies to the dealer, an innocent old man who is clearly in mortal danger. And yet the subjective camerawork asks us to imagine what it would be like to kill another human being, as if Brahm were saying, "Look how easily a film can get you to identify with a murderer." The shot's artiness—its flamboyant switching from outside to inside, from objective to subjective—supports its reflexive critique. The film manipulates our emotions, but we see the manipulation in action because we see the camera shifting registers before our eyes.

Extended point-of-view sequences were technically demanding, even when the crew did not have to build an oversize hand holding a pistol. Some producers thought they were not worth the trouble. Architect turned production designer William Pereira wrote a long memo to producer David O. Selznick outlining his plan to apply subjective technique to *Since You Went Away* (1944).[29] Perhaps resenting the idea of having to read someone else's multipage memo, Selznick did not take the suggestion. When Twentieth Century-Fox was preparing the amnesia-themed thriller *Somewhere in the Night* (1946), producer Darryl F. Zanuck encouraged director Joseph L. Mankiewicz to adopt *Laura* and *Hangover Square* as models, but he also gave Mankiewicz a warning: "I am not interested so much in exotic camera setups, which I think distort the viewpoint of an audience."[30] After Mankiewicz and cinematographer Norbert Brodine completed several successful point-of-view shots for the opening sequence, Zanuck made his warning more explicit: "I realized that you used this technique purposely for this situation. But please do not let it become a habit. It is my opinion that prolonged scenes where the camera moves back and forth are more harmful than helpful."[31] According to Zanuck, spectators rarely appreciated camera movement—or even noticed it.

The examples so far might serve to normalize *Lady in the Lake*, suggesting that the moving point-of-view shot had already joined (or rejoined) the family of acceptable storytelling conventions by the time Robert Montgomery's film premiered in early 1947. But "normalization" is not quite right, for the moving point-of-view shot had become an increasingly normal way of representing the abnormal.[32] In his screenplay for *Heart of Darkness* in 1940, Orson Welles had proposed to represent the point of view of a man being executed. Since then, filmmakers had used the technique to represent the perspective of a murderer, a suicide, and an amnesiac, among other extreme situations. *Lady in the Lake* exploited this abnormal norm, depicting the point of view of a man experiencing one violent encounter after another. The film's ad campaign emphasized the most extreme moments: "You get socked in the jaw by a murder suspect! You slug the crooked cop who tries to frame you!"[33] To identify with the camera was to have a gun pointed at your head. Even the film's romantic moments were treated as threats. *LIFE* magazine's review of the film noted that the scene showing Adrienne (Audrey Totter) leaning in to kiss the protagonist, Philip Marlowe (Montgomery), was sure to make "male members of the audience squirm in their seats."[34]

When Raymond Chandler, the author of the novel on which the film was based, wrote the initial screenplay for *Lady in the Lake*, he made no attempt to replicate Marlowe's point of view.[35] But a few months later pulp novelist Steve Fisher wrote another draft, rigorously applying the point-of-view technique. Fisher's screenplay was 113 pages long, but it listed only sixty-three shots, an unusually low number, reflecting the filmmakers' desire to rely on the moving camera more than on cuts. The script's instructions were remarkably precise: "CAMERA MOVES FORWARD, past the receptionist. Marlowe's hand enters SHOT, opens the door to Adrienne's office, and MOVES THRU TO: INT. ADRIENNE'S OFFICE—DAY. IN CONTINUOUS MOVEMENT, CAMERA TRAVELS a few steps into the office, then STOPS DEAD."[36] In practice, the film employed more cuts, but the camerawork remained remarkably ambitious. When Marlowe walks through the doorway in the scene quoted, the camera tilts down to show his hand and then tilts back up again as the camera dollies forward past the opening door. When Adrienne asks Marlowe to sit down, the camera dollies forward one foot and then booms downward two feet. The film uses various tricks to remind us that the camera's point of view corresponds with Marlowe's. The detective lights a cigarette, and smoke billows upward into the frame. He follows Adrienne over to a mirror, and the mirror shows Marlowe's reflection. Most importantly, the camera's movements mimic the flow of Marlowe's attention, panning to a framed magazine cover when Marlowe is bored, then panning to follow the attractive receptionist when Marlowe leers at her. The camera represents not just Marlowe's optical point of view but also his desiring gaze.

As in Welles's *Heart of Darkness* screenplay, Montgomery's film begins with an explanatory sequence, spelling out the logic of the film's unusual approach, as if the filmmakers were unsure that the technique would work. Drawing on his own wartime experiences, cinematographer Paul Vogel used an Eyemo, a handheld 35-millimeter camera, for some shots, but the film as a whole does not appear to be an extended experiment in bumpy camerawork. Most of the time, the camera rests on a dolly, boom, or tripod, shifting to the operator's shoulder only for exceptional effects.[37] One scene shows Marlowe interrogating Chris Lavery, a gigolo. During the interrogation, actor Dick Simmons looks directly into a tripod-mounted camera. When Marlowe looks at a clock, the camera pans to the right and back to the left. During the second pan, the film cuts to a new shot, now handheld. The gigolo punches Marlowe, Lavery's brass knuckles filling the frame (fig. 5.4a). After another cut, the handheld camera wobbles back and forth, out of focus, and sinks to the floor, as if Marlowe were passing out from being sucker punched (fig. 5.4b). Such unusual fight scenes feel amusing rather than immersive, creating an incongruous juxtaposition

5.4 *Lady in the Lake* switches to a handheld camera when Marlowe gets socked.

between what we see and what we feel. Later, Marlowe fights with the corrupt detective DeGarmot (Lloyd Nolan). In the corresponding scene in the book, Marlowe describes his own body with precision: "He hit me across the face with an open hand. It jerked my head around hard. My face felt hot and large."[38] In the movie, the camera neatly conveys the effect of a head being jerked to the side, but the same trickery fails to convey the feeling of blood rushing to one's face.

Several other filmmakers tried the technique, usually in brief bursts. Curtis Bernhardt used a moving camera to represent the point of view of psychologically unstable characters in *High Wall* and *Possessed* (both 1947). Lewis Milestone revised the latter film's subjective gurney shot for *Arch of Triumph* (1948). In *Sleep, My Love* (1948), Douglas Sirk used a moving camera to represent the point of view of a somnambulist tricked into committing a murder. Most notably, Delmer Daves's film *Dark Passage* featured dozens of extended point-of-view shots, approaching the extended immersion of *Lady in the Lake*. According to Norris Pope, it was Daves who gave his friend Montgomery the initial idea for the technique, even though Daves's film came out later.[39] Daves's cinematographer, Sid Hickox, took advantage of another wartime technology: the Arriflex, a German camera equipped with a reflex viewfinder, which allowed the operator to look directly through the lens while shooting. As Joshua Gleich reports, the Warner Bros. Camera Department even tinkered with a gyroscopic stabilizer, recalling Welles's proposals for *Heart of Darkness* and foreshadowing the Steadicam of the 1970s.[40]

A highly portable camera proved to be particularly useful because much of *Dark Passage* was photographed on location in San Francisco. Nevertheless, the film relied extensively on dollies and tripods, saving handheld work for technically challenging situations. One scene shows Vincent (Humphrey Bogart), an escaped convict, approaching the apartment building of Irene (Lauren Bacall), a mysterious woman who is helping him for as yet undisclosed reasons. Vincent opens a car door, and the camera (not yet handheld) whip-pans right and left, as if checking to see that all is clear, before dollying in toward a stairway. After an undisguised cut, the camera (now handheld) represents Vincent's point of view as he follows Irene into a tiny elevator. The shot would be impossible on a dolly. In less than a minute, the camera pans to the right, enters the tight space of the elevator, pans to the right again to reveal Irene as she pushes the buttons, holds on Irene as the elevator ascends to the third floor, and then pans to the right again as Irene exits the elevator. Curiously, the camera then moves closer to the back of Irene's head, creating a black screen that disguises the next cut to a stationary view of the upstairs hallway. Even when equipped with an Arriflex, cinematographers remained reluctant to embrace the handheld camera as an everyday tool for studio films.

Dark Passage alternates between point-of-view shots and more traditional outside views, eventually abandoning the point-of-view conceit altogether after the protagonist has plastic surgery. When compared to Montgomery's work, the film develops a very different relationship with the spectator. *Lady in the Lake* offers itself as a sort of puzzle. In the explanatory opening, Marlowe lays out the rules of the game: "You'll see it just as I saw it. You'll meet the people. You'll find the clues. And maybe you'll solve it quick, and maybe you won't." Though Marlowe cockily assures us that he is the only one who knows the whole truth, the game works because Marlowe originally knew nothing about the case. We will see the clues when he sees the clues. *Dark Passage* is more complicated. Although Vincent does not know everyone he meets, he does know some of them, creating distance between the protagonist and the spectator. The camera must jump *out* of its protagonist's head in order to bridge the gap. In one scene, Vincent is alone in Irene's apartment when he hears a knock on the door. A woman calls for Irene, and a voiceover communicates Vincent's thoughts: "That's Madge's voice." Consistent with Vincent's point of view, the camera dollies in, as if walking toward the door. Then, breaking the pattern, a dissolve takes us to the other side of the door, echoing the through-the-door dissolves from *A Woman of Affairs* and *Citizen Kane*. Once confined to Vincent's consciousness, the camera has attained the power to pass through solid objects. One might assume that the effect of this transmigration is to give us privileged knowledge, allowing us to see someone that Vincent does not. In fact, the result is closer to the reverse, compensating for our lack of knowledge by revealing information that he takes for granted. Vincent recognizes Madge's voice immediately, and he already knows what she looks like. Confining our view to Vincent's optical perspective would have made it harder for us to understand his worldview because he knows so much more than what he sees.

No matter how expert the camerawork, the spectator can never occupy the character's position in the world. The point-of-view fad of 1947 seems like a case of filmmakers taking the camera–person analogy to its logical conclusion, requiring the camera to imitate a person—not just an observer, but a character—from beginning to end. But none of the films applied this logic so rigorously—not *Dark Passage*, not *Lady in the Lake*, not even Welles's unmade *Heart of Darkness*. They treated the point-of-view shot as one storytelling option among many, and they were always prepared to slip outside their characters' heads to produce a different effect.

Significantly, the director who seemed to take the technique the furthest, Robert Montgomery, abandoned the extended point-of-view shot in his next film, *Ride the Pink Horse* (1947), produced by Hitchcock's former collaborator Joan Harrison. Montgomery instead explored the rich territory between the subjective and the objective. In the opening scene, Montgomery's character Lucky enters a bus station, places a sheet of paper in a locker, and uses some chewing gum to hide the locker key behind a map. Technically, the three-minute shot is as impressive as anything in *Lady in the Lake*. Starting in the bright

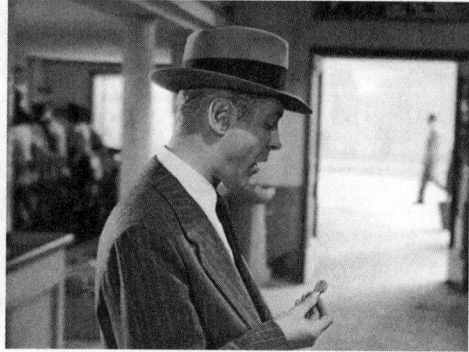

5.5 In *Ride the Pink Horse*, the camera observes the protagonist from the outside.

outdoor sun (fig. 5.5a), the camera dollies inside the station, and the aperture opens up, allowing us to see the dim interior. Once inside, the camera pans around 180 degrees to show the protagonist standing in front of the entrance (fig. 5.5b); then it reverses its movements, ending up back outside in the sun.

More important than the technique is the effect; the shot addresses its spectator differently. *Lady in the Lake* says, "Imagine that you are this man." *Ride the Pink Horse* says, "You are not this man. He is a mystery to you. Watch him. He knows what he is doing, but you do not. Why does he open up a locker? Watch and find out. Why does he start to chew gum? Watch and find out. Why is he sticking the gum to the key? Watch and find out." If *Lady in the Lake* offers the amped-up thrills of subjective storytelling—the pleasure of guessing along with a detective, the pleasure of identifying with his lustful gaze, the pleasure of getting socked in the jaw without feeling a thing—then *Ride the Pink Horse* offers its own, more muted pleasures—the pleasure of observation, the pleasure of seeing a process unfold over time, the pleasure of figuring out what someone else is doing and why.

Fictions and Functions

In his article "The Subjective Camera," Lightman had defined the terms *subjective* and *objective* in opposition to one another. Either the film presented the scene through a character's eyes, or the film did not. In this section, I shift briefly from a historical mode to a historical-theoretical approach, drawing on some general ideas from narrative theory to clarify the nature of this subjective–objective distinction—and to suggest some of its limitations.

One of Lightman's key examples, John Brahm's film *The Lodger*, features two murder scenes where the distinction between objective and subjective appears

to be quite sharp. In the opening scene, the camera cranes past some policemen and introduces a woman named Katie (Thora Hird). Exiting a bar, she
laughs as her friends joke about Jack the Ripper (fig. 5.6a). After a cut, the camera tracks alongside Katie before craning away as she steps behind a wall
(fig. 5.6b). When she screams, the camera cranes back down, revealing a broken bottle on the other side of the wall, its shattered glass symbolizing the murder that has just occurred. Following Lightman's either–or logic, the camerawork seems unambiguously objective, craning alongside a character without
looking through the character's eyes. A later murder unfolds differently. Jennie
(Doris Lloyd) hears a suspicious sound in her bedroom. Suddenly, the light
goes out, and the film cuts to a shot representing the murderer's point of view,
inching toward the victim as she struggles to scream (fig. 5.7a–b). Here, the
shot seems unambiguously subjective. Resembling a handheld camera, the
dolly-mounted camera pans left and right and tilts up and down erratically to
represent the killer's uneven steps as he lumbers closer and closer.

5.6 In *The Lodger*, a murder takes place unseen behind a wall.

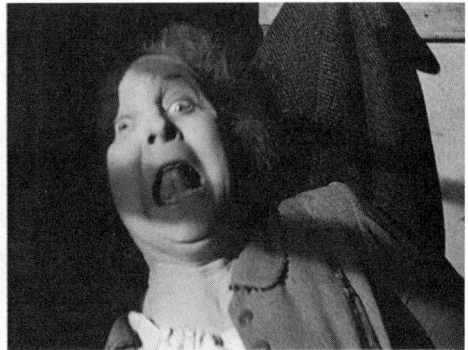

5.7 Later in *The Lodger*, the camera represents the murderer's moving point of view.

In comparison to the first scene's objectivity, the second scene's subjectivity seems so obvious that we may overlook a fundamental fact: only some of the point-of-view shot's visible features are subjective. The image is in black-and-white, but the film does not ask us to imagine that the murderer sees the world in black-and-white. The frame is rectangular, but the film does not ask us to imagine that the murderer sees the world through a moving rectangle. These traits are pictorial. When we watch a film, we do not share the storyworld's space. We see pictures of the storyworld.[41] To borrow a famous phrase, we might say that we see the storyworld *in* the pictures. Some of the visible traits we see, such as the monochrome appearance and the rectangular shape of the frame, belong only to the film's configuration, not to its representational subject.[42]

To be sure, there is nothing mysterious about the monochrome appearance and the rectangular shape; they are familiar pictorial features. More puzzling are other features that depart from our expectations. In the first murder scene in *The Lodger*, the camera follows Katie closely, but then it unexpectedly disconnects from her and cranes away at the crucial moment. In the second example, the camera is stationary, and then it bizarrely starts to wobble as it approaches the victim. Though small scale, such shifts might provoke questions: Why does the camera crane away? Why does the camera wobble?

Questions about why a film contains puzzling traits are questions of motivation. As Meir Sternberg explains, the motivation for a device may be *fictional* or *functional*. Confronted with a narrative artwork, we make sense of its peculiar features by situating them within the logic of the (fictional) storyworld and/ or by situating them within the logic of the work's (functional) purposes.[43] An analogy with lighting may make the distinction clearer. Why is the second murder scene so dark? If we answer, "Because the murderer has extinguished the lamp," then we are appealing to the logic of the storyworld. If we answer, "Because the filmmakers are creating an atmosphere of dread," then we are appealing to a means–end logic manifest in the film's design. The same dual logic applies to camera movement. In the first murder scene, the motivation for the unusual camerawork is functional. Why does the camera crane away? For a purpose: to conceal the identity of the murderer. The second murder scene is more complex, appealing to both fictional and functional motivation simultaneously. Why does the camera start to wobble? If we answer, "Because the murderer is walking forward erratically," then we are finding a reason within the storyworld. If we answer, "To create suspense while concealing the murderer's identity," then we are appealing to means–end thinking. Fictional motivation looks for an answer in the storyworld; functional motivation looks for an answer in the aesthetic-rhetorical situation.

Crucially, the two logics are not equal. As Sternberg writes, the tensions between the fictional and the functional modes "are always resolvable and

always in favor of the second mode, by way of a higher teleological explanation."[44] Once we assume that the feature in question was designed for a purpose (and not there by accident or rote convention), we can always ask what
effects the work was designed to achieve. The traits of the storyworld (its objects,
its characters, its events) become means to functional ends. But fictional motivation is optional. Many lighting techniques—from expressionist shadows to
showy Hollywood backlights—are highly functional, even when they make little sense according to the laws of physics. Similarly, a camera may move to
accomplish a function, whether its movement makes sense in the storyworld
or not—a world where the camera typically does not exist.

Within this theoretical framework, the mobile point-of-view shot acquires
a special status. It is the rare example of a shot where the movement of the camera is motivated functionally *and* fictionally. Normally, we may explain the
camera's movement perfectly well in functional terms alone. Why does the camera move? To reveal a clue, to follow a character, to offer an ironic juxtaposition. The status of the film's frame is comparable to the status of monochrome
in a black-and-white movie; the frame is part of the pictures that we see, not
part of the storyworld that the characters inhabit. But a moving point-of-view
shot is mimetic, imitating a movement in the fictional world. Like the extinguished lamp that creates a mood for murder, the point-of-view shot works
through the mediating level of the fictional world to accomplish its functional
ends. To make sense of the second scene's bumpy camerawork, we must revise
our understanding of the storyworld. The murderer is in the room; he is advancing toward his victim; he is tall; he is slow; he walks with a lumbering gait.
Even more, we must revise our understanding of the film's storytelling
perspective—its mediation via a character's experience. Unlike the camerawork
of the first scene, the camerawork of the second scene depicts the murder
through the eyes of a character—in this case, the murderer.[45] Notice that fictional mediation has enabled rather than replaced the second scene's functional
logic. As in the first scene, the camerawork generates mounting suspense while
concealing the murderer's identity. But it is only by working through the level
of the storyworld that the camerawork is able to accomplish an additional
function, asking us to imagine what it would be like to commit murder. It is
the latter function that delighted Lightman so much.

As noted in chapter 2, the subjective–objective distinction cuts across other
distinctions, such as the distinction between a camera that moves like a person and a camera that does not. Even an objective camera might be anthropomorphic, restricting itself to humanly possible perspectives. Similarly, the
subjective–objective distinction does not line up with the distinction between
restricted and unrestricted range. Drawing on Sternberg's work, David Bordwell
has explained how the concept of range applies to the cinema. A film with a
restricted range may follow a single character from scene to scene, thereby

limiting the film's revelations to the character's range of awareness, as in *The Big Sleep* (1946), where we learn the clues as Philip Marlowe learns them. Such a film might dip into a character's mind or it might not.[46] Similarly, George M. Wilson has proposed the term *restricted authority* to make sense of films such as *To Have and Have Not* (1944)—another Bogart film directed by Howard Hawks. The film does not get inside the protagonist's head, but it does adhere to an internal norm, showing scenes only as Bogart's character encounters them. This narrowly focused approach stands in contrast to the unrestricted mode of many Hollywood films, whereby the movie remains free to show whatever "dramatic effectiveness" demands.[47]

Both theorists insist that these restrictions may vary as a movie unfolds. Bordwell's recent book on cinema of the 1940s examines several intricate variations, such as the "moving spotlight" approach, whereby a film's narration examines one character closely before jumping to another.[48] Given this flexibility, it would be perfectly normal for a film to remain within a single character's range of knowledge for a few minutes, only to shift away at a key moment, revealing something that the character does not know or concealing something that the character does know. The opening murder scene in *The Lodger* follows a variable pattern. At first, the camera roams freely through the neighborhood. Then it attaches itself to Katie, disclosing details as she discovers them. Then the camera detaches from her decisively to offer a strikingly uninformative high-angle view just before her death. Such shifting patterns remain purposeful, hinting at threats without disclosing them fully. Whether attached to a single character's experience or not, whether delving into a character's mind or not, the camera remains a storyteller's tool.

Further complicating the objective–subjective divide, Wilson extols the affordances of another approach, which he calls "indirect or reflected subjectivity." Operating somewhere between the purely objective and the purely subjective, a sequence in the indirect mode will "let properties of the way in which the fictional world looks to us on the screen *stand in for* properties of the way in which that world is experienced by the character."[49] A film might use an unusual color palette or disturbing music to express what a character is feeling, without suggesting that the character sees that color or hears that music. Such indirectness characterizes the semisubjective examples discussed in the first half of this book, such as the shot of the troubled acrobat in *Variety* or the dancing sibling in *The Barretts of Wimpole Street*. In this mode, the camera's movements express emotions that the character is feeling while observing that character from the outside.

Many filmmakers of the 1940s believed that *Lady in the Lake*'s single-minded exploration of subjectivity went too far; Hitchcock mocked the film, claiming that Montgomery failed to understand that a subjective scene needs to show what the character sees *and* the character's reactions.[50] The semisubjective mode proved to be much more durable. Describing the waltz sequence in *Madame Bovary* (1949), the director Vincente Minnelli explained, "The camera movement suggested her dizziness and breathlessness."[51] The sequence features one whirling point-of-view shot, but the most astonishing shot reflects the protagonist's experience rather than representing it directly, panning 360 degrees to convey the delirium of Emma (Jennifer Jones) as she spins around the dance floor. Like the point-of-view shot, the semisubjective shot is mimetic; the camera moves to imitate an aspect of the storyworld—in this case, an emotional experience.

Such mimicry may be very subtle indeed. Curtis Bernhardt's thriller *High Wall* (1947) features a pair of sequences in the *Lady in the Lake* mold, but the film's most impressive shot works semisubjectively. Steve (Robert Taylor) is locked in an insane asylum because he has been accused of killing his wife—an accusation that he (wrongly) believes. Dr. Lorrison (Audrey Totter), a tough but wise psychologist, tells him that he is afraid to leave the asylum because he is afraid to face his son with the (supposed) truth about the wife's murder. Working with *Lady in the Lake* cinematographer Paul Vogel, director Curtis Bernhardt stages the first half of the scene in shot-reverse-shot, relying on cuts to shift from one angle to another. When Lorrison advances toward Steve and confronts him with a series of hard truths, the camera photographs the exchange in a fifty-four-second fluid take, tightening as the conversation intensifies. First, the camera follows Lorrison as she walks from a single into an over-the-shoulder composition (fig. 5.8a). Then the framing gets tighter: Steve steps forward, and Lorrison follows (fig. 5.8b). Then, tighter still: the camera cranes down to look over Lorrison's shoulder as Steve gradually turns to face her (fig. 5.8c). Then, as tight as possible: the camera cranes up to a close-up single of Steve as he realizes that Lorrison is right (fig. 5.8d). It is easy to imagine this portion of the scene broken down into four separate shots. Instead, the crew captured this sequence of compositions in a single shot, using movement itself to amplify the dramatic structure of the scene. Gradually, Lorrison presses her case. Gradually, Steve realizes that she speaks the truth. Gradually, Lorrison grows more determined. Gradually, Steve grows more afraid. The camera's movements—tighter and tighter—underline these gradual upticks in intensity. We see the doctor, the patient, and the ever-shrinking space between them. The camera never looks through anyone's eyes, and, indeed, its movements remain visibly machinelike, craning up and down several times. But the quality of mimicry remains, imitating Lorrison's determination as she steps closer and closer to Steve to force him to confront the truth.

This brief detour into narrative theory might seem like a digression from my historical argument, but it makes a historical point. The filmmakers of the 1940s were keen to explore these very distinctions—if not in print, then on the screen. In a time of narrative experimentation, filmmakers thought deeply

5.8 In *High Wall*, the camera fluidly shifts between four distinct compositions.

about the differences between subjective and objective storytelling. In a time of camera fluidity, they thought just as deeply about how the moving camera might complement and complicate these storytelling patterns.

Sympathy and Detachment

Like the subjective camera, the objective camera could take many forms. This section and the next explore a range of approaches, from the detached films of Otto Preminger to the earnest semidocumentaries of the postwar period. First, I consider objectivity as a particular tone expressing a distinct attitude toward a subject, from detachment to sympathy. Next, I consider objectivity as a style, adopting and transforming the visual markers of the documentary.

In the noir cycle, hard-boiled fiction modeled one form that objective storytelling might take. Inspired by the cinema, many hard-boiled novelists favored a "camera–eye" approach to narration, simply describing their characters from the outside, as if restricted to what a camera might record.[52] Robert Siodmak's film *The Killers* (1946) was based on Ernest Hemingway's nine-page story, a classic example of the hard-boiled prose style. With its supplementary flashbacks, the film is more of an elaboration than a strict adaptation, but one sequence offers reflexive commentary on the very idea of objective storytelling. The insurance investigator Jim (Edmund O'Brien) has learned that the Swede (Burt Lancaster) was involved in a robbery several years earlier. He listens while his boss reads aloud from an old newspaper account. Onscreen, we see the robbery, which Siodmak has staged with panache in a single two-minute take. The voiceover mimics Hemingway's clipped style, stating the known information and adding speculations only when warranted. Meanwhile, the camera represents the same events with cold precision.

Is this precision a cinematic analog of Hemingway's prose? Although the rest of the film features subjective and semisubjective techniques, this particular scene never looks through anyone's eyes, and indeed it never shows anyone in close-up, instead depicting the entire robbery in a series of long-shot framings. The film initially seems to be proposing a close comparison between the reporter's prose and the camera's positioning—both favor facts over feelings. But the analogy proves to be unsustainable. The longer the two-minute take stretches on, the more it seems like the voiceover and the cinematography offer two incommensurate ways of representing an event, each shaped by its own potentials and limitations. The voiceover describes "four men, all wearing employee identification badges," blending into the crowd of workers. The reporter does not identify the robbers, but we recognize them at a glance (fig. 5.9a). Following journalistic norms, the voiceover hazards a few guesses but identifies its guesses as such: "Apparently, the strangers merely crossed the yard." Showing no such caution, the image shows the men crossing the yard definitively. The voiceover picks out specific details: the drawing of guns and the gagging of employees. The camera is also selective, but its selections paradoxically overwhelm us with detail. When the camera cranes up to a window to show the

5.9 A robbery scene is photographed in a bravura long take in *The Killers*.

robbery from the outside, we see some of the details mentioned in the report, including the guns and the gags, but we also see much more: a calendar on the wall, a lamp hanging from the ceiling, and a tree rustling in the foreground (fig. 5.9b). Unlike a reporter, the camera captures everything in front of it (including, at one point, a reflection of the camera itself). And yet the camera's inclusiveness does not imply omniscience at all. Peering through a window to show the robbery, the camera offers a remarkably uninformative view: a bunch of distant masked men rustling around, occluded by the window, the lamp, and the tree. Even the high-angle view that shows the violent getaway is so distant as to leave key facts obscure, such as the shooter's identity. One can imagine this sequence being played in a more character-centered way, perhaps empha-sizing the Swede's emotions as the heist goes awry. As it is, the camera's insis-tent distance mocks the studied neutrality of the reporter's ostensibly objective prose.

Other canonical examples of cinematic objectivity prove to be equally com-plex. Many film scholars have characterized Otto Preminger as a director with an "objective" or "detached" style. In 1962, *Movie* noted that the director's goal was "to show events, not demonstrate his feelings about them."[53] Curiously, when Herb Lightman profiled Preminger's cinematographer Joseph LaShelle, LaShelle insisted that the camera must not become "a mere onlooker detached from the scene." Instead, the camera must get involved in the action, moving with it in the manner of a "participant."[54] Far from setting the camera back in the manner of an impassive observer, LaShelle hoped to move the camera into each space.

The challenge is to reconcile these two views—the view that Preminger favored an unusually objective style and the view that LaShelle favored par-ticipatory camerawork. One promising solution is to approach the problem from a different direction, replacing the language of objectivity with the lan-guage of knowledge. John Gibbs and Douglas Pye have argued, "Preminger places us epistemologically in relation to the characters in something of the way they are placed to each other—except, of course, that for us they are characters seen through Preminger's direction, both of the actors and of the camera. But what we see of them is what they do."[55] Preminger prefers to represent situa-tions cleanly, keeping their complexity intact. For instance, in *Fallen Angel* (1945), one scene shows the effect that a woman has on three different men. After a brief disappearance, Stella (Linda Darnell) has just returned to the diner where she works. Judd (Charles Bickford), a former cop, eyes her possessively. Pop (Percy Kilbride), the owner of the diner, is so happy to see her that he gives her another customer's hamburger. The customer, a drifter named Stanton (Dana Andrews), sits back and watches the exchange. As spectators, we resemble Stan-ton; we are drifters who have to make sense of people we have just met. But Preminger does not place his camera in Stanton's position in space; he places it on the other side of the room, so we may observe Stanton observing everyone else. The scene's concluding shot lasts for ninety seconds, featuring several distinct compositions: a single on Pop (fig. 5.10a); a group composition with all four characters (fig. 5.10b); a three-shot after Judd leaves; a two-shot with Pop and Stella (fig. 5.10c); and another three-shot including Stanton (fig. 5.10d). With the help of the single, Pop proves easy to read, so obviously in love with Stella. Stella's contempt for Pop is also clear; she tells him he makes her sick. Judd does not speak very much, but his looming presence quickly conveys his jealous nature. If all we had to do was keep track of these three characters, then we might conclude that the film is offering us a kind of omniscience, allowing us to read a complex situation clearly and quickly. But Preminger gives us one more character to monitor: Stanton. Is Stanton annoyed when Pop gives Stella the burger—or amused? Is Stanton attracted to Stella—or disgusted by her? A master of understated performance, Dana Andrews gives us few definitive clues in his wry facial expressions. Meanwhile, Preminger has placed Stanton in the background of a busy composition, slightly out of focus, making his behavior even harder to read with certainty. A more subjective approach might have been more informative, perhaps using point-of-view shots to let us know exactly when Stanton was looking at Pop and when Stanton was looking at Stella.

5.10 In *Fallen Angel*, we must keep track of four characters at once.

Instead, we must take in all of the scene at once. By giving us more to see, the film makes us even less certain of what we know. In this way, Preminger's detached, evenhanded approach might evoke the feeling of participation that LaShelle hoped to achieve, sparking a desire to lean in and examine the scene more closely.[56]

Working with LaShelle, Preminger would employ a similar strategy five years later in the detective thriller *Where the Sidewalk Ends*, moving the camera repeatedly to register more and more details, making us wonder if we can ever understand them all. Dana Andrews plays a detective, Dixon, who unexpectedly kills a suspect during a scuffle. Dixon plants various clues to make it seem as if the victim escaped. At the police station, Lieutenant Thomas (Karl Malden) examines one of these clues (a bag) and presents it to a cab driver, a witness to the staged escape. The scene is richly ironic, simultaneously demonstrating that the lieutenant is a determined investigator and exposing the fact that his determination makes him easily deceived. Far from photographing the scene with distanced reserve, Preminger keeps the camera and the actors in near-constant motion. Eight men appear in the course of a single shot—in more than a dozen different combinations (table 5.1).

Looking at table 5.1, one might be surprised to learn that Dixon is the protagonist. The camera follows Klein to Thomas, Thomas to the driver, the driver to a detective, and the detective to Thomas, but it never follows Dixon's own movements. Instead of playing up the risk when Dixon walks by a witness who might identify him, the camera simply pans to follow the witness and then switches to follow another detective, as if Dixon were an afterthought. Instead of celebrating Dixon's uneasy satisfaction when he sees the lieutenant fall for his plan, the camera follows the lieutenant back and forth as he delegates tasks to the squad, only allowing us to glimpse Dixon occasionally in soft focus in the background. Defying the adage of the advantageous angle, it is as if Preminger intentionally refused to place the camera in the most informative position. Most Hollywood filmmakers would ask the actor playing the protagonist to give an expressive performance; then they would photograph that performance in close-up. Preminger asked his leading man to give an inexpressive performance, and then he stuck him in the back of the room while the camera followed other characters around. This is what Preminger's detachment looks like: not static, not removed, but mobile in counterintuitive ways, fighting against our urge to watch the protagonist by giving other characters more compositional weight.

LaShelle theorized his own camerawork in anthropomorphic terms, imagining the camera as a person who moves around, in and out, left and right, always seeking to get a better view of the scene. Far from remaining aloof, his camera moves in the manner of a person who wants to understand several characters at once, many of whom are working at cross-purposes with one another.

TABLE 5.1 A Single Shot in *Where the Sidewalk Ends* (1950)

Composition	Klein	Driver	Policeman	Thomas	Detective 1	Detective 2	Dixon	Casey
1	**onscreen**	onscreen						
2	**onscreen**		background	**onscreen**				
3		onscreen		**onscreen**				
4	onscreen			**onscreen**				
5		onscreen		**onscreen**				
6	onscreen			**onscreen**				
7		**onscreen**		**onscreen**				
8		**onscreen**						
9		**onscreen**	background		background			
10		**onscreen**				**onscreen**	onscreen	

(continued)

TABLE 5.1 (continued)

Composition	Klein	Driver	Policeman	Thomas	Detective 1	Detective 2	Dixon	Casey
11			background		background	**onscreen**		
12	onscreen			**onscreen**		**onscreen**	background	
13			background	**onscreen**	onscreen			
14			background	**onscreen**		onscreen	background	
15	onscreen			**onscreen**		background	background	
16				**onscreen**				onscreen
17				**onscreen**				

Note: The camera following characters is indicated by **onscreen** in bold print.

But it is useful to remember that such anthropomorphism is a useful fiction. LaShelle's camera was a machine, with no interests or sympathies of its own. The alleged objectivity of Preminger's style is a particular way of guiding *our* interests and sympathies, encouraging us to find multiple points of interest in the film's complex storyworld while preventing us from attaching too much sympathy to Stanton and Dixon, two difficult men who make dubious choices.

Max Ophuls's protagonists also make dubious choices, but his films push us to view them more compassionately. In a classic essay on *Letter from an Unknown Woman*, Robin Wood argued that Ophuls managed to balance two opposing tendencies, represented by Hitchcock on the one hand and Preminger on the other: "Equally removed from the audience-participation techniques of Hitch-cock and the clinical objectivity and detachment of Preminger, Ophuls's cam-erawork achieves a perfect balance—in terms of the spectator's involvement—between sympathy and detachment."[57] Like Hitchcock, Ophuls uses the moving camera to encourage our engagement with individual characters. Like Prem-inger, Ophuls represents his characters from the outside, avoiding Hitchcock's extended point-of-view sequences. The resulting films express a distinctive attitude—an attitude of caring for the characters while criticizing the society that constrains them.

One scene in *Letter from an Unknown Woman* shows the protagonist Lisa (Joan Fontaine) when she is still a teenager, watching the delivery men as they move Stefan's things into an apartment. The camera pans to reveal Lisa, dol-lies back as a mover unloads the harp from a carriage, tilts up to reveal Lisa's mother telling her to come inside, and dollies in to follow Lisa through the entryway. After a cut, the movement intensifies: the camera, mounted on Uni-versal's number 2 crane, follows Lisa into the foyer and up the stairway, past some workers complaining about the weight of the piano (fig. 5.11a–b).[58] One can imagine the same scene in a subjective mode, cutting back and forth between Lisa's face and her perspective on each new object. The camera instead follows Lisa into the building and up the stairs, keeping her in long shot or medium shot the entire time. The technique generates sympathy for Lisa not by representing her exact perceptions but by putting us in her position of under-standing. When Franz Planer's camera pans to reveal three men struggling with the piano, we discover the piano when she discovers it. She is surprised by these riches, and so are we. For all its sympathy, the follow shot creates distance not just because Ophuls refuses the close-up but because the scene's insistent movement blocks Lisa from view several times. Lutz Bacher has described the director's signature technique as the "rhythmic long take," favoring the "jux-taposition of the moving subject with elements of the setting."[59] We see that rhythm here. The harp, the carriage door, the piano, the movers—all are inter-posed between Lisa and the camera at some point during the sequence. Although Ophuls does not bury Joan Fontaine in the background of the shot, the way

5.11 In *Letter from an Unknown Woman*, the camera follows Lisa as delivery men struggle to lift a piano.

Otto Preminger buries Dana Andrews, he does create an alternating pattern whereby attention shifts from Lisa to the harp to Lisa to the movers to Lisa to the piano and back to Lisa again. Joan Fontaine executes several complicated maneuvers, sometimes turning her back to the camera, sometimes opening herself up to it, thereby adding another layer to the rhythm of shifting attention. By selectively obscuring the protagonist, these compositional strategies force us to attend to the workers as well as to Lisa; we must compare their attitudes to Lisa's own. The young, slightly dirty Lisa is fascinated by Stefan's things, which represent a world of wealth, culture, and beauty that she has never known. The workers share none of her fascination; they are just annoyed that the piano is so heavy. Crucially, the scene offers a third attitude to consider: that of Lisa as an adult. Her voiceover gives us insights into the young Lisa's thoughts, but there remains a clear discrepancy between the adult Lisa's words—spoken with mature wisdom—and young Lisa's appearance—childish, overwhelmed, perhaps even a little ridiculous. If the workers' sarcasm makes Lisa's youthful fascination seem silly, then the voiceover's depth makes the workers' sarcasm seem short-sighted, as if this young child has an insight that others lack. Meanwhile, the mature Lisa's philosophical pronouncements sound a little pretentious when juxtaposed against the comedy onscreen. In all, we have at least three different perspectives on the scene, each of which exposes the shortcomings of the other two.

The collaboration on display is extraordinary, fully justifying Ophuls's belief that "there are as many creators to a film as there are people who work on it."[60] Still, the director's own sensibility comes through. Cinematographer Lee Garmes, who photographed *Caught* (1949) for the director, offered an intriguing assessment of Ophuls's approach: "He is probably the only director I ever worked with in my life, that the final results of the picture did not look like a motion picture. It looked like you had stuck a camera through a window and stolen the scene. . . . The camera just happened to capture what the actors were doing."[61] Formally, Garmes seems to be describing the director's tendency to stage characters in the middle ground, blocking our view with foreground objects, such as the harp and the piano. Although the approach resembles that of Garmes's former collaborator Josef von Sternberg, the differences are instructive. In a von Sternberg film, a character may get lost amid the clutter, as if the character were just one more piece of decoration. Ophuls's characters remain richly developed people, even amid the clutter; his detachment never implies a loss of sympathy.

In an important essay on the ethical meanings of Ophuls's camerawork, Daniel Morgan has explained how Ophuls crafts a formal structure of "dual attunement, taking account of the subjective states of characters while at the same time revealing their place within a social world."[62] In both his Hollywood films and his European works, Ophuls tells stories about characters—in particular women—who lose autonomy as a result of social constraints. The camerawork encourages us to understand the characters' thoughts, feelings, and attitudes while providing a perspective that the characters lack.[63] Consider the celebrated end to *The Reckless Moment* (1949). The protagonist Lucia (Joan Bennett) walks down the stairs, where she is told that her blackmailer Donnelly (James Mason) has died in a car crash, that her daughter is no longer a suspect in a murder, and that her husband is on the telephone. In many films, this confluence of events would qualify as a happy ending: the death of a criminal, the salvation of a daughter, the reunion of the married couple. However, the scene plays out as a tragedy because Lucia has come to value Donnelly, a criminal who showed her more kindness than her own family members could muster. Initially framing a long shot of Lucia on the second floor, the camera cranes down, moving closer and closer to Lucia until it arrives at the final composition: the protagonist, behind the banister, turning away from her family and away from the camera. The bars of the banister represent the home as a prison, and this closing composition represents the children as guards, watching over their mother and enforcing her entrapment. The social world imprisons Lucia by forcing her to conform to postwar norms of suburban motherhood.

With the Proteus principle in mind, we should resist the temptation to assign a specific function to a specific technique, as if a point-of-view shot always encourages sympathy or a distant frame always produces detachment. It is more useful to think of "subjective" and "objective" as inevitably partial frameworks that explain some features of films and not others. When the camera moves in one scene, we might make sense of its movement by appealing to the concept of "point of view" even though some pictorial features are not mimetic at all. When the camera moves in a superficially similar way in another scene, we might make sense of the movement by appealing to the concept of the "detached observer." Each framework offers a way of gaining provisional understanding without explaining all there is to see. The same logic applies to all the other figures I have discussed in this book: camera as engaged participant, camera as impassive witness, camera as recording machine, camera as emotional mimic. A camera may imitate all of these figures or none of them. Films are dynamic; their meanings change as they unfold.

Documentary as Style

The documentary provided a very different model for what the objective camera could be: not coolly detached, in the manner of *The Killers* or *Fallen Angel*, but immersed and engaged, in the manner of a combat cameraman. Some filmmakers found this model to be fully compatible with Hollywood norms, adding emotional intensity to familiar tales of war and crime. At least one theorist-practitioner, cinematographer James Wong Howe, disagreed, insisting that Hollywood should adopt the documentary as a model because it presented a radical challenge to existing conventions.

Before wartime documentaries shaped Hollywood, Hollywood shaped wartime documentaries. During the war, the Academy of Motion Picture Arts and Sciences' Research Council had recruited studio workers, newsreel photographers, and skilled amateurs to serve as combat photographers. M-G-M's John Arnold, Karl Freund, and Joseph Ruttenberg provided training in camera technology and shooting techniques.[64] Together, they taught recruits to work quickly but carefully. Far from advising their recruits to shake their cameras, they instilled familiar rules of balanced compositions. Captain M. S. Blankfort, a marine who lectured at the school, stressed three principles: planning, purpose, and clarity. "One way of helping to keep the content of your film clear," he said, "is by trying to tell a story with it."[65] Such classes encouraged military photographers to imitate Hollywood, presenting story information as clearly as possible.

For all his apparent classicism, Captain Blankfort recognized an opposing principle—the principle of surprise. By focusing on planning, he hoped to prepare photographers to react to the unexpected: "These 'surprises,' the unpredictable turns of war, may turn out to be the most important things you photograph."[66] During these moments of surprise, the style of the camerawork changes by necessity, no matter how hard the photographer tries to keep things clear. The era's documentarians had to reconcile two opposing tendencies, crafting stories about the world while recognizing that the world could not be controlled.

We see this odd mixture of clarity and chaos in *The Battle of Midway* (1942), directed by John Ford, with additional photography by Jack Mackenzie and

Kenneth Pier. As Mark Harris explains, Ford and his collaborators photographed the battle from the roof of the power station; the director sustained an arm injury from shrapnel during the attack.[67] The camerawork in the scenes before and after the battle is handheld but smooth, with the crisp beauty we might expect from the director of How Green Was My Valley. The combat scenes are visibly rougher, totally unlike a Ford film. Working with only five minutes of actual combat footage, Ford used editing to construct meaningful events, as in a four-shot sequence of a plane crashing. First, we see two American gunners huddling behind a barricade of sandbags. The next shot depicts an airplane plummeting toward the ground; sandbags are visible in the foreground. The soundtrack (added later) plays a plane crash, and the film cuts to a handheld shot of the sandbags, the camera panning left and right uncontrollably, as if shaken by the crash. The fourth shot shows a Japanese plane on fire, flames rising symbolically from the red circle on the wing. As in a fiction film, this sequence of pictures and sounds creates meaning, first by suggesting (perhaps inaccurately) that the American gunners are looking at this particular descending plane from their position behind the sandbags and then by suggesting (perhaps inaccurately) that they experience a concussion from this particular crash. The handheld camera fails to capture the crash itself, which is blocked by the sandbags; instead, the uncontrolled movement conveys what it feels like to experience the shock of battle. Here, "documentary technique" is not just sober and factual but messy and expressive.

Other documentaries followed the traditional newsreel model more closely. Newsreel expert Louis De Rochemont produced The Fighting Lady (1944), featuring photography by a group of navy cameramen working under the supervision of Edward Steichen. One sequence introduces sailors working at a variety of jobs, from baker to barber to butcher. The stationary camerawork represents the carrier as an orderly community, with each man assigned a job that suits his skills. Although the lighting is simple, the composition is clear and balanced; none of these shots would look out of place in a studio film. But the battle scenes look completely different—so strange that the film's narrator, M-G-M star Robert Taylor, has to explain what we are seeing. Cameras were placed on airplanes and set to run automatically, with no human operator to guide them. Because the cameras pointed forward, they could not record the bombs from their respective planes; rather, they photographed explosions from the bombs of unseen planes up ahead. Onscreen, the movement seems uncertain in its bumpiness but relentless in its forward progress. At this distance, the landscape looks abstract, like a miniature, becoming recognizable only when the bombs explode below. Reinforcing the sense of strangeness, Taylor describes the camerawork as inhuman: these cameras record, "as no human eye or memory could record, just what our guns and bombs do to the enemy." The sequence is hypnotic and oddly beautiful—until you recall that each shot is a real document of real destruction.

In interviews, De Rochemont situated *The Fighting Lady* and its odd mixture of the communal and the inhuman within the familiar context of the Hollywood fiction film. Favoring the terms *screen journalism* and *facts films*, De Rochemont pointed out that Hollywood had been using documentary technique for some time, most notably in the ripped-from-the-headlines films of producer Darryl F. Zanuck, as in Ford's *The Grapes of Wrath*.[68] Whereas Ford discovered the expressive power of the uncontrolled camera, De Rochemont looked back at Ford's sober-minded fiction films. For De Rochemont, the term *documentary* did not refer to films with a special ontological relationship to reality. Rather, it referred to a particular kind of technique (plain and unglamorous) that was appropriate for certain kinds of stories (serious and fact based), whether staged or not.

For the fiction filmmaker, documentaries provided a mixed model, simultaneously bumpy and still, rough and clear. Like De Rochemont, cinematographer James Wong Howe argued that Hollywood had been making films with the "documentary technique" for years, even in works of fiction. His examples ranged from the dynamic *All Quiet on the Western Front* to the steady *The Grapes of Wrath*.[69] When Howard Hawks asked Howe to apply the documentary technique to the fictional drama *Air Force* (1943), Howe adopted a two-pronged approach to camera movement: more but also less. As in *The Battle of Midway*, the battle scenes in *Air Force* called for extra camera movement. Describing an attack on a Japanese ship, Howe explained, "I directed an operator to shake his camera as if from concussion, let the actors blur out of focus, and tip the camera sharply as the decks tipped high into the air. This gave the audience a sense of real participation." By placing the camera on the deck of the ship, Howe applied the analogical theory of camerawork that he had been advocating for years. A person would shake from a blast; so should a camera. Standard studio cameras were too large to be shaken effectively, so Howe gave his operator a 35-millimeter Eyemo. He predicted that Hollywood filmmakers would soon adopt 16-millimeter cameras, which could squeeze into the tight spaces that a 35-millimeter Mitchell camera could not.[70]

But Howe's approach to *Air Force* also required *less* camera movement than usual. Elsewhere in the same article, Howe defined "documentary technique" in negative terms, noting that the documentarian seeks to avoid many of the flourishes that characterized the Hollywood A-film: no glamour, no unmotivated lighting effects, and "no unnecessary dollies, or panning, or other artificial movement."[71] Simplicity and common sense became his guiding ideals. For much of the film, Howe's camerawork was not handheld at all but steady and balanced. For instance, when the pilot (John Ridgely) greets his crew for the first time, a simple pan shot follows him as he walks toward the plane. The camera comes to a rest, and a cut introduces a new composition, featuring the captain and the crew chief in the bottom half of the frame and the enormous propeller in the top half. The focus is sharp and deep, rendering the machinery with all the meticulousness of a Steichen photograph. Movement would spoil the precision; the camera does not budge an inch.

Once the plane starts to fly, Howe introduces subtle movements, panning and tilting slightly—almost imperceptibly—to give the impression of a craft flying through the sky. During the battle scenes, the camera usually remains on a tripod, shaking only when a bomb explodes. The blurry shot that Howe describes is actually one of the few truly erratic handheld shots in the film. The camera wobbles unpredictably for a few seconds, pans awkwardly to the left, and then wobbles some more. Meanwhile, rubble crashes down, a flame ignites, and sailors fall to the deck (fig. 5.12a–b). Howe's comment that the shot gives the audience a sense of "real participation" is intriguingly ambiguous. Perhaps he meant that audiences would take vicarious delight in the attack, as if they were children grabbing a toy ship and shaking it. Or perhaps he meant that the audience would feel what it was like to be on a bombed ship, providing a brief moment of identification with the Japanese sailors in a film that is otherwise notable for its anti-Japanese racism.

Fiction filmmakers quickly adopted Howe's technique of shaking the camera during battle scenes. The Warner Bros. film *Destination Tokyo* (1943) used the same shot of the convulsing Japanese ship in its climactic scene. Not a similar shot—the exact same one. After the war, *Lady in the Lake*'s cinematographer Paul Vogel, a veteran of the Signal Corps, won the Best Cinematography Oscar for his work on William Wellman's film *Battleground* (1949). His crew had assembled a special rig that would hold the camera with springs. Striking the steel framework during a blast would create the appropriate concussion effect.[72] Documentarians also adopted the shaky aesthetic, even when they did not need to do so, as in John Huston's visceral film *The Battle of San Pietro* (1944,

5.12 *Air Force* uses shaky camerawork during battle scenes.

released to the public in 1945). Because Huston arrived in San Pietro as the fighting was ending, he ended up staging most of the film's battle footage. According to Mark Harris, the film "was a scripted, acted, and directed movie that contained barely two minutes of actual, unreconstructed documentation."[73] The chaotic handheld camerawork created such a powerful impression that many reviewers described Huston's film as the most realistic war documentary yet made.[74]

Because the shaking camera has become such a familiar war-film technique, it is easy to overlook the fact that many filmmakers of the 1940s photographed battle scenes differently. Lewis Milestone experimented with several possible approaches. For the Soviet-themed *The North Star* (1943), Milestone collaborated with James Wong Howe and designer William Cameron Menzies. The film depicts a roadside bombing with a stationary camera, creating Eisensteinian juxtapositions between the diagonal bursts and the vertical telephone poles. In *Edge of Darkness* (1943), the decisive battle features a series of zooms, still a rarely used technique. Milestone's best-remembered film of the period, *A Walk in the Sun* (1945), relies on a technique the director had pioneered in *All Quiet on the Western Front*: montages interspersed with lateral camera movement. The climactic scene shows American soldiers attacking a nest of machine guns in a country house. Instead of using a handheld camera to produce the effect of chaos, Milestone builds intensity through patterns of contrast, cutting back and forth between stationary shots of the firing machine guns and lateral dolly shots of the soldiers falling to the ground. The rhythm of the montage—stasis, movement, stasis, movement, all in one-second bursts—approximates the horrible rhythm of the machine guns.

Filmmakers were soon applying "documentary technique"—in all its contradictory senses—to other genres, as in Henry Hathaway's cycle of crime films (*The House on 92nd Street*, 1945; *13 Rue Madeleine*, 1947; *Call Northside 777*, 1948), many of which were produced by Louis De Rochemont. As Peter Lev explains, the series "is usually praised as an aesthetic innovation, but much of the motivation for shooting on location was to avoid union trouble and save money."[75] Films in the postwar location cycle favor restrained camera movement. It is not convenient to transport a crane to a faraway location, and it is not easy to push a dolly in a small room lacking the "wild walls" that came standard in a studio setting. This pared-down aesthetic reflected a stance of sober simplicity.[76] Significantly, Hathaway's cinematographers usually abjured handheld camerawork, even though the Eyemo would have offered practical advantages on location. In the era of the fluid camera, semidocumentaries favored clarity and directness. They functioned like training films, explaining how institutions worked. The camera moved only when doing so made an instructive point. *The House on 92nd Street* tells the story of a German American FBI agent, Dietrich

(William Eythe), who helps uncover a Nazi spy ring. In one scene, the narrator explains how Dietrich works with the FBI to mislead his contacts in Germany. Each movement of the camera reinforces a specific piece of the narrator's argument (table 5.2).

When the voiceover explains that the shack was in a rural location, the camera pans from the ocean to the shack (shot 1). When the voiceover explains that Dietrich sent messages through the airwaves, the camera pans from Dietrich to his transmitter (shot 2). When the voiceover explains that the FBI intercepted his messages, the camera pans from the antenna to the FBI office (shot 3). Each pan reinforces a specific verbal claim: space to individual, individual to action, action to effect. Even the direction of the movement is subtly informative, building a pattern of repetition and variation (right, right, then a surprise shift left) that underscores the key idea: Dietrich appears to be sending messages to the Germans, but he is actually sending them somewhere else. A movement in one direction is actually a movement the other way. The operator executes each pan with professional expertise; note the skillful aperture change to compensate for the shift in brightness when the camera pans from the exterior to the interior in the first shot. After this trio of pans, the film returns to its default stationary style, depicting the FBI office with an efficiency that mirrors the FBI's own. The model here is not the handheld chaos of *The Battle of San Pietro* or the Eyemo concussions of *Air Force* but the straightforward clarity of

TABLE 5.2 **Voiceover Coordinated with Camera Movements in *The House on 92nd Street* (1945)**

Shot	Voiceover	Camera Movement
1	"In a secluded cottage less than an hour's drive from Manhattan, Agent Dietrich set up a short-wave radio transmitter. Hamburg complimented Dietrich on the speed and efficiency . . .	Pan left to right, from a view of the ocean to an interior view of Dietrich at the controls of his transmitter. Cut to . . .
2	". . . with which he got his reports through to Germany and their instructions back to the United States. They did not know that Dietrich's little short-wave radio . . .	. . . pan left to right, from Dietrich at the controls of his transmitter to the transmitter's wires. Dissolve to . . .
3	". . . had a limited range and that all his messages were beamed to a secret FBI long-range radio station not far away."	. . . pan right to left, from a large outdoor antenna to the radio station. Cut.

The Fighting Lady.[77] The camerawork is not objective so much as it is directive, unambiguously reinforcing the film's arguments.

With their plain surfaces, the semidocumentaries did not look like typical Hollywood romances, but they did not look like World War II combat docs, either. William Daniels won an Oscar for his work on Jules Dassin's film *The Naked City* (1948). Uncomfortable with the word *documentary*, he explained, "We were after—well, let's call it realism. I dislike the term 'documentary' because the word has come to mean badly shot 16mm. footage."[78] The same year cinematographer Robert Surtees photographed the war-themed noir drama *Act of Violence* (1948) on location in Los Angeles; he hoped "to blend the best of the documentary technique with a more dramatic approach."[79] Both Daniels and Surtees argued that it was a mistake to pursue documentary realism at the expense of other virtues. Rather than run through the streets with Arriflexes on their shoulders, most cinematographers adhered to staid professional standards, using tripods and dollies to secure balanced compositions in sharp focus.

Nevertheless, the best semidocumentaries offered fresh visual ideas, taking full advantage of the camera's capacity to render the world in exceptional detail. *The Naked City* features a daringly hybrid style, mixing together helicopter cityscapes, stationary shots staged in real locations, dramatic dollies during action scenes, and fascinating footage of New York City streets photographed with a hidden camera. One scene shows the murderer, Garzah (Ted De Corsia), walking down a busy sidewalk. The camera is hidden in a car with darkened windows that drives alongside the sidewalk (and is even occasionally visible in passing reflections [fig. 5.13a]). Instead of explaining police procedures point by point, the narrator (producer Mark Hellinger) jabs at his villain: "The cops are on a manhunt, Garzah. You need a plan. You've got to get out of this neighborhood. Stop and look at a tie. Maybe you're being shadowed." Hellinger

5.13 In *The Naked City*, a hidden camera follows the murderer as he walks down a New York City street.

revels in his powers as an all-knowing narrator, telling us what Garzah thinks the moment Garzah thinks it. As soon as Hellinger says, "Stop and look at a tie," Garzah stops and looks at a tie. The camera also stops, framing a new composition: Garzah, looking at a tie on the right, and a detective, looking for Garzah on the left (fig. 5.13b). Garzah does not see the detective right away, and the detective fails to see Garzah at all, but the camera allows us to spot both of them easily. Underlining the detective's ignorance, Hellinger quotes him in voiceover: "Lady, ever seen a man [who] looks like this?" Hellinger's narration may be omniscient, but the spectator is not; the scene instills a feeling of uncertainty rather than mastery. To watch this shot is to be overwhelmed with detail: Garzah, yes, but also the man in sunglasses, the Old Gold poster, the woman with the baby carriage, the short man in an oversize suit, the woman with the white purse and the matching shoes, the carefully lettered sign of the delicatessen, and the man taking a huge bite out of an ear of corn. The reflection of the camera car in the windows, technically a mistake, adds to the effect of complexity, suggesting that a real camera went into a real space, making us wonder which people were staged and which were caught unawares.

Given the popularity of voiceover narration, we might expect semidocumentary camerawork to offer spectators a sense of empowering omniscience. But we should remember that the semidocumentaries tell stories—specifically crime stories, which produce many of their effects by playing games of concealment and revelation. Jacques Tourneur's film *Berlin Express* (1948) problematizes its own apparently omniscient narration. It combines studio scenes with documentary footage and location work in war-torn Europe; cinematographer Lucien Ballard even experimented with a handheld camera he bought in Germany.[80] An unseen narrator, with a deep voice and precise diction, functions as an authority figure, standing above the storyworld and speaking to us directly. However, the knowledge he offers proves to be incomplete, failing to explain the strange world we discover. In one early scene, several characters board a train bound for Berlin. Rather than offer privileged information, the narrator simply recites facts on record: "Compartment A. His travel orders read, 'Name: Robert J. Lindley. Birthplace: Quincy, Illinois. Occupation: United States government agricultural expert.'" After a few more introductions, the voiceover notes that Compartment D is unoccupied, "but being held for person of importance." At the end of the sequence, the narrator is about to reveal the occupation of a German man when a train whistle interrupts his narration. Far from offering a comprehensive account, the narrator has given us fragments, in the manner of a reporter who is working with a limited set of available facts.

Meanwhile, the camera, positioned outside the train car, dollies from window to window to offer a glimpse of each character in turn. A space of convergence, the train brings together strangers who are American, French, German, British, and Soviet. They represent the nations competing to rebuild postwar Europe.

Like the voiceover, the camerawork initially promises knowledge. The voyeuristic technique, peeking through one window after another, implies the revelation of hidden secrets, exposing connections the characters do not yet see. But the camera's promise of knowledge soon proves hollow. The rigorous pattern of the lateral dolly, moving from one window to the next, provides only a brief glimpse of each character, and we spend almost as much time looking at the partitions between the windows as we do looking at the characters themselves. The frame of each window echoes the frame of the film itself, serving as a reminder that our access to a film's storyworld remains limited, no matter how stentorian the narrator's voice may seem.

The postwar surge in location filmmaking introduced new conventions of camera movement while altering several old ones. One popular strategy was to introduce a shot on a recognizable landmark before panning to reveal a character. Early in *Night Has a Thousand Eyes* (1948), the camera pans more than 180 degrees to introduce the protagonist's Bunker Hill neighborhood; the camera follows the Angel's Flight funicular up the hill and then it continues panning past a tangle of trees and wires to locate Triton (Edward G. Robinson) on the stairs, approaching his run-down apartment building. Similarly, in George Cukor's *The Marrying Kind* (1952), one shot begins with a low-angle view of the Woolworth Building; then the camera moves in for a closer view of Florence (Judy Holiday), visible through the window of a fluorescent-lit office. These techniques vouched for each film's authenticity, proving that real cameras photographed real actors in real spaces. At the same time, location photography provided new forms of expressivity. In *D.O.A* (1950), when the protagonist (Edmund O'Brien) discovers that he has been poisoned, he runs outside the medical building and sprints through the street of San Francisco. The camera follows him from a camera car, zipping through the streets at astonishing speed. The fast-motion photography recalls the zany city sequences of the silent period, as in *My Best Girl* and *Speedy* (1928), but the connotations have shifted from dynamism to pure chaos. Far from looking like a documentary, the sequence shifts into the semisubjective mode, using a burst of bewildering movement to express the protagonist's confusion as he faces an inexplicable threat in the middle of an unfamiliar city.

After the war, Hollywood adapted army trucks, Jeeps, and helicopters to the problems of location filmmaking.[81] Designed by a grip, the "Blue Goose" featured a hydraulic lift mounted onto a four-wheel-drive army truck.[82] Powerful enough to lift an eight-hundred-pound Technicolor camera, the vehicle allowed crews to shoot Westerns and adventure films in increasingly remote rural locations.[83] Although it was possible to use the Blue Goose for running shots, its primary purpose was to move the camera into position for stationary frames.[84] The helicopter promised even greater mobility; *American Cinematographer* described the aircraft as the "biggest camera crane in the world."[85] Perhaps the most common use of the helicopter was to provide aerial views to appear underneath a film's opening credits, as in *Side Street* (1949). *Johnny Belinda* (1948) employed a helicopter to introduce its primary location—the California coast, standing in for Nova Scotia.[86] More creatively, Nicholas Ray's *They Live by Night* (1948) used a helicopter to follow a trio of thieves walking behind an outdoor billboard (fig. 5.14a–b). Ray could have used a crane and a wide-angle lens to juxtapose the three men and the billboard, but the helicopter allowed him to shoot the scene from farther away with a telephoto lens, registering the human figures and the billboard at a comparable scale. As the helicopter-mounted camera follows the thieves from above, the billboard appears out of nowhere, popping into the frame from below. This strange composition, with its flattened space and its unpredictable scaling, mocks the absurdity of postwar consumer culture.

For car scenes, most studios continued to rely on rear projection, but some location-heavy films featured shots with the camera perched on top of an actual moving automobile, as in Hathaway's *13 Rue Madeleine*. On *The Captive City* (1952), Lee Garmes's crew removed the driver-side door and mounted a camera with a 40-millimeter lens. Then they attached a generator to the front of the car, powering a set of lamps to illuminate the actors.[87] The results are exceptionally eerie, using camera movement to express the film's fears of urban decay. In voiceover, the protagonist regrets what has happened to his beloved town. In the background, the town whizzes by, just a blur of white neon lights sliding through pitch-black backgrounds.

In some cases, filmmakers had to scale back their plans when confronted with a difficult location. Writing the screenplay to *The Window* (1949), Mel Dinelli proposed a virtuoso opening shot, introducing a tenement neighborhood and then moving past a condemned building before settling on a specific

5.14 In *They Live by Night*, the helicopter frames an unusual composition.

apartment building. This proposal situated the movie within the established tradition of the apartment movie, including *Sunnyside Up* and *Street Scene*. In one passage, Dinelli wrote: "The CAMERA MOVES UP the concrete steps and THROUGH the front doors, abruptly leaving the glaring sunlight for the shadowy hallway. MED shot—the hallway. At first we are unable to distinguish anything in the shadows. (The impression is that which one experiences when moving from bright daylight into dark interiors.)"[88] The frugal finished film does not follow these instructions. Instead of dollying past a series of buildings, the film zooms in to introduce the neighborhood; instead of craning through a doorway, the camera cranes up to a darkened window, leading to a dissolve inside. Director Ted Tetzlaff explained that the exigencies of location filmmaking required constant changes: "I worked with writer Mel Dinelli on the script, but much of the screenplay is being altered or thrown out of the window when it comes to actual shooting. It is impossible to plan a shooting script 100% in advance."[89] The war was over, but the combat cameramen's advice lingered on: plan everything in advance but be ready to change those plans in the face of surprises.

Whereas Daniels had insisted that the semidocumentary technique was compatible with Hollywood's existing standards, the uncompromising James Wong Howe took a radical position, arguing that documentary technique offered a refreshing break from Hollywood norms. He continued to endorse a two-pronged aesthetic. On the one hand, he argued that his colleagues in Hollywood were moving the camera too much, pursuing a pointless fluidity: "Camera gymnastics and strange angles are not what I would call the stock of the 'brilliant cameraman.'"[90] A documentary approach would return the cinematographer to the virtues of simplicity. On the other hand, Howe was excited about the possibilities of the handheld camera. In an interview in 1945, Howe admitted that his own camerawork in *Objective Burma!* (1945) was too mechanical. Favorably recalling Karl Freund's handheld camerawork in *The Last Laugh* and *Variety*, Howe argued that handheld operation would have been more responsive to the players' movements. He predicted that he might be able to obtain a greater effect of immediacy if he operated a camera while on roller skates.[91] A few years later Howe put the idea to the test, donning roller skates to photograph the fight scenes in *Body and Soul* with a handheld Eyemo (fig. 5.15).[92] The resulting shots are unlike anything in Hathaway's semidocumentaries. Brodine's cinematography in *The House on 92nd Street* was impeccable, with sharp focus, balanced compositions, and pristine pans. Howe's fight cinematography is gloriously flawed: the lenses lose their focus, the compositions lose their centers, and the movements lose their fluidity. In one shot, Howe's camera pursues Charley (John Garfield) as he maneuvers his opponent Marlowe (Artie Dorrell) toward the ropes. In two seconds, Charley's body shifts from the far right side of the frame to the far left; Marlowe veers from

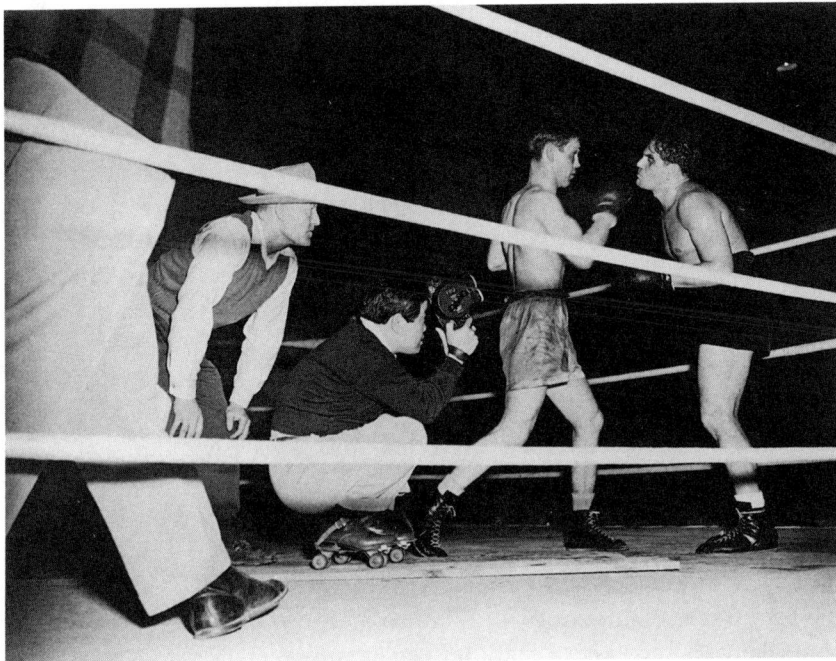

5.15 For *Body and Soul,* director Robert Rosson and cinematographer James Wong Howe film John Garfield boxing. (Courtesy of the Everett Collection)

the far left to the far right and back to the center; the focus changes from Charley's head to Charley's back to Marlowe's left arm. We never see the star's face, and his opponent looks blurry and occluded from view. By itself, the shot looks like an outtake. In the context of the scene as a whole, the shot evokes the feeling of "participation" that Howe had been aiming to achieve since *Air Force.*

A few filmmakers heeded Howe's call to experiment, but Howe's prediction of radical change proved to be incorrect. The handheld camera soon became a fight-scene cliché, as in the boxing movie *Champion* (1949) and the crime film *The Narrow Margin* (1952).[93] Meanwhile, the bulky Mitchell BNC continued to dominate the field throughout the 1950s, even in the face of competition from the Arriflex 35. The Arriflex had the advantage for location work in tight spaces, but the Mitchell was quieter, and professionals admired its reputation for quality and reliability.[94]

Howe's other prediction—that the seriousness of the war would discourage frivolous camera movement—proved to be only slightly more accurate as the trend toward fluidity continued. But a few filmmakers embraced the mood of sobriety that Howe endorsed. Gregg Toland noticed a shift in William Wyler's approach: "Willy had been thinking a lot, too, during the war. He had seen a lot of candid photography and lots of scenes without a camera dolly or boom. He used to go overboard on movement, but he came back with, I think, a better perspective on what was and wasn't important."[95] Here we see another kind of objectivity—not the cool detachment of the distant follow shot, not the visceral engagement of the immersive handheld shot, but the thoughtful gravity of the simple stationary shot. Perhaps the quiet stasis of *The Best Years of Our Lives* expressed the war's impact in a way that the concussive camerawork of the studio combat film never could.

* * *

Throughout the 1940s, Hollywood filmmakers explored a wide range of styles: semisubjective, sympathetic, documentary, detached, observational, mock objective, and more. All of these modes were partial and provisional, introducing as many contradictions as they resolved. The point-of-view shot could mimic the movements of a person ever more closely—and yet the camera's mobility might remind us of its inhuman machinery. The detached camera could deny easy access to a character's emotions—thereby making that character's emotions even more salient to the story. The semidocumentary camera could move into the city to record the world as it was—while using the mobile frame to achieve heightened expressivity. Trade journals continued to speak of the subjective–objective split as a defining feature of cinematic storytelling, but filmmakers were already leaving the opposition behind.

CHAPTER 6

AN ART OF DISCLOSURES

During the 1950s, new dollies and cranes enabled fluid camera-work within and beyond the studio walls. The era's most prominent new technology—widescreen—had more complicated implications for camera movement. Consider Howard Hawks's blunt assessment of the most familiar widescreen process, CinemaScope: "We have spent a lifetime learning how to compel the public to concentrate on one single thing. Now we have something that works in exactly the opposite way, and I don't like it very much. . . . Contrary to what some think, it is easier to shoot in CinemaScope—you don't have to bother about what you should show—everything's on the screen. I find that a bit clumsy. Above all, in a motion picture, is the story."[1] For Hawks, the art of cinematic storytelling required selection, picking out specific details and presenting them to the spectator in sequence. The trouble with the wider screen was that it was insufficiently selective, pushing the filmmaker to include "everything" on the screen, from the crucial plot point to the irrelevant detail.

This chapter critically examines both of Hawks's guiding assumptions: that the filmmakers of the previous years had used the frame to focus attention on one thing at a time and that widescreen technologies forced filmmakers to use the frame less selectively, with attendant costs to the craft of storytelling. Rather than argue that Hawks was right or wrong, I explain how the shifting status of these widely shared assumptions shaped the history of camera movement in the postwar period, before and after the explosion of widescreen techniques. Before the transition, Hollywood filmmakers were already exploring the possibilities of the inclusive frame, fitting more and more components into increasingly complex compositions. After the transition, the challenges of CinemaScope and other technologies proved to be real—but not insurmountable. Where Hawks saw a grave threat to cinematic storytelling, others saw an opportunity.

The first section focuses on examples from the late 1940s and proposes a set of terms—*revelation, concealment, emphasis,* and *understatement*—that can help us think about the moving camera's contribution to the cinema's art of disclosures. These familiar functions were not specific to the postwar years; indeed, I have been discussing them throughout this book. I spell out the distinctions here because increasingly long takes and increasingly wide screens would force filmmakers to rethink and reassert the value of these functions. The second section examines how the strategy of selective framing grew more refined in a series of films with unusually long takes. Many of these roving shots flaunted the camera's seeming ability to go anywhere—while retaining tight control over what the spectator could and could not see. The third section turns to CinemaScope, Cinerama, and other widescreen formats of the 1950s. Although the formats' failings seemed obvious to skeptics such as Hawks, directors such as Otto Preminger and Vincente Minnelli quickly discovered that CinemaScope did not fatally compromise the art of cinematic storytelling. These innovative filmmakers called for a newly modulated approach, rebalancing the functions of revelation, concealment, emphasis, and understatement.

Revelation, Concealment, Emphasis, and Understatement

According to V. F. Perkins, a movie "can never escape the necessity of viewpoint itself."[2] As we watch a movie, our understanding of its world remains partial not just because our access to it is mediated but because our ability to understand any world—even our own—is limited. The necessity of viewpoint is not a flaw but a source of the medium's power. As Perkins explains, "One of the arts of the movie is to turn this condition to advantage—for instance, by articulating the condition as a topic within the film—by dramatizing the distinction between the seen and unseen, or the relations between seeing and knowing."[3] Instead of aspiring toward the all-seeing view, a film might foreground its own limitations for thematic and tonal effect.

Perkins offers these remarks while meditating on the significance of *Citizen Kane*'s Rosebud shot, discussed in chapter 4. No one in the storyworld will ever know the truth about Rosebud, a sled soon to suffer a fiery demise. The crane shot grants us privileged knowledge, but the film's protagonist remains unknown to us in many ways. The shot takes a basic fact about cinematic storytelling—that stories take place within worlds—and turns it into a commentary on our inability to know any world fully.

Welles remained alive to this paradox for the rest of his career. His virtuosic movements prove that the camera *could* show us details that the film, in fact, withholds. Early in *The Stranger* (1946), the former Nazi Meinike (Konstantin Shayne) disembarks a ship and passes through immigration in a Latin American country. The American agent Wilson (Edward G. Robinson) follows him with the help of some local spies. The film's final shooting script called for the camera to swoop around the port, indicating where various characters are located.[4] Although Welles had less freedom than usual on this production, he staged this sequence with panache.[5] When Meinike anxiously approaches the immigration officials, one uniformed man steps into the background and looks up (fig. 6.1a). The camera cranes up and reveals a man with a pipe (known to be Wilson), standing next to a woman in an elegant dark suit (fig. 6.1b). The effect is thrilling: we see what Meinike does not. And yet our knowledge remains partial: a large sign occludes Wilson's face. The technique probably involves some sleight of hand, allowing a double to play Robinson's part, but the trick is meaningful nonetheless, enhancing the atmosphere of lies and uncertainty. Hypothetically, one could convey the same information through editing. (Cut to the official looking up. Cut to the mysterious figure up above.) Instead, the crane heightens our awareness of the camera's ability to go anywhere, which only heightens our awareness that Welles has refused to put the camera in the most informative spot.

Another filmmaker who thought deeply about the spectator's knowledge (or lack of it) was Alfred Hitchcock. In writings and interviews, he consistently

6.1 In *The Stranger*, the camera cranes up to reveal two figures while keeping their faces hidden.

argued that it was better to let spectators know all the important facts about the storyworld. Withholding information produces the short-term effect of surprise. Disclosing information produces something better: the long-term effects of suspense. If you show a bomb exploding, the resulting surprise engages spectators for a moment. If you show an unexploded bomb under a table, the resulting suspense may engage spectators for several minutes—as long as the bomb does not go off.[6] We might take Hitchcock's defense of suspense as a variation on the familiar idea that filmmakers should offer the most "advantageous" view on the scene, as in the theories of A. Lindsley Lane (chapter 2) and Garson Kanin (chapter 4). However, the distinction between surprise and suspense is not as clear-cut as Hitchcock was at such pains to suggest; even a suspenseful sequence may bring knowledge and ignorance into play.

Consider a famously suspenseful shot in Hitchcock's film *Notorious* (1946). A dissolve introduces an extreme high angle on a party; the camera gradually moves closer to Alicia (Ingrid Bergman), and the composition eventually settles on a tight close-up of her hand, which holds the crucial key to the wine cellar (fig. 6.2a–b). Cinematographer Ted Tetzlaff relied on a technique often used in silent films, suspending the camera from the ceiling, as in *Hotel Imperial* and *The Crowd*. As Bill Krohn reports, an optical zoom, added in postproduction, amplified the effect, making the key seem unusually close.[7] With Hitchcock's theory of suspense in mind, we might say that the shot offers us superior knowledge. Alicia knows about the key in her hand, but she has no way of seeing the room as a whole. The guests on the stairway can see the room as a whole, but they have no idea that Alicia has a key in her hand. The camera "knows" all, and so do we. In an article published in 1948, Hitchcock summarized his attitude to the spectator: "Let 'em play God."[8]

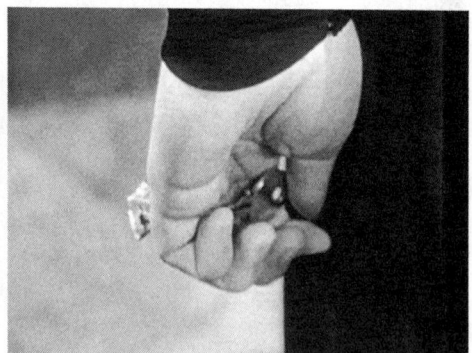

6.2 In *Notorious*, the camera locates a tiny detail in the middle of a large crowd.

But there are good reasons to question the idea that this shot (or any shot) offers spectators a truly omniscient perspective. The spectator in suspense does not know everything; the spectator just knows enough to ask what happens next. Even in that same article about suspense, Hitchcock defined the emotion in terms of unanswered questions. Knowing that Alicia has the key in her hand opens up new possibilities. Will someone at the party see the key? Will she be able to pass the key to Devlin (Cary Grant)? How will they get to the cellar to use the key? In its specific design, the shot offers not a feeling of mastery but an experience of uncertainty. At first, the camera pans across the crowd in the manner of a conventional establishing shot. We might expect the camera to locate Alicia or Sebastian (Claude Rains) or Devlin or some combination of the three, but we cannot be sure which one will appear. When the camera spots Alicia and Sebastian and starts to descend, we might expect it to pick out a detail, but we cannot be certain what that detail will be. (The last time we saw the key, Alicia was kicking it under a table, so we cannot know in advance that she is holding the key in her hand.) If anything, the camera appears to be moving toward Sebastian, not Alicia. When Sebastian steps out of the frame, Alicia's hand remains on the far right side of the frame, slightly out of focus. Suddenly, at the last possible moment, Alicia's hand slides into the center, snapping into sharpness, and she unclenches her fist just enough to reveal the key. On a macrolevel, the shot produces suspense, generating questions about what happens next. On a microlevel, the shot produces surprise, withholding information about what is in Alicia's hand until the last possible moment.

In 1935, A. Lindsley Lane had defined the camera as an "all-seeing" or "omniscient" eye.[9] In the mid-1940s, Herb Lightman invoked the same metaphor, describing the fluid camera as an "all-seeing eye."[10] Years later director Alexander Mackendrick taught his students cinematic technique by asking them to imagine the movements of an "Invisible Imaginary Ubiquitous Winged Witness."[11] Clearly, Hollywood filmmakers delighted in the idea that the camera could go anywhere and find anything, and I do not want to deny that the moving camera may offer the thrill of discovering the unknown or forbidden. Craning through space, the camera may find a prisoner rotting away in solitary (*Passage to Marseille*) or a killer hiding above a train station (*Union Station*, 1950) or a failure lying in shame in a flophouse (*Carrie*, 1952). With the help of special effects, the camera may even dissolve through the window of a moving train and fly down the street to find a man hiding out in a cheap hotel, as in *The Unsuspected* (1947). However, such feats of superhuman mobility rarely produce a true sense of omniscience. Even when the camera flies through space, it reveals some things and conceals others, passing by an untold number of untold stories. Setting aside talk of the "all-seeing eye," it is useful to recall that the camera is not a bodily organ but a mechanical tool. The camera does not see; it makes pictures for the movie to show. To photograph a scene is to photograph it selectively. To show the wide view is to avoid the close one. To follow the protagonist is to ignore the villain. Films produce patterns of disclosures, releasing information bit by bit or many bits at a time, but never all at once.

With respect to the moving camera, four related functions seem particularly important: revelation, concealment, emphasis, and understatement.[12] First, the camera might reveal something previously unseen, as when a dolly opens up an area of offscreen space. Alternatively, the camera might conceal something we have seen already, as when the camera pans off an already-established character. The processes are complementary: revealing one thing conceals another. A third possible function is emphasis: rather than reveal something previously unseen, the camera might draw more attention to an object or person *already* in our existing field of view, as when the camera dollies toward a person who currently occupies some position on the screen. A fourth possibility, understatement, serves as the opposite of emphasis: the filmmaker refuses to use camera movement to give extra priority to a subject even though that subject seems important to the story.

The terms may seem obvious or even tautological. Doesn't the rectangular frame conceal an infinite number of things by definition, whether it moves or not? The distinctions become meaningful only when we think of patterns of disclosure in light of a film's ongoing concerns. The unfolding story marks certain facts and possibilities as relevant and others as insignificant; relevant revelations matter more. To tell a story, filmmakers must decide when to reveal which details and in what order. In the film noir *Murder, My Sweet* (1944), detective Philip Marlowe (Dick Powell) sits down to examine a clue, a photograph that may or may not depict the missing Velma. The camera frames a balanced over-the-shoulder shot, offering a clear view of the picture (fig. 6.3a). Then the music shifts to a more menacing register, and the camera booms back and up,

6.3 In *Murder, My Sweet*, the camera booms up to reveal that Moose is standing behind Marlowe.

revealing Moose (Mike Mazurki) standing directly behind Marlowe (fig. 6.3b). When the boom completes its ascent, Marlowe senses Moose's presence and turns around. The story situation seems simple: a detective realizes that another man has entered the room. But think of all the choices the filmmakers must make. Do you reveal Moose before Marlowe notices him? At the same time? Or after? Do you reveal Moose with a straight cut? If so, do you employ a point-of-view shot? Do you reveal Moose via camera movement? If so, should the boom be synchronized with Marlowe's own movement or not? Each decision produces its own effects in context.

The film's director, Edward Dmytryk, insisted that framing was an essential task of the director, who must decide "what he wants to include in the frame and, just as important, what he wants to exclude."[13] Here, Dmytryk has opted for revelation *before* recognition, disclosing Moose's presence a few seconds before Marlowe notices him.[14] The strategy increases suspense because the threat of Moose seems even greater as long as Marlowe does not know he is there. Notice how the camera movement allows the viewer's suspense to rise in stages. When the boom begins, we quickly learn that someone is standing behind Marlowe, but we might not know right away that this man is the dangerous Moose. As the boom continues, we realize that the man is indeed our familiar hulk, and the threat rises. As the boom nears its end, Moose's menace increases even more; he just keeps filling more and more of the frame! A straight cut would have revealed Moose's presence right away, offering a jolt of surprise. The boom discloses the threat gradually, amplifying suspense.

In this example, revelation occurs before recognition. *Dead Reckoning* (1947) reverses the order. Rip (Humphrey Bogart) wakes up in a strange room after he has been knocked unconscious. Wondering why he was slugged, Rip turns over and sees something. A stinger on the soundtrack underscores his moment of recognition, but the film does not cut to the expected point-of-view shot. For several seconds, we are left to wonder what Rip has seen. Finally, Rip stands up, and the camera follows him as he turns over a dead body in the second bed. The approach here generates morbid curiosity: we know that something bad has happened, but we do not know what. The effect on our engagement with Rip is complex. On the one hand, the film introduces a significant discrepancy in knowledge: Rip knows what is offscreen, and we do not. On the other hand, the resulting feelings of confusion may actually amplify identification with Rip. Still recovering from his beating, Rip cannot make sense of his situation. The delayed revelation puts the spectator in a similarly confused state.

I have discussed Meir Sternberg's distinction between the changes in the storyworld and the changes in our understanding of that storyworld.[15] This distinction underscores the contrast I am making here between revelation and recognition. A revelation belongs to the film's "flow of disclosures," regulating our ever-shifting understanding of the storyworld. A recognition belongs to the storyworld's "flow of developments," as a character passes from ignorance to knowledge. Shifting the relationships between revelation and recognition alters a film's emotional effects, albeit in ways that cannot be predicted in advance without seeing the narrative unfold in context. I take this claim to be broadly applicable—true of narrative films in general and not just of Hollywood films of the 1940s. However, as David Bordwell has pointed out, the filmmakers of the 1940s took a heightened interest in problems of narrative construction, actively discussing "ways information could be manipulated."[16] Experimentation took place at many levels, from the crafting of the screenplay to the design of the dolly shot.

Whether executed via camera movement, editing, or staging, revelations rely on corresponding acts of concealment. In order to reveal that Moose is already standing there, *Murder, My Sweet* must hide his entrance. Other films make concealment itself the point of a scene, asking us to consider what is not shown. Censorship mandated evasive tactics; certain stories required filmmakers to make those acts of concealment paradoxically noticeable. For instance, the story line of Lewis Milestone's wartime drama *Edge of Darkness* (1943) turns on a war crime, when a Nazi soldier rapes the Norwegian resistance fighter Karen, played by Ann Sheridan. For reasons of censorship and dramatic impact, the filmmakers elected not to show the assault. The camera instead frames a view of Karen's feet as she walks through a church. When the Nazi pulls her offscreen, the camera dollies back—away from the characters and indeed all the way outside, where the camera cranes up the church steeple to frame a symbolic image of a cross and a clock. Simply cutting away from the scene might have satisfied the Production Code, but it would do so at the risk of leaving the story point unclear. Craning away from the scene makes the act of concealment visible, forcing us to think about what cannot be shown. It is not enough to conceal the scene; the film must dramatize the concealment itself.

These examples of revelation and concealment involve the interplay between onscreen and offscreen space. Alternatively, a moving camera might place extra *emphasis* on a person or object already onscreen. Consider again the problem of representing a moment of recognition. One popular technique was to dolly in toward a character's face right at the moment when understanding dawns, as in *Mrs. Miniver* and *Phantom Lady*, discussed in the introduction. Filmmakers could execute this convention in countless ways, varying the camera placement, the speed, and the timing of the dolly. In *Sorry, Wrong Number* (1948), directed by Anatole Litvak, the protagonist, Leona (Barbara Stanwyck), attempts to report a possible murder plot. After making several phone calls, Leona receives a message that her husband is not coming home, and she realizes that she is the intended victim. As a look of terror comes across her face, the camera dollies in slowly, from a tight medium close-up to an even tighter close-up (fig. 6.4a–b). In comparison to the lively *Phantom Lady* and the sympathetic *Mrs. Miniver*, *Sorry, Wrong Number* registers as a cruel, misogynistic film,

6.4 In *Sorry, Wrong Number*, the camera dollies in to frame an extremely tight composition.

presenting Leona as a manipulative, self-deceiving woman who deserves her fate. An extreme wide-angle lens allows the camera to approach within a few inches of Barbara Stanwyck's face, resulting in a grotesque close-up of the star. The insistent tightness of the frame expresses a sense of increasing entrapment; the too-close positioning of the camera expresses a corresponding sense of impending violence. Significantly, the dolly-in does not reveal anything new. Leona is onscreen; then she is a little bit closer. The camera simply rivets our attention onto Leona's face, encouraging us to savor a moment of recognition that we have been anticipating for some time. She hasn't realized the truth just yet, but she is going to. Not yet . . . not yet . . . now.

A filmmaker might emphasize a detail in a thousand ways: via color as well as camerawork, via cutting as well as composition. In the right context, a dolly-out might emphasize a point more effectively than a dolly-in. Just as important, a filmmaker might choose to represent a relevant detail with *less* emphasis than we might expect it to warrant. Such understatement is itself a cinematic gesture—a refusal of obvious rhetoric. For the filmmakers of the 1940s, the wedding scene in *How Green Was My Valley* and the kitchen scene in *The Magnificent Ambersons* served as impressive demonstrations of the power of understatement, paring movement to a minimum. *Out of the Past* (1947) takes another approach to understatement, moving the camera to follow one thing but not another. When Jeff (Robert Mitchum) visits his nemesis Whit (Kirk Douglas), Kathie (Jane Greer) is the last person Jeff expects to see. In walks Kathie. This revelation is shocking—all the more so because the filmmakers reintroduce their femme fatale so casually. The camera simply dollies to follow Jeff as he approaches a breakfast table. This lateral movement reveals a room in the background, where Kathie is walking to join the men (fig. 6.5a–b). At first,

6.5 A simple dolly reveals Kathie in the background in *Out of the Past*.

Kathie is hard to recognize. She is dozens of feet away, and Jeff's body partially occludes her. When Kathie gets close enough to be recognized, the film cuts away from her and shows a closer angle of Jeff, who is still oblivious. My description may sound innocuous, but the scene's innocuousness produces its effect. For this shocking plot twist, one might expect some cinematic device to heighten the drama: perhaps a musical flourish, perhaps a cut to a close-up of Kathie, perhaps an emphatic dolly-in. The camerawork instead remains as understated as Robert Mitchum's performance; a short dolly follows Jeff as he walks to a table. The absence of rhetorical heightening might even raise doubts in the viewer's mind. Wait, was that Kathie? The timing of the cut is perfectly judged: a split second after the shot has given us a clear view of Kathie, the film cuts away, leaving us to wonder if we have seen her correctly. After an excruciating few seconds, Whit asks from offscreen, "You remember Kathie, don't you?" No whip-pan to Kathie, no dolly-in to Jeff's shocked face: just a few more seconds of Robert Mitchum's exquisitely underplayed performance and then a workmanlike arcing pan to follow Jeff as he walks over to assist with Kathie's chair. Only then is the truth confirmed: she is really there.

Throughout this section, I have avoided the question of whether these movements are "motivated" or not, in the narrow sense of the term. Hollywood filmmakers drew a distinction between "motivated" dolly shots that followed characters in motion and "unmotivated" dolly shots that operated independently of character movements. In spite of my interest in practitioners' working theories, I have been reluctant to use this distinction because I think that it misleadingly suggests that unmotivated movements are somehow aberrant. But Hollywood filmmakers were perfectly willing to use "unmotivated" (i.e., nonfollowing) camera movements as long as they performed a dramatic function, such as revealing what a character does not know (as in *Murder, My*

Sweet) or emphasizing what a character does know (as in *Sorry, Wrong Number*). Alexander Mackendrick provides support for this view. While drawing the traditional distinction between motivated and unmotivated moves, he explains, "If the camera either pans, tracks, cranes, or tilts without motivation from the subject . . ., this is clearly intervention from the filmmaker and is a much more conscious move. The audience may sense it is therefore of some significance."[17] In other words, the allegedly unmotivated movement turns out to be one where the shot's purpose is *more* prominent, not less. Whether the camera follows a character or not, the camera's movement is usually motivated in the deeper sense of the term—executed for a rhetorical or aesthetic point.

Although these terms—*revelation, concealment, emphasis,* and *understatement*—are admittedly broad, they help describe how a film might deploy the moving camera to tell its story with heightened narrative effect. In particular, they offer a new way of thinking about the "omniscient eye" and its alternatives. For years, Hollywood's practical theorists had insisted that the filmmaker's job was to put the camera in the most "advantageous" position at all times. Surely, they did not mean that the camera should reveal everything; such a task would be impossible. A more plausible reading is that they were proposing a guideline for selection: the camera should reveal the most relevant events and conceal the rest. It is not a question of what the camera sees but of what the movie shows. Many filmmakers strived for this always-advantageous ideal, but the system remained flexible enough to allow for alternatives.

The previous chapter examined some of these alternatives, such as the point-of-view craze of 1947. The next two sections look at two more trends, one from the late 1940s and one from the 1950s. First, several directors began staging increasingly audacious long takes, relying on figure movement and camera movement to create variable framing over the course of a scene. Second, the industry's adoption of widescreen processes forced filmmakers to devise new compositional strategies without unduly compromising narrative effects. Both trends proved controversial precisely because they forced filmmakers to rethink the moving camera's contributions to the functions of revelation, concealment, emphasis, and understatement.

The Longest Takes

As discussed in chapter 4, the term *fluid camera* describes a specific method of scene construction whereby filmmakers design compositions ahead of time and then lace them together with camera movement. As the cinematographer Boris Kaufman explained in 1960, "The continuity can be fragmentary, formed by cuts of close-ups, long shots, etc.; or it can take a legato form—the so-called fluid camera technique—when the moving camera combines several camera set-ups in one continuous scene."[18] This account described the moving camera as a substitute for a cut—another way to produce familiar patterns of scene construction, from establishing shot to close-ups. However, Kaufman's use of the term *legato* introduced a fresh musical analogy, suggesting that a moving camera might do more than just replace the cut—it might alter the flow of a scene. Analyzing the increasingly fluid camerawork of the late 1940s and early 1950s, we must keep both points in mind—that the camera could perform the everyday functions of the cut and that its movement made meanings and moods above and beyond what a cut could provide.[19]

Building on the long takes of the early 1940s, many films of the late 1940s pushed the aesthetic of fluidity even further, as if directors were engaged in a competition to see who could craft the most elaborate shot. John Farrow staged three-minute shots in *The Big Clock* (1948) and *Night Has a Thousand Eyes* (1948). Preston Sturges staged a four-minute shot in *Unfaithfully Yours* (1948). In *Lady from Shanghai* (1947), Orson Welles set out to design the slowest possible dolly shot, creaking forward just a few feet during the course of a three-minute scene. The following year, he set out to record the longest possible take, staging a ten-minute shot for *Macbeth* (1948). The technique may seem like an extravagance, but it was not necessarily expensive. The shooting script for *The Big Clock* called for 255 setups. Long takes allowed Farrow to cover the entire script in only 183 setups. The crew executed less than five setups per day, but they managed to complete the film roughly on schedule.[20] Cinematographer John F. Seitz even had time to devise a new lighting scheme for the film, relying on overhead reflected light to minimize the risk of the camera recording its own shadow.[21]

Some of the era's most impressive long takes were created with the aid of special effects, echoing the virtuosic displays of *Citizen Kane*. *The Big Clock* opens with a spectacular sequence: an artificially constructed long take that introduces the problem of omniscience as an overriding theme. At first, the camera pans over the skyline of New York at night (fig. 6.6a). After a hidden dissolve, the pan continues across a miniature of a modernistic office building (fig. 6.6b). With the help of an optical effect, the camera appears to enter the building (fig. 6.6c). Once inside, the camera locates the hunted protagonist, George (Ray Milland), who evades discovery by hiding inside a huge clock (fig. 6.6d). Meanwhile, the soundtrack introduces a subjective voiceover, allowing us to hear George's thoughts: "How'd I get into this rat race anyway? I'm no criminal. What happened? When did it all start?" The scene develops a contrast between the incomprehension of the voiceover and the uninhibited range of the camera, which is able to move anywhere without a (visible) cut. At first, the privileged knowledge seems empowering to the spectator. There are dozens of guards looking for the protagonist, but we spot him right away! However, the voiceover's questions actually reinforce our awareness of our own ignorance. George knows

6.6 In *The Big Clock*, the camera dollies toward a miniature of a modernistic office building and locates the protagonist trying to hide.

exactly where he is, and we do not; George knows when it all started, and we do not. The subjective voiceover reveals one sort of information; the hypermobile camera reveals another; neither provides complete understanding. Here, the film brilliantly establishes its themes. In the flashback, George will act like a near-omniscient figure, solving crimes that the police cannot. But omniscience proves to be self-destructive as George is forced to conduct an investigation that will implicate himself. By staging such an audacious shot, the movie encourages us to see the camera metaphorically as an all-seeing eye. By using that all-seeing eye to introduce such a persecuted protagonist, the movie implicates the cinema as just another technology of surveillance in a society increasingly under constant watch. Merrill Schleier's discussion of this sequence is instructive. Depression-era films such as *Skyscraper Souls* had represented the skyscraper lobby as a "microcosm of urban life," where meetings could happen by chance. The postwar film *The Big Clock* represents the same space as a site of regulation and control.[22]

This synthetic long take relies on the resources of a powerful studio: a crack special-effects team, a distinguished cinematographer, a director with a history of fluid camerawork, a continuity script that described the shot in detail, a budget that made a boom available for every day of shooting, and a professional crew with the skills to swing the set's wild walls in and out as the camera moved into and out of the clock.[23] By contrast, the crew of the low-budget thriller *Gun Crazy* (1950) shot the film's most celebrated long take on the cheap. According to director Joseph H. Lewis, the original script for the bank robbery sequence ran to seventeen pages. He said to himself, "My gosh, this is just another bank hold-up, and it isn't interesting. To me, it's boring. People are way ahead of you."[24] He decided instead to stage the scene in a single take photographed from the back of the getaway car—actually, a stretch Cadillac with the rear seats taken out. The crew greased some wooden boards and placed them in the back of the car; then they mounted a saddle onto the boards and attached the camera head to the saddle. Sliding back and forth on the greased boards, the operator created the effect of a dolly shot in a moving vehicle. This ingenious solution saved time and money. Lewis photographed a practice take in 16-millimeter to give his crew an idea of what he wanted; then they shot the scene in a single morning.[25] The result exhibits a wonderful new pattern of revelation and concealment. Recall Lewis's critique of the conventional approach: people are way ahead of you. This shot leaves spectators behind, struggling to catch up. The characters know the directions to the bank, but we do not, so every turn (left, right, then left again) comes as a surprise. When Bart (John Dall) enters the bank, the camera remains in the car, inciting curiosity about the offscreen robbery (fig. 6.7a). When the couple drives away, Annie (Peggy Cummins) knows whether they are being followed or not, but the camera does not turn around to show us what she sees. Instead, it dollies in on her, emphasizing the perverse delight on her face (fig 6.7b). Over the course of the scene, the camera car spins around 360 degrees, but the effect does not feel remotely empowering because our view remains locked inside a vehicle that someone

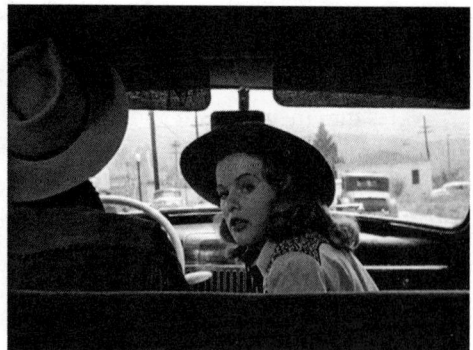

6.7 The highlight of *Gun Crazy* is a three-minute-long take in the back of a car.

else is driving. As in *Citizen Kane*, the more virtuosic the shot, the more we realize that we are under the film's control.

Perhaps the most surprising contributor to the long-take trend was Alfred Hitchcock. Back in 1937, Hitchcock had complained, "If I have to shoot a long scene continuously I always feel I am losing grip on it, from a cinematic point of view."[26] Ten years later he was photographing *Rope* (1948), featuring the longest takes Hollywood had ever seen. In keeping with the emerging discourse of the fluid camera, Hitchcock presented his experiments as extensions of his long-standing commitment to planning sequences ahead of time. *Rebecca* and *Shadow of a Doubt* had demonstrated the merits of cutting in the camera, shifting from one effective angle to another. The long takes of *The Paradine Case* (1947), *Rope*, and *Under Capricorn* (1949) followed a similar logic much more fluidly.

All three of Hitchcock's long-take films received considerable attention in the trade press, which highlighted the grips' contributions. While directing *The Paradine Case* for producer David O. Selznick, Hitchcock had asked his crew to create a small-scale dolly with improved maneuverability. Working with engineer Steve Krilanovich and cinematographer Lee Garmes, Selznick's grip, Morris Rosen, constructed a prototype crab dolly, which came to be known as the "Rosie" dolly in the grip's honor. The prototype was not much to look at: four wheels, a platform, and a camera post. But each wheel could swivel 360 degrees, and a chain connected all four wheels together so that the entire dolly could be steered in a different direction in the middle of a take. Introducing the dolly, an article in *American Cinematographer* argued that it fulfilled, at long last, the go-anywhere ideal: "It carries the camera not only in a straight line, but around corners and at an infinite number of angles."[27] The filmmakers used this dolly to photograph several complex shots for *The Paradine Case*, including one that reportedly ran for three and a half minutes, capturing an exchange between protagonist Anthony (Gregory Peck) and his wife, Gay (Ann Todd). As David Bordwell points out, the shot does not survive intact in the finished film because producer David O. Selznick elected to cut in the additional angles that Hitchcock had provided (counter to the director's stated practice of limiting his domineering producer's choices).[28] The remaining portions of the shot still demonstrate the Rosie dolly's remarkable flexibility. At first, the camera frames a medium close-up of Gay (fig. 6.8a). The camera dollies back and to the right, booming downward to frame a two-shot (fig. 6.8b-c). It is a nice move—but nothing the Raby dolly couldn't handle. Then Rosen does something remarkable—he pushes the dolly in toward Anthony, allowing operator Eddie Fitzgerald to frame an over-the-shoulder composition looking toward Gay (fig. 6.8d). Notice that Rosen has not simply pushed the dolly back to where it started. Repositioning the wheels midshot, he has changed the dolly's orientation toward the action. The fact that the adjustment is so subtle is what makes

6.8 In *The Paradine Case*, the crab dolly follows a subject and moves in at a different angle.

it so revolutionary. One measured the power of a crane by asking how many feet it could fly into the air; one measured the power of the Rosie dolly by considering how it might change a composition by half an inch.

Rosen devised an improved version of his dolly for another Selznick film, *Portrait of Jennie* (1948).[29] Soon Selznick was renting the "all-angle dolly" out to other companies.[30] Sensing a market, Krilanovich began manufacturing crab dollies for widespread use. This improved model offered the option of either a "square" pattern, whereby the dolly could travel in a straight line and then turn to go in another straight line, or a "round" pattern, whereby the dolly could trace an arc or circle of any diameter. An added feature was a small boom, in the manner of the Velocilator. With the help of hydraulics, this miniature arm could rise from fifteen inches to fifty-two inches.[31] Lee Garmes used the new crab dolly to shave several days off the shooting schedule of William Wyler's film *Detective Story* (1951). According to Garmes, Wyler "was delighted with the idea of a camera he could move wherever he wanted."[32] Over the course of the 1950s, several other crab dollies appeared, such as Houston-Fearless's Cinemobile and Moviola's Crab Dolly. Karl Freund, whose career stretched from *The Last Laugh* in 1924 to *I Love Lucy* in the 1950s, quickly recognized the dolly's potential for television production.[33]

Freed from Selznick's meddling, Hitchcock pushed the long take even further on his next movie, the independently produced film *Rope*.[34] The film comprises exactly eleven shots, some of which are linked with traditional cuts and some of which are linked with "hidden" cuts, as when the camera dollies in toward a character's coat in order to disguise the transition from one shot to another. Many of these shots run for nearly ten minutes, close to the maximum length of a film magazine. Joseph Valentine and Technicolor man William Skall were the cinematographers. Eddie Fitzgerald operated the camera. Morris Rosen served as the dolly grip, using his latest model; photographs show that the Rosie dolly now came equipped with a midsize boom.[35] The entire camera crew even received screen credit as "operators of camera movement." They photographed the film on a stage at Warner Bros., featuring a special raised floor lined with felt. Numbered markers were placed on the floor, one for each camera stop. A technician would point to each marker, and the grip would make his move. A small flashlight suspended from the camera's lens would illuminate the marker, and Rosen would know that he had hit the spot.[36]

American Cinematographer covered the experiment with interest, recounting many of these technical details. *Showmen's Trade Review* suggested that the film's "revolutionary" use of the "fluid camera" might serve as a primary audience appeal, especially in light of Hitchcock's reputation as an innovator. Outside the industry, articles in *Popular Photography* and *Look* celebrated the film's constantly moving camera.[37] Together, these sources provided two distinct frameworks for understanding the film—an authorial framework centered around Hitchcock and a technical framework centered around the ideal of fluidity. One could see the film as an extension of an individual's long-standing interest in visual storytelling or as the culmination of the industry's exploration of the mobile long take as a viable method of scene construction.

Whereas *American Cinematographer* described *Rope* as a collaborative effort, Irving Pichel fit the movie into his proto-auteurist theory (discussed in chapter 4), crediting the director with the power to make all the relevant choices—for the film crew and for the spectator. Defending the film from charges that it was overly theatrical, Pichel drew a sharp contrast between the theater and the cinema. A theater director may induce us to look here or there, but a director such as Hitchcock has absolute control: "He shows us what we are going to see at a given moment. He shows it to us at a scale that measures the importance and emphasis of what we are seeing at that moment. Above all, he excludes at that moment everything we are not to see."[38] *Rope* may have depicted one hundred minutes of continuous action in the manner of a stage play, but Hitchcock had not abandoned his long-standing determination to control the flow of information bit by bit.

We can see this piecemeal logic at work in the film's eighth shot, which begins with a straight cut to the maid (Edith Evanson) and ends eight minutes later with a hidden cut on the back of a killer's coat. The camera moves dozens of times; just as significantly, it does not move all the time. It instead frames several discrete compositions, all linked together with fluid movement. With Hitchcock's history of cutting in the camera in mind, one might reimagine the entire shot as a series of distinct groupings.

Hypothetically, the Hitchcock of 1940 might have broken this shot down into thirty shots or more, as shown in table 6.1. Individual sequences of shots would have followed familiar patterns of scene construction, such as the glance–object–reaction pattern of stages 19, 20, and 21 (figs. 6.9a–b), when Rupert (James Stewart) looks at an incriminating clue (the murder victim's hat) and reacts with suppressed alarm, or the two-shot–single–two-shot pattern of stages 24, 25, and 26 (figs. 6.9c–d), when Brandon (John Dall) changes tactics in the middle of a conversation with Philip (Farley Granger). Hitchcock himself encouraged such a reading. In his *Popular Photography* article, Hitchcock explained that he prepared the shot breakdown with the film's editor, William Ziegler, effectively "cutting" the film ahead of time.[39] Years later Hitchcock told François Truffaut, "The mobility of the camera and the movement of the players closely followed my usual cutting practice."[40] Truffaut's mentor André Bazin agreed, suggesting that Hitchcock's long takes were less revolutionary than Welles's and Wyler's long takes. Summarizing Bazin's views, John Belton notes that Hitchcock's "continual re-framing" breaks the scene down into a series of actions rather than placing those actions onscreen together in deep focus.[41]

Although Hitchcock, Pichel, and others encouraged observers to think of the long take as a variation on cutting in the camera, it is important to recognize that the experience of watching the eight-minute take is somewhat different. *Rope*'s compositions do not simply progress from cut to cut; they change before our eyes. Looking at table 6.1, one might imagine a quick transition from the seventh composition, showing Brandon confronting Rupert over the chest, to the eighth, showing Janet (Joan Chandler), Mrs. Atwater (Constance Collier), Mr. Kentley (Cedric Hardwicke), and Kenneth (Douglas Dick). The shift instead takes several seconds, passing through a series of ephemeral compositions as Mrs. Wilson exits and Mrs. Atwater enters. In this way, the camera ends up framing many more groupings than my thirty-point chart can suggest. The pattern of movement—indeed, the ever-present possibility of movement—adds enormously to the scene's effects. Consider the moment when the camera pans past Brandon, past Philip, and onto Rupert, listed as stages 9, 10, and 11. Given the film's well-established pattern of panning to establish a new stationary composition, we might expect the camera to stop at any time. Will the frame settle on Brandon? No. Maybe it will stop on Philip? . . . No. Will it stop on Rupert? Yes! A simple cut to Brandon followed by a cut to Philip followed by a cut to Rupert would not have produced the same sense of anticipation that we get here. As V. F. Perkins explains, "A good deal of the suspense in the film comes from

TABLE 6.1 **Thirty Separate Stages of a Single Shot in *Rope* (1948)**

Stage	Rupert	Brandon	Philip	Mrs. W	Janet	Mrs. A	Mr. K	Kenneth	Chest
1				onscreen					
2	onscreen	onscreen	onscreen	onscreen					
3				onscreen		onscreen			onscreen
4	partial			onscreen					onscreen
5	onscreen			onscreen					onscreen
6	onscreen	onscreen		onscreen					onscreen
7	onscreen	onscreen							onscreen
8					onscreen	onscreen	onscreen	onscreen	
9		onscreen							
10			onscreen						

(continued)

TABLE 6.1 (continued)

Stage	Rupert	Brandon	Philip	Mrs. W	Janet	Mrs. A	Mr. K	Kenneth	Chest
11	onscreen								
12		onscreen			partial		onscreen		
13		onscreen			onscreen		onscreen		
14		onscreen			onscreen	onscreen	onscreen	onscreen	
15					onscreen			onscreen	
16		onscreen			onscreen			onscreen	
17	onscreen		onscreen						
18	onscreen								
19	onscreen			onscreen					

20	partial		
21	onscreen		onscreen
22	onscreen	onscreen	
23	onscreen		
24	onscreen	onscreen	
25	onscreen		
26	onscreen	onscreen	
27	onscreen		
28	onscreen		onscreen
29	onscreen		
30	partial		

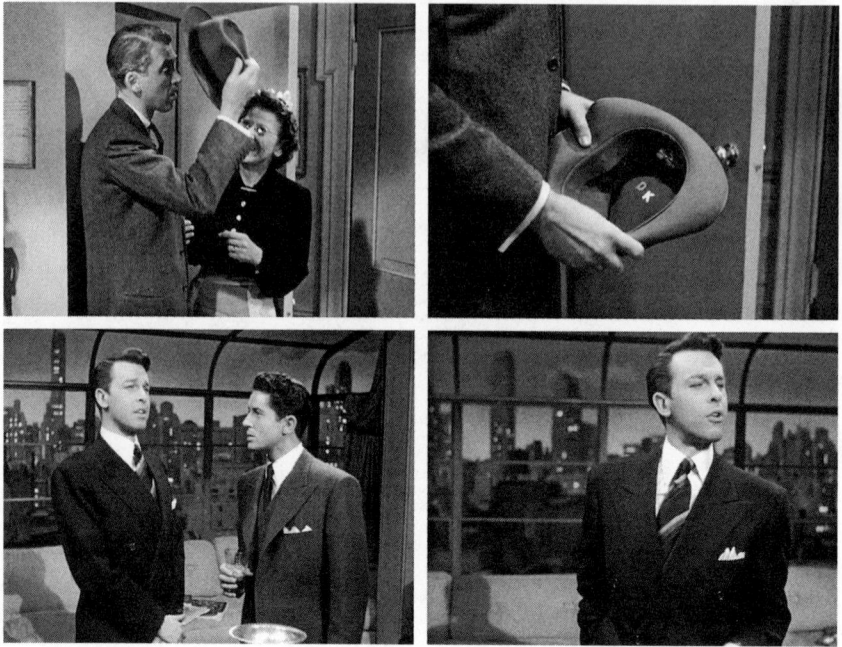

6.9 The variable framing follows the patterns of an edited scene in *Rope*.

the fact that one is seldom sure just where one is being taken by any particular camera movement."[42] As the camera sweeps past Brandon to Philip to Rupert, one expects the camera to rest on someone but cannot know who that someone will be.

Even the camera's moments of stasis become meaningful. Early in the shot, the camera remains locked in an awkward composition for nearly two minutes, with a corpse-filled chest to the left and Rupert's partly offscreen body to the right (stage 4 in table 6.1). Given the camera's proven fluidity, we might expect it to move to a more informative angle: a view of the chest, of Mrs. Wilson, of Rupert, of anything. The camera's near-total stasis produces its own kind of suspense, making us wonder what is happening offscreen. The example supports Hitchcock's definition of suspense as an effect of superior knowledge—but only partly. We know that there is a dead body in the chest, but Mrs. Wilson and Rupert do not. In that sense, the framing reminds us that we have privileged information. But our privileged knowledge still remains maddeningly restricted. Brandon and Philip stand offscreen. Rupert, in a brilliantly frustrating bit of blocking, stands just at the edge of the screen, his face turned away and his back cut in half by the frame line. The "all-angle" dolly only amplified the cinema's selectivity.

Hitchcock's next film, *Under Capricorn*, featured another audacious long take: a six-minute virtuoso shot that required grips and actors to remove a table, piece by piece, as the camera approached.[43] In the next decade, Hitchcock resumed his practice of planning and sketching sequences of shorter shots ahead of time.[44] By the 1960s, he was telling interviewers that *Rope* had betrayed his core belief that montage constituted the essence of the cinema: "I abandoned pure cinema in an effort to make the stage play mobile."[45]

Other filmmakers showed more commitment to the long take as a viable shooting strategy rather than a stunt. While Hitchcock was filming *Under Capricorn* in the United Kingdom, George Cukor was filming the M-G-M production *Edward, My Son* on the stage next door.[46] Cukor had been tinkering with long takes for nearly two decades, as in *Little Women* (1933) and *Keeper of the Flame* (1942). *Edward, My Son*, released in 1949, pushed the director's long-take aesthetic to the limits—for instance, in a remarkable ten-minute scene photographed in exactly three shots. The middle shot, just shy of six minutes long, is almost the length of a typical shot in *Rope*, but Cukor's staging differs from Hitchcock's in instructive ways. *Rope* constantly shifts its groupings; we see empty frames, singles, two-shots, three-shots, and group shots in every conceivable variation. *Edward, My Son* has one default grouping: the two-shot. The six-minute shot begins with a cut to Arnold, the boorish businessman played by Spencer Tracy. After nine seconds, Arnold steps into a two-shot with his wife, Evelyn (Deborah Kerr), who is seeking a divorce. The composition then remains in a two-shot for the next five minutes and thirty-nine seconds. Finally, Evelyn steps into the foreground; the resulting single lasts for only five more seconds before the next cut.

Though based on a play, the staging is richly cinematic. The scene depicts Evelyn's attempt to separate herself from her cruel husband. Over the course of this six-minute shot, she gets closer and closer to her goal; in the third shot, he counterattacks and humiliates her. In this context, the two cuts that open and close the six-minute shot form a despairing pattern: in each instance, a single of Evelyn is replaced with a single of the more powerful Arnold. In between, the actors hit a series of carefully judged marks. Sometimes the composition gives priority to Arnold, as when he sits smugly on the table while Evelyn stands partially occluded and in soft focus in the background (fig. 6.10a). Sometimes the composition gives priority to Evelyn, as when she steps forward to express her fear that their son is adopting Arnold's brutishness, while Arnold simmers a few feet behind her (fig. 6.10b). But these shifts in emphasis are never absolute. Both actors deliver demanding performances, and the two-shot composition asks us to keep our eyes on both of them at all times. As Arnold sits on the table, his smugness visibly contrasts with Evelyn's nervousness. As she steps to the fore, her fear visibly contrasts with his anger. In place of revelation and concealment, we have the unfolding play of emphasis and understatement.

6.10 In *Edward, My Son*, a six-minute-long take captures two extraordinary performances.

Cukor later insisted, "If you do a lot of fancy footwork, maybe they notice you as a director, but I think it hurts the story."[47] The footwork here is subtle but intricate. Working at M-G-M's British studios, Cukor took full advantage of an excellent crew headed by F. A. Young, a future three-time Oscar winner for his work with David Lean. When the actors move laterally, operator Skeets Kelly pans to keep both of them in the frame. When the tension rises in the middle of the shot, the camera dollies in for emphasis. When the tension eases temporarily, the camera dollies back out. Focus puller Christopher Doll controls the flow of the scene by shifting back and forth between the two characters, pulling to Arnold in the foreground, Evelyn in the background, Evelyn in the foreground, Arnold in the background. The scene may be a showcase for Tracy and Kerr, but the camera crew shapes the arc of the scene from moment to moment.[48]

In his autobiography, Young dismissed the long takes of the late 1940s as a "craze." They were "exciting" to shoot, but they required extra camera movement to be effective, which in turn made lighting and sound recording more difficult: "All in all we found long takes a lot more trouble than they were worth, and within a few months the idea had gone out of fashion."[49] Back in Hollywood, the long take remained essential to the musical genre, allowing filmmakers to preserve the integrity of each performance. As Vincente Minnelli explained, "Many short takes using several cameras from different angles tended to interrupt the flow of movement. . . . Sometimes I might use as many as twenty different stops on the camera to accommodate different details."[50] On Minnelli's film *An American in Paris* (1951), "cuts were avoided whenever possible," in dramatic scenes and musical numbers alike.[51] Minnelli extended his fluid, musical techniques to other genres, such as the comedy *Father of the Bride* (1950) and the melodrama *The Bad and the Beautiful* (1952).[52]

After leaving Selznick, dolly grip Morris Rosen went on to collaborate with several filmmakers discussed in this book. Working with cinematographer Lee Garmes, he served as the grip on Ophuls's film *Caught*. With Ophuls's long-time collaborator Franz Planer, Rosen provided the grip work for *Champion* (1949) and *Not as a Stranger* (1955). For Fred Zinnemann, Rosen gripped *The Men* (1950) and *High Noon* (1952). These collaborations led to a long relationship with producer-director Stanley Kramer. Many critics scoff at Kramer's plodding directorial style, but some of his films feature intricate camerawork—see especially the arcing dolly work in *Judgment at Nuremberg* (1961), which recalls Rosen's work in the trial scenes in *The Paradine Case*. Capping off a distinguished career, Rosen became a regular contributor to Preminger's films, lending his expert touch to *The Man with the Golden Arm* (1955), *Exodus* (1960), and *Advise & Consent* (1962).

The combination of the long take with elaborate camera movement provoked some resistance from budget-minded producers. Watching the dailies for Twentieth Century-Fox's *A Letter to Three Wives* (1949), studio boss Darryl F. Zanuck was impressed by the skill on display but worried about the time spent on set. In a memo addressed to key members of the production team, Zanuck wrote, "Almost every scene involves camera movement, change in focus, change in lighting, dolly shots, etc. The photography is beautiful and the result is very effective. I do not believe, however, that the success or failure of the film will depend upon this treatment, which takes additional time."[53] In a period of post-war budget-cutting, Zanuck was looking to shorten shooting times.[54] Significantly, he did not object to long takes per se. He later encouraged his directors to take Minnelli's *Father of the Bride* as a model because Minnelli had proven that a good crew could complete a quality film on a tight shooting schedule.[55] On *A Letter to Three Wives*, the problem was not the length of the takes but the intricacy. All those little moves, a few inches left and a few inches right, could add days to a shooting schedule.

Whether for practical or dramatic reasons, some filmmakers opted to combine long takes with relatively simple camerawork, as in nearly stationary four-minute scenes in George Stevens's *A Place in the Sun* (1951) and George Cukor's *The Marrying Kind* (1952), which subordinate camerawork to brilliant performances. Some television dramas favored this low-key approach; the corresponding film adaptations featured economical, unobtrusive long takes, as in *Marty* (1955).[56] At its best, this modest approach could produce moments of exquisite understatement. In Mankiewicz's hospital drama *No Way Out* (1950), Cora (Mildred Joanne Smith in her only screen performance) delivers a long monologue, reassuring her husband, Luther (Sidney Poitier), that he is a good doctor even though a recent confrontation with a racist patient has given him self-doubt. As Cora reaches her arm around Luther, the camera dollies in to emphasize the intimacy between them. Then the camera does a remarkable thing: nothing.

Rather than dolly in relentlessly to amplify the intensity, the camera simply pans and tilts to keep Cora and Luther in the center of the frame, granting Smith's sensitive performance a respect rarely accorded to African American actors. In its own quiet way, *No Way Out*'s two-minute take was as radical as a flamboyant crane.

The camera had grown more fluid, but its increasing mobility made familiar rhetoric about the "all-seeing eye" seem ever more problematic. Instead of cutting to the most advantageous angle at every possible moment, filmmakers used the camera to make the cinema's essential selectivity ever more salient. The camera's gestures could be forceful, as in *Rope*, or gentle, as in *No Way Out*, but they were visibly gestures, producing effects not of omniscience but of revelation, concealment, emphasis, and understatement.

Widescreen Cinema as a Storytelling Problem

Many established Hollywood directors were unimpressed with the new widescreen formats, especially CinemaScope, which often employed an aspect ratio of 2.55 to 1. George Cukor said, "CinemaScope is such an unfortunate shape."[57] Rouben Mamoulian called it "the worst shape ever devised."[58] Billy Wilder joked that the format might be suitable for a love story between two dachshunds.[59] John Ford offered a more specific critique: "You've never seen a painter use that kind of composition—even in the great murals, it wasn't this huge tennis court. Your eyes pop back and forth, and it's still very difficult to get a close-up."[60] Ford's observations echoed those of Howard Hawks, quoted at the beginning of this chapter. Hollywood directors had spent decades learning how to control the spectator's attention. Now they had to fill much larger frames, and they worried that the new formats offered them less control.

David Bordwell has examined how early CinemaScope filmmakers devised various solutions to the problem: for instance, by blocking off large sections of the screen.[61] The new formats posed particular problems for camera movement. While Ford and Hawks were proud of their minimalism, many of their peers had mastered a more dynamic approach over the course of the 1940s. By the early 1950s, the camera's fluidity seemed like an established fact. It could inch toward the actors on a crab dolly or fly through the air on a helicopter; it could creep past wild walls on a studio set or drive alongside an actor walking anywhere in the United States or abroad. Widescreen cinema threatened to end this line of progress toward fluidity—or, at least, to change its trajectory.

In practice, the relationship between camera movement and widescreen cinema was complex. There were many widescreen processes, each presenting its own technological problems and opportunities, and there were competing widescreen aesthetics, some discouraging camera movement, some pushing filmmakers to move the camera even more. In this section, I move broadly from technology to aesthetics, first summarizing the major widescreen systems and then turning to the solutions that filmmakers found for emerging aesthetic problems. Many of the solutions required filmmakers to rebalance functional priorities, favoring smaller gestures of emphasis and understatement without abandoning the tools of revelation and concealment.

By 1955, filmmakers already had several widescreen systems to choose from, including Cinerama, CinemaScope, Todd-AO, and VistaVision.[62] The Cinerama camera employed three separate lenses to expose three separate negatives. Projecting the three resulting prints simultaneously onto a curved screen would create an ultrawide image with an aspect ratio up to 2.77 to 1. The anamorphic CinemaScope process used a single lens to squeeze the image onto a 35-millimeter negative. During projection, another lens would unsqueeze the image. Todd-AO produced a wide image by using wide-gauge film: 65-millimeter for photography, 70-millimeter for projection. Paramount's VistaVision ran the negative past the lens horizontally, thereby exposing a larger picture area, equivalent to two frames of standard 35-millimeter film. The additional negative produced a higher-quality image with a less-extreme aspect ratio: often 1.66 to 1. Various alternatives proliferated, such as masking off the top and bottom of an Academy ratio image (1.37 to 1) to produce a moderately wide aspect ratio (e.g., 1.85 to 1) or shooting on 55-millimeter film. Many of these systems incorporated stereophonic sound, which helped guide the spectator's attention to particular sides of the screen.[63]

Widescreen technologies made certain types of camera movement more difficult. The Cinerama image comprised three separate images, connected by two lightly visible joins. With careful composition, a filmmaker could make the joins less noticeable, but they stood out more clearly whenever the camera moved, especially in lateral dolly shots. The anamorphic CinemaScope process avoided the problem of the joins but introduced another challenge: the original CinemaScope lenses contained an optical flaw that made faces appear bloated whenever the camera got too close. Until Panavision corrected the "CinemaScope mumps" with its superior anamorphic lenses, filmmakers were reluctant to deploy one of Hollywood's most familiar techniques: the dolly-in to a close-up.[64] Lateral dollies remained problematic in CinemaScope as flat walls appeared to curve toward the center of the screen. An additional challenge involved depth of field, which was narrower than usual in anamorphic and wide-gauge formats. The reduced depth of field placed special pressure on assistants, who had to execute their focus pulls with less room for error. Meanwhile, camera operators had to adjust to new viewfinders, with an unfamiliar parallax calibrated to accommodate the wider angle of view.[65]

Listing the era's obstacles to camera movement tells only one side of the story, however; several new technologies made camera movement easier for standard and widescreen films alike. In 1949, the Research Council of the Academy of Motion Picture Arts and Sciences had introduced a new crane, big enough to carry a camera ten feet into the air but small enough to fit through a regular doorway on location.[66] The following year Steve Krilanovich put his crab dolly on the market, inspiring a wave of imitations. Most importantly, studios and supply companies introduced a new line of cranes mounted on the backs of Jeeps and trucks, which enabled tremendous mobility outdoors and on location. The Blue Goose had previously facilitated outdoor work, but its hydraulic lift did not offer much flexibility; in contrast, the new cranes were truly mobile.[67] On *High Noon* (not widescreen), Fred Zinnemann and his crew used a Jeep-mounted crane, probably an early Chapman model, to produce the acclaimed shot of Will Kane (Gary Cooper) standing alone in the street after everyone in town has abandoned him. The shot works because of its double movement: the Jeep moves backward while the arm rises up and away from Kane, who looks increasingly vulnerable in the engulfing space. Zinnemann described the crane as an "enormous monster which could be rented for the day."[68] The Chapman Studio Equipment Company gave its monsters mythological names: the Electra, the Atlas, the Hercules, and the Titan.[69] In 1956, Chapman designed a new model for Cecil B. DeMille's superproduction *The Ten Commandments* (1956), photographed in Hollywood and in Egypt on Paramount's VistaVision format. The boom could rotate a full 360 degrees, and the crane could ascend to a height of twenty-eight feet. Cost: $50,000.[70] Directors admired the expertise of the Chapman crews: "The people who run it look like ordinary workmen, but they move it like a Swiss watch."[71] Within a few years, the Chapman crane had become standard equipment on spectacular fare, such as *Ben-Hur* (1959, photographed in M-G-M Camera 65, a 65-millimeter process) and *Spartacus* (1960, photographed in Technirama, a horizontal format similar to VistaVision).[72] Universal-International, once the home of the Broadway Boom, acquired its own Chapman crane.[73] The opening shot of *Touch of Evil* (1958, shot flat) would have been impossible without it.

While acknowledging the technical challenges, the discourse surrounding Cinerama actively encouraged filmmakers to move the camera more, not less, on the theory that forward movement created a more participatory experience. Taking the camera–person analogy to its logical conclusion, cinematographer Joseph Brun insisted that Cinerama was "essentially a subjective medium." The technology had fulfilled the long-standing desire to turn the camera into the "eye" of the spectator: "The Cinerama camera can 'see' not only as the actor does," Brun argued, "but can reach total identification with the spectator, as if he were himself present in the environment of the actor or also involved in the action."[74] In response to Cinerama's critics, Brun claimed that all of the cinema's traditional devices, from editing to camera movement, remained available. His camera operator, Gayne Rescher, went even further. Although acknowledging that lateral movement posed a problem because it looked distorted on the curved screen, Rescher urged his colleagues not to abandon one of Cinerama's signature techniques—the wide-angle forward-motion shot, as in the roller coaster sequence in *This Is Cinerama* (1952): "The feeling of participation—which is really the only added dimension of Cinerama—is there only when wide screen is combined with wide angle and with movement."[75] The key advantage of Cinerama was its immersive appeal. To reject forward movement was to misunderstand the point of the process.

Ariel Rogers has argued that widescreen systems "offered moviegoers an experience portrayed as both empowering and overpowering."[76] In part a claim about the sheer size of the image, this argument also applies to the spectacular forward-moving shot. On the one hand, the technique empowered spectators by giving them the thrilling experience of flying through the air or skiing down the slopes. On the other hand, the technique imposed itself on the spectators, forcing them to experience these vertiginous jolts whether they liked it or not.

The first Cinerama films were travelogues with little narrative content, but Twentieth Century-Fox had different ambitions for CinemaScope. According to Lisa Dombrowski, "While Cinerama and 3-D were designed to produce visceral thrills in a manner that harkened back to the early 'cinema of attractions,' CinemaScope and other widescreen systems aimed to integrate spectacle with narrative."[77] In place of the fairground model, CinemaScope appealed to the model of the legitimate theater. John Belton explains how this theatrical model merged two competing ideals: "The theater emerged as the one traditional form of entertainment that possessed the participatory effect of outdoor recreational activities and a strong sense of presence, and, at the same time, retained a strong identification with the narrative tradition in which Hollywood remained steadfastly rooted."[78]

Modeling the cinema on the legitimate theater posed problems for the advocates of camera movement. For decades, practical theorists such as F. W. Murnau, Alfred Hitchcock, and Irving Pichel had argued that camera movement helped to distinguish the cinema from the stage. In comparison to the theater director, the film director had much more power to control the spectator's attention by repositioning the camera from moment to moment via editing or camera movement. CinemaScope challenged this aesthetic not just because it was overly spectacular but because it was overly inclusive, stretching to allow more things into each frame. By making the frame itself less salient, the process forced filmmakers to rethink established strategies of controlling the spectator's attention.

Whereas camera movement made a clear contribution to the immersive art of Cinerama, its value to narrative widescreen filmmaking was a matter for dispute. Disagreements raged even within the walls of Twentieth Century-Fox. Producer Darryl F. Zanuck spent the postwar years searching for ways to cut costs. CinemaScope initially offered an ideal solution: it looked more expensive than prewidescreen films, but it could save money if used correctly. The director Robert Wise attended an early demonstration of the format, and he emerged from the meeting deeply skeptical of Zanuck's intentions: "Zanuck's idea was that CinemaScope was going to be a great time- and money-saver for films. . . . He had in mind to simply shoot everything right out in front. You had a three-page scene with five actors, and you'd stage it and your camera would be there and that would be all, no coverage, no alternate angles, nothing."[79]

Abandoning his earlier commitment to master-and-coverage technique, Zanuck had become a champion of the long take—not the finicky long takes of a Hitchcock or a Welles but simplified takes that took advantage of Cinema-Scope's wide screen. "I am still opposed to too much camera movement," Zanuck wrote to his stable of directors. "I fully believe that while we have to occasionally move the camera we should put the emphasis on moving the actors."[80] Elaborate camerawork would defeat the purpose, wasting money by lengthening the shooting schedule.

Zanuck tapped the workmanlike Henry Koster to direct the studio's first CinemaScope feature, the biblical drama *The Robe* (1953). In a contemporary article, Koster praised the new technology as a form of liberation for the film director: "Now he doesn't have to worry about 'dolly shots' and 'pan shots' and 'boom shots' and all other camera movements."[81] Koster's cinematographer, the color specialist Leon Shamroy, toed the party line. In an article in *American Cinematographer*, he explained that the wide screen had rendered many of the cinema's traditional techniques unnecessary: "If Griffith were using CinemaScope, he would seldom have to move in close with the camera, nor would he change angles often."[82] Shamroy planned to save Zanuck some money by shooting less than two hundred setups for *The Robe*, and he explicitly abjured camera movement: "If the camera moves too much it wastes the ability of our lens to see more at once than ever before."[83] Years later Shamroy recanted this opinion, saying that the static, distant compositions of CinemaScope "wrecked the art of film for a decade."[84] For now, though, he conceded that films should be more like plays.

Shamroy's colleague Charles Clarke offered a more nuanced opinion. Like Zanuck and Shamroy, he agreed that the larger screen made complicated shot breakdowns less necessary; Clarke even mocked the close-up as a "relic of the silent film." Pans were no longer necessary, especially because stereophonic sound could direct the spectator's attention to characters who did not occupy the center of the frame. However, Clarke refused to renounce camera movement altogether, for two reasons. First, given the proven delights of the forward-moving vehicle shot, Clarke advised that "they should be used whenever logically possible," even in CinemaScope. Spectacle was a plus; the trick was to make it logical. Second, he argued that the film director could stage scenes in the manner of the theater director, "with the added advantage of being able to move in with the camera to accentuate the most important portions of a scene."[85] If the camera was to be a theater spectator, then it should be a theater spectator under the filmmaker's control, subject to cinematic gestures of emphasis.

In practice, the early Scope films employ camera movement rarely but judiciously. *The Robe* features several stationary long takes, but it also includes carefully placed dollies and cranes, which shape the tone of the story's key turning points. When the Roman tribune Marcellus (Richard Burton) receives the order to crucify Jesus, the camera dollies from medium long shot to medium shot, emphasizing the fact that Marcellus alone is aware of the gravity of his assignment. The subtle movement—slow, measured—is appropriate to the moment, showing a man who is experiencing the first glimmer of conscience rather than the sudden sway of conversion. Subsequent films employ such understatement even more effectively. Consider an example of Clarke's work in *Black Widow* (1954), a mystery directed by erstwhile Ford collaborator Nunnally Johnson. In a five-minute dialogue scene, the shot breakdown alternates between long takes and brief shot-reverse-shot exchanges. The longest take lasts for 104 seconds, gradually shifting from a four-shot to a three-shot to a two-shot to a single. As in a Ford film, the actors do most of the work, walking across the room, stepping into the background, or exiting through the door. The camera simply follows the actors, and yet the camerawork follows a clear pattern of accentuation, gradually placing more emphasis on a relatively minor character who delivers a piece of devastating news. In the early part of the scene, Brian (Reginald Gardiner) twice turns his back to the camera, allowing us to concentrate on the other three characters: Peter (Van Heflin), a playwright under suspicion of murder; Lottie (Ginger Rogers), a Margo Channing–like star who casts aspersions on Peter; and Iris (Gene Tierney), Peter's wife, who is beginning to doubt her husband's innocence (fig. 6.11a). When Brian follows Lottie to the door, the camera gives Brian a little more compositional weight, following his movements to the exclusion of Iris. But Brian quickly steps into the background of the scene, letting the other two characters dominate the screen (fig. 6.11b). When Lottie exits, Brian steps into a clean two-shot. The composition seems to be perfectly balanced, but the staging actually grants Peter primacy: a colorful painting draws attention to the left, and Van Heflin's head movements attract the eyes (fig. 6.11c). Finally, Peter steps offscreen, and the camera pans to place Brian in the center at last, where he delivers his shocking news: the murder victim was pregnant (fig. 6.11d). The scene has followed a logical progression, slowly granting more importance to Brian while paradoxically reminding us how unimportant he is. In the group shot, he has the fourth-best position. In the three-shot, he has the third-best position. In the two-shot, he has the second-best position. Only in the single does he have compositional

6.11 In the early CinemaScope production *Black Widow,* a long take includes four characters.

priority, and even here he delivers his jolt of information in a medium-long-shot profile. The filmmakers have taken advantage of the CinemaScope format to solve a difficult storytelling problem, emphasizing a minor character without letting him upstage the stars.

In the quest to integrate narrative and spectacle, one option was to alternate between extravagant movement and calm stasis, favoring the former for astonishing set pieces while returning to the latter for ordinary narrative scenes. The original Todd-AO production *Oklahoma!* (1955) clearly saved its forward-moving "immersion" shots for spectacular moments: the opening (the camera pushes through the cornfields to reveal an expansive landscape), a musical number (the camera rides underneath the surrey with the fringe on top), and an action scene (the camera hurtles forward, representing the point of view of a team of runaway horses as they race past trees and through a fence). By contrast, the dialogue scenes show considerable restraint, suggesting that director Fred Zinnemann had heeded Ford's personal advice: "You know, you could be a pretty good director if you'd stop fooling around with that boom."[86] The contrast is palpable, but such a reading runs the risk of reinstating a binary opposition that I have been at pains to question throughout this book—the opposition between spectacle and narrative. In fact, Zinnemann's achievement is to use immersive cinematography to develop the story's themes. When Curly (Gordon MacRae) sings "Surrey with the Fringe on Top," Laurey (Shirley Jones) listens with fascination, imagining what it would be like to ride in such a surrey. She eventually decides that Curly is lying about the surrey, and she makes the fateful decision to attend the dance with Jud (Rod Steiger) instead. By placing the camera in such an unlikely spot, suspended underneath the carriage as it moves past a gaggle of geese, the filmmakers align us with Laurey's position—not her literal position in space but something akin to her imaginative position, astonished by a strange and spectacular sensory experience that seems too vivid to be true. Later, the action scene with Jud's runaway horses employs a nearly identical shot, suspending the camera underneath the carriage. The repetition asks us to compare the two sensory experiences—the lightly amusing experience of driving through a gaggle of geese and the terrifying experience of being dragged by runaway horses through a puddle of water. In so doing, the film asks us to compare the two narrative situations—Laurey's imagined delight with Curly versus Laurey's actual fear of Jud.

My point here is not to say that spectacle must be subordinated to narrative or vice versa, but that the two principles may be mutually intensifying. While preparing the CinemaScope production *Lust for Life* (1956), producer John Houseman articulated this idea in a memo: "This, then, is the basic concept behind the pre-production footage—it is not a Cinerama tour of pretty fields, but a dramatic event—a terribly important one—in the life of our protagonist."[87] The Cinerama travelogue had become a symbol of empty spectacle, which is what Houseman wanted to avoid. He instead called on his cinematographers to produce pictorial beauty for a dramatic purpose: to express the landscape's impact on the character. Similarly, the immersive train shots at the beginning of Elia Kazan's film *East of Eden* (1955) express the alienation of Cal (James Dean), sitting alone on top of the train as it hurtles through an empty void, just as the immersive dance shots at the beginning of the Gene Kelly–Stanley Donen musical *It's Always Fair Weather* (1955) express the delight of the three soldiers as they experience the sensory richness of New York City together. One of the most powerful fusions of spectacle and narrative appeared in *The House of Bamboo* (1955), a CinemaScope thriller that Samuel Fuller directed for Twentieth Century-Fox. The film ends with a dramatic action scene set in an amusement park built at the top of a Tokyo skyscraper. Spectacle does not compete with narrative; it intensifies the narrative. The more we experience a perceptual illusion of being at the top of a skyscraper, the more suspense we feel because we gain a deeper, almost tactile understanding of the dangers the hero faces.[88]

Spectacular sequences aside, with widescreen cameras filmmakers faced the same problems that they had always faced: how to construct a scene. Here, widescreen filmmakers found themselves in a paradoxical position. As Robert Surtees, the first-unit cinematographer for *Oklahoma!*, explained, "We had too much of a good thing. . . . There is so much to look at in the huge Todd-AO frame that at times we were forced to use special measures to focus audience attention on the one single element that was important."[89] The very size of the screen made the problem of directing the spectator's attention more consequential than before, but the basic techniques of attention management, such as the rapid dolly-in to a close-up, were temporarily out of service. The widescreen filmmaker had fewer tools to accomplish a much more difficult job.

In a landmark essay on CinemaScope, Charles Barr explained that this apparent disadvantage was actually an advantage. The "closed-in" Academy frame (1.37 to 1) did not have enough room to admit casual details, so every detail seemed as if it had been placed there deliberately. By contrast, the wider aspect ratios encompassed more details by definition. "If I had to sum up [CinemaScope's] implications," Barr wrote, "I would say that it gives a greater range for *gradation of emphasis*."[90] A filmmaker might choose to train the camera on the most important story point, but the larger frame would take in other details as well, both stressed and unstressed. Following V. F. Perkins, Barr pointed to a particular moment in Otto Preminger's *River of No Return* (1954) as a demonstration of CinemaScope's potential. When Harry (Robert Mitchum) rescues Kay (Marilyn Monroe) from a raft, she drops a bundle, which floats away (fig. 6.12a–b). When the camera pans, the bundle appears again, drifting far into the background of the shot (fig. 6.12c–d). On the one hand, the moment carries symbolic meaning: the loss of the bag represents the loss of Kay's former life. On the other hand, the framing allows the spectator to discover the symbolic meaning in the event itself. Preminger does not cut to the bag or dolly toward it; he simply lets the bag drift away. For Perkins, even the word *understatement* was too emphatic to describe such a choice: "The symbolism is in the event, not in the visual pattern, so the director presents the action clearly and leaves the interpretation to the spectator."[91] My own inclination is to see the scene as an extension of the understatement found in *How Green Was My Valley*. In both scenes, the camera is mobile but modest, refusing obvious gestures of emphasis in favor of a more basic function, opening up an inclusive view onto a multifaceted storyworld.

6.12 In *River of No Return*, CinemaScope allows for the "gradation of emphasis."

To say that Preminger used the wide screen to capture the world's complexity is not to say that he just planted his camera and let it record whatever was in front of it. In fact, Preminger's camera could be quite mobile, even in Cinemascope. In *Bonjour Tristesse* (1958), there is a beautiful scene where Cecile (Jean Seberg) and her father, Raymond (David Niven), bang on the doors to their summer house to awaken Raymond's companion, Elsa. In contrast to the clothesline staging of *River of No Return*, this shot unfolds in depth. First, Cecile and Raymond walk into the background of the shot (fig. 6.13a). Then Raymond steps outside, and the camera recedes in time with his movement (fig. 6.13b). When Raymond stops to bang on a door, Cecile steps to the fore, her pace perfectly in tune with the camera's continuing retreat (fig. 6.13c). The dance continues: Cecile stops, and Raymond steps back into the foreground for a moment before both characters exit to the background (fig. 6.13d). The staging allows each performer to dominate the composition for a moment before ceding the foreground to the other, expressing the dynamic of this curious father–daughter relationship, a dynamic of friendly give-and-take. Later, we will learn about the relationship's lethal flaws, but for now the shot expresses pure delight, using the spectacle of an unfolding space for narrative ends. With its backward movement, the camera discloses the gorgeous French location bit by bit, offering us an experience of discovery as we catch glimpses of blue ocean and green landscape along the way. With a narrower frame, Raymond and Cecile might dominate the frame too strongly. The wide frame instead introduces the characters in the context of a larger world, a beautiful site that delights us as much as it delights them.

Perhaps the language of "attention" is too dry to account for the power of a scene like this one. We should remember that guiding attention (gently or

6.13 In *Bonjour Tristesse*, the camera reveals space as the characters discover it.

aggressively, rapidly or slowly, with simplicity or with nuance) is a means to other ends: emotion, tone, point of view. Here, the dance of attention, shifting from Raymond to Cecile to Raymond to Cecile while catching glimpses of the house and the ocean and the sky and the trees, produces an experience of sensory engagement that is crucial to the scene's tonal effect. It is a joyous presentation of a joyful event—made all the more devastating because we know from the film's flashback structure that this story will not end well.

Alternatively, a filmmaker might craft the gradations of emphasis to give subtle priority to a character's ideological point of view, thereby altering a scene's tone. In a four-minute scene in *Tea and Sympathy* (1956), Vincente Minnelli imposes a hierarchy on each CinemaScope composition by designing frames within frames (see table 6.2). The story concerns the physical and verbal abuse of Tom (John Kerr), a sensitive young man at a prep school. (In the original play, the young man is gay.) In this scene, the boy's father, Herb (Edward Andrews), visits his old friend Bill (Leif Erickson), the coach at the school. Before Bill enters the room, his wife, Laura (Deborah Kerr), tries to reassure Herb, and there is a brief moment when it seems as if Herb might respond to her with understanding. But then Bill enters, and Herb's personality completely changes; Herb insists that he will be proud of his son only if Tom becomes a "regular guy." The scene features several rigorous patterns. In the first shot, the camera pans to follow Herb. In the second, it pans to follow Bill walking in the same direction through the same room, creating a parallel between the two men. Later in the second shot, Laura stands in the center, close to Bill on the left, and Herb stands farther away on the right. The fourth shot repeats this composition, but now Herb is the one in the middle, standing closer to Bill, and Laura is the one isolated on the right, as if the old friend has usurped Laura's role.

Throughout the scene, Minnelli and cinematographer John Alton follow most of the early CinemaScope rules: no lateral dollies, no big close-ups, just a few quick pans and some modest reframes. Working within these restrictions, they rely on blocking and set design to shape our interests, giving top priority to Laura, second priority to the two men, and third priority to Laura's impeccably maintained house. After the initial introductions of the two men, Laura dominates the composition, even as she fails to steer the conversation in a more productive direction. Look at shots 3 through 5 in table 6.2: the camera follows Laura's movements, keeps Laura in focus, and allows Laura to occupy the foreground. When the men insist that Tom should not spend so much time in the company of women, the camera stubbornly remains with Laura in the kitchen while the men appear and disappear behind the window. Another director might have cut back and forth between Laura inside the house and the men outside. Minnelli situates all the characters within the wide CinemaScope frame, favoring Laura while acknowledging her entrapment, asking

TABLE 6.2 A Five-Shot Scene in *Tea and Sympathy* (1956)

Shot	Seen in Foreground Room	Seen Through Glass	Seen Through Doorway	Unseen (Behind Wall)	Unseen (out of Frame)	Subsequent Camera Movement
1	Herb				Laura	Pan to follow Herb
	Herb		Laura			Dolly in to follow Herb
			Laura, Herb			Dolly out to follow Laura
		Laura	Herb			Dolly in to follow Laura
			Laura, Herb			
2	Bill				Herb, Laura	Pan to follow Bill
	Bill		Laura, Herb			Dolly in to follow Bill and Herb
			Bill, Laura, Herb (door not visible)			Dolly back to follow Laura
	Laura		Herb	Bill		

(continued)

TABLE 6.2 (continued)

Shot	Seen in Fore-ground Room	Seen Through Glass	Seen Through Doorway	Unseen (Behind Wall)	Unseen (out of Frame)	Subsequent Camera Movement
3	**Laura**			Herb, Bill		Boom down as Laura enters
	Laura	**Bill**		Herb		
	Laura	**Herb, Bill**				Rack focus to follow Laura
	Laura	**Bill**		Herb		
	Laura	**Herb, Bill**				
	Laura	**Herb**		Bill		Pan to follow Laura
4	**Laura**		**Bill, Herb**			Dolly in to follow L
			Bill, Laura, Herb (door not visible)			Dolly out to follow Laura
	Laura		**Bill, Herb**			
5	**Laura**	**Herb**		Bill		Pan to follow Laura
	Laura				Herb, Bill	Dolly out to follow Laura

Note: Names of visible figures are given in bold type.

us to understand the ramifications of the scene through her values and perspective.

Widescreen filmmaking partially overlapped with another important trend—runaway productions, or, Hollywood films photographed abroad. Daniel Steinhart has detailed many of the challenges filmmakers faced when shooting overseas.[92] Cinematographers preferred to work with their regular crews, but budgets and union regulations often prevented them from taking Hollywood crews to other countries. Even worse, they struggled to find the right equipment in these locations. For the costume drama *Quo Vadis* (1951, not widescreen), M-G-M shipped a huge camera crane to Italy to support the Technicolor camera.[93] On John Huston's *Beat the Devil* (1954, not widescreen), cinematographer Oswald Morris obliged his crew to construct a huge ramp on a hillside to mimic the effect of an extravagant crane shot in an otherwise unreachable location.[94] On *Funny Face* (1957, VistaVision), Paramount's Parisian representative Edouard de Segonzac spent several weeks hunting for a crane that could hold the heavy VistaVision camera.[95] Happily, working overseas also exposed Hollywood filmmakers to some valuable new technologies. On Minnelli's *Gigi* (1958, CinemaScope), cinematographer Joseph Ruttenberg worked with a French technician who had devised an innovative system for laying down tracks by hooking together pieces of tubular steel.[96] These tracks facilitated the extensive location work when Louis Jourdain walked and talked his way through the title number.

Back in Hollywood, Alfred Hitchcock had little trouble playing his familiar games of revelation and concealment, especially because he favored less-extreme aspect ratios. *Rear Window* (1954) relied on matting to produce images with a 1.66-to-1 aspect ratio; later productions, such as *To Catch a Thief* (1955) and *The Man Who Knew Too Much* (1956) achieved similar aspect ratios via VistaVision.[97] In *Rear Window*'s celebrated opening sequence, the camera surveys the courtyard before examining the apartment of voyeuristic protagonist L. B. Jefferies (James Stewart). This movement, from one neighbor to another, revises the existing motif of the window-to-window shot, as seen in films from *Sunnyside Up* to *Gold Diggers of 1933*. As Pamela Robertson Wojcik explains, "The courtyard represents a particular form of urban community that navigates carefully between separation and togetherness."[98] The opening sequence depicts strangers while pointing ahead toward the possibility of convergence.

The first shot promises immersion in the manner of a widescreen film: the camera dollies toward an open window as if entering a new world. But the remaining shots of the sequence—indeed, of the film as a whole—follow a different logic, using the rectangular frame to control the flow of disclosures. The fourth shot lasts for eighty-six seconds, framing at least ten distinct compositions: the married couple on the balcony, the dancer Miss Torso (fig. 6.14a), Jefferies's face (fig. 6.14b), Jefferies's broken leg, Jefferies's entire body, a broken

6.14 In *Rear Window,* the camera reveals the protagonist's backstory by showing a succession of visual details.

camera (fig. 6.14c), a photograph of a car crash, a photograph of a fire, a framed negative, and a positive image of the same negative on the cover of a magazine (fig. 6.14d). Cinematographer Robert Burks explained that the crew mounted the camera on "the biggest boom on the Paramount lot, augmented by an extension."[99] After one afternoon of rehearsal and one morning of shooting, the crew completed the shot on the tenth take. Production documents indicate that they used a Chapman boom, budgeted at $750 per week.[100] An article in *American Cinematographer* singled out this sequence for attention. In just a few paragraphs, writer Arthur Gavin used the word *reveal* four times and the word *show* five times.[101] Far from offering the experience of entering a world, *Rear Window* offered the experience of watching a story unfold via a sequence of carefully composed pictures. In later interviews, Hitchcock affirmed his belief that the cinema was a two-dimensional medium: "Mustn't forget that. You have a rectangle to fill. Fill it. Compose it."[102]

The director described *Rear Window* as the clearest example "of a purely cinematic subjective treatment in my own work."[103] Note that the film is not subjective in the sense that a Cinerama travelogue is subjective, offering the perceptual illusion of riding in a roller coaster. Nor is *Rear Window* subjective in the sense that *Lady in the Lake* is subjective, representing a single character's point of view from beginning to end. *Rear Window* instead follows Hitchcock's preferred strategy of integrating point-of-view shots with reaction shots and other seemingly external techniques. In the opening scene, *Rear Window* bypasses its sleeping protagonist and introduces the neighbors directly. Later, when the film deploys a series of point-of-view shots, the decision feels like a restriction precisely because we have seen how informative the film can be.

Douglas Pye has observed that Hitchcock's films often express a playful tone, precisely by flaunting their "ability to restrict what we see and know."[104] This sense of playfulness characterizes the eighty-six-second shot, which works like a riddle, revealing a set of effects (the broken leg, the broken camera) before revealing their cause (the car crash). A montage expert such as Hitchcock could have produced a similar effect by cutting from one composition to the next, but the movement of the camera enhances the sense of playfulness by toying with the spectator's expectations moment by moment. Three strategies are at work; call them "Hint-and-Reveal," "Hint-and-Conceal," and "Surprise!" First, Hint-and-Reveal. Because the camera is in motion, it often provides a preliminary glimpse of an object before revealing it completely; the movement encourages us to guess the nature of the object a split second before its identity is revealed. For instance, the film could have cut from Jefferies's face to the cast on his leg. Instead, the operator spends four seconds panning and tilting across Jefferies's body to reveal the cast. The technique produces a quick flurry of miniature revelations: What is that blurry thing? Oh, it's a cast! Oh, it covers his entire leg! Later, the film whip-pans to Jefferies's broken camera. The framing is wide enough to allow us to catch a glimpse of the car crash photo, but the photo remains out of focus, and the dolly-in forces us to attend to the broken camera first. Again, the film offers a teasing hint a couple seconds before delivering the crucial revelation. By contrast, some movements drop hints without providing the corresponding acts of disclosure; they hint and conceal. Early in the shot, the camera cranes back from Miss Torso's apartment to Jefferies's face. Along the way, we catch a glimpse of an anonymous woman's arm, reaching out of a window to remove the cover from a bird cage. The assistant cameraman, Lennie South, pulls the focus to ensure that the detail is visible, but then he pulls the focus again, so that the bird cage goes soft just as its cover is removed. This hint-and-conceal technique functions as a sexual joke, drawing an analogy between the quick revelation and concealment of the bird and the film's previous revelation and concealment of Miss Torso's body. Elsewhere in the same shot, the camera glides past many other important details (the telephone, the drinks, the flashes), even as it lingers on less important ones. Again, Hitchcock toys with us. The camera frames a clear view of the car-crash photo, which will play no role in the ensuing story beyond its simple expository function. But the camera pans right past the flashes, which will end up saving Jefferies's life. A third game involves surprise in spite of Hitchcock's oft-stated preference for suspense. Twice during the opening scene (and once during this shot), the camera pans and dollies back to reveal Jefferies in the foreground. Each time, his appearance registers as a perceptual jolt. The camera was outside; now it is inside. The focus was distant; now it is close. The subjects looked small; now the subject looks big. We expect a cut to generate such shifts instantaneously; we do not expect a camera to render them so quickly in a single shot.

Hitchcock's VistaVision films followed similar principles, using carefully designed shot breakdowns and the occasional long take to manage the flow of disclosures. Two of the director's most famous moving-camera shots appear in *Vertigo* (1958): the dolly–zoom shot and the 360-degree kiss. Both shots are innovative solutions to difficult technical problems. Just as important, both solve a difficult conceptual problem—the problem of representing subjectivity onscreen. For the dolly–zoom shot, the crew, led by second-unit director Irmin Roberts, constructed a miniature of the stairway and laid it on its side. The camera dollied in and zoomed out simultaneously, creating the effect of "stretching" the space.[105] I have said very little about zooms in this book, in part because they were not really movements of the camera and in part because zooms remained relatively rare through the 1950s. New lenses were available, such as the Zoomar and the Pan-Cinor, but professional norms held that the zoom was an inferior substitute for a dolly. As one article stated in 1957, "Only the dolly shot gives the impression that the camera is actually going somewhere."[106] The discourse defined the dolly and the zoom in oppositional terms: a film zoomed when it couldn't dolly. Hitchcock's real insight was to understand that this either–or logic was flawed: the techniques could be combined to produce a new effect.

A brief technical explanation is in order. Why does *Vertigo*'s technique seem to stretch the space? It is tempting to suppose that a telephoto lens "flattens" space and that a deep-focus lens "stretches" it out. However, Bruce Block provides a more convincing explanation, emphasizing how the movement of the camera manipulates various depth cues, such as relative size.[107] Suppose you place a camera four feet away from a wooden board. Now you place a wooden board of the same size four feet behind the first one, eight feet from the camera. Regardless of the lens on the camera, the second wooden board's size onscreen (that is, its occlusion size) will be one-quarter the occlusion size of the first wooden board—that is, half the height and half the width. Now suppose you move the camera in two feet. The first wooden board is now two feet away. The second wooden board is now six feet away. The second board's occlusion size is now one-ninth the occlusion size of the first—that is, one-third the height and one-third the width. The difference in relative occlusion size is now more extreme, resulting in a stronger depth cue. Moving the camera affects other depth cues as well: for instance, the first wooden board will overlap different parts of the second wooden board simply because their position vis-à-vis the camera has changed. A moving camera will record these shifting depth cues without a zoom, which is why cinematographers insisted for years that the dolly shot produced a strong sense of moving in space. By contrast, a zoom merely magnifies or demagnifies the center of the image without changing an image's perspective. Put these techniques together, and you have the dolly–zoom effect. The image's depth cues constantly change (thanks to the movement of the camera), and yet the frame remains eerily still (thanks to the coordination of the dolly with the counteracting zoom).[108] If you take a look at the wooden boards in *Vertigo*'s stairway miniature, you will see the effect in action. At first, the steps on the left side of the screen are about twice as tall as the steps directly behind them in terms of occlusion size (fig. 6.15a). Later, those same steps are about three times as tall precisely because the movement of the camera has changed the relative distance (fig. 6.15b).

It is hard to watch this shot without imagining being in Scottie's position, experiencing the world slip away. But notice that this example actually problematizes the familiar idea that the camera is the eye of the spectator. The physical camera that took the shot was moving in, toward the stairway. We see something very different onscreen: a stable frame around an elastic space. No matter how immersive the shot may be, it remains a shot: a rectangle filled with a dynamic composition, relying on that composition to produce its effects. We do not see the filmed world from within, as if occupying the camera's position; we see moving pictures of a stretching storyworld.

The technology behind *Vertigo*'s 360-degree shot was equally ingenious. In this scene, Scotty kisses Judy, now remade as Madeleine. Scotty briefly has the impression that he is standing in a dark stable, located near the church where Madeleine died. The moment passes, and he finds that he is in the neon-lit hotel room once more. The screenplay featured an unusual instruction: "He opens his eyes—the CAMERA SWIMS AROUND the room."[109] How do you make a camera swim? Hitchcock explained: "I had the whole set built in a circle—the stable and the hotel room—a 360-degree set. And we put the camera in the

6.15 In *Vertigo*, the dolly–zoom shot appears to stretch the space.

middle and panned it right around. Then we put it on a flat screen. I put them on a turntable and just twisted the turntable in front of the screen and photographed it straight."[110]

The shot recalls a scene from Murnau's film *The Last Laugh,* discussed in chapter 1, showing the drunken porter sitting still in the middle of the frame while the background spins behind him. Hitchcock's version triples the movement: the world spins around the characters, the characters spin around each other, and the camera moves in and out. However intense the result, the shot remains semisubjective. Rather than look through the character's eyes, *Vertigo* momentarily depicts its protagonist from the outside, while representing the character's world as he might see it.

As Scotty finds himself back in the stable, we find ourselves back in 1924. Technologies had changed—from silent to sound, from the Academy ratio to the wide screen, from Karl Freund's turntable to the crab dolly and the Chapman crane. But Hitchcock remained in dialogue with Murnau's ideas—the idea that the camera may reveal and conceal, the idea that the camera may represent thought, and, most of all, the idea that movies must move. Filmmakers soon solved the lingering technical problems of widescreen: Panavision lenses would cure the CinemaScope mumps, and faster stocks would allow greater depth of field, even in color. The deepest problem would remain the same: how to tell a story in movement.

＊＊＊

In 1953, *American Cinematographer* published another Herb Lightman article on camera movement. Titled "The Function of Boom Shots in Feature Film Production," the article offered a helpful list of six functions: following action, capturing the scope of a sweeping subject, establishing spatial relationships, focusing attention, adding movement to a static situation, and tying together two elements of a composition.[111] The exact particulars of the list may be debated. Indeed, this book has pointed to several functions that did not make the cut in Lightman's article: representing subjectivity, commenting on modernity, concealing information discreetly, concealing information overtly, ironizing, understating, mimicking, misleading, playing, hinting, and more. Indeed, I am not sure we can list all the functions of camera movement. If we narrowed the list down to fifty, some filmmaker would discover the fifty-first.

What is valuable about Lightman's article is not its list of six functions but its elaboration of a tradition. Thirty years earlier, Rouben Mamoulian had declared that the moving camera must serve a purpose. Hollywood filmmakers still agreed. When Mamoulian made his claim, the moving camera was under attack—most notably from hostile cinematographers. Now everyone accepted that the moving camera was a normal part of modern cinematic technique. A history had formed—a tradition. To make his case, Lightman pointed to canonical examples of each function, such as the opera shot in *Citizen Kane* and the key shot in *Notorious*. Filmmakers now made sense of camera movement by looking at other films. Some they copied, some they rejected, and some they revised, but the dialogue continued.

In 1958, another film would join the list of canonical examples: *Touch of Evil*.

CONCLUSION

Over the course of several decades, the moving camera took many forms, from the crossing-the-street shots of *Sunrise* (1927) to the train station shots of *The Clock* (1945), from the introduction of John Wayne in *Stagecoach* (1939) to the introduction of the apartment in *Rear Window* (1954), from the witty staging of *Design for Living* (1933) to the forced gimmickry of *Lady in the Lake* (1947). This book concludes with an analysis of the most canonical crane of all: the spectacular first shot in Orson Welles's film *Touch of Evil* (1958), photographed by Russell Metty. Summarizing the major themes of this book, my analysis proceeds in six parts, one for each chapter. Because the most recent chapters offer the most proximate contexts, I offer these observations in reverse order, moving from the immediate concerns of chapter 6 to the lingering echoes of chapter 1.

Chapter 6 argued that the cinema is an art of disclosures and that the moving camera makes this art unusually salient. Like most Hollywood filmmakers, Welles insisted that he never moved the camera without purpose: "Only when there's a reason to—not just for the fun of it, or to show off."[1] At the most basic level, *Touch of Evil*'s opening shot is a masterpiece of revelation and concealment. The camera starts up close, disclosing a pair of hands setting the timer on a bomb (fig. C.1a). Immediately, a question forms: Who is this person? There follows a flurry of almost revelations. The camera pans quickly to the left, but the man (Victor Millan) spins away to the right, denying us a clear view of his face. When the bomber enters the frame again, he remains unidentifiable because he steps to the very edge of the frame line. Then he turns his profile

C.1 *Touch of Evil* draws on more than thirty years of moving-camera traditions.

to the camera and sprints off-screen right, too fast to be seen. A split second later, the camera turns to the right, far enough to reveal the man's cast shadow but not far enough to show his body. The bomber runs into the shot to hide the bomb in the trunk of a Cadillac, but his face is turned away from the light. The shot is less than thirty seconds old, and already the film has cycled through five different ways to show a man's actions while concealing his identity.

The game of revelation and concealment continues, with the bomb-laden car as the new subject. The mysterious man exits the shot, and the camera cranes up to frame a high-angle view of the Cadillac (fig. C.1b). An older man and a blond woman step into the car and drive away; the car disappears behind a building. The camera finds the Cadillac and holds it in the center of the frame, only to obscure the vehicle in other ways as traffic occludes our view. Up in the air, the camera continues its retreat, making the Cadillac seem small. Soon, the camera shifts its focus, following the protagonist Mike Vargas (Charlton Heston) and his wife, Susie (Janet Leigh), instead. Now we get a close view of the couple in the Cadillac—but only when they are speeding through the foreground and only after our attention has turned to someone else.

After following Mike and Susie for a while, the camera picks up the Cadillac again. For more than a minute, both remain visible in the frame. The game of revelation and concealment becomes a dance of emphasis and understatement, sometimes bringing the Cadillac to the fore, sometimes focusing on Mike and Susie, sometimes placing equal emphasis on both couples, and sometimes allowing both couples to slide into the background, overwhelmed by the swirl-ing crowd around them (fig. C.1c). After the Cadillac crosses the U.S.–Mexico border, crossing outside the frame, the camera booms in to frame a closer view of Mike and Susie kissing (fig. C.1d). At last, after all this clutter and movement, all this shifting and turning, we get an idealized image: a stationary frame with an unobstructed view of a couple in love. For three minutes, we have been waiting for clarity. Finally, the film provides it . . . for approximately one second. Cut as the bomb explodes offscreen. The art of *Touch of Evil* is an art of disclosures, using the moving camera to hint at details that emerge only over time.

Chapter 5 explained that filmmakers theorized camera movement in "sub-jective" and "objective" terms, even as they explored the ambiguous territory between these two alternatives. At first, the shot in *Touch of Evil* seems reso-lutely objective. The scene depicts its characters from the outside, never once assuming anyone's point of view. The characters do not know what is in the trunk of the car; we do. As a result, our experience of the scene is very different from theirs. Every time we lose sight of the Cadillac, we must scan the compo-sition to find it. Every time the car pulls alongside Mike and Susie, we must recalculate the odds. Has it been three minutes yet? How dangerous is it to be three feet from an exploding car? How about twenty feet?

The objective view offers additional pleasures, not so tightly connected to the unfolding narrative. Welles and his crew photographed the scene in Ven-ice, California, and the city space provides a source of endless fascination: the perspectival order of the porticoes; the neon signs, some on, some off; the cars with their sporty fins and their whitewall tires; the men's hats; the women's coats; the peeling paint and the decaying posters; the telephone poles against the early morning sky; the crosswalks, the carts, and the goats. In the restored version of the film, the sound design reinforces the sense that we are experi-encing this world through the camera's mediation and not through a charac-ter's consciousness.[2] The Cadillac plays a jazzy tune, which fades in and out several times, depending on how close the Cadillac gets to the camera. Mean-while, the camera travels through dense layers of sonic space: a mélange of music tracks and wallah that rises and falls with the presence of the crowd.

And yet this objective shot remains intensely expressive, suggesting that it, too, may fall into the category that I have called the "semisubjective." On one level, the scene is about the border town itself—its density, its energy, its com-plexity. On another level, the scene is about Mike and Susie's *experience* of this town. Mike and Susie enjoy the unpredictability of the urban environment: they smile when they notice the goats on the street; they smile again when a man walks by with a cart of flowers; they even smile when they must step out of the way to allow the Cadillac to drive past. Significantly, the camera moves backward and sideways as it follows Mike and Susie on their stroll through town. The result is a composition filled with surprises as people and objects pierce the boundary of the frame. Suddenly, a man in a hat enters the shot from the right side. Suddenly, goats enter from the left. Suddenly, a cart enters from the right. Unlike the bomb-laden car, there is nothing threatening about these incursions. They make the town seem full of life, at once vibrant and unpredictable, encouraging us to share in Mike and Susie's delight.

Chapter 4 offered an overview of Hollywood's division of labor and explained how three different methods of scene construction—master and coverage, cutting in the camera, and the long take—altered the balance of power among industry professionals. Many Hollywood producers preferred directors who constructed their scenes with the master-and-coverage approach, which allowed more leeway to reshape each scene in postproduction. Ever since *Citizen Kane*, Orson Welles had championed the long take, a method that gave the director more power to control the sequence of angles from beginning to end. On *Touch of Evil*, Welles continued to use the long take as a weapon against studio control. Charlton Heston liked to tell a story about anxious executives huddling in the shadows as the crew spent an entire day preparing to shoot the later scene when Mike discovers an empty shoebox. When the crew finally finished the scene, covering more than a dozen pages of script in a single take with a crab dolly, Welles turned to the executives and said, "We're two days ahead of schedule." Worried that he would try the pugnacious stunt again, the astonished executives decided not to challenge him for the rest of the shoot.[3] However, the studio still managed to meddle with Welles's work in postproduction: the original release version layered credits on top of the introductory shot and added a musical theme by Henry Mancini.[4]

Clearly, Welles enjoyed playing the role of the auteur. When *Cahiers du Cinéma* asked him about his characteristic combination of figure movement and camera movement, he replied that the technique "corresponds to my vision of the world; it reflects that sort of vertigo, uncertainty, lack of stability, that mélange of movement and tension that is our universe."[5] While defining his own worldview as the source of the film's visual style, Welles paid tribute to his collaborators. Indeed, his remarks stand as a great testament to the studio system at its best: "I could never have done all that I did in *Touch of Evil* elsewhere. And it is not only a question of technique; it essentially concerns the human competence of the men with whom I worked. All this stems from the economic security they enjoy, from the fact that they are well paid, from the fact that they do not think of themselves as belonging to another class."[6]

Welles admitted that the European industry had a few great cinematographers, but he insisted that the American industry was exceptional because it employed skilled artisans at every level of the operation, from the camera operator to the dolly grip to the person who operated the crane. These practitioners thought of themselves as contributors; they recognized that every shift of the camera shaped the meaning of the film. They were right: just look at the opening movements of *Touch of Evil*. As actor Victor Millan pirouettes away from the camera, the camera tilts and pans to a new composition, with an abruptness that hints at the violence to come. As Millan runs across the screen, the camera pans to follow, slowly enough to allow the actor to exit frame quickly but quickly enough to catch his shadow before it disappears. The operator, the assistant, the grip, the driver—each member of the crew was a contributor who had to think carefully about timing, speed, and placement.[7] Although Welles plausibly took credit for the overall authorial vision, bringing that vision to life required the depth of talent and skill that Hollywood's mode of production provided.

Chapter 3 proposed that Hollywood filmmakers developed a set of shared strategies, using the moving camera to comment on three distinct aspects of modern life: dynamism, seriality, and convergence. *Touch of Evil* proves to be particularly concerned with the theme of convergence. As we have seen, Hollywood found convergence in many types of settings, from the heart of the American city (*42nd Street*, 1933) to unfamiliar neighborhoods on distant continents (*Algiers*, 1938). *Touch of Evil* locates convergence at the U.S.–Mexico border. As Robin Wood explains, the opening shot establishes one of the film's central concerns: "the idea of connectedness."[8] The film's story develops the theme in various ways: Mike and Susie emerge as the central couple, even though they come from different worlds; like the blonde in the car, Susie will be subject to violence because of events that originally have nothing to do with her; a bomb planted in one country goes off in another, forcing Mike to work with his corrupt American counterpart to solve the crime. In addition to motivating several plot points, convergence becomes a defining aspect of the film's visual style. As the camera gets closer to the border, the composition grows increasingly complex, taking in ever more visual contrasts: the shiny Cadillac and the humble pushcarts; the shop signs in Spanish and in English; the cowboy hats and the fedoras; the people walking left to right, right to left, background to foreground, and foreground to background. Rather than restrict convergence, the border amplifies it.

In response to Eisenhower-era racist crackdowns on undocumented workers, *Touch of Evil* critically depicts the border as a fundamentally arbitrary divide. The camera's movement develops this critique in two ways.[9] First, the camera shows how permeable the border is in the most literal way imaginable—by crossing it. Cutting across the border would not have produced the same effect. The camera's movement perfectly captures the ineradicable continuity of the spaces. Second, the camera's backward trajectory represents the border as a surprise. Imagine the scene with the camera following Mike and Susie from behind. The camera would get closer and closer to the checkpoint, firmly establishing it as the defining landmark in the space. Instead, the checkpoint pops into the frame unexpectedly—a brightly lit octagonal structure that clashes with the dimly lit porticoes that have defined the space so far. The camerawork makes the checkpoint seem strange and out of place, foreshadowing the film's treatment of the border as a manufactured political concept.

Chapter 2 argued that Hollywood's practical theorists were not as hostile to camera movement as they appeared to be in print. Although cinematographers wrote articles with titles such as "Let's Stop Abusing Camera Movement," they were willing to countenance a variety of mobile techniques as long as those techniques served a definite purpose. Permissible purposes ranged widely, from familiar functions such as following and emphasis to more ambitious goals such as irony and rhythm. Taking advantage of newly invented cranes and dollies, many films from the early 1930s featured spectacular opening sequences. *Touch of Evil* revived this tradition, using extravagant technical skill to accomplish a complex combination of functions to artistic effect.

At Welles's request, Metty photographed the scene with a wide-angle lens. The resulting images look strange and distorted, but the decision clearly serves a purpose, amplifying the strategy of surprise that dominates the opening of the film. A wide-angle lens allowed the filmmaker to place the camera very close to subjects entering the frame. From this position, small differences in absolute distance produced large differences in relative distance.[10] Welles exploited this compositional principle relentlessly, juxtaposing characters who are close to the camera with characters who are far: the close ones look huge, and the far ones look tiny. Even better, Welles put this principle in motion. Character and camera move simultaneously: a huge figure becomes a tiny one in a matter of moments. As Mike and Susie approach the checkpoint, two men enter the frame from the right. Because they enter so close to the camera, they look enormous. After just a few steps, though, they look small. This approach might seem like mindless virtuosity, but these little perceptual jolts serve several purposes: amplifying suspense by calling attention to the crowd of potential victims; helping us understand Mike and Susie, who delight in the town's surprises; characterizing Welles's "vertiginous" vision of the universe; and developing the theme of the permeable border by drawing our attention to a constant flow of entrances and exits.

Since the silent era, Hollywood's working theories of camera movement had appealed to conflicting ideals. On the one hand, some filmmakers assumed that the camera represented the eye of the audience; they concluded that its movements should be restricted to those an actual person might perform. On the other hand, these restrictions seemed to betray the very idea of the cinema, which surpassed human perception in its ability to show an event from any angle. Early dollies such as the Rotambulator and the Velocilator followed the logic of the camera–person analogy; early cranes such as the Broadway Boom seemed to fulfill the cinema's promise to go anywhere. A second wave of technological innovations revived this long-standing contrast. In the 1950s, the crab dolly was the successor to the Rotambulator: mobile but built to a human scale. The Chapman cranes recalled the Broadway Boom. Even these contraptions' names—the Hercules, the Titan—expressed a desire to break free from human limitations.

Touch of Evil took full advantage of the Chapman crane, which featured a heavy-duty arm mounted on the back of a truck. At first, the framing seems to adopt a human scale, echoing the bomber's movements without looking through his eyes. When he focuses on the bomb, so does the camera. When he swings around to look at the victims, so does the camera. When he runs by the wall, so does the camera. Without being fully subjective, the camera mimics the bomber's movements. But then—shockingly, gloriously—the camera vaults up to the sky. It remains in this elevated position for nearly a minute as the Chapman vehicle drives to the left and back and to the left again, traveling down an entire city block. Only when Mike and Susie appear does the camera return to eye level, participating in their walk through the lively center of town. In Welles's film, anthropomorphism is at best a temporary state. The opening shot announces that the camera will remain unambiguously what it always was: a machine.

The book's first chapter, "American Cinema, German Angles," may seem as if it is the least relevant to my final example. The chapter explained how the films of F. W. Murnau and E. A. Dupont had inspired Hollywood to take a fresh look at camera movement at the end of the silent period. In 1958, those years must have seemed distant indeed. Yet the tradition remained. *Touch of Evil*'s opening shot may be read as a descendant of *Sunrise*'s marsh scene. The link had little to do with technology: nobody dangled the camera from the ceiling anymore. The link involved ideas. *Sunrise* had shown that a shot's meaning could change radically from moment to moment, transforming before our very eyes. In Murnau's marsh scene, a follow shot becomes a point-of-view shot—without a cut. A trailing shot becomes a profile, which becomes a frontal view—without a cut. A shot where the protagonist is present becomes a shot where the protagonist is absent—without a cut. Subjective becomes objective, obscurity becomes beauty, motion becomes stasis—all without a cut. This is the tradition that culminates in *Touch of Evil*: a tradition of using the moving camera as a tool of transformation. The camera starts out too close, as an enormous hand reaches into the frame to set the explosive's timer. Then a movement, and the camera is too far away as a distant couple appears in the background and walks off. The camera also starts out close to the ground. Then a movement, and the camera is looking down from above. The camera starts out on the bomber and the victims. Then a movement, and the camera is following Mike and Susie. The camera starts out on one side of the border. Then a movement, and the camera is on the other side. The camera starts out focusing on an individual. Then a movement, and the camera is in the midst of a crowd, and then another, and the camera is isolating a couple. All of these transformations and more happen over the course of three and a quarter minutes, all through movement.

Murnau once wrote that the camera "must whirl and peep and move from place to place as swiftly as thought itself."[11] He called for a camera with superhuman mobility put in the service of human stories. The history of camera movement is not just a history of technologies. It is also a history of concepts—theories, strategies, and motifs. Murnau and Welles used the camera in different ways, for different purposes, but they shared an ideal. By expanding the camera's mobility, they expanded the cinema's powers of expression.

NOTES

Introduction

1. Rouben Mamoulian, quoted in Hal Hall, "Cinematographers and Directors Meet: Discuss Camera Trucking Problems," *American Cinematographer* 13, no. 4 (August 1932): 10.
2. James Wong Howe, quoted in Victor Milner, "Let's Stop Abusing Camera Movement," *American Cinematographer* 16, no. 2 (February 1935): 46.
3. Darryl F. Zanuck to Joseph L. Mankiewicz, memo, November 26, 1945, Joseph L. Mankiewicz Papers, Academy of Motion Picture Arts and Sciences, Margaret Herrick Library, Beverly Hills, CA.
4. George Cukor, in Peter Bogdanovich, *Who the Devil Made It: Conversations with Legendary Film Directors* (New York: Knopf, 1997), 444.
5. Chris Cagle has called this process the "adaptation-evolution" model of technological history ("Technology and Aesthetic Adaptation," *Category D: A Film and Media Studies Blog*, February 19, 2010, http://categoryd.blogspot.com/2010/02/technology -and-aesthetic-adaptation.html).
6. David Bordwell, *Poetics of Cinema* (New York: Routledge, 2008), 42.
7. V. F. Perkins, "Where Is the World? The Horizon of Events in Movie Fiction," in *Style and Meaning: Studies in the Detailed Analysis of Film*, ed. John Gibbs and Douglas Pye (Manchester, UK: Manchester University Press, 2005), 20.
8. For more on the meanings of *viewpoint*, see Douglas Pye, "Movies and Point of View," *Movie* 36 (2000): 2, and Deborah Thomas, *Beyond Genre: Melodrama, Comedy, and Romance in Hollywood Film* (Moffat, UK: Cameron and Hollis, 2000), 20.
9. See the insightful discussion of Kansas as a "working-girl investigator" in Helen Hanson, *Hollywood Heroines: Women in Film Noir and the Female Gothic Film* (New York: I. B. Tauris, 2007), 20–32.

10. Tamar Yacobi, "Package Deals in Fictional Narrative: The Case of the Narrator's (Un)Reliability," *Narrative* 9, no. 2 (May 2001): 223. Sternberg has discussed the Proteus principle in many articles. See, for instance, the account of "the many-to-many correspondence between form and function" in Meir Sternberg, "The 'Laokoon' Today: Interart Relations, Modern Projects, and Projections," *Poetics Today* 20, no. 2 (Summer 1999): 291–379.
11. Janet Bergstrom reports that there was a special screening of *The Last Laugh* for American film executives and the press in December 1924 (*William Fox Presents F. W. Murnau and Frank Borzage*, booklet in *Murnau, Borzage, and Fox*, DVD box set [Los Angeles: Twentieth Century-Fox Home Entertainment, 2008], 17).
12. The discussion of space draws on Bruce Block, *The Visual Story: Creating the Visual Structure of Film, TV, and Digital Media*, 2nd ed. (Burlington, MA: Focal Press, 2008). See, in particular, Block's appendix on lenses.
13. I borrow the term *occlusion size* from the philosophy of pictures. See, for instance, John Hyman, *The Objective Eye: Color, Form, and Reality in the Theory of Art* (Chicago: University of Chicago Press, 2006), 98.
14. Many introductory textbooks explain that zooming in is a way to "flatten" the image on the grounds that the telephoto lens produces a flatter sense of space, whereas the wide-angle lens seems to stretch the space. Following Block, I prefer to say that zooming in magnifies the image, whereas zooming out demagnifies the image.

1. American Cinema, German Angles

1. Maurice Kann, "Tricks," *Film Daily*, October 27, 1926, 1.
2. One article in 1937 claimed that *The Last Laugh* "marked the advent of the 'moving camera'" ("'Last Laugh' Revived by Art Film Library," *Film Daily*, January 22, 1937, 6). An article in *American Cinematographer* in 1942 argued that cinematographer Karl Freund "pioneered" the moving camera in *The Last Laugh* and *Variety* (William Stull, "Through the Editor's Finder," *American Cinematographer* 23, no. 4 [April 1942]: 159).
3. Barry Salt notes that there was "a new explosion of camera mobility in France and Germany" in 1923 (*Film Style and Technology: History and Analysis*, 3rd ed. [London: Starword, 2009], 174).
4. For these three shots, see *Scene from the Elevator Ascending Eiffel Tower* (James White, 1900), *Skyscrapers of New York City from North River* (J. B. Smith, 1903), and *The Georgetown Loop* (unknown filmmaker, 1903).
5. Lauren Rabinovitz, *Electric Dreamland: Amusement Parks, Movies, and American Modernity* (New York: Columbia University Press, 2012), 67–94.
6. Tom Gunning, "The Cinema of Attractions: Early Film, Its Spectator, and the Avant-Garde," in *Early Cinema: Space, Frame, Narrative*, ed. Thomas Elsaesser (London: British Film Institute, 1990), 56–62.
7. Charles Musser, *The Emergence of Cinema: The American Screen to 1907* (Berkeley: University of California Press, 1990), 386.
8. Tom Gunning has argued that the narrative "sublates" the energy of the attraction, harnessing that energy within a larger organizational system ("Modernity and Cinema: A Culture of Shocks and Flows," in *Cinema and Modernity*, ed. Murray Pomerance [New Brunswick, NJ: Rutgers University Press, 2006], 312).
9. Noël Carroll, "Toward a Theory of Film Suspense," in *Theorizing the Moving Image* (New York: Cambridge University Press, 1996), 94–117.

10. This discussion of narrative and attractions draws on my account in Patrick Keating, "Emotional Curves and Linear Narratives," *Velvet Light Trap* 58 (Fall 2006): 4–15.

11. G. W. Bitzer, *Billy Bitzer: His Story* (New York: Farrar, Straus and Giroux, 1973), 135. Elsewhere, the director Allan Dwan claims that the idea for the device was his (Kevin Brownlow, *The Parade's Gone By . . .* [Berkeley: University of California Press, 1968], 100–101). Dwan's film *David Harum* (1915) features several ambitious following shots.

12. See the reviews of *Regeneration* and *The Silent Voice* (1915) in *Wid's Films and Film Folk*, September 23, 1915. I quote these passages in more detail in Patrick Keating, "The Silent Screen, 1894–1927," in *Cinematography*, ed. Patrick Keating (New Brunswick, NJ: Rutgers University Press, 2014), 30.

13. Salt, *Film Style and Technology*, 138.

14. See Kristin Thompson's discussion of the "soft style" in "Major Technological Changes of the 1920s," in David Bordwell, Janet Staiger, and Kristin Thompson, *The Classical Hollywood Cinema: Film Style and Mode of Production to 1960* (New York: Columbia University Press, 1985), 287–293.

15. The technology of the Akeley camera is discussed in Ira Hoke, "What Is an Akeley?" *American Cinematographer* 9, no. 1 (April 1928): 20–21. See also Salt, *Film Style and Technology*, 171–173.

16. Hoke, "What Is an Akeley?" 21.

17. See George Meehan, "Filming 'Ben Hur' Chariot Race Scenes," *American Cinematographer* 6, no. 10 (January 1926): 5–6.

18. The cinematographer Charles Clarke explains that an Akeley camera with a long lens was designed to photograph "cross-camera action"—that is, action moving from left to right or right to left. Long lenses were less effective when photographing action moving toward or away from the camera because it would appear that the subject was "never getting anywhere" (*Highlights and Shadows: The Memoirs of a Hollywood Cameraman*, ed. Anthony Slide [Metuchen, NJ: Scarecrow Press, 1989], 73).

19. Fred Jackman, "Comedy 'Kicks' Require Courage and Skill," *American Cinematographer* 3, no. 9 (December 1922): 5–6, 23.

20. Sam Taylor, "New Styles in Comedy," *Film Daily*, June 7, 1925, 111.

21. Walter Lundin, "Drama Treatment Enters Comedy Photography," *American Cinematographer* 5, no. 3 (June 1924): 10. I discuss this article in more detail in Patrick Keating, *Hollywood Lighting from the Silent Era to Film Noir* (New York: Columbia University Press, 2010), 95–96. The Lundin article may be a direct response to Jackman's, "Comedy 'Kicks' Require Courage and Skill," written a year and a half earlier.

22. For a similar analysis, see the discussion of the "switch image" in Noël Carroll, "Notes on the Sight Gag," in *Theorizing the Moving Image* (New York: Cambridge University Press, 1996), 151–152.

23. My analysis of the shot's depth cues draws on the chapter on space in Bruce Block, *The Visual Story: Creating the Visual Structure of Film, TV, and Digital Media*, 2nd ed. (Burlington, MA: Focal Press, 2008), 13–86.

24. It was common for major films to use two cameras, one to produce a negative for domestic release, another to produce a nearly identical negative for foreign release.

25. "Again the Foreign Director Steps In," *Film Daily*, June 7, 1925, 111.

26. For a detailed history featuring chapters on Ernst Lubitsch, F. W. Murnau, Victor Sjöström, Mauritz Stiller, and others, see Graham Petrie, *Hollywood Destinies: European Directors in America, 1922–1931*, rev. ed. (Detroit: Wayne State University Press, 2002).

27. Janet Bergstrom, *William Fox Presents F. W. Murnau and Frank Borzage*, booklet in *Murnau, Borzage, and Fox*, DVD box set (Los Angeles: Twentieth Century-Fox Home Entertainment, 2008), 17.
28. Mordaunt Hall, "A Remarkable Film," *New York Times*, January 28, 1925, 14.
29. Mordaunt Hall, "A German Masterpiece," *New York Times*, June 28, 1926, 15. For a compilation of *Film Daily*'s top-ten lists from the 1920s, see "The Best Pictures of Previous Years," in *The 1930 "Film Daily" Year Book of Motion Pictures*, ed. Jack Alicoate (Los Angeles: Film Daily, 1930), 49–51.
30. Statements from *New York Daily News* quoted in "Newspaper Opinions," *Film Daily*, July 4, 1926, 7; Lilian W. Brennan, "A Review of Reviews," *Film Daily*, July 6, 1926, 7.
31. "Simc.," "*Variety*," *Variety*, June 30, 1926, 10. Note that this was the trade journal's second review of the film. Its first review, appearing on January 20, 1926, well before the film's American release, was more hostile.
32. For instance, the critic Harry Alan Potamkin used the terms *angle* and *mobile camera* interchangeably in an article in 1930 listing the greatest cinematographers. After introducing the subject of the "camera angle," he referred to the elevator-dolly shot in *Intolerance* and then argued that American filmmakers neglected the technique until *Variety* employed the "angle" as a structuring technique ("Knights of the Camera," *International Photographer* 2, no. 8 [September 1930]: 14). Similarly, Gilbert Seldes explained that German directors of the silent period contributed "camera angles" to the technique of the moving pictures (*The Movies Come from America* [1937; reprint, New York: Arno Press, 1978], 76–77). A hypothetical example concerning a trapeze sequence is almost certainly a reference to *Variety*, suggesting that the term is used broadly enough to include the mobile camera.
33. "Trask," "*Varietee*," *Variety*, January 20, 1926, 40.
34. Evelyn Gerstein, "*Variety*," *New Republic*, July 28, 1926, 281; Edwin Seaver, "A Bunkless Movie," *New Masses*, September 1926, 28.
35. F. W. Murnau, quoted in "Murnau Insists Camera Angles Shall Be 'Dramatic,' If Anything," *Moving Picture World* 85, no. 5 (April 2, 1927): 490.
36. "Freund Wins Academy Honors," *American Cinematographer* 19, no. 3 (March 1938): 92.
37. F. W. Murnau, "Real 'Motion' Pictures," *Film Daily*, June 7, 1925, 21, emphasis in the original.
38. Maurice Kann, "*Variety*," *Film Daily*, April 29, 1926, 1; Gerstein, "*Variety*," 280.
39. Jean Mitry, *The Aesthetics and Psychology of the Cinema*, trans. Christopher King (1997; reprint, Bloomington: Indiana University Press, 2000), 214–219.
40. See Karl Freund's article "A Film Artist," which appears as an appendix in Paul Rotha, *The Film till Now: A Survey of World Cinema*, 3rd ed. (New York: Twayne, 1960), 716–717. In this article, Freund gives screenwriter Carl Mayer the credit for *The Last Laugh*'s visual design. In response, Lotte Eisner offers evidence to support her claim that Murnau should be given most of the credit (*Murnau* [Berkeley: University of California Press, 1973], 71–88).
41. Petrie, *Hollywood Destinies*, 208.
42. "Camera Dynamics," *Film Daily*, June 27, 1926, 25.
43. Set designer Robert Herlth explains that the goal was "to represent a sound travelling through space" (quoted in Eisner, *Murnau*, 65; see also Freund, "A Film Artist," 717).
44. Maurice Kann, "What Does the Future Hold?" *Film Daily*, June 27, 1926, 23.
45. Jan-Christopher Horak, "Sauerkraut & Sausages with a Little Goulash: Germans in Hollywood, 1927," *Film History* 17, nos. 2–3 (2005): 244.

46. Foster Goss, "The Editor's Lens: New or Old?" *American Cinematographer* 7, no. 5 (August 1926): 5.
47. Charles Sewell, "Films from Across the Sea," *Moving Picture World* 85, no. 4 (March 26, 1927): 438.
48. Peter Decherney, *Hollywood and the Culture Elite: How Movies Became American* (New York: Columbia University Press, 2005), 102–103.
49. Petrie, *Hollywood Destinies*, 10.
50. Thomas Saunders, *Hollywood in Berlin: American Cinema and Weimar Germany* (Berkeley: University of California Press, 1994), 126.
51. Hermann Bing, interviewed in "Murnau to Produce for Fox Film Corp.," *Moving Picture World* 78, no. 1 (January 2, 1926): 69.
52. Bing, in "Murnau to Produce for Fox Film Corp.," 69.
53. F. W. Murnau, quoted in "Murnau Insists Camera Angles Shall Be 'Dramatic,'" 490.
54. Maurice Kann, "1902–1926," *Film Daily*, July 9, 1926, 1. A fan magazine covered the same dinner and noted that Murnau had praised "the energy, the youth, and the vital freshness of America" (L. R., "Flash Backs," *Motion Picture Classic* 24, no. 1 [September 1926]: 54).
55. Bergstrom, *William Fox Presents F. W. Murnau and Frank Borzage*, 19.
56. William Fox, quoted in "Murnau's 'Sunrise' to Open in Month," *Moving Picture World* 87, no. 6 (August 6, 1927): 402.
57. Janet Gaynor also won the Best Actress Academy Award for her work in three films, including *Sunrise*.
58. Richard Koszarski discusses this shot in "The Cinematographer," in *New York to Hollywood: The Photography of Karl Struss*, ed. Barbara McCandless, Bonnie Yochelson, and Richard Koszarski (Fort Worth, TX: Amon Carter Museum, 1995), 177.
59. Struss claimed that the suspended dolly had a "wedge shaped thing" on the front to push the foliage out of the way (interview in Scott Eyman, *Five American Cinematographers* [Metuchen, NJ: Scarecrow Press, 1987], 9).
60. Karl Struss, "Dramatic Cinematography," *Transactions of the Society of Motion Picture Engineers* 12, no. 34 (October 1928): 318.
61. Susan Harvith and John Harvith, *Karl Struss: Man with a Camera* (Bloomsfield Hills, MI: Cranbrook Academy of Art, 1976), 15.
62. Caitlin McGrath, "Captivating Motion: Late–Silent Film Sequences of Perception in the Modern Urban Environment," PhD diss., University of Chicago, 2010, 222.
63. For more information on this shot, see *Murnau, Borzage, and Fox*, DVD box set.
64. Maurice Kann, "*Sunrise* and Movietone," *Film Daily*, September 25, 1927, 4.
65. Pare Lorentz, "The Stillborn Art" (1928), in *Lorentz on Film: Movies, 1927–1941* (Norman: University of Oklahoma Press, 1986), 25.
66. "Rush.," "*Sunrise*," *Variety*, September 28, 1927, 21.
67. "*Sunrise*," *Moving Picture World* 88, no. 5 (October 1, 1927): 312.
68. Donald Crafton reports that *Sunrise* "sank like a stone" in New York after a strong opening. Its run at the Cathay Circle Theatre in Los Angeles was more successful (*The Talkies: American Cinema's Transition to Sound, 1926–1931* [Berkeley: University of California Press, 1997], 525–527).
69. Janet Bergstrom carefully details the making of both films in "Murnau in America: Chronicle of Lost Films," *Film History* 14, nos. 3–4 (2002): 430–460.
70. Bergstrom, *William Fox Presents F. W. Murnau and Frank Borzage*, 10.
71. Clarence Brown, quoted in Brownlow, *The Parade's Gone By . . .* , 146. A decade later, the director repeated the trick in *Anna Karenina* (1935).

72. "The Gyroscopic Camera and Future Production Possibilities," *Film Daily*, June 7, 1925, 5.

73. Maurice Kann, "Fred Thomson," *Film Daily*, July 14, 1926, 1, and Maurice Kann, "More Pictures," *Film Daily*, July 15, 1926, 1. Elsewhere, a fan commented on the fact that *You Never Know Women* copied its angles from *Variety* (Richard Roland, "What the Foreigners Have Done for Us," *Picture-Play Magazine* 26, no. 1 [March 1927]: 12). Largely conventional, *Mantrap* (1926) featured one spectacular montage showing a dynamic trip from the country to the city.

74. Gilbert Seldes, "Camera Angles," *New Republic* 50, no. 640 (March 9, 1927): 72–73.

75. "The Shadow Stage," *Photoplay* 31, no. 4 (March 1927): 94.

76. Ken Chamberlain, "Camera Angles," *Motion Picture* 23, no. 3 (April 1927): 25. The tone of the article is mocking, accompanied by four cartoons depicting four bizarre techniques.

77. Harold R. Hall, "Camera Angles—the Bunk," *Motion Picture Classic* 24, no. 6 (February 1927): 18, 79.

78. F. W. Murnau, quoted in Matthew Josephson, "F. W. Murnau: The German Genius of the Films," *Motion Picture Classic* 24, no. 2 (October 1926): 16.

79. Murnau, "Real 'Motion' Pictures," 21.

80. Karl Freund, quoted in "Camera Dynamics," 25.

81. Erich Pommer, quoted in "Angles," *Motion Picture News* 34, no. 26 (December 25, 1926): 2407. According to Fritz Lang, it was Pommer who told him, "Fritz, you have to tell a story with the camera" (in Bogdanovich, *Who the Devil Made It*, 183).

82. E. A. Dupont, quoted in "Camera Dynamics," 25.

83. Pommer, quoted in "Angles," 2407.

84. Vsevolod Pudovkin, *Film Technique and Film Acting*, trans. Ivor Montagu (New York: Bonanza Books, 1949), 39–45. On these early theories of the "invisible observer," see David Bordwell, *Narration in the Fiction Film* (Madison: University of Wisconsin Press, 1985), 9–10.

85. Pommer, quoted in "Angles," 2407.

86. Maurice Kann, "Murnau," *Film Daily*, July 2, 1926, 1.

87. Eisner, *Murnau*, 72.

88. F. W. Murnau, "Films of the Future" (1927), in *Hollywood Directors, 1914–1940*, ed. Richard Koszarski (New York: Oxford University Press, 1976), 219. I quote this passage in *Hollywood Lighting from the Silent Era to Film Noir*, 119.

89. F. W. Murnau, "The Ideal Picture Needs No Titles: By Its Very Nature the Art of the Screen Should Tell a Complete Story Pictorially" (1928), in *German Essays on Film*, ed. Alison Guenther-Pal and Richard W. McCormick (New York: Continuum, 2004), 68.

90. In a German publication, Murnau once wrote that his strongest wish was for a camera "that at any moment can go anywhere, at any speed" (quoted in Eisner, *Murnau*, 84). For a more detailed discussion of Murnau's theoretical statements, including some useful passages from German publications, see Lutz Bacher, *The Mobile Mise-en-Scène: A Critical Analysis of the Theory and Practice of Long-Take Camera Movement in the Narrative Film* (New York: Arno Press, 1978), 210–226.

91. Gilbert Seldes, *The 7 Lively Arts* (1924; reprint, New York: Dover, 2001), 324.

92. Gilbert Seldes, "The Theatre," *The Dial* 82, no. 5 (May 1927): 440.

93. Alexander Bakshy, "The New Art of the Motion Picture," *Theatre Arts Monthly* 11, no. 4 (April 1927): 281.

94. Bakshy, "The New Art of the Motion Picture," 281.

95. Bakshy, "The New Art of the Motion Picture," 280.
96. Alexander Bakshy, "The Talkies," *The Nation* 128 (February 20, 1929): 238.
97. On these distinctions, see Bordwell, *Narration in the Fiction Film*, 57–58.
98. Ernest Palmer, quoted in Richard Koszarski, "Ernest Palmer on Frank Borzage and F. W. Murnau," *Griffithiana* 46 (December 1992): 117. Earlier that year, a less-ambitious stairway shot had appeared in Raoul Walsh's bizarre film *The Monkey Talks* (1927).
99. See the useful account, along with the photograph, in Hervé Dumont, *Frank Borzage: The Life and Films of a Hollywood Romantic* (Jefferson, NC: McFarland, 2006), 116–117.
100. King Vidor, *A Tree Is a Tree: An Autobiography* (1953; reprint, Hollywood, CA: Samuel French, 1981), 150–151.
101. Vidor, *A Tree Is a Tree*, 151.
102. For technical details, see George Turner, "*Wings*: Epic of the Air," *American Cinematographer* 66, no. 4 (April 1985): 36–38.
103. In this chapter, my analyses of *Wings*, *The Cat and the Canary*, *It*, *Hotel Imperial*, and *Street Angel* draw on my remarks in Patrick Keating, "A Homeless Ghost: The Moving Camera and Its Analogies," *[in]Transition: A Journal of Videographic Film & Video Criticism* 2, no. 4 (2016), http://mediacommons.futureofthebook.org/intransition/issue-2-4.
104. Turner, "*Wings*," 40.
105. See the illustration in Brownlow, *The Parade's Gone By . . .* , 214.
106. See the illustration in "Camera Angles," *Screenland* 17, no. 3 (July 1928): 24.
107. Production photographs, *The Last Performance*, Hal Mohr and Evelyn Venable Papers, Academy of Motion Picture Arts and Sciences, Margaret Herrick Library, Beverly Hills, CA.
108. George Kent Shuler, "Pictures and Personalities," *Motion Picture Classic* 28, no. 4 (December 1928): 15.
109. Bergstrom, "Murnau in America," 431.
110. Bergstrom, "Murnau in America," 438. An illustration of the Go-Devil appears in *Photoplay* 34, no. 4 (September 1928): 104.
111. F. W. Murnau, quoted in Bergstrom, "Murnau in America," 438; the original passage appears in Murnau, "Films of the Future," 219.
112. Here my argument echoes that of Robert Spadoni, who has examined the strangeness of sound in films from the early sound period in *Uncanny Bodies: The Coming of Sound Film and the Origins of the Horror Genre* (Berkeley: University of California Press, 2007), 11.
113. The shot looks like a crane-down, even though the modern crane had not yet been invented in 1927. Perhaps Leni and his crew had jerry-rigged a makeshift crane, or perhaps they assembled a simple elevator-like device.
114. For this alternate arrangement, see the illustration in Petrie, *Hollywood Destinies*, 201.
115. Ernest Palmer reports that this early crane was made of wood (quoted in Koszarski, "Ernest Palmer on Frank Borzage and F. W. Murnau," 118). See also the well-illustrated account of early cranes in Jakob Isak Nielsen, "En scenes anatomi: *Sunnyside Up*," *16:9* 43 (September 2011), http://www.16-9.dk/2011-09/side07_anatomi.htm.
116. Dumont, *Frank Borzage*, 127.
117. Laura Mulvey, "Visual Pleasure and Narrative Cinema," in *Narrative, Apparatus, Ideology: A Film Theory Reader*, ed. Philip Rosen (New York: Columbia University Press, 1986), 203.
118. Michael Baxandall, *Patterns of Intention: On the Historical Explanation of Pictures* (New Haven, CT: Yale University Press, 1985), 59.

119. Robert Herring, "Synthetic Dawn," *Close Up* 2, no. 3 (March 1928): 38–45. The same journal mocked Dupont's camerawork when he came to the United Kingdom to make *Piccadilly* (1929). See Hugh Castle, "Some British Films," *Close Up* 5, no. 1 (July 1929): 45–46.

120. Production photographs for *My Best Girl* (Mary Pickford Papers, Margaret Herrick Library) show the actors performing in a studio street and on a moving truck, confirming my sense that neither scene uses a traveling matte, though the film's climactic scene does.

121. Harold Lloyd would repay the favor. His comedy *Speedy* (1928) contains a comedic scene with the two lovers on the back of a very bumpy truck, clearly derived from the gag in *My Best Girl*.

122. "Ford Praises Murnau's Film," *Moving Picture World* 85, no. 1 (March 5, 1927): 35.

123. "Fox Films Production Costs for Next Season, $15,000,000," *Moving Picture World* 85, no. 3 (March 19, 1927), 192. Tag Gallagher notes in *John Ford: The Man and His Films* (Berkeley: University of California Press, 1986) that the footage was unused (50).

124. *Murnau, Borzage, and Fox*, DVD box set.

125. Gallagher describes *Four Sons* as "an almost self-effacing imitation of Murnau's style" (*John Ford*, 50).

126. Ford used variants of this plot structure in several subsequent films. See Lea Jacobs, "Making John Ford's *How Green Was My Valley*," *Film History* 28, no. 2 (2016): 60–61.

127. Bergstrom, *William Fox Presents F. W. Murnau and Frank Borzage*, 17.

128. Horak, "Sauerkraut & Sausages with a Little Goulash," 254–256.

129. The quotation appears in "The Big Gun Group Jewels Among the Big Guns," *Moving Picture World* 85, no. 9 (May 2, 1927): 813. The article is essentially a press release for Universal.

130. Petrie, *Hollywood Destinies*, 268.

131. Dupont's early attachment to the project is announced in "Dupont Remaining with 'U,'" *Film Daily*, July 2, 1926, 1.

132. For a summary of Leni's career, see Petrie, *Hollywood Destinies*, 185–189.

133. In a lecture at a symposium, Miriam Hansen compared *Lonesome* and *The Crowd* as examples of vernacular modernism (cited in Mike Hammond, "Film: The First Global Vernacular?" *History Workshop Journal* 58 [Autumn 2004]: 356).

134. Maurice Kann, quoted in Crafton, *The Talkies*, 584.

135. Paul Fejos, "Illusion on the Screen" (1929), in *Hollywood Directors, 1914–1940*, ed. Richard Koszarski (New York: Oxford University Press, 1976), 225.

2. Purposes and Parallels

1. Set designer Robert Herlth describes a brainstorming session on the set of *The Last Laugh* that resulted in the decision to use a firemen's ladder to move the camera (in Lotte Eisner, *Murnau* [Berkeley: University of California Press, 1973], 63).

2. David Bordwell contrasts "romantic anecdotes" about bicycles with the fact that camera departments "coolly and carefully" designed new dollies ("Camera Movement: The Coming of Sound and the Classical Hollywood Style," in *The Hollywood Film Industry*, ed. Paul Kerr [London: Routledge, 1984], 150).

3. Karl Freund, quoted in "Looking Ahead," *International Photographer* 16, no. 1 (February 1934): 17.

4. Donald Crafton, *The Talkies: American Cinema's Transition to Sound, 1926–1931* (Berkeley: University of California Press, 1997), 230.

5. William Stull, "Solving the 'Ice-Box' Problem," *American Cinematographer* 10, no. 6 (September 1929): 7.

6. Stull, "Solving the 'Ice-Box' Problem," 7.

7. King Vidor, *A Tree Is a Tree: An Autobiography* (1953; reprint, Hollywood, CA: Samuel French, 1981), 181.

8. William Wyler, in Bernard Kantor, Irwin Blacker, and Anne Kramer, *Directors at Work: Interviews with American Film-Makers* (New York: Funk and Wagnalls, 1970), 411.

9. Crafton, *The Talkies*, 247.

10. Janet Staiger describes the continuity script as a "blueprint" that fulfilled the industry's profit-oriented goals by enabling "efficient and cost-effective work processes" ("Blueprints for Feature Films: Hollywood's Continuity Scripts," in *The American Film Industry*, rev. ed., ed. Tino Balio [Madison: University of Wisconsin Press, 1985], 173).

11. Bess Meredyth, "A Woman of Affairs," shooting script, n.d., Clarence Brown Collection, Special Collections, University of Tennessee–Knoxville.

12. Barry Salt, *Film Style and Technology: History and Analysis*, 3rd ed. (London: Starword, 2009), 192, 237. See also the extensive data available on the Cinemetrics website at www.cinemetrics.lv.

13. Edward Sheldon, "Romance," shooting script, n.d., Clarence Brown Collection.

14. All of these continuity scripts can be found in the Clarence Brown Collection at the University of Tennessee–Knoxville. Some scripts appear in multiple drafts; there is usually variation in shot count across drafts. I use the word *shot* in the modern sense; in fact, however, the scripts refer to each shot as a separate scene.

15. Salt, *Film Style and Technology*, 204. Donald Crafton quotes this same passage in *The Talkies*, 232.

16. In "Cinematography: Film, Tape, and Honesty," *Journal of the University Film Association* 26, no. 4 (1974), the cinematographer Lee Garmes explains how the crew attached a viewfinder to the outside of the booth (60). The film in question is probably Michael Curtiz's *Bright Lights* (1930).

17. The names are listed in Stull, "Solving the 'Ice-Box' Problem," 6–7, 36. Descriptions of the various materials appear in Elmer Richardson, "Tilt Heads and Rolling Tripods for Camera Blimps," *Journal of the Society of Motion Picture Engineers* 15, no. 1 (July 1930): 46.

18. The attachments are illustrated in "New Apparatus," *Journal of the Society of Motion Picture Engineers* 20, no. 1 (January 1933): 85. The "Rolls Royce" comparison appears in Fred Westerberg, "Camera Equipment Demonstration Shows Much Has Been Accomplished," *International Photographer* 4, no. 5 (June 1932): 5.

19. Richardson, "Tilt Heads and Rolling Tripods for Camera Blimps," 46.

20. William Stull, "Evolution of Cinema Tripods for Studio Use," *American Cinematographer* 13, no. 12 (April 1933): 7.

21. David Bordwell and Kristin Thompson, "Technological Change and Classical Film Style," in Tino Balio, *Grand Design: Hollywood as a Modern Business Enterprise, 1930–1939* (Berkeley: University of California Press, 1993), 126.

22. "Crane Mechanical Marvel," *American Cinematographer* 10, no. 2 (May 1929): 14–15; William Stull, "Development of Mobile Camera-Carriages and Cranes," *American Cinematographer* 14, no. 1 (May 1933): 12–13. In some documents, credit for the design of the crane is attributed to Fejos, but in others to Mohr.

23. Hal Mohr, quoted in Richard Koszarski, "Moving Pictures: Hal Mohr's Cinematography," *Film Comment* 10, no. 5 (September 1974): 52.

24. In this chapter, my analyses of *Broadway*, *The Bat Whispers*, *Chandu the Magician*, *Gold Diggers of 1933*, and *The Barretts of Wimpole Street* draw on my remarks in Patrick Keating, "A Homeless Ghost: The Moving Camera and Its Analogies," [*in*]*Transition: A Journal of Videographic Film & Video Criticism* 2, no. 4 (2016), http://mediacommons.futureofthebook.org/intransition/issue-2-4.

25. Lutz Bacher, *The Mobile Mise-en-Scène: A Critical Analysis of the Theory and Practice of Long-Take Camera Movement in the Narrative Film* (New York: Arno Press, 1978), 26–27.

26. Fritz Lang, in Peter Bogdanovich, *Who the Devil Made It: Conversations with Legendary Film Directors* (New York: Knopf, 1997), 185–186.

27. "This Giant Camera Crane May Pick Out a New Star," *Photoplay* 41, no. 5 (April 1932): 72; Ty [*sic*], "Looking About on Location and Set," *International Photographer* 5, no. 1 (February 1933): 5.

28. Stull, "Development of Mobile Camera-Carriages," 12–13.

29. See the chart in *International Photographer* 9, no. 12 (January 1938): 12.

30. E. H. Heyer and E. L. Fischer, "A New Motion Picture Camera Crane," *Journal of the Society of Motion Picture Engineers* 30, no. 5 (May 1938): 586–591.

31. Hal Mohr, in Leonard Maltin, *The Art of the Cinematographer: A Survey and Interviews with Five Masters* (New York: Dover, 1978), 86.

32. Joseph Dubray of Bell and Howell explained the device in "New Motion Picture Apparatus: The Rotambulator—a New Motion Picture Stand," *Journal of the Society of Motion Picture Engineers* 22, no. 3 (March 1934): 200–205. For M-G-M's version, see "M-G-M Rotambulator," *International Photographer* 4, no. 9 (October 1932): 24–25. For the criticism, see Westerberg, "Camera Equipment Demonstration," 5. According to Barry Salt, the highly maneuverable dolly used in Lewis Milestone's film *The Front Page* (1931) served as the prototype for the Rotambulator (*Film Style and Technology*, 227).

33. On the original Velocilator design, see J. Henry Kruse, "Kamera Kiddie Kars," *International Photographer* 5, no. 2 (May 1933): 44–45, and the unsigned article "Cinematic Progress During 1933: A Technical Review," *American Cinematographer* 14, no. 12 (April 1934): 490. On the new rotating Velocilator, see "Progress in Motion Picture Industry," *Journal of the Society of Motion Picture Engineers* 27, no. 1 (July 1936): 11.

34. For use of the term *perambulator*, see "Mole-Richardson Construct Perambulator to Eliminate Shifting on Travel Shots," *International Photographer* 2, no. 11 (December 1930): 45, and "New Perambulator and Camera," *American Cinematographer* 13, no. 2 (June 1932): 16, 47. For use of the term *baby carriage*, see Joseph August, "Cinematographers Have Language All Their Own," *American Cinematographer* 18, no. 2 (February 1937): 76.

35. Edgar Ulmer, in Bogdanovich, *Who the Devil Made It*, 569.

36. Photographs of the Rotambulator appear in publicity photographs for *Romeo and Juliet* (1936) in Metro-Goldwyn-Mayer Production and Biography Photographs and for *Ninotchka* (1939) in Bison Archives Photographs Collected by Marc Wanamaker—Camera Dollies, Academy of Motion Picture Arts and Sciences, Margaret Herrick Library, Beverly Hills, CA.

37. "Progress in the Motion Picture Industry," *Journal of the Society of Motion Picture Engineers* 27, no. 1 (July 1936): 11.

38. For the Warner Bros. small-arm dolly, see Arthur Edeson, "Utility Features New Light Crane," *American Cinematographer* 15, no. 1 (May 1934): 10, 22. For a photograph of Paramount's small-arm dolly, see "Progress in Motion Picture Industry," *Journal of the Society of Motion Picture Engineers* 25, no. 1 (July 1935): 11. For RKO's version, see "RKO's Camera and Dolly Unit," *International Photographer* 9, no. 3 (April 1937): 9.

39. "New Perambulator and Camera," 47.

40. Virgil Miller, *Splinters from Hollywood Tripods* (New York: Exposition Press, 1964), 105, quoting an unidentified essay Miller wrote in the early 1930s.

41. Lewis Physioc summarizes the meeting in "Unterrified Inventors Show Work," *International Photographer* 4, no. 5 (June 1932): 4–5.

42. David Bordwell, "The Mazda Tests of 1928," in David Bordwell, Janet Staiger, and Kristin Thompson, *The Classical Hollywood Cinema: Film Style and Mode of Production to 1960* (New York: Columbia University Press, 1985), 296–297.

43. Leigh Aman, "In Leo's Den," *The Cine-Technician* 3, no. 12 (October–November 1937): 138.

44. "The Technique of Follow-Focus," *American Cinematographer* 42, no. 1 (January 1961): 49–50. This article is unsigned, but it is probably by Joseph V. Mascelli.

45. For a technical description and illustrations, see John Arnold, "The Metro-Goldwyn-Mayer Semi-automatic Follow-Focus Device," *Journal of the Society of Motion Picture Engineers* 32, no. 4 (April 1939): 419–423.

46. See Mamoulian's discussion of variable diffusion in *Interviews with Film Directors*, ed. Andrew Sarris (New York: Avon Books, 1967), 347–348.

47. Emil Oster, "Device for Producing Variable Diffusion Effects," *American Cinematographer* 18, no. 2 (February 1937): 52.

48. Nick Hall, *The Zoom: Drama at the Touch of a Lever* (New Brunswick, NJ: Rutgers University Press, 2018), 28.

49. "New B.&H. Lens Eliminates Crane Shots in Professional Movies," *American Cinematographer* 12, no. 10 (February 1932): 31; "A New Zoom Lens," *American Cinematographer* 12, no. 11 (March 1932): 16, 37.

50. Allan Dwan, in Bogdanovich, *Who the Devil Made It*, 97.

51. Photographs show that M-G-M, Fox, Paramount, Warner Bros., Universal, Columbia, and Republic, among other studios, owned camera cars at some point during the studio period. See Bison Archives Photographs Collected by Marc Wanamaker—Camera Cars.

52. "Progress in the Motion Picture Industry," *Journal of the Society of Motion Picture Engineers* 17, no. 1 (July 1931): 75.

53. Hans F. Koenekamp, "An Insert-Car to Meet Today's Need," *American Cinematographer* 17, no. 1 (January 1936): 11.

54. See Dyer's advertisement in *American Cinematographer* 12, no. 5 (September 1931): 22.

55. Vernon Walker, "Special Process Technic," *Journal of the Society of Motion Picture Engineers* 18, no. 5 (May 1932): 662.

56. Fred Jackman, "The Evolution of Special-Effects Cinematography from an Engineering Viewpoint," *Journal of the Society of Motion Picture Engineers* 29, no. 3 (September 1937): 293.

57. For technical details, see Frank Williams, "Trick Photography," *Transactions of the Society of Motion Picture Engineers* 12, no. 34 (April 1928): 537–538. The patents are discussed in H. D. Hineline, "Composite Photographic Processes," *Journal of the Society of Motion Picture Engineers* 20, no. 4 (April 1933): 285–286. Barry Salt speculates that big-budget films used a more painstaking version of the Williams process,

painting countersilhouettes onto sheets of paper by hand and photographing the papers to produce the mattes (*Film Style and Technology*, 188).

58. See the original explanation of the Dunning process in C. Dodge Dunning, "Composite Photography," *Transactions of the Society of Motion Picture Engineers* 12, no. 36 (September 1928): 976–977; a later and somewhat clearer explanation appears in Gordon A. Chambers, "Process Photography," *Journal of the Society of Motion Picture Engineers* 18, no. 6 (June 1932): 785–786. H. D. Hineline argues that Roy Pomeroy's patents of 1928 were just as important as Dunning's patent of 1927 ("Composite Photographic Processes," 294–295).

59. Writing in the 1960s, after the traveling matte had returned to prominence, Raymond Fielding provided a useful comparison of matte and rear-screen projection, clearly enumerating the advantages and disadvantages of each, in *The Technique of Special Effects Cinematography*, 3rd ed. (New York: Hastings House, 1974), 249–252.

60. Farciot Edouart, "The Evolution of Transparency Process Photography," *American Cinematographer* 24, no. 10 (October 1943): 359.

61. Julie Turnock analyzes rear-screen projection as a "crack in the system" of classical Hollywood filmmaking, placing efficiency above the practitioners' stated aesthetic ideals ("The Screen on the Set: The Problem of Classical-Studio Rear Projection," *Cinema Journal* 51, no. 2 [Winter 2012]: 160).

62. Bacher, *The Mobile Mise-en-Scène*, 29.

63. On the value of studying production cultures, see John Thornton Caldwell, *Production Culture: Industrial Reflexivity and Critical Practice in Film and Television* (Durham, NC: Duke University Press, 2008), 14. Caldwell's book offers a critical ethnography of working professionals in the contemporary film industry of Los Angeles.

64. Hal Hall, "Cinematographers and Directors Meet: Discuss Camera Trucking Problems," *American Cinematographer* 13, no. 4 (August 1932): 10.

65. John F. Seitz, paraphrased in Hall, "Cinematographers and Directors Meet," 10.

66. Victor Milner, paraphrased in Hall, "Cinematographers and Directors Meet," 10.

67. Rouben Mamoulian, quoted in Hall, "Cinematographers and Directors Meet," 10.

68. Rouben Mamoulian, quoted in William Stull, "Common Sense and Camera Angles," *American Cinematographer* 12, no. 10 (February 1932): 9.

69. Mamoulian, quoted in Stull, "Common Sense and Camera Angles," 9.

70. Richard Koszarski, "The Greatest Film Paramount Ever Made," *Film History* 15, no. 4 (2003): 440.

71. These words appear in a Paramount press release ("Drama, Love Stir Hearts in New Film," *Applause* press book, Paramount Pictures Press Sheets, Academy of Motion Picture Arts and Sciences, Margaret Herrick Library).

72. V. F. Perkins, "Where Is the World? The Horizon of Events in Movie Fiction," in *Style and Meaning: Studies in the Detailed Analysis of Film*, ed. John Gibbs and Douglas Pye (Manchester, UK: Manchester University Press, 2005), 30.

73. For a thoughtful analysis of these and other shots in *Applause*, see Jeffrey P. Smith, "'It Does Something to a Girl. I Don't Know What': The Problem of Female Sexuality in *Applause*," *Cinema Journal* 30, no. 2 (Winter 1991): 47–60.

74. See, for example, Rouben Mamoulian, in Charles Higham and Joel Greenberg, *The Celluloid Muse: Hollywood Directors Speak* (London: Angus and Robertson, 1969), 130.

75. Clemens was Struss's regular operator in the early 1930s (George Blaisdell, "Looking in on Just a Few New Ones," *International Photographer* 3, no. 12 [January 1932]: 30).

76. Richard Koszarski, "The Cinematographer," in *New York to Hollywood: The Photography of Karl Struss*, ed. Barbara McCandless, Bonnie Yochelson, and Richard Koszarski (Fort Worth, TX: Amon Carter Museum, 1995), 185.

77. Gerald Mast, *The Comic Mind: Comedy and the Movies*, 2nd ed. (Chicago: University of Chicago Press, 1979), 207.

78. Ernst Lubitsch, quoted in Herman Weinberg, *The Lubitsch Touch: A Critical Study* (New York: Dutton, 1968), 259. Weinberg took the quote from an article he wrote in 1951, where he recalled a meeting with Lubitsch in 1928.

79. Graham Petrie notes that Ernst Lubitsch, Harold Lloyd, and Buster Keaton employed a comedy technique that he calls "the misreading of visual evidence" (*Hollywood Destinies: European Directors in America, 1922–1931*, rev. ed. [Detroit: Wayne State University Press, 2002], 48).

80. Kristin Thompson, *Herr Lubitsch Goes to Hollywood: German and American Film After World War I* (Amsterdam: Amsterdam University Press, 2005), 120.

81. Mellor is credited as the film's camera operator (or "operative cameraman") in "Brulatour Bulletin," *International Photographer* 4, no. 12 (January 1933): 20. Soon promoted to cinematographer, Mellor had a distinguished career, winning two Oscars.

82. The head of the Studio Relations Committee, James Wingate, commented on the first draft of the script: "This type of story will need great care in treatment and direction to avoid making loose and unconventional habits of living appear attractive or condoned" (James Wingate to A. M. Botsford, June 19, 1933, *Design for Living*, Production Code Administration Files, Academy of Motion Picture Arts and Sciences, Margaret Herrick Library). On Hollywood's self-censorship system prior to 1934, see Lea Jacobs, "Industry Self-Regulation and the Problem of Textual Determination," *Velvet Light Trap* 23 (Spring 1989): 4–15.

83. René Clair used a similar technique in France (Bacher, *The Mobile Mise-en-Scène*, 43–44).

84. Rouben Mamoulian, quoted in "Entire Feature Length Talkie Filmed in Continuity with Mobile Camera," *Motion Picture News*, September 7, 1929, 908.

85. Ernst Lubitsch, quoted in Barney Hutchison, "Hollywood Still Leads . . . Says Ernst Lubitsch," *American Cinematographer* 13, no. 11 (March 1933): 8.

86. Victor Milner, "Let's Stop Abusing Camera Movement," *American Cinematographer* 16, no. 2 (February 1935): 46.

87. See the photographs in Ty, "Looking About on Location and Set," 5, and in Cecil B. DeMille, "How a Motion Picture Is Put Together," *International Photographer* 7, no. 4 (May 1935): 10.

88. Douglas Pye, "Movies and Point of View," *Movie* 36 (2000): 3.

89. On *The Song of Songs*, see "Photography of the Month," *American Cinematographer* 14, no. 1 (August 1933): 136; on *Rain*, see "Thru the Lens of the Critic," *American Cinematographer* 13, no. 7 (November 1932): 44; on *The Sign of the Cross*, see "Photography of the Month," *American Cinematographer* 13, no. 11 (March 1933): 17. The author of these reviews is anonymous, but I believe that Stull wrote them, given that the series was a continuation of his earlier series "Concerning Cinematography."

90. William Stull, "Concerning Cinematography: Critical Comments on Current Pictures," *American Cinematographer* 12, no. 10 (February 1932): 24.

91. "Daily Production Reports," RKO Production Files—*Prestige*, Special Collections, University of California–Los Angeles.

92. I borrow the term *visual intensity* from Bruce Block, *The Visual Story: Creating the Visual Structure of Film, TV, and Digital Media*, 2nd ed. (Burlington, MA: Focal Press, 2008), 11.

93. William Stull, "Concerning Cinematography: Critical Comments on Current Pictures," *American Cinematographer* 13, no. 2 (June 1932): 23.

94. Blanche Sewell, "Editing Is Easy When . . .," *American Cinematographer* 13, no. 9 (December 1932): 26.

95. A. Lindsley Lane, "The Camera's Omniscient Eye," *American Cinematographer* 16, no. 3 (March 1935): 95, 102.

96. The camera operator was Bob Pittack (Helen Boyce, "When Seen Through Feminine Eyes," *International Photographer* 4, no. 12 [January 1933]: 34).

97. In some shots, cinematographers Ray June and Robert Planck worked with technician Charles Cline to suspend the camera from the ceiling (Michael H. Price and George E. Turner, "Remembering How *The Bat Whispers*," *American Cinematographer* 67, no. 3 [March 1986]: 37).

98. Howard Hawks, in Bogdanovich, *Who the Devil Made It*, 262.

99. Edward Branigan, *Projecting a Camera: Language-Games in Film Theory* (New York: Routledge, 2006), 36–39.

100. Erik Charell, in "Erik Charell, Director of Fox 'Caravan,' Claims Something New in Camera Technique," *International Photographer* 6, no. 6 (July 1934): 21.

101. James Wong Howe, quoted in Milner, "Let's Stop Abusing Camera Movement," 47.

102. Miller, *Splinters from Hollywood Tripods*, 105.

103. L. M. Dieterich, "Camera Movement," *American Cinematographer* 13, no. 4 (August 1932): 14.

104. Summarizing this view, Jane Gaines writes: "This cinema's supreme achievement is that by using these narrative and imagistic economies it is able to convince viewers that it is one and the same with the physical world—thus its famous 'realistic effect'" ("Introduction: The Family Melodrama of Classical Narrative Cinema," in *Classical Narrative Cinema: The Paradigm Wars*, ed. Jane Gaines [Durham, NC: Duke University Press, 1992], 1).

105. Virgil Miller, "An Eternal Triangle," *International Photographer* 2, no. 5 (June 1930): 164.

106. Dieterich, "Camera Movement," 14.

107. Quoted in Harry Burdick, "David Abel Evolves New Technique," *American Cinematographer* 17, no. 7 (July 1936): 288.

108. Jerome Delamater, *Dance in the Hollywood Musical* (Ann Arbor, MI: UMI Research Press, 1981), 67–69.

109. H. C. Potter, quoted in Delamater, *Dance in the Hollywood Musical*, 69.

110. Sol Polito, quoted in "Riddle Me This," *American Cinematographer* 14, no. 3 (July 1933): 115.

111. Lane, "The Camera's Omniscient Eye," 95.

112. Lane, "The Camera's Omniscient Eye," 102.

113. Lane, "The Camera's Omniscient Eye," 95.

114. "Month's Photographic Honors Fall to Daniels on 'Marie Antoinette,'" *American Cinematographer* 19, no. 9 (September 1938): 395, including the quotation from William Daniels.

115. Robert B. Ray, *A Certain Tendency of the Hollywood Cinema, 1930–1980* (Princeton, NJ: Princeton University Press, 1985), 33.

116. Marilyn Fabe, *Closely Watched Films: An Introduction to the Art of Narrative Film Technique* (Berkeley: University of California Press, 2004), 72.

117. A. Lindsley Lane lists elimination and suggestion as functions of framing in "Rhythmic Flow—Mental and Visual," *American Cinematographer* 16, no. 4 (April 1935): 139. He mentions selection, synthesis, and emphasis in "Cinematographer Plays Leading Part in Group of Creative Minds," *American Cinematographer* 16, no. 2 (February 1935): 48.

118. Lane, "Rhythmic Flow," 139. See also Lane's argument that the film guides the spectator's imagination "so that there is indicated a fuller significance in the picture's philosophy than is specifically delineated" ("Cinematographer Plays Leading Part," 48). I take this passage as another allusion to offscreen space.

119. Lane, "Rhythmic Flow," 138–139.

120. David Bordwell, *Reinventing Hollywood: How 1940s Filmmakers Changed Movie Storytelling* (Chicago: University of Chicago Press, 2017), 508 n. 5. Bordwell's warning may seem surprising, given that many scholars take *The Classical Hollywood Cinema* by Bordwell, Staiger, and Thompson as the definitive statement of the view that Hollywood cinema favors omniscient narration. However, nuances to that book's argument are often overlooked. For instance, the claim that the classical narrative is a linear chain of causes and effects is qualified by the argument that a film is like a "winding corridor," telling the story in ways that are not entirely predictable (David Bordwell, "Classical Narration," in Bordwell, Staiger, and Thompson, *The Classical Hollywood Cinema*, 30, 37).

121. Pye, "Movies and Point of View," 9.

122. Photographs show Arthur Miller's crew working with a Raby on the set of *Wee Willie Winkie* (Core Collection—Production Files, Academy of Motion Picture Arts and Sciences, Margaret Herrick Library).

123. Meir Sternberg, "Narrativity: From Objectivist to Functional Paradigm," *Poetics Today* 31, no. 3 (Fall 2010): 637. For additional discussion of this passage, see Patrick Keating, "Narrative and the Moving Image," in *The Palgrave Handbook for the Philosophy of Film and Motion Pictures*, ed. Noël Carroll, Laura T. DiSumma-Knoop, and Shawn Loht (New York: Palgrave Macmillan, forthcoming).

124. Sternberg compares and contrasts his theory of the twinned sequences of narrativity with some related pairs, such as story/discourse and *fabula/syuzhet*. On the former, see Seymour Chatman, *Story and Discourse: Narrative Structure in Fiction and Film* (Ithaca, NY: Cornell University Press, 1978), 19–26. On the latter, see David Bordwell, *Poetics of Cinema* (New York: Routledge, 2008), 98.

125. While *Angels with Dirty Faces* was in the writing stage, Joseph Breen warned Jack Warner, "It is important to avoid any flavor of making a hero and sympathetic character of a man who is at the same time shown to be a criminal, a murderer and a kidnapper" (Joseph I. Breen to J. L. Warner, memo, January 19, 1938, in *Inside Warner Bros. [1935–1951]*, ed. Rudy Behlmer [New York: Viking, 1985], 66).

126. Fritz Lang, in Higham and Greenberg, *The Celluloid Muse*, 127.

127. Fritz Lang, in George Stevens Jr., *Conversations with the Great Moviemakers of Hollywood's Golden Age at the American Film Institute* (New York: Vintage Books, 2006), 67.

128. In a provocative analysis of *You Only Live Once*, George M. Wilson discusses this sequence and others as "rudimentary but classic illustrations of the potential unreliability of film" (*Narration in Light: Studies in Cinematic Point of View* [Baltimore: Johns Hopkins University Press, 1986], 18).

129. Fritz Lang, quoted in Lewis Jacobs, "Film Directors at Work," *Theatre Arts* 25, no. 3 (March 1941): 230.

130. Fritz Lang, quoted in Saverio Giovacchini, *Hollywood Modernism: Film and Politics in the Age of the New Deal* (Philadelphia: Temple University Press, 2001), 69. See also Giovacchini's excellent discussion of *Fury* as a whole.

131. Lane, "Rhythmic Flow," 138.

132. Lane, "Rhythmic Flow," 138.

133. Daniel Morgan has recently argued that Richard Wollheim's theory of the internal spectator (in *Painting as an Art* [Princeton, NJ: Princeton University Press, 1987], 102) can help us understand shots like my example from *The Barretts of Wimpole Street*: "Rather than increasing immersion in the world of the film, or securing identifications in it, this construction establishes positions from which we can imagine how that world is being experienced" ("Where Are We? Camera Movements and the Problem of Point of View," *New Review of Film and Television Studies* 14, no. 2 [2016]: 238). Significantly, Morgan's proposal need not rely on cameras at all. A film might ask us to imagine seeing the story world from many perspectives, not just the specific point in space that the camera occupied when filming the actors on the set. Nevertheless, in the right context a moving camera may prove to be a powerful way of constructing an internal spectator. These comments place Lane's participatory camera in another light—as an appeal to imagination, not to illusion. Prompted by this shot, we may choose to imagine seeing the events from within the storyworld, caught up in Henrietta's joy and taken aback by Mr. Barrett's intrusion. Such a choice may prompt other imaginings, such as imagining the scene from Elizabeth's viewpoint—not so much her viewpoint in space but her viewpoint in the situation, more mature than Henrietta but vicariously exulting in her sister's dancing. By prompting such imaginings, the film works to align our sympathies on the side of the siblings, against the cruel parent.

134. As Janet Bergstrom writes, "Kate finds herself back in the thankless servant role she has just escaped in the city: serving food to men who measure her up sexually and make jokes about her" ("Murnau in America: Chronicle of Lost Films," *Film History* 14, nos. 3–4 [2002]: 446).

135. "Adjustment for Dolly Head," *American Cinematographer* 16, no. 6 (June 1935): 246.

136. The dolly-head article cited in the previous note does not mention Shipham by name, but International Movie Database (IMDb) online indicates that he worked with Toland on several projects, including *Les Misérables, The Grapes of Wrath* (1940), and *The Best Years of Our Lives* (1943). The Toland–Shipham collaboration is noted as early as 1932 (Clara Sawdon, "When Seen Through Feminine Eyes," *International Photographer* 4, no. 4 [(May 1932]: 33).

137. Jean Mitry, *The Aesthetics and Psychology of the Cinema*, , trans. Christopher King (1997; reprint, Bloomington: Indiana University Press, 2000), 214, 215, 216.

138. See, for instance, the analysis of a still photograph to make a larger point about the "negation of the female gaze in the classical Hollywood cinema" in Mary Ann Doane, "Film and the Masquerade: Theorizing the Female Spectator," in *Femmes Fatales: Feminism, Film Theory, Psychoanalysis* (New York: Routledge, 1991), 28–31.

139. Laura Mulvey, "Visual Pleasure and Narrative Cinema," in *Narrative, Apparatus, Ideology: A Film Theory Reader*, ed. Philip Rosen (New York: Columbia University Press, 1986), 204.

140. Oster, "Device for Producing Variable Diffusion Effects," 52.

141. Lee Garmes, quoted in "Can't Combine Jobs of Director and Cinematographer, Says Garmes," *American Cinematographer* 20, no. 4 (April 1939): 158.

142. John Arnold, "M-G-M's New Camera Boom," *Journal of the Society of Motion Picture Engineers* 37, no. 3 (September 1941): 278.

3. Dynamism, Seriality, and Convergence

1. William Stull, "Evolution of Cinema Tripods for Studio Use," *American Cinematographer* 13, no. 12 (April 1933): 7.
2. Miriam Bratu Hansen, "The Mass Production of the Senses: Classical Cinema as Vernacular Modernism," in *Reinventing Film Studies*, ed. Christine Gledhill and Linda Williams (London: Arnold, 2000), 341.
3. Miriam Bratu Hansen, "Vernacular Modernism: Tracking Cinema on a Global Scale," in *World Cinemas, Transnational Perspectives*, ed. Natasa Ďurovičová and Kathleen A. Newman (New York: Routledge, 2010), 301.
4. Daniel Morgan, " 'Play with Danger': Vernacular Modernism and the Problem of Criticism," *New German Critique* 122, no. 2 (Summer 2014): 69.
5. Charlie Keil, "To Here from Modernity: Style, Historiography, and Transitional Cinema," in *American Cinema's Transitional Era: Audiences, Institutions, Practices*, ed. Charlie Keil and Shelley Stamp (Berkeley: University of California Press, 2004), 52–53.
6. The uncredited Fitzgerald is listed as the operator in George Blaisdell, "Looking in on Just a Few New Ones," *International Photographer* 4, no. 1 (February 1932): 30.
7. The continuity script does not mention camera movement, instead recommending more editing than appears in the finished film ("Continuity Script," *Emma*, October 17, 1931, Turner/M-G-M Scripts, Academy of Motion Picture Arts and Sciences, Margaret Herrick Library, Beverly Hills, CA).
8. Rick Jewell makes this point eloquently in "How Howard Hawks Brought Baby Up," in *Howard Hawks: American Artist*, ed. Jim Hillier and Peter Wollen (London: British Film Institute, 1996), 175–184.
9. My discussion of themes and motifs is similar to David Bordwell's discussion of the cinematic schema, defined as "a pattern with parts that can be creatively varied" (*Reinventing Hollywood: How 1940s Filmmakers Changed Movie Storytelling* [Chicago: University of Chicago Press, 2017], 41). However, as I read it, the schema is more open-ended than my theme–motif pairing. A schema is a "hollow form" (42), capable of being slotted into a wide range of situations. The repetitions I have in mind are more specific: not just repeated shots and not just repeated situations but recognizably similar shots in recognizably similar situations.
10. Kristen Whissel, *Picturing American Modernity: Traffic, Technology, and the Silent Cinema* (Durham, NC: Duke University Press, 2008), 1, 5.
11. I analyze examples of the crossing-the-street shot and the seriality shot in my video essay "Motifs of Movement and Modernity," *Movie: A Journal of Film Criticism* 7 (May 2017), http://www2.warwick.ac.uk/fac/arts/film/movie/.
12. Keil, "To Here from Modernity," 60.
13. Slavko Vorkapich, "Motion and the Art of Cinematography," *American Cinematographer* 7, no. 8 (November 1926): 19.
14. Vorkapich, "Motion and the Art of Cinematography," 11.
15. Vorkapich, "Motion and the Art of Cinematography," 19.
16. Slavko Vorkapich, "Cinematics: Some Principles Underlying Effective Cinematography," in *The Cinematographic Annual*, vol. 1, ed. Hal Hall (Los Angeles: American Society of Cinematographers, 1930), 32.

17. Vorkapich designed montages for dozens of films, and his ideas retained currency for quite some time: as late as 1945, a profile in *American Cinematographer* was quoting Vorkapich's theory approvingly (Ezra Goodman, "Movement in Movies," *American Cinematographer* 26, no. 6 [June 1945]: 206). Don Siegel, who created montages at Warner Bros., claimed that he looked to Vorkapich's work at M-G-M for inspiration (in Peter Bogdanovich, *Who the Devil Made It: Conversations with Legendary Film Directors* [New York: Knopf, 1997], 724–725). The RKO effects master Linwood Dunn also named Vorkapich as an influence (interviewed in Scott Eyman, *Five American Cinematographers* [Metuchen, NJ: Scarecrow Press, 1987], 112).

18. Harry Perry, "Cinematic Rhythm in Film-Editing," *American Cinematographer* 15, no. 8 (December 1934): 345, 352.

19. Milestone cited Murnau as an inspiration in his essay "All Quiet on the Western Front?," unpublished manuscript, Lewis Milestone Papers, Academy of Motion Picture Arts and Sciences, Margaret Herrick Library.

20. Photographs confirm that the crew used the Broadway Boom to photograph the film's trench sequences (George J. Mitchell, "Making *All Quiet on the Western Front*," *American Cinematographer* 66, no. 9 [September 1985]: 39).

21. Tom Gunning, "Modernity and Cinema: A Culture of Shocks and Flows," in *Cinema and Modernity*, ed. Murray Pomerance (New Brunswick, NJ: Rutgers University Press, 2006), 312. See also Ben Singer, "The Ambimodernity of Early Cinema: Problems and Paradoxes in the Film-and-Modernity Discourse," in *Film 1900: Technology, Perception, Culture*, ed. Annemone Ligensa and Klaus Kreimeier (New Barnet, UK: John Libbey, 2009), 38.

22. René Clair, "Talkie Versus Talkie" (1929), in *French Film Theory and Criticism*, vol. 2: *1929–1939*, ed. Richard Abel (Princeton, NJ: Princeton University Press, 1988), 39.

23. "Maxi.," "*À nous la liberté*," *Variety*, January 5, 1932, 23.

24. Charles Beard and Mary Beard, *The Rise of American Civilization: The Industrial Era* (New York: Macmillan, 1927), 713–714.

25. Frances Marion, *How to Write and Sell Film Stories* (1937; reprint, New York: Garland, 1978), 77.

26. Lenore Coffee, "Mirage" ["Possessed"], shooting script, n.d., Clarence Brown Collection, Special Collections, University of Tennessee–Knoxville.

27. Nikil Saval, *Cubed: A Secret History of the Workplace* (New York: Doubleday, 2014), 44.

28. King Vidor, "The March of Life: Treatment," October 21, 1926, Turner/M-G-M Scripts, Academy of Motion Picture Arts and Sciences, Margaret Herrick Library.

29. Saval, *Cubed*, 77–78.

30. Gwendolyn Audrey Foster, "Performing Modernity and Gender in the 1930s," in *Cinema and Modernity*, ed. Pomerance, 96.

31. William Leach, *Land of Desire: Merchants, Power, and the Rise of a New American Culture* (New York: Vintage Books, 1993), 273, 372.

32. George Cukor, in Bogdanovich, *Who the Devil Made It*, 450.

33. "Corkscrew Camera Effect," *International Photographer* 6, no. 7 (August 1934): 28.

34. Siegfried Kracauer, "The Mass Ornament" (1927), in *The Mass Ornament: Weimar Essays*, ed. and trans. Thomas Y. Levin (Cambridge, MA: Harvard University Press, 1995), 79.

35. Faith Baldwin, *Skyscraper* (1931; reprint, New York: Feminist Press, 2003), 5, 6.

36. David Bordwell, *Poetics of Cinema* (New York: Routledge, 2008), 191. For a closer look at *Grand Hotel* and its immediate successors, see Bordwell's blog entry "1932: M-G-M

Invents the Future (Part 2)," David Bordwell's Website on Cinema, posted March 22, 2015, http://www.davidbordwell.net/blog/2015/03/22/1932-mgm-invents-the-future-part-2/.

37. Edgar Selwyn, in "Story Conference Notes," February 25, 1932, *Skyscraper Souls*, Turner/M-G-M Scripts.

38. Bernard Hyman, in "Story Conference Notes," February 25, 1932, *Skyscraper Souls*.

39. Merrill Schleier, *Skyscraper Cinema: Architecture and Gender in American Film* (Minneapolis: University of Minnesota Press, 2009), 66.

40. Whissel, *Picturing American Modernity*, 3.

41. The film *Grand Hotel* was based on a novel adapted into a play, allowing filmmakers to adapt the formula before the screen version came out.

42. For *Transatlantic*'s credits, see George Blaisdell, "Looking in on Just a Few New Ones," *International Photographer* 3, no. 8 (September 1931): 31

43. In a classic passage, Siegfried Kracauer associates "haphazard contingencies" with the street, broadly defined to included "railway stations, dance and assembly halls, bars, hotel lobbies, airports, etc." (*Theory of the Film: The Redemption of Physical Reality* [Princeton, NJ: Princeton University Press, 1997], 62).

44. Jules Furthman, "Final Screenplay," *Morocco*, July 12, 1930, Paramount Pictures Scripts, Academy of Motion Picture Arts and Sciences, Margaret Herrick Library.

45. Baron Basil Wrangell, "Cutting to Balance Atmosphere and Action," *American Cinematographer* 18, no. 1 (January 1937): 27.

46. Wrangell, "Cutting to Balance Atmosphere and Action," 26.

47. For production details and a photograph of the trolley, see George Blaisdell, "James Wong Howe Wins Honors for His Photography on 'Algiers,'" *American Cinematographer* 19, no. 8 (August 1938): 312–315.

48. Working with camera operator Michael Joyce, Sol Polito photographed the films *Union Depot*, *42nd Street*, and *Gold Diggers of 1933* as well as the musical numbers in Busby Berkeley's *Footlight Parade*. See the credits listed in *International Photographer* 4, no. 3 (April 1932): 30; 4, no. 9 (October 1932): 25; 5, no. 2 (March 1933): 21; and 5, no. 6 (July 1933): 24.

49. Compare this example to a shot in *The Great Lie* (1941), where a crane makes us aware that two contiguous spaces are in fact segregated.

50. Louis Wirth, "Urbanism as a Way of Life" (1938), in *On Cities and Social Life: Selected Papers*, ed. Albert J. Reiss Jr. (Chicago: University of Chicago Press, 1964), 79, 69.

51. Lewis Mumford, "Landscape and Townscape" (1960–1961), in *The Urban Prospect* (New York: Harcourt, Brace and World, 1968), 88.

52. Alison Isenberg, *Downtown America: A History of the Place and the People Who Made It* (Chicago: University of Chicago Press, 2004), 5.

53. Mervyn LeRoy, as told by Dick Kleiner, *Take One* (New York: Hawthorn Books, 1974), 21.

54. Jacob Isak Nielsen, "En scenes anatomi: *Sunnyside Up*," 16:9 43 (September 2011), http://www.16-9.dk/2011-09/side07_anatomi.htm. Director David Butler had acted in Borzage's film *7th Heaven* (1927).

55. Larry R. Ford, *Cities and Buildings: Skyscrapers, Skid Rows, and Suburbs* (Baltimore: Johns Hopkins University Press, 1994), 206.

56. Donald Crafton argues that *Sunnyside Up*'s neighborhood sequence became an "early-sound cliché" because it provided the opportunity for an exciting "symphony" of urban sounds (*The Talkies: American Cinema's Transition to Sound, 1926–1931* [Berkeley: University of California Press, 1997], 338).

57. Elmer Rice, "The Playwright as Director," *Theatre Arts Monthly* 13, no. 5 (May 1929): 355.
58. Elmer Rice, *Three Plays* (New York: Hill and Wang, 1993), 70, 85.
59. King Vidor, *A Tree Is a Tree: An Autobiography* (1953; reprint, Hollywood, CA: Samuel French, 1981), 203.
60. Ira Katznelson, *Fear Itself: The New Deal and the Origins of Our Time* (New York: Liveright, 2013), 17–18.
61. On the conflicting ideals of the 1930s, see Warren Susman, "The Culture of the Thirties," in *Culture as History: The Transformation of American Society in the Twentieth Century* (Washington, DC: Smithsonian Institution Press, 2003), 150–183, and Lawrence Levine, "American Culture and the Great Depression," in *The Unpredictable Past: Explorations in American Cultural History* (New York: Oxford University Press, 1993), 206–230.
62. As on *Emma*, Brown worked with his regular team consisting of cinematographer Oliver Marsh and operator Eddie Fitzgerald ("Brulatour Bulletin," *International Photographer* 5, no. 2 [March 1933]: 20).
63. *Sweepings* is more complex, juxtaposing two competing philosophies of capitalism. Barrymore's character, Daniel, ascends to the upper class, but then he reasserts distinctions of class and ethnicity, passing his fortune along to his heirs and refusing to allow his hard-working assistant Abe (Gregory Ratoff) to buy into the company. In some scenes, Abe comes across as an anti-Semitic stereotype—for instance, when he takes over Daniel's business without his knowledge. In the end, however, the film shows sympathy for Abe's position, arguing that capitalism works best as an unsentimental meritocracy in which the advantages of inheritance fall to the ethic of hard work.
64. Morris Dickstein, *Dancing in the Dark: A Cultural History of the Great Depression* (New York: Norton, 2009), 217, 219.
65. Brown's characterization of himself as a "red hot conservative" is discussed in Gwenda Young, "Clarence Brown: From Knoxville to Hollywood and Back," *Journal of East Tennessee History* 73 (2002): 64. The other comments can be found in interview transcripts in the Clarence Brown Collection.
66. Saverio Giovacchini, *Hollywood Modernism: Film and Politics in the Age of the New Deal* (Philadelphia: Temple University Press, 2001), 5, 47.
67. Gregg Toland, quoted in Lester Koenig, "Gregg Toland, Film-Maker," *The Screen Writer* 3, no. 7 (December 1947): 29. Toland claimed, incorrectly, that this shot is the only example of camera movement in the entire film.
68. Otis Ferguson, *The Film Criticism of Otis Ferguson*, ed. Robert Wilson (Philadelphia: Temple University Press, 1971), 283.
69. For examples of such rhythmic repetitions, see John Steinbeck, *The Grapes of Wrath* (1939; reprint, New York: Penguin, 2006), 65, 113.
70. See Robert Lord to Irene Lee, memo, December 23, 1941, in *Inside Warner Bros. (1935–1951)*, ed. Rudy Behlmer (New York: Viking, 1985), 196.
71. M. Todd Barnett, *One World, Big Screen: Hollywood, the Allies, and World War II* (Chapel Hill: University of North Carolina Press, 2012), 107–109.
72. Ronald Takaki, *Double Victory: A Multicultural History of America in World War II* (New York: Back Bay Books, 2000), 20–21.
73. Clayton R. Koppes and Gregory D. Black, *Hollywood Goes to War: How Politics, Profits, and Propaganda Shaped World War II Movies* (Berkeley: University of California Press, 1990), 69.

74. Koppes and Black, *Hollywood Goes to War*, 67.

75. Koppes and Black, *Hollywood Goes to War*, 179.

76. Jeanine Basinger, *The World War II Combat Film: Anatomy of a Genre* (Middletown, CT: Wesleyan University Press, 2003), 46.

77. I offer a different analysis of this same scene in Patrick Keating, *Hollywood Lighting from the Silent Era to Film Noir* (New York: Columbia University Press, 2010), 238–240.

78. Elizabeth Reich, *Militant Visions: Black Soldiers, Internationalism, and the Transformation of American Cinema* (New Brunswick, NJ: Rutgers University Press, 2016), 36.

79. Vincent Brook, *Driven to Darkness: Jewish Émigré Directors and the Rise of Film Noir* (New Brunswick, NJ: Rutgers University Press, 2009), 206–207.

80. Helen Deutsch, "The Seventh Cross—Screenplay," October 22, 1943, Fred Zinnemann Papers, Academy of Motion Picture Arts and Sciences, Margaret Herrick Library. The script is marked "F.Z."

81. Fred Zinnemann to Pandro Berman, July 28, 1943, "The Seventh Cross—Screenplay," Fred Zinnemann Papers.

82. For more on the film's unusual narrator, see Bordwell, *Reinventing Hollywood*, 253–254.

83. William Saroyan, *The Human Comedy* (1943; reprint, New York: Dell, 1971), 123.

84. Takaki, *Double Victory*, 134.

85. Saroyan, *The Human Comedy*, 179.

86. See Howard Estabrook, "Complete OK Script," *The Human Comedy*, August 28, 1942, Turner/M-G-M Scripts.

87. Stephen Longstreet, "Setting Back the Clock," *The Screen Writer* 13 (August 1945): 12; James Agee, review of *The Clock*, in *Agee on Film: Criticism and Comment on the Movies* (New York: Modern Library, 2000), 345, a review originally published in 1945.

88. Paul Gallico and Pauline Gallico, "Story Outline," *The Clock*, Turner/M-G-M Scripts.

89. Robert Nathan and Joseph Schrank, "Complete Composite Script," *The Clock*, Turner/M-G-M Scripts.

4. Constructing Scenes with the Camera

1. For a definitive account of the Hollywood mode of production, with emphasis on the division of labor, see Janet Staiger, "The Producer–Unit System: Management by Specialization After 1931," in David Bordwell, Janet Staiger, and Kristin Thompson, *The Classical Hollywood Cinema: Film Style and Mode of Production to 1960* (New York: Columbia University Press, 1985), 320–329.

2. For a philosophical defense of the collaborative approach, see Berys Gaut, *A Philosophy of Cinematic Art* (New York: Cambridge University Press, 2010), 128–133. For a more historical defense, see Christopher Beach, *A Hidden History of Film Style: Cinematographers, Directors, and the Collaborative Process* (Berkeley: University of California Press, 2015), 3–4.

3. Frances Marion, *How to Write and Sell Film Stories* (1937; reprint, New York: Garland, 1978), 219.

4. Casey Robinson, *Now, Voyager*, revised final screenplay, ed. Jean Thomas Allen (Madison: University of Wisconsin Press, 1984), 172.

5. Irving Rapper, in Charles Higham and Joel Greenberg, *The Celluloid Muse: Hollywood Directors Speak* (London: Angus and Robertson, 1969), 200.

6. Fritz Lang, in Peter Bogdanovich, *Who the Devil Made It: Conversations with Legendary Film Directors* (New York: Knopf, 1997), 197.

7. Gregg Toland, quoted in Lester Koenig, "Gregg Toland, Film-Maker," *The Screen Writer* 3, no. 7 (December 1947): 32.

8. Lutz Bacher, *Max Ophuls in the Hollywood Studios* (New Brunswick, NJ: Rutgers University Press, 1996), 10–11.

9. Daily production reports for *The Devil and Daniel Webster* are in the RKO Production Files, Special Collections, University of California–Los Angeles; for *Passage to Marseille* in the Warner Bros. Archives, University of Southern California–Los Angeles; for *Sleep, My Love*, in the Mary Pickford Papers, Academy of Motion Picture Arts and Sciences, Margaret Herrick Library, Beverly Hills, CA. Some daily production reports list script scenes but not setups; others list setups but not script scenes. By the 1940s, it was fairly common for reports to list both.

10. Daily production reports for *The Magnificent Ambersons*, Orson Welles Papers, Lilly Library, Indiana University–Bloomington.

11. Richard B. Jewell, *RKO Radio Pictures: A Titan Is Born* (Berkeley: University of California Press, 2012), 134.

12. Joseph H. Lewis, in Bogdanovich, *Who the Devil Made It*, 654.

13. Lewis once said, "I decided every single set-up in every single film I ever made" (in *Film Noir Reader 3: Interviews with Filmmakers of the Classic Noir Period*, ed. Robert Porfirio, Alain Silver, and James Ursini [New York: Limelight Editions, 2002], 83).

14. Herb Lightman, "The Camera and Production Value," *American Cinematographer* 27, no. 9 (September 1946): 312.

15. Budget accounts for *Torrid Zone* are in the Warner Bros. Archive; for *The More the Merrier* in the George Stevens Papers, Academy of Motion Picture Arts and Sciences, Margaret Herrick Library; for *Double Indemnity* in the Paramount Pictures Production Records, Academy of Motion Picture Arts and Sciences, Margaret Herrick Library. In some cases, I have consulted preliminary budgets, estimated before shooting; in others, I have consulted final budgets, calculated after completion.

16. David Bordwell, "William Cameron Menzies: One Forceful, Impressive Idea," blog entry, David Bordwell's Website on Cinema, posted March 2010, http://www.davidbordwell.net/essays/menzies.php.

17. James Wong Howe, "Visual Suggestion Can Enhance 'Rationed' Sets," *American Cinematographer* 23, no. 6 (June 1942): 246. See also "Camera Rehearsals," *International Photographer* 12, no. 4 (May 1940): 17.

18. Ezra Goodman, "Production Designing," *American Cinematographer* 26, no. 3 (March 1945): 83.

19. Victor Milner, "Creating Moods with Light," *American Cinematographer* 16, no. 1 (January 1935): 14.

20. Victor Milner, "Preparation Pays a Profit," *American Cinematographer* 24, no. 6 (June 1943): 211.

21. George Cukor, in Bernard Kantor, Irwin Blacker, and Anne Kramer, *Directors at Work: Interviews with American Film-Makers* (New York: Funk and Wagnalls, 1970), 96.

22. John Huston, in *Interviews with Film Directors*, ed. Andrew Sarris (New York: Avon Books, 1967), 268.

23. Clarence Brown, interview transcript, n.d., Clarence Brown Collection, Special Collections, University of Tennessee–Knoxville. There is no date on the interview, but it certainly occurred after Brown's retirement in 1952.

24. John Ford, in *Interviews with Film Directors*, ed. Sarris, 198.

25. Max Ophuls, in *Interviews with Film Directors*, ed. Sarris, 360.

26. Frank Capra, quoted in James R. Silke and Bruce Henstell, "Frank Capra: 'One Man—One Film,'" in *Frank Capra Interviews*, ed. Leland Poague (Jackson: University Press of Mississippi, 2004), 81, 79, 89.

27. King Vidor, *A Tree Is a Tree: An Autobiography* (1953; reprint, Hollywood, CA: Samuel French, 1981), 278.

28. King Vidor, interview in George Stevens Jr., *Conversations with the Great Moviemakers of Hollywood's Golden Age at the American Film Institute* (New York: Vintage Books, 2006), 50.

29. William Clothier, interview in Scott Eyman, *Five American Cinematographers* (Metuchen, NJ: Scarecrow Press, 1987), 126.

30. Karl Struss, quoted in Susan Harvith and John Harvith, *Karl Struss: Man with a Camera* (Bloomsfield Hills, MI: Cranbrook Academy of Art, 1976), 17.

31. Joseph Ruttenberg, interview in Eyman, *Five American Cinematographers*, 41.

32. Hal Mohr, in Leonard Maltin, *The Art of the Cinematographer: A Survey and Interviews with Five Masters* (New York: Dover, 1978), 91.

33. Gregg Toland, "The Motion Picture Cameraman," *Theatre Arts* 25, no. 9 (September 1941): 649.

34. Hal Hall lists several of LaShelle's operating credits in "Aces of the Camera," *American Cinematographer* 26, no. 5 (May 1945): 170.

35. As indicated in credits provided on the pages for *The Maltese Falcon* at the AFI Catalog and IMDb websites. Both sources list E. F. Dexter as the "grip," which may mean "dolly grip."

36. Hal Wallis to Raoul Walsh, memo, November 8, 1940, in *Inside Warner Bros. (1935–1951)*, ed. Rudy Behlmer (New York: Viking, 1985), 130. The picture in question is *The Strawberry Blonde* (1941).

37. Jack L. Warner to Michael Curtiz, memo, July 13, 1938, in *Inside Warner Bros.*, ed. Behlmer, 69. The picture in question is *Four Daughters* (1938).

38. See the quotation from Robert Florey in Tino Balio, *Grand Design: Hollywood as a Modern Business Enterprise, 1930–1939* (Berkeley: University of California Press, 1995), 337.

39. Margaret Booth, "The Cutter," in *Behind the Screen*, ed. Stephen Watts (London: Arthur Barker, 1938), 148–149.

40. I. J. Wilkinson and W. H. Hamilton, "Motion Picture Editing," *Journal of the Society of Motion Picture Engineers* 36, no. 1 (January 1941): 103.

41. John Boyle, "Black and White Cinematography," *Journal of the Society of Motion Picture Engineers* 39, no. 2 (August 1942): 89.

42. Photographs show LaShelle working with a Raby on *Laura* (1944) (Core Collection—Production Files, Academy of Motion Picture Arts and Sciences, Margaret Herrick Library) and Miller working with a Raby on *Anna and the King of Siam* (1946) (American Society of Cinematographers—Member Files: Arthur Miller, Academy of Motion Picture Arts and Sciences, Margaret Herrick Library).

43. See the advertisement for Houston-Fearless's various offerings in *American Cinematographer* 34, no. 6 (June 1953): 2.

44. William Stull, "M-G-M Builds Unique Camera Boom," *American Cinematographer* 20, no. 12 (December 1939): 572. Two years later the same article was reprinted with only minor revisions but credited to John Arnold. See John Arnold, "M-G-M's New Camera Boom," *Journal of the Society of Motion Picture Engineers* 37, no. 3 (September 1941): 278–282.

45. Arthur Rowan, "Technicolor Cameras Now Ride the RO Crane," *American Cinematographer* 33, no. 2 (February 1952): 65. Lutz Bacher proposes an alternative account: the abbreviation RO stood for "Reverse Oscillator" (*The Mobile Mise-en-Scène: A Critical Analysis of the Theory and Practice of Long-Take Camera Movement in the Narrative Film* [New York: Arno Press, 1978], 50).

46. E. A. Hunter, "Speed Boom," *American Cinematographer* 29, no. 7 (July 1948): 234; Rowan, "Technicolor Cameras Now Ride the RO Crane," 83.

47. Joseph Ruttenberg, "Assignment Overseas," *American Cinematographer* 31, no. 10 (October 1950): 353.

48. Frederick Foster, "The Development of Follow-Focus in Cinematography," *American Cinematographer* 33, no. 12 (December 1952): 523, 552.

49. Gregg Toland, "Practical Gadgets Expedite Camera Work," *American Cinematographer* 20, no. 5 (May 1939): 218.

50. John McCullough, "Servo Mechanism for Remote Control of Mitchell BNC Lens and Finder," *American Cinematographer* 33, no. 1 (January 1953): 18.

51. Gregg Toland, "Realism for 'Citizen Kane,'" *American Cinematographer* 22, no. 2 (February 1941): 80. See also Patrick Ogle, "Technological and Aesthetic Influences on the Development of Deep-Focus Cinematography in the United States," in *Movies and Methods*, vol. 2, ed. Bill Nichols (Berkeley: University of California Press, 1985), 58–83.

52. Maurice Pivar, "Film Editing," *Journal of the Society of Motion Picture Engineers* 29, no. 4 (October 1937): 368.

53. John Huston, in *Interviews with Film Directors*, ed. Sarris, 272. For a similar account of Huston's approach, see Oswald Morris and Geoffrey Bull, *Huston, We Have a Problem* (Lanham, MD: Scarecrow Press, 2006), 96.

54. Rouben Mamoulian, in Higham and Greenberg, *The Celluloid Muse*, 141.

55. James Wong Howe argued that directors who preferred "protection shooting," such as Wyler and Stevens, were "not quite so secure" as directors who "cut with the camera," such as Hawks (in Stevens, *Conversations with the Great Moviemakers*, 134).

56. Timothy Barnard, in an extensive footnote to André Bazin, "William Wyler, the Jansenist of Mise-en-Scène," in *What Is Cinema?* trans. Timothy Barnard (Montreal: Caboose Books, 2009), 265–266.

57. Melvin LeRoy, as told to Alyce Canfield, *It Takes More Than Talent* (New York: Knopf, 1953), 85.

58. Edward Bernds, quoted in Joseph McBride, *Frank Capra: The Catastrophe of Success* (Jackson: University Press of Mississippi, 2011), 347. Bernds worked as a sound engineer on several Capra films in the 1930s.

59. Capra explains the method in Stevens, *Conversations with the Great Moviemakers*, 84–85.

60. Capra discusses this scene in Silke and Henstell, "Frank Capra," 83. Cinematographer Lee Garmes discusses *The Paradine Case* in Lee Garmes, "Cinematography: Film, Tape, and Honesty," *Journal of the University Film Association* 26, no. 4 (1974): 60.

61. Frank Capra, quoted in Silke and Henstell, "Frank Capra," 79.

62. Daily production reports for *Gunga Din*, RKO Production Files.

63. I am setting aside setup I, which appears at the end of the scene, after Connie stands up. As for setup A, it is possible that this angle was part of the scene's coverage, but it is possible that it was a brief shot intended only for use at the start of the scene. See table 4.1.

64. The cinematographer for *Johnny Eager* was the reliable M-G-M pro Harold Rosson. On its page for *Johnny Eager*, IMDb lists Harkness Smith as the operator.

65. On piecemeal *découpage*, see David Bordwell, *Poetics of Cinema* (New York: Routledge, 2008), 359; on "segment shooting," see David Bordwell, *Planet Hong Kong: Popular Cinema and the Art of Entertainment* (Cambridge, MA: Harvard University Press, 2000), 129.

66. An article on UFA in 1932 noted that German directors employed "far fewer 'protection shots' than is customary here" (Robert Low, "UFA," *American Cinematographer* 13, no. 5 [September 1932]: 23).

67. Ernst Lubitsch, quoted in William Stull, "Concerning Cinematography," *American Cinematographer* 10, no. 8 (November 1929): 5.

68. Mollie Merrick, "25 Years of the 'Lubitsch Touch' in Hollywood," *American Cinematographer* 28, no. 7 (July 1947): 239.

69. William Paul, *Ernst Lubitsch's American Comedy* (New York: Columbia University Press, 1983), 32.

70. Vincent Brook, *Driven to Darkness: Jewish Émigré Directors and the Rise of Film Noir* (New Brunswick, NJ: Rutgers University Press, 2009), 109, 156, 170.

71. Howard Hawks, in *Interviews with Film Directors*, ed. Sarris, 233–234.

72. Robert Parrish, quoted in Peter Bogdanovich, *John Ford* (Berkeley: University of California Press, 1967), 9.

73. Hal Wallis to Michael Curtiz, memo, April 17, 1936, in *Inside Warner Bros.*, ed. Behlmer, 31.

74. See, for instance, the account of Thalberg's contributions to *Grand Hotel* (1932) in Thomas Schatz, *The Genius of the System: Hollywood Filmmaking in the Studio Era* (New York: Holt, 1988), 118–119.

75. Lee Garmes, *Lee Garmes: An American Film Institute Seminar on His Work* (Glen Rock, NJ: Microfilming Corporation of America, 1977), 87.

76. Jackson Rose, "Wartime Economies by 'Pre-photographing' Scripts," *American Cinematographer* 23, no. 3 (March 1942): 110.

77. Robert Carringer, *The Making of "Citizen Kane,"* rev. ed. (Berkeley: University of California Press, 1996), 110.

78. Orson Welles and Peter Bogdanovich, *This Is Orson Welles*, ed. Jonathan Rosenbaum (New York: Da Capo, 1998), 255.

79. Alfred Hitchcock, "Direction" (1937), in *Hitchcock on Hitchcock: Selected Writings and Interviews*, ed. Sidney Gottlieb (Berkeley: University of California Press, 1997), 253.

80. Hitchcock, "Direction," 254.

81. "Alfred Hitchcock: England's Best Director Starts Work in Hollywood," *LIFE*, June 19, 1939, 66.

82. Lewis Jacobs, "Film Directors at Work," *Theatre Arts* 25, no. 1 (January 1941): 42.

83. Jacobs, "Film Directors at Work" (January 1941), 41.

84. Anonymous editor, quoted in Herb Lightman, "Cameraman's Director," *American Cinematographer* 28, no. 4 (April 1947): 125.

85. Hitchcock attributed these words to David O. Selznick in his conversation with Peter Bogdanovich in Bogdanovich, *Who the Devil Made It*, 516. See also Hitchcock's account in François Truffaut, *Hitchcock*, rev. ed. (New York: Touchstone, 1985), 194–195.

86. Bill Krohn, *Hitchcock at Work* (London: Phaidon Press, 2000), 10.

87. Krohn, *Hitchcock at Work*, 144.

88. For *Casablanca*, Arthur Edeson was the cinematographer. On its page for the film, IMDb lists Michael Joyce as the operator and Wally Meinardus as the assistant.

89. Joseph Walker and Juanita Walker, *The Light on Her Face* (Los Angeles: ASC Press, 1984), 250.

90. David O. Selznick to Jock Whitney and John Wharton, memo, September 1, 1937, and to Alfred Hitchcock, memo, September 19, 1939, in *Memo from David O. Selznick*, ed. Rudy Behlmer (New York: Modern Library, 2000), 167, 306.

91. Barry Salt, "Up and Down and Back and Forth," in *Moving Into Pictures* (London: Starword, 2006), 286.

92. Universal marketed *Magnificent Obsession* by noting that director John Stahl had "the most fluid camera in Hollywood" ("Stahl Regards 'Magnificent Obsession' as a Formula for Living," *Universal Weekly* 37, no. 20 [December 14, 1935]: 20).

93. As Robert Carringer explains, Toland worked with several longtime crew members on *Citizen Kane*: operator Bert Shipham (sometimes spelled "Shipman"), assistant cameraman Eddie Garvin, and grip Ralph Hoge (*The Making of "Citizen Kane,"* 69).

94. Toland, "Realism for 'Citizen Kane,'" 54.

95. George Blaisdell, "*Citizen Kane*'s New Technique," *Movie Makers* 16, no. 3 (March 1941): 127, giving a quote from Welles.

96. Alexander Kahle, "Welles and the Cameraman," *International Photographer* 12, no. 2 (January 1941): 7.

97. André Bazin, *Orson Welles: A Critical View*, trans. Jonathan Rosenbaum (Los Angeles: Acrobat Books, 1991), 76–77. Rosenbaum points out in a note that the phrase "breakdown into shots" is his translation of Bazin's term *découpage*. As already noted, this term bears some affinities with *cutting in the camera*, though they are not identical.

98. William Wyler, "No Magic Wand," *The Screen Writer* 2, no. 9 (February 1947): 10.

99. Joseph H. Lewis, in Bogdanovich, *Who the Devil Made It*, 657.

100. Lewis, in Bogdanovich, *Who the Devil Made It*, 657.

101. Welles and Bogdanovich, *This Is Orson Welles*, 201.

102. See the detailed account in Bacher, *The Mobile Mise-en-Scène*, 115–188.

103. Bacher, *The Mobile Mise-en-Scène*, 112. See also Bacher, *Max Ophuls in the Hollywood Studios*, 81–82.

104. V. F. Perkins, *The Magnificent Ambersons* (London: British Film Institute, 1999), 61.

105. Otis Ferguson, "The Camera Way Is the Hard Way" (1941), in *The Film Criticism of Otis Ferguson*, ed. Robert Wilson (Philadelphia: Temple University Press, 1971), 13.

106. Garson Kanin, "I Direct," *Theatre Arts* 25, no. 9 (September 1941): 643.

107. Kanin was one of Ferguson's favorite directors (David Bordwell, *The Rhapsodes: How 1940s Critics Changed American Film Culture* [Chicago: University of Chicago Press, 2016], 51).

108. Kanin, "I Direct," 641–642.

109. In this brief passage, Kanin looks ahead to Noël Carroll's more fully developed argument that the director's primary job is directing the audience's attention. Carroll explains how filmmakers employ variable framing (including both cutting and camera movement) to perform functions of bracketing (keeping important details onscreen), indexing (pointing toward important details), and scaling (making important details larger) (*The Philosophy of Motion Pictures* [Malden, MA: Blackwell, 2008], 124–133).

110. Garson Kanin, quoted in Lewis Jacobs, "Film Directors at Work," *Theatre Arts* 25, no. 3 (March 1941): 225.

111. Herb Lightman, "The Fluid Camera," *American Cinematographer* 27, no. 3 (March 1946): 103. Lightman repeated these ideas in various articles over the years, sometimes verbatim, as in "'Fluid' Camera Gives Dramatic Emphasis to Cinematography," *American Cinematographer* 34, no. 3 (February 1953): 63, 76–77.

112. Lightman, "The Fluid Camera," 102–103.
113. Lightman, "The Fluid Camera," 82.
114. Lightman, "The Fluid Camera," 82.
115. Lightman, "Cameraman's Director," 151.
116. Lightman, "The Fluid Camera," 103.
117. Otto Preminger, in Bogdanovich, *Who the Devil Made It*, 634.
118. Irving Pichel, "Seeing with the Camera," *Hollywood Quarterly* 1, no. 2 (January 1946): 143, 140.
119. Pichel, "Seeing with the Camera," 143, 141, 144.
120. Pichel, "Seeing with the Camera," 142.
121. Kanin, "I Direct," 642; Lightman, "The Fluid Camera," 82; Joseph LaShelle, quoted in Herb Lightman, "*My Cousin Rachel*," *American Cinematographer* 34, no. 2 (February 1953): 87; Hitchcock, "Direction," 9.
122. Bazin, *Orson Welles*, 80.
123. Bazin, *Orson Welles*, 73–74. The quotations are drawn from a footnote in which Jonathan Rosenbaum translates Bazin's essay "L'apport d' Orson Welles" (1948).
124. Pichel, "Seeing with the Camera," 142.
125. Carringer, *The Making of "Citizen Kane,"* 92.
126. On Linwood Dunn's contribution to this shot, see Carringer, *The Making of "Citizen Kane,"* 94.
127. Robert Rahtz, "The Traveling Camera," *Hollywood Quarterly* 2, no. 3 (April 1947): 299.
128. See, for instance, the opening sequence of *Four Daughters* and the airplane scene in *Foreign Correspondent*.
129. John Ford, quoted in Joseph McBride and Michael Wilmington, *John Ford* (New York: Da Capo, 1975), 47.
130. Pichel, "Seeing with the Camera," 143.
131. Miller attributes these words to Ford in McBride and Wilmington, *John Ford*, 26.

5. Between Subjective and Objective

1. Charles G. Clarke, "Story Telling with Film," *American Cinematographer* 30, no. 12 (December 1949): 452.
2. David Bordwell identifies sources for the cinema's "subjective turn," including middlebrow modernism, pulp novels, and radio dramas (*Reinventing Hollywood: How 1940s Filmmakers Changed Movie Storytelling* [Chicago: University of Chicago Press, 2017], 276–277).
3. Robert Carringer, *The Making of "Citizen Kane,"* rev. ed. (Berkeley: University of California Press, 1996), 14.
4. "Plot Treatment," September 15, 1939, Welles Manuscripts, Films—*Heart of Darkness*, Orson Welles Papers, Lilly Library, Indiana University–Bloomington. This document refers to Welles in the third person. Although unsigned as far as I can tell, its bombastic tone suggests that it is a faithful rendering of Welles's ideas circa 1940. Marguerite Rippy quotes the same passage in *Orson Welles and the Unfinished RKO Projects: A Postmodern Perspective* (Carbondale: Southern Illinois University Press, 2009), 190 n. 108.
5. "Plot Treatment," Welles Manuscripts, Films—*Heart of Darkness*.
6. James Naremore, *The Magic World of Orson Welles*, rev. ed. (Dallas: Southern Methodist University Press, 1989), 22. A copy of the screenplay for this sequence appears in

Jonathan Rosenbaum, "The Voice and the Eye: A Commentary on the *Heart of Darkness* Script" (1972), in *Discovering Orson Welles* (Berkeley: University of California Press, 2007), 42–48.

7. Orson Welles, "Estimating Script," November 30, 1939, Welles Manuscripts, Films—*Heart of Darkness*.

8. Welles, "Estimating Script," Welles Manuscripts, Films—*Heart of Darkness*.

9. Carringer, *The Making of "Citizen Kane,"* 12.

10. Orson Welles, "Estimating Script," August 15, 1941, Welles Manuscripts, Films—*The Magnificent Ambersons*, Orson Welles Collection.

11. Welles, "Estimating Script," Welles Manuscripts, Films—*The Magnificent Ambersons*.

12. Welles, "Estimating Script," Welles Manuscripts, Films—*The Magnificent Ambersons*.

13. See the daily production reports in Welles Manuscripts, Films—*The Magnificent Ambersons*.

14. "Vital Statistics," RKO press release, Welles Manuscripts, Films—*The Magnificent Ambersons*.

15. Orson Welles and Peter Bogdanovich, *This Is Orson Welles*, ed. Jonathan Rosenbaum (New York: Da Capo Press, 1998), 31.

16. "Cutting Continuity," March 12, 1942, Welles Manuscripts, Films—*The Magnificent Ambersons*. In a useful footnote in his book about the film, Robert Carringer discusses the omission and speculates that Welles had Cortez shoot the sequence just to give the estranged cinematographer something to do (*"The Magnificent Ambersons": A Reconstruction* [Berkeley: University of California Press, 1993], 245).

17. I analyze this sequence in more detail in a video essay: Patrick Keating, "The Strange Streets of a Strange City: The *Ambersons* Montage," *NECSUS: European Journal of Media Studies* (Spring 2018), https://necsus-ejms.org/journal/.

18. Booth Tarkington, *The Magnificent Ambersons* (1918; reprint, New York: Barnes and Noble, 2005), 212.

19. Alfred Hitchcock, in Peter Bogdanovich, *Who the Devil Made It: Conversations with Legendary Film Directors* (New York: Knopf, 1997), 544.

20. Hitchcock, in Bogdanovich, *Who the Devil Made It*, 507.

21. See Robin Wood, "The Use of Cinematic Devices," in *Hitchcock's Films Revisited* (New York: Columbia University Press, 1989), 309–310. Wood outlines several variations on the point-of-view shot, including the one I am calling the "amplified" point-of-view shot.

22. Hitchcock claimed that Barnes rejected the obvious solution—deep focus—because he was a "woman's cinematographer"—that is, a glamour specialist who insisted on composing images with a degree of softness (in Bogdanovich, *Who the Devil Made It*, 513). This explanation is consistent with another strange feature of this shot—the clear shift in focus from the top background to the bottom foreground, as if it were shot with a swing-mount lens (with a focus pull to provide an additional complication). Together, these techniques allowed Barnes to capture Bergman's face and most of the gun in focus while throwing the rest of her body and the background into soft focus.

23. James Agee, *Agee on Film: Criticism and Comment on the Movies* (New York: Modern Library, 2000), 205.

24. Herb Lightman, "The Subjective Camera," *American Cinematographer* 27, no. 2 (February 1946): 46.

25. Lightman, "The Subjective Camera," 46.
26. Lightman, "The Subjective Camera," 67, 66.
27. Susan Smith, *Hitchcock: Suspense, Humour, and Tone* (London: British Film Institute, 2000), 18–25.
28. For further discussion of *Hangover Square*, see Vincent Brook, *Driven to Darkness: Jewish Émigré Directors and the Rise of Film Noir* (New Brunswick, NJ: Rutgers University Press, 2009), 190–192.
29. William Pereira to David O. Selznick, memo, May 17, 1943, Story Files, *Since You Went Away*, David O. Selznick Collection, Harry Ransom Humanities Research Center, University of Texas–Austin.
30. Darryl F. Zanuck to Andy Lawler and Joseph L. Mankiewicz, memo, November 7, 1945, Joseph L. Mankiewicz Papers, Academy of Motion Picture Arts and Sciences, Margaret Herrick Library, Beverly Hills, CA.
31. Darryl F. Zanuck to Joseph L. Mankiewicz, memo, November 26, 1945, Joseph L. Mankiewicz Papers.
32. See the argument that the point-of-view shot often puts the spectator in a position of sadism or masochism in Dana Polan, *Power & Paranoia: History, Narrative, and the American Cinema, 1940–1950* (New York: Columbia University Press, 1986), 224.
33. Advertisement for *Lady in the Lake*, *LIFE*, January 20, 1947, 50.
34. "Movie of the Week: *Lady in the Lake*," *LIFE*, January 13, 1947, 66.
35. Raymond Chandler, screenplay draft, *Lady in the Lake*, July 5, 1945, Turner/M-G-M Scripts, Academy of Motion Picture Arts and Sciences, Margaret Herrick Library.
36. Steve Fisher, screenplay draft, *Lady in the Lake*, March 22, 1946, Turner/M-G-M Scripts.
37. Herb Lightman, "M-G-M Pioneers with Subjective Feature," *American Cinematographer* 27, no. 11 (November 1946): 401.
38. Raymond Chandler, *The Lady in the Lake* (1943; reprint, New York: Vintage Books, 1992), 153.
39. Norris Pope, *Chronicle of a Camera: The Arriflex 35 in North America, 1945–1972* (Jackson: University Press of Mississippi, 2013), 17–18. Thanks to Andrew Patrick Nelson for alerting me to the connection between Daves and Montgomery. Because *Dark Passage* was released later than *Lady in the Lake*, contemporary reviews assumed that Daves simply borrowed the idea of extended point-of-view shots from Montgomery. See, for instance, "Reviews: Dark Passage," *Film Daily* 92, no. 45 (September 3, 1947): 8.
40. Joshua Gleich, *Hollywood in San Francisco: Location Shooting and the Aesthetics of Urban Decline, 1945–1975* (Austin: University of Texas Press, 2018), 36–37. I first read this work in manuscript form.
41. For a defense of the idea that we see films as pictures, see Robert Hopkins, "Depiction," in *The Routledge Companion to Philosophy and Film*, ed. Paisley Livingston and Carl Plantinga (New York: Routledge, 2011), 69.
42. Richard Wollheim, "Seeing-as, Seeing-in, and Pictorial Representation," in *Art and Its Objects*, 2nd ed. (New York: Cambridge University Press, 1980), 212. See also the contrast between "representational aspect" and "configurational aspect" in Richard Wollheim, *Painting as an Art* (Princeton, NJ: Princeton University Press, 1987), 73. Jordan Schonig applies Wollheim's theory to camera movement in "Seeing Aspects of the Moving Camera: On the Twofoldness of the Mobile Frame," *Synoptique* 5, no. 2 (Winter 2017): 59.

43. Meir Sternberg, "Mimesis and Motivation: The Two Faces of Fictional Coherence," *Poetics Today* 33, nos. 3–4 (Fall–Winter 2012): 368.

44. Sternberg, "Mimesis and Motivation," 411. A note on Sternberg's use of the word *teleological*: In film studies, this term is often used to criticize quasi-biological theories of film history as a process of evolutionary improvement. By contrast, Sternberg uses it to indicate that we approach a text not as a biological being but as a purposeful construction.

45. See Sternberg's discussion of the "existential mechanism," whereby we appeal to our understanding of the storyworld's "objective makeup," and the "perspectival mechanism," whereby we appeal to our understanding of the narrators, perceivers, dreamers, and other figures who mediate our access to the storyworld ("Mimesis and Motivation," 453).

46. David Bordwell, *Narration in the Fiction Film* (Madison: University of Wisconsin Press, 1985), 57–58. In contrast to *range*, Bordwell uses the term *depth* to characterize patterns of subjectivity and objectivity.

47. George M. Wilson, *Narration in Light: Studies in Cinematic Point of View* (Baltimore: Johns Hopkins University Press, 1986), 87–88.

48. Bordwell, *Reinventing Hollywood*, 219–227.

49. Wilson, *Narration in Light*, 87, italics in the original.

50. Alfred Hitchcock, in "On Style: An Interview with *Cinema*," in *Hitchcock on Hitchcock: Selected Writings and Interviews*, ed. Sidney Gottlieb (Berkeley: University of California Press, 1997), 291.

51. Vincente Minnelli and Hector Arce, *I Remember It Well* (Hollywood, CA: Samuel French, 1974), 206.

52. For a theoretically nuanced account of camera–eye narration in relation to other forms of literary and cinematic narration, see Seymour Chatman, "A New Point of View on 'Point of View,'" in *Coming to Terms: The Rhetoric of Narrative in Fiction and Film* (Ithaca, NY: Cornell University Press, 1990), 139–160.

53. V. F. Perkins, "Why Preminger?" (1962), in *"Movie" Reader*, ed. Ian Cameron (New York: Praeger, 1972), 43. In the original publication, the essay was unsigned.

54. Joseph LaShelle, quoted in Herb Lightman, "Exponent of the Moving Camera," *American Cinematographer* 29, no. 11 (November 1948): 376.

55. John Gibbs and Douglas Pye, "Revisiting Preminger: *Bonjour Tristesse* (1958) and Close Reading," in *Style and Meaning: Studies in the Detailed Analysis of Film*, ed. John Gibbs and Douglas Pye (Manchester, UK: Manchester University Press, 2005), 121. I discuss this passage in Patrick Keating, "Otto Preminger," in *Fifty Hollywood Directors*, ed. Suzanne Leonard and Yvonne Tasker (London: Routledge, 2014), 190.

56. *Fallen Angel* adopts a more elliptical approach elsewhere, concealing pieces of information to enhance the mystery plot.

57. Robin Wood, *Personal Views: Explorations in Film*, rev. ed. (Detroit: Wayne State University Press, 2006), 157.

58. For a photograph of the crane shooting this scene, see Lutz Bacher, *Max Ophuls in the Hollywood Studios* (New Brunswick, NJ: Rutgers University Press, 1996), 146. Elsewhere in the book, Bacher identifies Les Kahn as the grip who had operated the Universal number 2 crane since its introduction in 1937.

59. Bacher, *Max Ophuls in the Hollywood Studios*, 5.

60. Max Ophuls, quoted in Lutz Bacher, *The Mobile Mise-en-Scène: A Critical Analysis of the Theory and Practice of Long-Take Camera Movement in the Narrative Film* (New York: Arno Press, 1978), 152.

61. Lee Garmes, *Lee Garmes: An American Film Institute Seminar on His Work* (Glen Rock, NJ: Microfilming Corporation of America, 1977), 60.

62. Daniel Morgan, "Max Ophuls and the Limits of Virtuosity: On the Aesthetics and Ethics of Camera Movement," *Critical Inquiry* 38 (Autumn 2011): 135.

63. Morgan, "Max Ophuls and the Limits of Virtuosity," 138.

64. Herb Lightman, "The Men Behind the Combat Cameramen," *American Cinematographer* 26, no. 10 (October 1945): 355.

65. M. S. Blankfort, "The Camera Is a Weapon," *American Cinematographer* 25, no. 1 (January 1944): 14.

66. Blankfort, "The Camera Is a Weapon," 16.

67. Mark Harris, *Five Came Back: A Story of Hollywood and the Second World War* (New York: Penguin Press, 2014), 147–148.

68. Louis De Rochemont, quoted in Ezra Goodman, "Fact Films to the Front," *American Cinematographer* 26, no. 2 (February 1945): 46, 66.

69. James Wong Howe, "The Documentary Technique in Hollywood," *American Cinematographer* 25, no. 1 (January 1944): 10.

70. Howe, "The Documentary Technique in Hollywood," 10, 32.

71. Howe, "The Documentary Technique in Hollywood," 10.

72. Paul Vogel, "Different . . . and Difficult," *American Cinematographer* 30, no. 12 (December 1949): 448.

73. Harris, *Five Came Back*, 280.

74. Harris, *Five Came Back*, 383–384.

75. Peter Lev, *Twentieth Century-Fox: The Zanuck–Skouras Years, 1935–1965* (Austin: University of Texas Press, 2013), 107.

76. Herb Lightman, "13 Rue Madeleine: Documentary Style in the Photoplay," *American Cinematographer* 28, no. 3 (March 1947): 89. On de Rochemont's preference for an unpolished, plain style of camerawork, see R. Barton Palmer, *Shot on Location: Postwar American Cinema and the Exploration of Real Place* (New Brunswick, NJ: Rutgers University Press, 2016), 139, 157.

77. Herb Lightman, "New Horizons for the Documentary Film," *American Cinematographer* 26, no. 12 (December 1945): 418.

78. William Daniels, quoted in Herb Lightman, " 'The Naked City': Tribute in Celluloid," *American Cinematographer* 29, no. 5 (May 1948): 178.

79. Robert Surtees, "The Story of Filming 'Act of Violence,' " *American Cinematographer* 29, no. 8 (August 1948): 268.

80. Lucien Ballard, in Leonard Maltin, *The Art of the Cinematographer: A Survey and Interviews with Five Masters* (New York: Dover, 1978), 110.

81. For more on the technologies of location cinematography, see Lisa Dombrowski, "Postwar Hollywood, 1947–1967," in *Cinematography*, ed. Patrick Keating (New Brunswick, NJ: Rutgers University Press, 2014), 61–70.

82. John del Valle, "Boom Shots Anywhere!" *American Cinematographer* 31, no. 8 (August 1950): 270.

83. William Mellor, "No Time for Weather," *American Cinematographer* 32, no. 4 (May 1951): 178–179.

84. Frederick Foster, "Location Camera Carriers," *American Cinematographer* 37, no. 8 (August 1956): 495. Del Valle lists George Dye and John Cooley as the inventors of the Blue Goose ("Boom Shots Anywhere!" 270), but Foster credits Howard Cooley.

85. Paul Ivano, "We Operate the Biggest Camera Crane in the World," *American Cinematographer* 28, no. 9 (September 1947): 312.

86. Herb Lightman, "'Johnny Belinda,'" *American Cinematographer* 29, no. 10 (October 1948): 338.

87. Garmes, *Lee Garmes*, 13–14.

88. Mel Dinelli, script, *The Window*, April 15, 1947, RKO Scripts Collection, Special Collections, University of California–Los Angeles.

89. Ted Tetzlaff, quoted in Ezra Goodman, "Motion Picture Photographer to Director," *American Cinematographer* 29, no. 3 (March 1948): 102.

90. James Wong Howe, "The Cameraman Talks Back," *The Screen Writer* 1, no. 5 (October 1945): 35.

91. Ezra Goodman, "Post-war Motion Pictures," *American Cinematographer* 26, no. 5 (May 1945): 160.

92. Howe later said he was surprised to learn that director Sidney Franklin had used the technique in *Quality Street* (1927) (James Wong Howe, in *Film Noir Reader 3: Interviews with Filmmakers of the Classic Noir Period*, ed. Robert Porfirio, Alain Silver, and James Ursini [New York: Limelight Editions, 2002], 138).

93. Ralph Lawton, "*Champion* . . . A Two-Fisted Picture Made Startlingly Real by Skillful Photography," *American Cinematographer* 30, no. 6 (June 1949): 196, 218.

94. For examples of Hollywood films that employed the Arriflex 35 during the 1950s, see Pope, *Chronicle of a Camera*, 33–37.

95. Gregg Toland, quoted in Lester Koenig, "Gregg Toland, Film-Maker," *The Screen Writer* 3, no. 7 (December 1947): 29.

6. An Art of Disclosures

1. Howard Hawks, in *Interviews with Film Directors*, ed. Andrew Sarris (New York: Avon Books, 1967), 231.

2. V. F. Perkins, "Where Is the World? The Horizon of Events in Movie Fiction," in *Style and Meaning: Studies in the Detailed Analysis of Film*, ed. John Gibbs and Douglas Pye (Manchester, UK: Manchester University Press, 2005), 20.

3. Perkins, "Where Is the World?" 20.

4. Orson Welles, "Final Shooting Script," *The Stranger*, September 24, 1945, Orson Welles Papers, Lilly Library, Indiana University–Bloomington.

5. James Naremore, *The Magic World of Orson Welles*, rev. ed. (Dallas: Southern Methodist University Press, 1989), 125.

6. Hitchcock explains his view on revealing information in François Truffaut, *Hitchcock*, rev. ed. (New York: Touchstone, 1985), 73.

7. Bill Krohn, *Hitchcock at Work* (London: Phaidon Press, 2000), 98.

8. Alfred Hitchcock, "Let 'Em Play God," in *Hitchcock on Hitchcock: Selected Writings and Interviews*, ed. Sidney Gottlieb (Berkeley: University of California Press, 1997), 114.

9. A. Lindsley Lane, "The Camera's Omniscient Eye," *American Cinematographer* 16, no. 3 (March 1935): 95.

10. Herb Lightman, "The Fluid Camera," *American Cinematographer* 27, no. 3 (March 1946): 102.

11. Alexander Mackendrick, *On Film-Making: An Introduction to the Craft of the Director*, ed. Paul Cronin (New York: Faber and Faber, 2004), 198.

12. Jakob Isak Nielsen has proposed a different but overlapping list of functions in "Five Functions of Camera Movement in Narrative Cinema," in *Transnational*

Cinematography Studies, ed. Lindsay Coleman, Daisuke Miyao, and Roberto Schaeffer (Lanham, MD: Lexington Books, 2017), 26.

13. Edward Dmytryk, *On Directing* (Boston: Focal Press, 1984), 72.

14. I owe the distinction between revelation and recognition to the screenwriting teacher Frank Daniel. See also the discussion of dramatic irony in David Howard and Edward Mabley, *The Tools of Screenwriting* (New York: St. Martin's Press, 1995), 68–70.

15. Meir Sternberg, "Narrativity: From Objectivist to Functional Paradigm," *Poetics Today* 31, no. 3 (Fall 2010): 637. See the discussion of Sternberg's distinction in chapter 2.

16. David Bordwell, *Reinventing Hollywood: How 1940s Filmmakers Changed Movie Storytelling* (Chicago: University of Chicago Press, 2017), 200.

17. Mackendrick, *On Film-Making*, 276.

18. Boris Kaufman, "Film Making as an Art," *Daedalus* 89, no. 1 (Winter 1960): 141.

19. See also Boris Kaufman's discussion of *Twelve Angry Men*, which combines long takes with cut-in-the-camera sequences, in "Filming '12 Angry Men' on a Single Set," *American Cinematographer* 37, no. 12 (December 1956): 725.

20. See the production reports for *The Big Clock*, Paramount Pictures Production Records, Academy of Motion Picture Arts and Sciences, Margaret Herrick Library, Beverly Hills, CA. The schedule called for forty-three shooting days. The crew initially used only forty-one, though production was reopened a few times to shoot pickups.

21. John F. Seitz, in *Film Noir Reader 3: Interviews with Filmmakers of the Classic Noir Period*, ed. Robert Porfirio, Alain Silver, and James Ursini (New York: Limelight Editions, 2002), 210.

22. Merrill Schleier, *Skyscraper Cinema: Architecture and Gender in American Film* (Minneapolis: University of Minnesota Press, 2009), 155–156.

23. Gordon Jennings, in charge of the film's special photographic effects, traveled to New York to photograph the skyline shot (Production Files, *The Big Clock*, Paramount Pictures Production Records).

24. Joseph H. Lewis, in *Film Noir Reader 3*, ed. Porfirio, Silver, and Ursini, 70.

25. See Lewis's account in *Film Noir Reader 3*, ed. Porfirio, Silver, and Ursini, 70–73.

26. Alfred Hitchcock, "Direction" (1937), in *Hitchcock on Hitchcock*, 6.

27. Bart Sheridan, "Three and a Half Minute Take . . .," *American Cinematographer* 29, no. 9 (September 1948): 305.

28. Two long portions of the shot remain, one lasting fifty-seven seconds, the other lasting forty-eight (David Bordwell, *Poetics of Cinema* [New York: Routledge, 2008], 437 n. 65).

29. "Wider Scope Seen in New Dolly Design," *Film Daily* 92, no. 47 (September 5, 1947): 2.

30. Legal Files—1936–1954—All Angle Dolly, David O. Selznick Collection, Harry Ransom Humanities Research Center, University of Texas–Austin.

31. For technical specs of Rosen's crab dolly, see Lee Garmes, "New 'All-Direction' Baby Camera-Dolly," *American Cinematographer* 31, no. 9 (September 1950): 307, 321.

32. Lee Garmes, quoted in Charles Higham, *Hollywood Cameramen: Sources of Light* (Bloomington: Indiana University Press, 1970), 51–52.

33. Karl Freund, "A New Camera Dolly for Films and Television," *American Cinematographer* 34, no. 6 (June 1953): 273. Freund's article was about Cinetel's Multidolly. Houston-Fearless later sold the same device as the Cinemobile (Lutz Bacher, *The Mobile Mise-en-Scène: A Critical Analysis of the Theory and Practice of Long-Take Camera Movement in the Narrative Film* [New York: Arno Press, 1978], 87–88).

34. Bordwell, *Poetics of Cinema*, 37.

35. See the first photograph of the Rosie dolly in Alfred Hitchcock, "My Most Exciting Picture," *Popular Photography* 23, no. 5 (November 1948): 48.
36. Hitchcock describes Rosen's contributions in "My Most Exciting Picture," 96–98.
37. In addition to Hitchcock, "My Most Exciting Picture," see Virginia Yates, "'Rope' Sets a Precedent," *American Cinematographer* 29, no. 7 (July 1948): 231, 246; "*Rope*," *Showmen's Trade Review* 49, no. 9 (August 28, 1948): 20; and "*Look* Movie Review: *Rope*," *Look*, September 14, 1948, 92–94.
38. Irving Pichel, "A Long Rope," *Hollywood Quarterly* 3, no. 4 (Summer 1948): 419.
39. Hitchcock, "My Most Exciting Picture," 103.
40. Hitchcock, in Truffaut, *Hitchcock*, 180.
41. John Belton, "*Under Capricorn*: Montage Entranced by Mise-en-Scène," in *Cinema Stylists* (Metuchen, NJ: Scarecrow Press, 1983), 42.
42. V. F. Perkins, "*Rope*" (1963), in "*Movie*" *Reader*, ed. Ian Cameron (New York: Praeger, 1972), 36.
43. Jack Cardiff, "The Problems of Lighting and Photographing 'Under Capricorn,'" *American Cinematographer* 30, no. 10 (October 1949): 359.
44. Hilda Black, "The Photography Is Important to Hitchcock," *American Cinematographer* 33, no. 12 (December 1952): 525.
45. Alfred Hitchcock, in Peter Bogdanovich, *Who the Devil Made It: Conversations with Legendary Film Directors* (New York: Knopf, 1997), 517.
46. Freddie Young, *Seventy Light Years: A Life in the Movies* (London: Faber and Faber, 1999), 74.
47. George Cukor, in Bogdanovich, *Who the Devil Made It*, 445.
48. Kelly's name appears in the credits; Doll's name does not. The IMDb page for *Edward, My Son* credits Doll as the film's assistant. Young's autobiography mentions both Kelly and Doll in connection with other films (*Seventy Light Years*, 68–69, 74).
49. Young, *Seventy Light Years*, 74.
50. Vincente Minnelli and Hector Arce, *I Remember It Well* (Hollywood, CA: Samuel French, 1974), 232.
51. Alfred Gilks, "Some Highlights in the Filming of . . . 'An American in Paris,'" *American Cinematographer* 33, no. 1 (January 1952): 36.
52. James Naremore, *The Films of Vincente Minnelli* (New York: Cambridge University Press, 1993), 101–102, 128–130.
53. Darryl F. Zanuck to Sol Siegel, Joseph L. Mankiewicz, and Arthur Miller, memo, June 26, 1948, Joseph L. Mankiewicz Papers, Academy of Motion Picture Arts and Sciences, Margaret Herrick Library.
54. See Darryl F. Zanuck to All Executives, Producers, and Directors, memo, May 27, 1947, in Darryl F. Zanuck, *Memo from Darryl F. Zanuck: The Golden Years at Twentieth Century-Fox*, ed. Rudy Behlmer (New York: Grove Press, 1993), 143, in which Zanuck warned against two competing tendencies: the habit of shooting too many angles and the urge to complete a perfect master.
55. Darryl F. Zanuck to Henry King, memo, November 25, 1950, Henry King Papers, Academy of Motion Picture Arts and Sciences, Margaret Herrick Library.
56. See the discussion of *Marty* in Chris Cagle, *Sociology on Film: Postwar Hollywood's Prestige Commodity* (New Brunswick, NJ: Rutgers University Press, 2017), 20–22.
57. George Cukor, in *Interviews with Film Directors*, ed. Sarris, 106.
58. Rouben Mamoulian, in Charles Higham and Joel Greenberg, *The Celluloid Muse: Hollywood Directors Speak* (London: Argus and Robertson, 1969), 143.

59. Billy Wilder, in Cameron Crowe, *Conversations with Wilder* (New York: Knopf, 1999), 205.

60. John Ford, quoted in Peter Bogdanovich, *John Ford* (Berkeley: University of California Press, 1967), 92.

61. Bordwell, *Poetics of Cinema*, 302–303.

62. "Summary of Current Wide-Screen Systems of Photography," *American Cinematographer* 36, no. 11 (November 1955): 654–656, 674–676.

63. For a thorough account of these various widescreen systems, see John Belton, *Widescreen Cinema* (Cambridge, MA: Harvard University Press, 1992). Belton looks to the industrial and social context to explain why these systems came to prominence during the 1950s, even though the underlying technologies had been around for years.

64. Bordwell, *Poetics of Cinema*, 288–289.

65. Frederick Foster, "Photography Sharp, Clear, and Incisive," *American Cinematographer* 40, no. 8 (August 1959): 504.

66. For technical specs of this new crane, see André Crot, "Research Council Camera Crane," *Journal of the Society of Motion Picture Engineers* 52, no. 3 (March 1949): 273–279.

67. Frederick Foster, "Location Camera Carriers," *American Cinematographer* 37, no. 8 (August 1956): 496.

68. Fred Zinnemann, in Brian Neve, "A Past Master of His Craft: An Interview with Fred Zinnemann," *Cineaste* 23, no. 1 (1997): 18.

69. Joseph Henry, "Superior Maneuverability in Boom Shot Photography," *American Cinematographer* 43, no. 11 (November 1962): 681.

70. Arthur Rowan, "Cinematography Unsurpassed," *American Cinematographer* 37, no. 11 (November 1956): 680. DeMille had used an earlier Chapman crane in *The Greatest Show on Earth* (1952). See the illustration in Arthur Rowan, "Filming the Circus," *American Cinematographer* 32, no. 1 (December 1951): 494.

71. Frank Tashlin, in Bogdanovich, *Who the Devil Made It*, 777.

72. "Boom-Shot Technique," *American Cinematographer* 42, no. 1 (January 1961): 30–31.

73. Herb Lightman, "Filming 'Spartacus' in Super-Technirama," *American Cinematographer* 42, no. 11 (January 1961): 43.

74. Joseph Brun, "The Cinerama Technique," *American Cinematographer* 35, no. 6 (June 1954): 291.

75. Gayne Rescher, "Wide Angle Problems in Wide Screen Photography," *American Cinematographer* 37, no. 5 (May 1956): 300.

76. Ariel Rogers, " 'Smothered in Baked Alaska': The Anxious Appeal of Widescreen Cinema," *Cinema Journal* 51, no. 3 (Spring 2012): 75.

77. Lisa Dombrowski, "Postwar Hollywood, 1947–1967," in *Cinematography*, ed. Patrick Keating (New Brunswick, NJ: Rutgers University Press, 2014), 73.

78. Belton, *Widescreen Cinema*, 191.

79. Robert Wise, in "An American Film Institute Seminar with Robert Wise and Milton Krasner, ASC," *American Cinematographer* 61, no. 3 (March 1980): 292.

80. Darryl F. Zanuck to Nunnally Johnson, Jean Negulesco, Sid Rogell, Sol Halprin, and Earl Sponable, memo, March 25, 1953, in *Memo from Darryl F. Zanuck*, 236.

81. Henry Koster, "Directing in CinemaScope," in *New Screen Techniques*, ed. Martin Quigley (New York: Quigley, 1953), 171.

82. Leon Shamroy, "Filming the Big Dimension," *American Cinematographer* 34, no. 5 (May 1953): 217.

83. Shamroy, "Filming the Big Dimension," 232.

84. Leon Shamroy, quoted in Higham, *Hollywood Cameramen*, 30.

85. Charles G. Clarke, "CinemaScope Photographic Techniques," *American Cinematographer* 36, no. 6 (June 1955): 362, 363. This article was based on a pamphlet that Clarke wrote for the benefit of his colleagues at Twentieth Century-Fox.

86. John Ford, quoted in Joe McBride and Michael Wilmington, *John Ford* (New York: Da Capo, 1975), 146.

87. John Houseman to J. J. Cohn, memo, February 1955, *Lust for Life*—Production, Vincente Minnelli Papers, Academy of Motion Picture Arts and Sciences, Margaret Herrick Library.

88. For a detailed analysis of this scene in *The House of Bamboo*, see Lisa Dombrowski, *The Films of Samuel Fuller: If You Die, I'll Kill You!* (Middletown, CT: Wesleyan University Press, 2008), 85–89.

89. Robert Surtees, quoted in Herb Lightman, "Shooting 'Oklahoma!' in Todd-AO," *American Cinematographer* 36, no. 5 (April 1955): 210.

90. Charles Barr, "CinemaScope: Before and After," *Film Quarterly* 16, no. 4 (Summer 1963): 19, 18, emphasis in original.

91. V. F. Perkins, "*River of No Return*," *Movie* 2 (September 1962): 18.

92. Daniel Steinhart, *Runaway Hollywood: Internationalizing Postwar Production and Location Shooting* (Berkeley: University of California Press, forthcoming). I read this work in manuscript form.

93. Robert Surtees, "The Filming of *Quo Vadis* in Italy," *American Cinematographer* 32, no. 19 (October 1951): 399.

94. Oswald Morris and Geoffrey Bull, *Huston, We Have a Problem* (Lanham, MD: Scarecrow Press, 2006), n.p., in the photograph section after page 44.

95. See various memos in "*Funny Face*—Production," Paramount Pictures Production Records.

96. Arhur Gavin, "Location-Shooting in Paris for 'Gigi,'" *American Cinematographer* 39, no. 7 (July 1958): 425.

97. Scott Curtis, "The Making of *Rear Window*," in *Alfred Hitchcock's "Rear Window*," ed. John Belton (New York: Cambridge University Press, 2000), 39–40.

98. Pamela Robertson Wojcik, *The Apartment Plot: Urban Living in American Film and Popular Culture, 1945 to 1975* (Durham, NC: Duke University Press, 2010), 85.

99. Robert Burks, quoted in Arthur Gavin, "*Rear Window*," *American Cinematographer* 35, no. 2 (February 1952): 102.

100. For costs, see "*Rear Window*—Budgets," and for the reference to the Chapman crane, see "*Rear Window*—Camera Reports," both in Paramount Pictures Production Records.

101. Gavin, "*Rear Window*," 100–101.

102. Hitchcock, in Bogdanovich, *Who the Devil Made It*, 515.

103. Alfred Hitchcock, in Higham and Greenberg, *The Celluloid Muse*, 97.

104. Douglas Pye, "Movies and Tone," in *Close Up 02*, ed. John Gibbs and Douglas Pye (London: Wallflower, 2007), 41.

105. For a useful account of the dolly–zoom shot in *Vertigo*, see Christopher Beach, *A Hidden History of Film Style: Cinematographers, Directors, and the Collaborative Process* (Berkeley: University of California Press, 2015), 129.

106. Joseph Mascelli, "The Use and Abuse of the Zoom Lens," *American Cinematographer* 38, no. 10 (October 1957): 652.

107. Bruce Block, *The Visual Story: Creating the Visual Structure of Film, TV, and Digital Media*, 2nd ed. (Burlington, MA: Focal Press, 2008), chapter 3 on space and the appendix.

108. I discuss lenses in more detail in Patrick Keating, "The Art of Cinematography," in *The Palgrave Handbook for the Philosophy of Film and Motion Pictures*, ed. Noël Carroll, Laura T. DiSumma-Knoop, and Shawn Loht (New York: Palgrave Macmillan, forthcoming).

109. "From Among the Dead," final shooting script, September 12, 1957, "*Vertigo*—Script Notes," Alfred Hitchcock Papers, Academy of Motion Picture Arts and Sciences, Margaret Herrick Library.

110. Hitchcock, in Bogdanovich, *Who the Devil Made It*, 530.

111. Herb Lightman, "The Function of Boom Shots in Feature Film Production," *American Cinematographer* 34, no. 4 (April 1953): 161. A few years later the magazine published a revised version of the same article, now unsigned. See "Boom-Shot Technique," *American Cinematographer* 42, no. 1 (January 1961): 31.

Conclusion

1. Orson Welles and Peter Bogdanovich, *This Is Orson Welles*, ed. Jonathan Rosenbaum (New York: Da Capo, 1998), 23.

2. Working from Welles's own notes, Walter Murch supervised the sound design for Universal's restoration of *Touch of Evil* in 1998.

3. Charlton Heston, quoted in James Delson, "Heston on Welles," in *"Touch of Evil": Orson Welles, Director*, ed. Terry Comito (New Brunswick, NJ: Rutgers University Press, 1998), 220–221.

4. James Naremore, *The Magic World of Orson Welles*, rev. ed. (Dallas: Southern Methodist University Press, 1989), 158.

5. Orson Welles, in *Interviews with Film Directors*, ed. Andrew Sarris (New York: Avon Books, 1967), 536.

6. Welles, in *Interviews with Film Directors*, ed. Sarris, 552–553.

7. Some sources credit Philip Lathrop as the operator (see, e.g., Bob Fisher, "Philip Lathrop, ASC, Steps Into the Spotlight," *American Cinematographer* 73, no. 2 [February 1992]: 35–36). Welles gave the credit to John Russell (Welles and Bogdanovich, *This Is Orson Welles*, 308).

8. Robin Wood, *Personal Views: Explorations in Film*, rev. ed. (Detroit: Wayne State University Press, 2006), 172.

9. Wood, *Personal Views*, 174.

10. On lenses and space, see Bruce Block, *The Visual Story: Creating the Visual Structure of Film, TV, and Digital Media*, 2nd ed. (Burlington, MA: Focal Press, 2008), 272–275.

11. F. W. Murnau, "Films of the Future" (1927), in *Hollywood Directors, 1914–1940*, ed. Richard Koszarski (New York: Oxford University Press, 1976), 219.

BIBLIOGRAPHY

Archival Sources

*Academy of Motion Picture Arts and Sciences, Margaret Herrick Library,
Beverly Hills, CA*

Alfred Hitchcock Papers
American Society of Cinematographers—Member Files
Bison Archives Photographs Collected by Marc Wanamaker
Core Collection—Production Files
Fred Zinnemann Papers
George Stevens Papers
Hal Mohr and Evelyn Venable Papers
Henry King Papers
Joseph L. Mankiewicz Papers
Lewis Milestone Papers
Mary Pickford Papers
Metro-Goldwyn-Mayer Production and Biography Photographs
Paramount Pictures Press Sheets
Paramount Pictures Production Records
Paramount Pictures Scripts
Production Code Administration Files
Turner/M-G-M Scripts
Vincente Minnelli Papers

Harry Ransom Humanities Research Center, University of Texas–Austin

David O. Selznick Collection

Lilly Library, Indiana University–Bloomington

Orson Welles Papers

Special Collections, University of California–Los Angeles

RKO Production Files
RKO Scripts Collection

Special Collections, University of Tennessee–Knoxville

Clarence Brown Collection

University of Southern California

Warner Bros. Archives

Periodicals and Trade Journals

For newspaper articles, magazine articles, blogs, video essays, and minor trade journal articles, see the notes.

American Cinematographer
The Cine-Technician
The Dial
Film Daily
Film Quarterly
Hollywood Quarterly
International Photographer
Journal of the Society of Motion Picture Engineers, formerly *Transactions of the Society of Motion Picture Engineers*
LIFE magazine
Look
Motion Picture
Motion Picture Classic
Motion Picture News
Movie
Movie Makers
Moving Picture World
The Nation
New Masses
New Republic
New York Times
Photoplay
Picture-Play Magazine
Popular Photography
The Screen Writer
Showmen's Trade Review
Theatre Arts, formerly *Theatre Arts Monthly*

Universal Weekly
Variety

Published Sources

This list includes books, scholarly journals, and major articles in trade journals.

Agee, James. *Agee on Film: Criticism and Comment on the Movies*. New York: Modern Library, 2000.

Alicoate, Jack, ed. *The 1930 "Film Daily" Year Book of Motion Pictures*. Los Angeles: Film Daily, 1930.

Bacher, Lutz. *Max Ophuls in the Hollywood Studios*. New Brunswick, NJ: Rutgers University Press, 1996.

——. *The Mobile Mise-en-Scène: A Critical Analysis of the Theory and Practice of Long-Take Camera Movement in the Narrative Film*. New York: Arno Press, 1978.

Bakshy, Alexander. "The New Art of the Motion Picture." *Theatre Arts Monthly* 11, no. 4 (April 1927): 277–282.

Baldwin, Faith. *Skyscraper*. 1931. Reprint. New York: Feminist Press, 2003.

Balio, Tino. *Grand Design: Hollywood as a Modern Business Enterprise, 1930–1939*. Berkeley: University of California Press, 1995.

Barnard, Timothy. Notes in André Bazin, *What Is Cinema?*, translated by Timothy Barnard. Montreal: Caboose Books, 2009.

Barnett, M. Todd. *One World, Big Screen: Hollywood, the Allies, and World War II*. Chapel Hill: University of North Carolina Press, 2012.

Barr, Charles. "CinemaScope: Before and After." *Film Quarterly* 16, no. 4 (Summer 1963): 4–24.

Basinger, Jeanine. *The World War II Combat Film: Anatomy of a Genre*. Middletown, CT: Wesleyan University Press, 2003.

Baxandall, Michael. *Patterns of Intention: On the Historical Explanation of Pictures*. New Haven, CT: Yale University Press, 1985.

Bazin, André. *Orson Welles: A Critical View*. Translated by Jonathan Rosenbaum. Los Angeles: Acrobat Books, 1991.

——. *What Is Cinema?* Translated by Timothy Barnard. Montreal: Caboose Books, 2009.

Beach, Christopher. *A Hidden History of Film Style: Cinematographers, Directors, and the Collaborative Process*. Berkeley: University of California Press, 2015.

Beard, Charles, and Mary Beard. *The Rise of American Civilization: The Industrial Era*. New York: Macmillan, 1927.

Behlmer, Rudy, ed. *Inside Warner Bros. (1935–1951)*. New York: Viking, 1985.

Belton, John. "*Under Capricorn*: Montage Entranced by Mise-en-Scène." In *Cinema Stylists*, 39–58. Metuchen, NJ: Scarecrow Press, 1983.

——. *Widescreen Cinema*. Cambridge, MA: Harvard University Press, 1992.

Bergstrom, Janet. "Murnau in America: Chronicle of Lost Films." *Film History* 14, nos. 3–4 (2002): 430–460.

——. *William Fox Presents F. W. Murnau and Frank Borzage*. Booklet in *Murnau, Borzage, and Fox*, DVD box set. Los Angeles: Twentieth Century-Fox Home Entertainment, 2008.

Bitzer, G. W. *Billy Bitzer: His Story*. New York: Farrar, Straus and Giroux, 1973.

Block, Bruce. *The Visual Story: Creating the Visual Structure of Film, TV, and Digital Media*. 2nd ed. Burlington, MA: Focal Press, 2008.

Bogdanovich, Peter. *John Ford*. Berkeley: University of California Press, 1967.
——. *Who the Devil Made It: Conversations with Legendary Film Directors*. New York: Knopf, 1997.
Booth, Margaret. "The Cutter." In *Behind the Screen*, edited by Stephen Watts, 147–153. London: Arthur Barker, 1938.
Bordwell, David. "Camera Movement: The Coming of Sound and the Classical Hollywood Style." In *The Hollywood Film Industry*, edited by Paul Kerr, 148–153. London: Routledge, 1984.
——. *Narration in the Fiction Film*. Madison: University of Wisconsin Press, 1985.
——. *Planet Hong Kong: Popular Cinema and the Art of Entertainment*. Cambridge, MA: Harvard University Press, 2000.
——. *Poetics of Cinema*. New York: Routledge, 2008.
——. *Reinventing Hollywood: How 1940s Filmmakers Changed Movie Storytelling*. Chicago: University of Chicago Press, 2017.
——. *The Rhapsodes: How 1940s Critics Changed American Film Culture*. Chicago: University of Chicago Press, 2016.
Bordwell, David, Janet Staiger, and Kristin Thompson. *The Classical Hollywood Cinema: Film Style and Mode of Production to 1960*. New York: Columbia University Press, 1985.
Bordwell, David, and Kristin Thompson. "Technological Change and Classical Film Style." In Tino Balio, *Grand Design: Hollywood as a Modern Business Enterprise, 1930–1939*, 109–141. Berkeley: University of California Press, 1993.
Branigan, Edward. *Projecting a Camera: Language-Games in Film Theory*. New York: Routledge, 2006.
Brook, Vincent. *Driven to Darkness: Jewish Émigré Directors and the Rise of Film Noir*. New Brunswick, NJ: Rutgers University Press, 2009.
Brownlow, Kevin. *The Parade's Gone By . . . .* Berkeley: University of California Press, 1968.
Cagle, Chris. *Sociology on Film: Postwar Hollywood's Prestige Commodity*. New Brunswick, NJ: Rutgers University Press, 2017.
Caldwell, John Thornton. *Production Culture: Industrial Reflexivity and Critical Practice in Film and Television*. Durham, NC: Duke University Press, 2008.
Carringer, Robert. *"The Magnificent Ambersons": A Reconstruction*. Berkeley: University of California Press, 1993.
——. *The Making of "Citizen Kane."* Rev. ed. Berkeley: University of California Press, 1996.
Carroll, Noël. "Notes on the Sight Gag." In *Theorizing the Moving Image*, 146–157. New York: Cambridge University Press, 1996.
——. *The Philosophy of Motion Pictures*. Malden, MA: Blackwell, 2008.
——. "Toward a Theory of Film Suspense." In *Theorizing the Moving Image*, 94–117. New York: Cambridge University Press, 1996.
Chandler, Raymond. *The Lady in the Lake*. 1943. Reprint. New York: Vintage Books, 1992.
Chatman, Seymour. "A New Point of View on 'Point of View.'" In *Coming to Terms: The Rhetoric of Narrative in Fiction and Film*, 139–160. Ithaca, NY: Cornell University Press, 1990.
——. *Story and Discourse: Narrative Structure in Fiction and Film*. Ithaca, NY: Cornell University Press, 1978.
Clair, René. "Talkie Versus Talkie" (1929). In *French Film Theory and Criticism*, vol. 2: *1929–1939*, edited by Richard Abel, 39–40. Princeton, NJ: Princeton University Press, 1988.
Clarke, Charles. *Highlights and Shadows: The Memoirs of a Hollywood Cameraman*. Edited by Anthony Slide. Metuchen, NJ: Scarecrow Press, 1989.

Crafton, Donald. *The Talkies: American Cinema's Transition to Sound, 1926–1931*. Berkeley: University of California Press, 1997.

Crowe, Cameron. *Conversations with Wilder*. New York: Knopf, 1999.

Curtis, Scott. "The Making of *Rear Window*." In *Alfred Hitchcock's "Rear Window,"* edited by John Belton, 21–56. New York: Cambridge University Press, 2000.

Decherney, Peter. *Hollywood and the Culture Elite: How Movies Became American*. New York: Columbia University Press, 2005.

Delamater, Jerome. *Dance in the Hollywood Musical*. Ann Arbor, MI: UMI Research Press, 1981.

Delson, James. "Heston on Welles." In *"Touch of Evil": Orson Welles, Director*, edited by Terry Comito, 213–222. New Brunswick, NJ: Rutgers University Press, 1998.

Dickstein, Morris. *Dancing in the Dark: A Cultural History of the Great Depression*. New York: Norton, 2009.

Dmytryk, Edward. *On Directing*. Boston: Focal Press, 1984.

Doane, Mary Ann. "Film and the Masquerade: Theorizing the Female Spectator." In *Femmes Fatales: Feminism, Film Theory, Psychoanalysis*, 17–32. New York: Routledge, 1991.

Dombrowski, Lisa. *The Films of Samuel Fuller: If You Die, I'll Kill You!* Middletown, CT: Wesleyan University Press, 2008.

——. "Postwar Hollywood, 1947–1967." In *Cinematography*, edited by Patrick Keating, 60–83. New Brunswick, NJ: Rutgers University Press, 2014.

Dumont, Hervé. *Frank Borzage: The Life and Films of a Hollywood Romantic*. Jefferson, NC: McFarland, 2006.

Eisner, Lotte. *Murnau*. Berkeley: University of California Press, 1973.

Eyman, Scott. *Five American Cinematographers*. Metuchen, NJ: Scarecrow Press, 1987.

Fabe, Marilyn. *Closely Watched Films: An Introduction to the Art of Narrative Film Technique*. Berkeley: University of California Press, 2004.

Fejos, Paul. "Illusion on the Screen" (1929). In *Hollywood Directors, 1914–1940*, edited by Richard Koszarski, 223–226. New York: Oxford University Press, 1976.

Ferguson, Otis. *The Film Criticism of Otis Ferguson*. Edited by Robert Wilson. Philadelphia: Temple University Press, 1971.

Fielding, Raymond. *The Technique of Special Effects Cinematography*. 3rd ed. New York: Hastings House, 1974.

Ford, Larry R. *Cities and Buildings: Skyscrapers, Skid Rows, and Suburbs*. Baltimore: Johns Hopkins University Press, 1994.

Foster, Gwendolyn Audrey. "Performing Modernity and Gender in the 1930s." In *Cinema and Modernity*, edited by Murray Pomerance, 93–109. New Brunswick, NJ: Rutgers University Press, 2006.

Freund, Karl. "A Film Artist." Appendix to Paul Rotha, *The Film till Now: A Survey of World Cinema*, 716–717. New York: Twayne, 1960.

Gaines, Jane. "Introduction: The Family Melodrama of Classical Narrative Cinema." In *Classical Narrative Cinema: The Paradigm Wars*, edited by Jane Gaines, 1–8. Durham, NC: Duke University Press, 1992.

Gallagher, Tag. *John Ford: The Man and His Films*. Berkeley: University of California Press, 1986.

Garmes, Lee. "Cinematography: Film, Tape, and Honesty." *Journal of the University Film Association* 26, no. 4 (1974): 59–60.

——. *Lee Garmes: An American Film Institute Seminar on His Work*. Glen Rock, NJ: Microfilming Corporation of America, 1977.

Gaut, Berys. *A Philosophy of Cinematic Art*. New York: Cambridge University Press, 2010.

Gibbs, John, and Douglas Pye. "Revisiting Preminger: *Bonjour Tristesse* (1958) and Close Reading." In *Style and Meaning: Studies in the Detailed Analysis of Film*, edited by John Gibbs and Douglas Pye, 108–126. Manchester, UK: Manchester University Press, 2005.

Giovacchini, Saverio. *Hollywood Modernism: Film and Politics in the Age of the New Deal*. Philadelphia: Temple University Press, 2001.

Gleich, Joshua. *Hollywood in San Francisco: Location Shooting and the Aesthetics of Urban Decline, 1945–1975*. Austin: University of Texas Press, 2018.

Gunning, Tom. "The Cinema of Attractions: Early Film, Its Spectator, and the Avant-Garde." In *Early Cinema: Space, Frame, Narrative*, edited by Thomas Elsaesser, 56–62. London: British Film Institute, 1990.

——. "Modernity and Cinema: A Culture of Shocks and Flows." In *Cinema and Modernity*, edited by Murray Pomerance, 297–315. New Brunswick, NJ: Rutgers University Press, 2006.

Hall, Hal. "Cinematographers and Directors Meet: Discuss Camera Trucking Problems." *American Cinematographer* 13, no. 4 (August 1932): 10, 47.

Hall, Nick. *The Zoom: Drama at the Touch of a Lever*. New Brunswick, NJ: Rutgers University Press, 2018.

Hammond, Mike. "Film: The First Global Vernacular?" *History Workshop Journal* 58 (Autumn 2004): 355–358.

Hansen, Miriam Bratu. "The Mass Production of the Senses: Classical Cinema as Vernacular Modernism." In *Reinventing Film Studies*, edited by Christine Gledhill and Linda Williams, 332–350. London: Arnold, 2000.

——. "Vernacular Modernism: Tracking Cinema on a Global Scale." In *World Cinemas, Transnational Perspectives*, edited by Natasa Ďurovičová and Kathleen A. Newman, 287–314. New York: Routledge, 2010.

Hanson, Helen. *Hollywood Heroines: Women in Film Noir and the Female Gothic Film*. New York: I. B. Tauris, 2007.

Harris, Mark. *Five Came Back: A Story of Hollywood and the Second World War*. New York: Penguin Press, 2014.

Harvith, Susan, and John Harvith. *Karl Struss: Man with a Camera*. Bloomsfield Hills, MI: Cranbrook Academy of Art, 1976.

Higham, Charles. *Hollywood Cameramen: Sources of Light*. Bloomington: Indiana University Press, 1970.

Higham, Charles, and Joel Greenberg. *The Celluloid Muse: Hollywood Directors Speak*. London: Angus and Robertson, 1969.

Hitchcock, Alfred. *Hitchcock on Hitchcock: Selected Writings and Interviews*. Edited by Sidney Gottlieb. Berkeley: University of California Press, 1997.

Hopkins, Robert. "Depiction." In *The Routledge Companion to Philosophy and Film*, edited by Paisley Livingston and Carl Plantinga, 64–74. New York: Routledge, 2011.

Horak, Jan-Christopher. "Sauerkraut & Sausages with a Little Goulash: Germans in Hollywood, 1927." *Film History* 17, nos. 2–3 (2005): 241–260.

Howard, David, and Edward Mabley. *The Tools of Screenwriting*. New York: St. Martin's Press, 1995.

Howe, James Wong. "The Documentary Technique in Hollywood." *American Cinematographer* 25, no. 1 (January 1944): 10, 32.

Hyman, John. *The Objective Eye: Color, Form, and Reality in the Theory of Art*. Chicago: University of Chicago Press, 2006.

Isenberg, Alison. *Downtown America: A History of the Place and the People Who Made It*. Chicago: University of Chicago Press, 2004.

Jacobs, Lea. "Industry Self-Regulation and the Problem of Textual Determination." *Velvet Light Trap* 23 (Spring 1989): 4–15.

——. "Making John Ford's *How Green Was My Valley*." *Film History* 28, no. 2 (2016): 32–80.

Jacobs, Lewis. "Film Directors at Work." *Theatre Arts* 25, no. 1 (January 1941): 40–48.

——. "Film Directors at Work." *Theatre Arts* 25, no. 3 (March 1941): 225–232.

Jewell, Richard. "How Howard Hawks Brought Baby Up." In *Howard Hawks: American Artist*, edited by Jim Hillier and Peter Wollen, 175–184. London: British Film Institute, 1996.

——. *RKO Radio Pictures: A Titan Is Born*. Berkeley: University of California Press, 2012.

Kanin, Garson. "I Direct." *Theatre Arts* 25, no. 9 (September 1941): 640–644.

Kantor, Bernard, Irwin Blacker, and Anne Kramer. *Directors at Work: Interviews with American Film-Makers*. New York: Funk and Wagnalls, 1970.

Katznelson, Ira. *Fear Itself: The New Deal and the Origins of Our Time*. New York: Liveright, 2013.

Kaufman, Boris. "Film Making as an Art." *Daedalus* 89, no. 1 (Winter 1960): 138–143.

Keating, Patrick. "The Art of Cinematography." In *The Palgrave Handbook for the Philosophy of Film and Motion Pictures*, edited by Noël Carroll, Laura T. DiSumma-Knoop, and Shawn Loht. New York: Palgrave Macmillan, forthcoming.

——. "Emotional Curves and Linear Narratives." *Velvet Light Trap* 58 (Fall 2006): 4–15.

——. *Hollywood Lighting from the Silent Era to Film Noir*. New York: Columbia University Press, 2010.

——. "Narrative and the Moving Image." In *The Palgrave Handbook for the Philosophy of Film and Motion Pictures*, edited by Noël Carroll, Laura T. DiSumma-Knoop, and Shawn Loht. New York: Palgrave Macmillan, forthcoming.

——. "Otto Preminger." In *Fifty Hollywood Directors*, edited by Suzanne Leonard and Yvonne Tasker, 186–194. London: Routledge, 2014.

——. "The Silent Screen, 1894–1927." In *Cinematography*, edited by Patrick Keating, 11–33. New Brunswick, NJ: Rutgers University Press, 2014.

Keil, Charlie. "To Here from Modernity: Style, Historiography, and Transitional Cinema." In *American Cinema's Transitional Era: Audiences, Institutions, Practices*, edited by Charlie Keil and Shelley Stamp, 51–65. Berkeley: University of California Press, 2004.

Koenig, Lester. "Gregg Toland, Film-Maker." *The Screen Writer* 3, no. 7 (December 1947): 27–33.

Koppes, Clayton R., and Gregory D. Black. *Hollywood Goes to War: How Politics, Profits, and Propaganda Shaped World War II Movies*. Berkeley: University of California Press, 1990.

Koster, Henry. "Directing in CinemaScope." In *New Screen Techniques*, edited by Martin Quigley, 171–173. New York: Quigley, 1953.

Koszarski, Richard. "The Cinematographer." In *New York to Hollywood: The Photography of Karl Struss*, edited by Barbara McCandless, Bonnie Yochelson, and Richard Koszarski, 167–205. Fort Worth, TX: Amon Carter Museum, 1995.

——. "Ernest Palmer on Frank Borzage and F. W. Murnau," *Griffithiana* 46 (December 1992): 115–120.

——. "The Greatest Film Paramount Ever Made." *Film History* 15, no. 4 (2003): 436–443.

——. "Moving Pictures: Hal Mohr's Cinematography." *Film Comment* 10, no. 5 (September 1974): 48–53.

Kracauer, Siegfried. "The Mass Ornament" (1927). In *The Mass Ornament: Weimar Essays*, edited and translated by Thomas Y. Levin, 75–86. Cambridge, MA: Harvard University Press, 1995.

———. *Theory of the Film: The Redemption of Physical Reality*. Princeton, NJ: Princeton University Press, 1997.

Krohn, Bill. *Hitchcock at Work*. London: Phaidon Press, 2000.

Lane, A. Lindsley. "The Camera's Omniscient Eye." *American Cinematographer* 16, no. 3 (March 1935): 95, 102 .

———. "Rhythmic Flow—Mental and Visual," *American Cinematographer* 16, no. 4 (April 1935): 138–139, 151–152.

Leach, William. *Land of Desire: Merchants, Power, and the Rise of a New American Culture*. New York: Vintage Books, 1993.

LeRoy, Mervyn, as told to Alyce Canfield. *It Takes More Than Talent*. New York: Knopf, 1953.

———, as told to Dick Kleiner. *Take One*. New York: Hawthorn Books, 1974.

Lev, Peter. *Twentieth Century-Fox: The Zanuck–Skouras Years, 1935–1965*. Austin: University of Texas Press, 2013.

Levine, Lawrence. "American Culture and the Great Depression." In *The Unpredictable Past: Explorations in American Cultural History*, 206–230. New York: Oxford University Press, 1993.

Lightman, Herb. "The Fluid Camera." *American Cinematographer* 27, no. 3 (March 1946): 82, 102–103.

———. "The Subjective Camera." *American Cinematographer* 27, no. 2 (February 1946): 46, 66–67 .

Lorentz, Pare. "The Stillborn Art" (1928). In *Lorentz on Film: Movies, 1927–1941*, 18–27. Norman: University of Oklahoma Press, 1986.

Mackendrick, Alexander. *On Film-Making: An Introduction to the Craft of the Director*. Edited by Paul Cronin. New York: Faber and Faber, 2004.

Maltin, Leonard. *The Art of the Cinematographer: A Survey and Interviews with Five Masters*. New York: Dover, 1978.

Marion, Frances. *How to Write and Sell Film Stories*. 1937. Reprint. New York: Garland, 1978.

Mast, Gerald. *The Comic Mind: Comedy and the Movies*. 2nd ed. Chicago: University of Chicago Press, 1979.

McBride, Joseph. *Frank Capra: The Catastrophe of Success*. Jackson: University Press of Mississippi, 2011.

McBride, Joseph, and Michael Wilmington. *John Ford*. New York: Da Capo, 1975.

McGrath, Caitlin. "Captivating Motion: Late–Silent Film Sequences of Perception in the Modern Urban Environment." PhD diss., University of Chicago, 2010.

Miller, Virgil. *Splinters from Hollywood Tripods*. New York: Exposition Press, 1964.

Milner, Victor. "Let's Stop Abusing Camera Movement." *American Cinematographer* 16, no. 2 (February 1935): 46–47, 58, 60.

Minnelli, Vincente, and Hector Arce. *I Remember It Well*. Hollywood, CA: Samuel French, 1974.

Mitry, Jean. *The Aesthetics and Psychology of the Cinema*. Translated by Christopher King. 1997. Reprint. Bloomington: Indiana University Press, 2000.

Morgan, Daniel. "Max Ophuls and the Limits of Virtuosity: On the Aesthetics and Ethics of Camera Movement." *Critical Inquiry* 38 (Autumn 2011): 127–163.

———. " 'Play with Danger': Vernacular Modernism and the Problem of Criticism." *New German Critique* 122, no. 2 (Summer 2014): 67–82.

———. "Where Are We? Camera Movements and the Problem of Point of View." *New Review of Film and Television Studies* 14, no. 2 (2016): 222–248.

Morris, Oswald, and Geoffrey Bull. *Huston, We Have a Problem*. Lanham, MD: Scarecrow Press, 2006.

Mulvey, Laura. "Visual Pleasure and Narrative Cinema." In *Narrative, Apparatus, Ideol-ogy: A Film Theory Reader*, edited by Philip Rosen, 198–209. New York: Columbia University Press, 1986.

Mumford, Lewis. "Landscape and Townscape" (1960–1961). In *The Urban Prospect*, 79–91. New York: Harcourt, Brace & World, 1968.

Murnau, F. W. "Films of the Future" (1927). In *Hollywood Directors, 1914–1940*, edited by Richard Koszarski, 215–221. New York: Oxford University Press, 1976.

——. "The Ideal Picture Needs No Titles: By Its Very Nature the Art of the Screen Should Tell a Complete Story Pictorially" (1928). In *German Essays on Film*, edited by Alison Guenther-Pal and Richard W. McCormick, 66–68. New York: Continuum, 2004.

Musser, Charles. *The Emergence of Cinema: The American Screen to 1907*. Berkeley: University of California Press, 1990.

Naremore, James. *The Films of Vincente Minnelli*. New York: Cambridge University Press, 1993.

——. *The Magic World of Orson Welles*. Rev. ed. Dallas: Southern Methodist University Press, 1989.

Neve, Brian. "A Past Master of His Craft: An Interview with Fred Zinnemann." *Cineaste* 23, no. 1 (1997): 15–19.

Nielsen, Jakob Isak. "En scenes anatomi: *Sunnyside Up*." *16:9* 43 (September 2011). http://www.16-9.dk/2011-09/side07_anatomi.htm.

——. "Five Functions of Camera Movement in Narrative Cinema." In *Transnational Cinematography Studies*, edited by Lindsay Coleman, Daisuke Miyao, and Roberto Schaeffer, 25–53. Lanham, MD: Lexington Books, 2017.

Ogle, Patrick. "Technological and Aesthetic Influences on the Development of Deep-Focus Cinematography in the United States." In *Movies and Methods*, vol. 2, edited by Bill Nichols, 58–83. Berkeley: University of California Press, 1985.

Palmer, R. Barton. *Shot on Location: Postwar American Cinema and the Exploration of Real Place*. New Brunswick, NJ: Rutgers University Press, 2016.

Paul, William. *Ernst Lubitsch's American Comedy*. New York: Columbia University Press, 1983.

Perkins, V. F. *The Magnificent Ambersons*. London: British Film Institute, 1999.

——. "*River of No Return*." *Movie* 2 (September 1962): 18–19.

——. "*Rope*" (1963). In *"Movie" Reader*, edited by Ian Cameron, 35–37. New York: Praeger, 1972.

——. "Where Is the World? The Horizon of Events in Movie Fiction." In *Style and Meaning: Studies in the Detailed Analysis of Film*, edited by John Gibbs and Douglas Pye, 16–41. Manchester, UK: Manchester University Press, 2005.

——. "Why Preminger?" (1962). In *"Movie" Reader*, edited by Ian Cameron, 43. New York: Praeger, 1972.

Petrie, Graham. *Hollywood Destinies: European Directors in America, 1922–1931*. Rev. ed. Detroit: Wayne State University Press, 2002.

Pichel, Irving. "Seeing with the Camera." *Hollywood Quarterly* 1, no. 2 (January 1946): 138–145.

Polan, Dana. *Power & Paranoia: History, Narrative, and the American Cinema, 1940–1950*. New York: Columbia University Press, 1986.

Pope, Norris. *Chronicle of a Camera: The Arriflex 35 in North America, 1945–1972*. Jackson: University Press of Mississippi, 2013.

Porfirio, Robert, Alain Silver, and James Ursini, eds. *Film Noir Reader 3: Interviews with Filmmakers of the Classic Noir Period*. New York: Limelight Editions, 2002.

Pudovkin, Vsevolod. *Film Technique and Film Acting.* Translated by Ivor Montagu. New York: Bonanza Books, 1949.

Pye, Douglas. "Movies and Point of View." *Movie* 36 (2000): 2–34.

——. "Movies and Tone." In *Close Up 02*, edited by John Gibbs and Douglas Pye, 1–80. London: Wallflower, 2007.

Rabinovitz, Lauren. *Electric Dreamland: Amusement Parks, Movies, and American Modernity.* New York: Columbia University Press, 2012.

Ray, Robert B. *A Certain Tendency of the Hollywood Cinema, 1930–1980.* Princeton, NJ: Princeton University Press, 1985.

Reich, Elizabeth. *Militant Visions: Black Soldiers, Internationalism, and the Transformation of American Cinema.* New Brunswick, NJ: Rutgers University Press, 2016.

Rice, Elmer. "The Playwright as Director." *Theatre Arts Monthly* 13, no. 5 (May 1929): 355–360.

——. *Three Plays.* New York: Hill and Wang, 1993.

Rippy, Marguerite. *Orson Welles and the Unfinished RKO Projects: A Postmodern Perspective.* Carbondale: Southern Illinois University Press, 2009.

Robinson, Casey. *Now, Voyager.* Revised final screenplay. Edited by Jean Thomas Allen. Madison: University of Wisconsin Press, 1984.

Rogers, Ariel. "'Smothered in Baked Alaska': The Anxious Appeal of Widescreen Cinema." *Cinema Journal* 51, no. 3 (Spring 2012): 74–96.

Rosenbaum, Jonathan. "The Voice and the Eye: A Commentary on the *Heart of Darkness* Script" (1972). In *Discovering Orson Welles*, 28–48. Berkeley: University of California Press, 2007.

Salt, Barry. *Film Style and Technology: History and Analysis.* 3rd ed. London: Starword, 2009.

——. "Up and Down and Back and Forth." In *Moving Into Pictures*, 285–291. London: Starword, 2006.

Saroyan, William. *The Human Comedy.* 1943. Reprint. New York: Dell, 1971.

Sarris, Andrew, ed. *Interviews with Film Directors.* New York: Avon Books, 1967.

Saunders, Thomas. *Hollywood in Berlin: American Cinema and Weimar Germany.* Berkeley: University of California Press, 1994.

Saval, Nikil. *Cubed: A Secret History of the Workplace.* New York: Doubleday, 2014.

Schatz, Thomas. *The Genius of the System: Hollywood Filmmaking in the Studio Era.* New York: Holt, 1988.

Schleier, Merrill. *Skyscraper Cinema: Architecture and Gender in American Film.* Minneapolis: University of Minnesota Press, 2009.

Schonig, Jordan. "Seeing Aspects of the Moving Camera: On the Twofoldness of the Mobile Frame." *Synoptique* 5, no. 2 (Winter 2017): 57–78.

Seldes, Gilbert. *The 7 Lively Arts.* New York: Dover, 2001.

——. *The Movies Come from America.* 1937. Reprint. New York: Arno Press, 1978.

Selznick, David O. *Memo from David O. Selznick.* Edited by Rudy Behlmer. New York: Modern Library, 2000.

Silke, James R., and Bruce Henstell. "Frank Capra: 'One Man—One Film.'" In *Frank Capra Interviews*, edited by Leland Poague, 72–92. Jackson: University Press of Mississippi, 2004.

Singer, Ben. "The Ambimodernity of Early Cinema: Problems and Paradoxes in the Film-and-Modernity Discourse." In *Film 1900: Technology, Perception, Culture*, edited by Annemone Ligensa and Klaus Kreimeier, 37–51. New Barnet, UK: John Libbey, 2009.

Smith, Jeffrey. "'It Does Something to a Girl. I Don't Know What': The Problem of Female Sexuality in *Applause*." *Cinema Journal* 30, no. 2 (Winter 1991): 47–60.

Smith, Susan. *Hitchcock: Suspense, Humour, and Tone*. London: British Film Institute, 2000.

Spadoni, Robert. *Uncanny Bodies: The Coming of Sound Film and the Origins of the Horror Genre*. Berkeley: University of California Press, 2007.

Staiger, Janet. "Blueprints for Feature Films: Hollywood's Continuity Scripts." In *The American Film Industry*, rev. ed., edited by Tino Balio, 173–192. Madison: University of Wisconsin Press, 1985.

Steinbeck, John. *The Grapes of Wrath*. 1939. Reprint. New York: Penguin, 2006.

Steinhart, Daniel. *Runaway Hollywood: Internationalizing Postwar Production and Location Shooting*. Berkeley: University of California Press, forthcoming.

Sternberg, Meir. "The 'Laokoon' Today: Interart Relations, Modern Projects, and Projections." *Poetics Today* 20, no. 2 (Summer 1999): 291–379.

——. "Mimesis and Motivation: The Two Faces of Fictional Coherence." *Poetics Today* 33, nos. 3–4 (Fall–Winter 2012): 329–483.

——. "Narrativity: From Objectivist to Functional Paradigm." *Poetics Today* 31, no. 3 (Fall 2010): 507–659.

Stevens, George, Jr. *Conversations with the Great Moviemakers of Hollywood's Golden Age at the American Film Institute*. New York: Vintage Books, 2006.

Stull, William. "Common Sense and Camera Angles." *American Cinematographer* 12, no. 10 (February 1932): 8–9, 26.

Susman, Warren. "The Culture of the Thirties." In *Culture as History: The Transformation of American Society in the Twentieth Century*, 150–183. Washington, DC: Smithsonian Institution Press, 2003.

Takaki, Ronald. *Double Victory: A Multicultural History of America in World War II*. New York: Back Bay Books, 2000.

Tarkington, Booth. *The Magnificent Ambersons*. 1918. Reprint. New York: Barnes and Noble, 2005.

Thomas, Deborah. *Beyond Genre: Melodrama, Comedy, and Romance in Hollywood Film*. Moffat, UK: Cameron and Hollis, 2000.

Thompson, Kristin. *Herr Lubitsch Goes to Hollywood: German and American Film After World War I*. Amsterdam: Amsterdam University Press, 2005.

Truffaut, François. *Hitchcock*. Rev. ed. New York: Touchstone, 1985.

Turnock, Julie. "The Screen on the Set: The Problem of Classical-Studio Rear Projection." *Cinema Journal* 51, no. 2 (Winter 2012): 157–162.

Vidor, King. *A Tree Is a Tree: An Autobiography*. 1953. Reprint. Hollywood, CA: Samuel French, 1981.

Vorkapich, Slavko. "Cinematics: Some Principles Underlying Effective Cinematography." In *The Cinematographic Annual*, vol. 1, edited by Hal Hall, 29–33. Los Angeles: American Society of Cinematographers, 1930.

Walker, Joseph, and Juanita Walker. *The Light on Her Face*. Los Angeles: ASC Press, 1984.

Weinberg, Herman. *The Lubitsch Touch: A Critical Study*. New York: Dutton, 1968.

Welles, Orson, and Peter Bogdanovich. *This Is Orson Welles*. Edited by Jonathan Rosenbaum. New York: Da Capo, 1998.

Whissel, Kristen. *Picturing American Modernity: Traffic, Technology, and the Silent Cinema*. Durham, NC: Duke University Press, 2008.

Wilson, George M. *Narration in Light: Studies in Cinematic Point of View*. Baltimore: Johns Hopkins University Press, 1986.

Wirth, Louis. "Urbanism as a Way of Life" (1938). In *On Cities and Social Life: Selected Papers*, edited by Albert J. Reiss Jr., 60–83. Chicago: University of Chicago Press, 1964.

Wojcik, Pamela Robertson. *The Apartment Plot: Urban Living in American Film and Popular Culture, 1945 to 1975*. Durham, NC: Duke University Press, 2010.

Wollheim, Richard. *Painting as an Art*. Princeton, NJ: Princeton University Press, 1987.

——. "Seeing-as, Seeing-in, and Pictorial Representation." In *Art and Its Objects*, 205–226. 2nd ed. New York: Cambridge University Press, 1980.

Wood, Robin. *Hitchcock's Films Revisited*. New York: Columbia University Press, 1989.

——. *Personal Views: Explorations in Film*. Rev. ed. Detroit: Wayne State University Press, 2006.

Yacobi, Tamar. "Package Deals in Fictional Narrative: The Case of the Narrator's (Un)Reliability." *Narrative* 9, no. 2 (May 2001): 223–229.

Young, Freddie. *Seventy Light Years: A Life in the Movies*. London: Faber and Faber, 1999.

Young, Gwenda. "Clarence Brown: From Knoxville to Hollywood and Back." *Journal of East Tennessee History* 73 (2002): 53–73.

Zanuck, Darryl F. *Memo from Darryl F. Zanuck: The Golden Years at Twentieth Century-Fox*. Edited by Rudy Behlmer. New York: Grove Press, 1993.

INDEX

Rosher, Charles, 29–30, 48
Rotambulator, 62–64, 160, 287–88
Ruttenberg, Joseph, 156, 160, 224, 275

Salt, Barry, 18–19, 57–58, 300n32
Saval, Nikil, 119
Schleier, Merrill, 123, 249
Secrets of a Co-ed (1942), 180
Seitz, John F., 9, 68, 248
Seldes, Gilbert, 35, 38, 294n32
Selznick, David O.: crab dolly, 251–52, 261;
    cutting in the camera, 168–69, 173; *Gone
    with the Wind*, 155, 173; Hitchcock, 169,
    173; *The Paradine Case*, 251–53; *Since
    You Went Away*, 203
semidocumentary, 7, 194–95, 228–34, 236
semisubjective mode: in German films,
    25–26, 30–31, 45; in Hollywood films,
    98, 132, 212–14, 232, 280, 284
seriality: in department store films, 135–37;
    in factory films, 115–18; in films of the
    Depression, 131–37; in films of World
    War II, 140–45; in office films, 118–20;
    in prison films, 115–18; in
    representations of women, 120–22; as
    theme, 7, 41, 103–6, 108, 150, 190. *See
    also* person-to-person shot
Seventh Cross, The (1944), 144–45
7th Heaven (1927), 35, 39–42, 47
Shadow of a Doubt (1943), 199–201, 251
Shamroy, Leon, 266
shared strategy, 3, 5–6, 14, 106–8, 110, 286
Sherlock Jr. (1924), 22–23
Shipham, Bert, 98
Show People (1928), 23–24
simultaneity, 124, 179
Siodmak, Robert, 4, 167, 215
Skyscraper Souls (1932), 122–23, 136, 249
Smith, Susan, 202–3
Somewhere in the Night (1946), 1, 204
special effects. *See* optical printer,
    rear-screen projection, traveling matte
Spellbound (1945), 201–3
Stagecoach (1939), 104, 282
Stahl, John, 177, 316n92
Staiger, Janet, 64, 299n10, 311n1
Steadicam, 67, 196, 206. *See also* gyroscope
Steichen, Edward, 225, 227
Steinhart, Daniel, 275

Sternberg, Meir: Proteus principle, 6, 104,
    115, 223; flow of disclosures, 91, 243;
    theory of motivation, 210–11, 320n45
Stevens, George, 162–66, 169, 261
Street Angel (1928), 35, 47, 129
Street Scene (1931), 105, 110, 129–31, 139, 234
Struss, Karl, 30–31, 48, 71, 156
Stull, William, 77–79, 103, 303n89
Sunnyside Up (1929), 129, 132, 234
Sunrise: A Song of Two Humans (1927):
    crossing-the-street shots, 33–34, 49, 51,
    109–11, 282; influence, 35–38, 47–54, 103,
    151, 180, 193; marsh shot, 30–31, 40, 50,
    71, 288; reception, 34–35; trolley shot,
    31–32, 49
Sunset Boulevard (1950), 9–14
Surtees, Robert, 230, 269
suspended camera, 27, 30, 40–41, 47, 61
Suspense (1913), 17–18
Sweepings (1933), 113, 135–36, 310n63

Taylor, Sam, 21–22, 24, 48
Tea and Sympathy (1956), 272–75
Technicolor, 110, 160, 232, 253
telephoto lens, 20–21, 23, 233, 278, 292n14.
    See also zoom lens
Thompson, Kristin, 65, 72, 293n14
360-degree shot: examples, 78, 110, 121, 213,
    250, 278–80; technology, 62, 251, 264,
    279
Todd-AO, 263, 268–69
Toland, Gregg: *The Best Years of Our Lives*,
    180, 236; *Citizen Kane*, 179–80, 192;
    collaboration, 153, 156, 168; focus,
    160–61, 201; *The Grapes of Wrath*,
    137–38; *The Little Foxes*, 180, 184; *Les
    misérables*, 97
Top Hat (1935), 85–86
Touch of Evil (1958), 7, 264, 281–89
traveling matte, 33–34, 49, 67, 110, 302n59
Turnock, Julie, 302n61
Twentieth Century-Fox: CinemaScope,
    265; velocilator, 159. *See also* Fox Films;
    Zanuck, Darryl F.
Two Seconds (1932), 128

Ulmer, Edgar, 62–63, 167
understatement: in the 1930s, 177; in the
    long take, 259, 261, 283; as storytelling

FILM AND CULTURE

A series of Columbia University Press

Edited by John Belton

Andrew Britton

Silent Film Sound
Rick Altman

Home in Hollywood: The Imaginary Geography of Cinema
Elisabeth Bronfen

Hollywood and the Culture Elite: How the Movies Became American
Peter Decherney

Taiwan Film Directors: A Treasure Island
Emilie Yueh-yu Yeh and Darrell William Davis

Shocking Representation: Historical Trauma, National Cinema, and the Modern Horror Film
Adam Lowenstein

China on Screen: Cinema and Nation
Chris Berry and Mary Farquhar

The New European Cinema: Redrawing the Map
Rosalind Galt

George Gallup in Hollywood
Susan Ohmer

Electric Sounds: Technological Change and the Rise of Corporate Mass Media
Steve J. Wurtzler

The Impossible David Lynch
Todd McGowan

Sentimental Fabulations, Contemporary Chinese Films: Attachment in the Age of Global Visibility
Rey Chow

Hitchcock's Romantic Irony
Richard Allen

Intelligence Work: The Politics of American Documentary
Jonathan Kahana

Eye of the Century: Film, Experience, Modernity
Francesco Casetti

Shivers Down Your Spine: Cinema, Museums, and the Immersive View
Alison Griffiths

Weimar Cinema: An Essential Guide to Classic Films of the Era
Edited by Noah Isenberg

African Film and Literature: Adapting Violence to the Screen
Lindiwe Dovey

Film, a Sound Art
Michel Chion

Film Studies: An Introduction
Ed Sikov

Hollywood Lighting from the Silent Era to Film Noir
Patrick Keating

Levinas and the Cinema of Redemption: Time, Ethics, and the Feminine
Sam B. Girgus

Counter-Archive: Film, the Everyday, and Albert Kahn's Archives de la Planète
Paula Amad

Indie: An American Film Culture
Michael Z. Newman

Pretty: Film and the Decorative Image
Rosalind Galt

Film and Stereotype: A Challenge for Cinema and Theory
Jörg Schweinitz

Chinese Women's Cinema: Transnational Contexts
Edited by Lingzhen Wang

Hideous Progeny: Disability, Eugenics, and Classic Horror Cinema
Angela M. Smith
Hollywood's Copyright Wars: From Edison to the Internet
Peter Decherney
Electric Dreamland: Amusement Parks, Movies, and American Modernity
Lauren Rabinovitz
Where Film Meets Philosophy: Godard, Resnais, and Experiments in Cinematic Thinking
Hunter Vaughan
The Utopia of Film: Cinema and Its Futures in Godard, Kluge, and Tahimik
Christopher Pavsek
Hollywood and Hitler, 1933–1939
Thomas Doherty
Cinematic Appeals: The Experience of New Movie Technologies
Ariel Rogers
Continental Strangers: German Exile Cinema, 1933–1951
Gerd Gemünden
Deathwatch: American Film, Technology, and the End of Life
C. Scott Combs
After the Silents: Hollywood Film Music in the Early Sound Era, 1926–1934
Michael Slowik
"It's the Pictures That Got Small": Charles Brackett on Billy Wilder and Hollywood's Golden Age
Edited by Anthony Slide
Plastic Reality: Special Effects, Technology, and the Emergence of 1970s Blockbuster Aesthetics
Julie A. Turnock
Maya Deren: Incomplete Control
Sarah Keller
Dreaming of Cinema: Spectatorship, Surrealism, and the Age of Digital Media
Adam Lowenstein
Motion(less) Pictures: The Cinema of Stasis
Justin Remes
The Lumière Galaxy: Seven Key Words for the Cinema to Come
Francesco Casetti
The End of Cinema? A Medium in Crisis in the Digital Age
André Gaudreault and Philippe Marion
Studios Before the System: Architecture, Technology, and the Emergence of Cinematic Space
Brian R. Jacobson
Impersonal Enunciation, or the Place of Film
Christian Metz
When Movies Were Theater: Architecture, Exhibition, and the Evolution of American Film
William Paul
Carceral Fantasies: Cinema and Prison in Early Twentieth-Century America
Alison Griffiths
Unspeakable Histories: Film and the Experience of Catastrophe
William Guynn
Reform Cinema in Iran: Film and Political Change in the Islamic Republic
Blake Atwood
Exception Taken: How France Has Defied Hollywood's New World Order
Jonathan Buchsbaum
After Uniqueness: A History of Film and Video Art in Circulation
Erika Balsom
Words on Screen
Michel Chion
Essays on the Essay Film
Edited by Nora M. Alter and Timothy Corrigan